Evenings with the Orchestra

BERLIOZ IN 1845,
by an unidentified artist

HECTOR BERLIOZ
Evenings
with the Orchestra

*Translated and edited with an
Introduction and Notes
by JACQUES BARZUN*
AT THE REQUEST OF THE BERLIOZ SOCIETY

THE UNIVERSITY OF CHICAGO PRESS
Chicago and London

The University of Chicago Press, Chicago 60637
The University of Chicago Press, Ltd., London
Copyright 1956, © 1973 by Jacques Barzun. All rights reserved
Published 1956. Phoenix Edition published 1973
Printed in the United States of America
International Standard Book Number: 0–226–04375–4
Library of Congress Catalog Card Number: 72–95224

▸ CONTENTS ◂

PREFACE TO THE PHOENIX EDITION by Jacques Barzun   viii

INTRODUCTION by Jacques Barzun   x

PROLOGUE   5

FIRST EVENING   9
The First Opera—Vincenza—The Vexations of Kleiner the Elder

SECOND EVENING   32
The Strolling Harpist—The Performance of an Oratorio —The Sleep of the Just

THIRD EVENING [*Der Freischütz*]   52

FOURTH EVENING   53
A Debut in Freischütz—*Marescot*

FIFTH EVENING   60
The S in Robert le diable

SIXTH EVENING   64
How a Tenor Revolves around the Public—The Vexations of Kleiner the Younger

SEVENTH EVENING   76
Historical and Philosophical Studies: De viris illustribus urbis Romæ—*A Roman Woman—Vocabulary of the Roman Language*

EIGHTH EVENING   99
Romans of the New World—Mr. Barnum—Jenny Lind's Trip to America

NINTH EVENING   105
The Paris Opéra and London's Opera Houses

Contents

TENTH EVENING   118
   *On the Present State of Music—The Tradition of Tack
—A Victim of Tack*

ELEVENTH EVENING [A Masterpiece]   133

TWELFTH EVENING   134
   Suicide from Enthusiasm

THIRTEENTH EVENING   152
   Spontini, a Biographical Sketch

FOURTEENTH EVENING   180
   *Operas off the Assembly Line—The Problem of Beauty—
Schiller's* Mary Stuart—*A Visit to Tom Thumb*

FIFTEENTH EVENING   187
   Another Vexation of Kleiner the Elder's

SIXTEENTH EVENING   188
   *Musical and Phrenological Studies—Nightmares—The Pu-
ritans of Sacred Music—Paganini*

SEVENTEENTH EVENING [*The Barber of Seville*]   200

EIGHTEENTH EVENING   201
   *Charges Leveled against the Author's Criticism—Analysis
of* The Lighthouse—*The Piano Possessed*

NINETEENTH EVENING [*Don Giovanni*]   221

TWENTIETH EVENING   222
   *Historical Gleanings: Napoleon's Odd Susceptibility—His
Musical Judgment—Napoleon and Lesueur—Napoleon
and the Republic of San Marino*

TWENTY-FIRST EVENING   228
   The Study of Music

TWENTY-SECOND EVENING [*Iphigenia in Tauris*]   253

TWENTY-THIRD EVENING   254
   *Gluck and the Conservatory in Naples—A Saying of
Durante's*

Contents

TWENTY-FOURTH EVENING [*Les Huguenots*]   257

TWENTY-FIFTH EVENING   258
  Euphonia, or the Musical City

EPILOGUE   298
  The Farewell Dinner

SECOND EPILOGUE   310
  *Corsino's Letter to the Author—The Author's Reply to
Corsino—Beethoven and His Three Styles—Beethoven's
Statue at Bonn—Méhul—Conestabile on Paganini—Vin-
cent Wallace*

INDEX   377

Berlioz would be pleased to know that the reissue of this book in paperback comes immediately after the conclusion, in London, of the first recording of his ill-fated but ever-living opera *Benvenuto Cellini*, which was sabotaged—also in London—one year after the completion of his *Evenings with the Orchestra*.

Whether Berlioz would approve the sound of recorded music or the merits of the first tape of *Benvenuto* is another question. But as the *Evenings* and others of his writings make clear, he was an eager and intelligent user of electronic technology, whether in coordinating the conducting of large groups of performers or in guiding his imagination so as to depict the "musical city," Euphonia.

It is this imaginative element that led Berlioz to call his book at first "Tales by the Orchestra." But since he was intermingling genuine biographies and high criticism with fanciful anecdotes and stories made out of whole cloth, he substituted the word *Evenings* (*soirées*), which fitted exactly the scheme he had hit upon for giving a lifelike and continuous setting to his various ideas.

To note this change of title is to imply that this collection reflects his characteristic genius, which is the dramatic: things happen, arguments go on, scenes and characters develop; and, as in *Benvenuto Cellini*, the prevailing tone is comic; the tone, that is, of high comedy, which includes the serious and even the tragic, but plays upon these in the spirit of ironic observation and social satire.

This tone and its modulations upwards and downwards are what makes the book difficult to translate. French in any case does not readily turn into English, being too close in vocabulary and too far in connotations; and Berlioz's French is sinewy, allusive, rapid in its shifts from grave to gay, rhythmically subtle and strong—just like his music—so that whoever tries to render the spirit alive within the word must first steep himself not just in this one emanation of it but in all the rest.

Indeed, Berlioz's prose style, including that of his treatise on orchestration, has defeated any number of English-speaking men and women. There are on the shelves three versions (or two and a half) of the *Evenings*. It is no boast at all to say that the present one surpasses the others in accuracy of text and tone. But simple truth compels one to add without any show of false modesty that the translator who looks again at his work side by side with the original is tossed up and down on alternate waves of resignation and despair. May the reader feel only the pleasures of a calm sea and prosperous voyage!

J.B.

Iɴ Mᴀʏ 1852 Berlioz was in London conducting the New Philharmonic Society and preparing a performance of the Ninth Symphony, the first—as the event proved—that the English deemed an exact and inspired rendering of the score. This was the final concert of the season. When Berlioz returned to France toward the end of June, he carried with him, besides British good will, the manuscript of a new book, which on May 5 he had asked his intimate friend, the musicologist Joseph d'Ortigue, to propose to the Paris publishers.

Berlioz had suggested two firms and described his work: "from 450 to 500 pages of mine entitled *Tales by the Orchestra*. They comprise short stories, anecdotes, romances, squibs, critiques, and discussions, in which music is treated only episodically and not theoretically. There are biographical sketches and formal dialogues, which are read or recounted by the musicians of an unnamed orchestra *during the performance of bad operas*. They attend to their parts only when a masterpiece is being played; the book is consequently divided into Evenings."

Neither publisher was interested and Berlioz himself made arrangements with a third, who brought out the work under its present title that same December. By January 1853 it was a best seller with an excellent critical press. A new, corrected, and slightly enlarged edition was called for a year and a half later, and from that time to the outbreak of the Second World War the book has rarely been out of print. In French and in translation it has been, with Berlioz's *Memoirs*, the best-known manifestation of his literary mind.

This is due partly to the ingenious device of "evenings"—perhaps the most economical scheme ever hit upon for conveying critical judgments while binding together a great variety of pieces; partly to the fact that despite the skillful dramatization of divergent views, the author's personality is intensely present on every page. The book is thus indirect autobiography, like a novel, and self-portraiture in the manner of the great painters. Even when we know nothing of Berlioz's achievements, tastes, trials, and love affairs, it is borne in upon us that such characters as Cellini's friend Della Viola, the concertmaster Corsino, the enthusiast Adolphe D., and the delineator of Euphonia the musical city, are speaking for the author, summing up his experience or projecting his artistic ideals.

At the same time the work is a historical source; for all its extended parts were written in the heat of action as articles for the press, and consequently upon subjects of contemporary importance —Jenny Lind's landing in America or the publication of *Beethoven and His Three Styles*. The earliest of the articles ("Vincenza") dates back to 1833, and the volume in effect spans twenty years of Berlioz's forty-year stretch of service as a critic. What he did in London in the spring of 1852 was to go through his files and sort, revise, and arrange those essays of his which seemed to him to belong to one genre. They are not necessarily his most profound or (as he told D'Ortigue) the most important theoretically; but they are the most popular in tone as well as the most amusing. Three main ideas emerge as leading themes: how is art to be financially supported in the modern world? How do music and its devotees actually live and behave in a commercial society? how should they? And what light do the lives of the great composers throw on these interrelated problems?

That Berlioz could invest these high matters with exuberant humor should not blind us to the seriousness of his arguments or the accuracy of his descriptions. He wrote both as a partisan in the struggle and as a philosophical observer—hence the continual modulating from strenuous advocacy to inexpressible gaiety. Hence also the dramatic truth, which implies the ability to understand the rightness of the wrongs. In the astronomical account of the popular tenor's rising and setting, for example, Berlioz represents with equal justice the pathos of fragile fame and the unforgivable crimes of an obtuse musical conscience. In the riotous extravaganza on the *claque*, he gives us also a piece of social and cultural history.

This habit of seeing life in the round sometimes creates the appearance of contradiction or reversal of opinion. We cannot tell from *The Evenings* whether the public at large is natively stupid and vulgar, or only corrupted by stupid and vulgar middlemen. The evidence points both ways: it did in Shakespeare's time and it does in ours, if only because we cannot get a public without managers to corral them and cater for them. This suggests a worthy project for a research foundation or study group: raising a pure public from the cradle and measuring its inborn immunity to trash.

If we had the results, the great question of patronage could be tackled with more chance of success. Until then it is instructive to read in Berlioz the concrete, detailed proof that our modern belief in the former prevalence of adequate support for the arts is sheer illusion. That "intelligent elite" we hear so much about, "trained to appreciate fine work and respectful of artistic integrity," has never existed—or rather, it was always mixed with and swamped by a larger body of dedicated philistines. We see that Berlioz feared the egalitarian Second Republic as a force that might lessen the slight influence of the best on the worst; but he was to find, precisely from the year of *The Evenings* to his death in 1869, that a Second Empire was as bad, if not worse—and with the same old badness. His knowledge of Mozart's life, of Gluck's and Spontini's careers, of Beethoven's slow acceptance in England and France, should have been sufficient warning that conditions are never right for art. They can only be more or less unfavorable.

For us today, at any rate, the warning in these pages is as much against the self-pity based on the myth of decline in taste as against its inversion into the creed: "good music has always been popular," which a recent very lively book manipulated history in order to maintain.[1] It is sobering to discover in the Ninth Evening and again in the Twenty-fifth that the Hollywood spirit is nothing new and that there is a natural connection between stars, lavish costuming, an absent-minded public, and industrial methods. As for the ultimate illusion that Berlioz inoculates us against, it is one from which we in the United States need special protection right now: the panacea of government support.

In one respect, I am glad to say, *The Evenings* enable us to note unmistakable progress. The standards of musical performance have risen to utopian heights since Berlioz's time. The innumerable malpractices which he denounces, derides, and deplores—from the insidious *Tack!* (see the Twelfth Evening) to the "embroidering" of parts ad lib.—would now be considered intolerable license. They were so to him, and because he fought them tirelessly, he was him-

---

[1] Henry Pleasants: *The Agony of Modern Music* (New York, 1955).

self called intolerant, fanatical, obsessed. Yet it is chiefly to his life-long warfare against bad musicianship, slovenliness, egotism, failure of mind, and love of noise that we owe our modern insistence on technical perfection and fidelity to the composer's will.

He and his century shouldered the task of educating the steadily rising populations of the West to the importance of music as an art, in contradistinction to music as a pastime. It was a long crusade, and its results became visible only toward the end of the century, with the cult of Wagner. They were to be democratically spread only in our time, with the development of the radio and phonograph. It is not surprising, then, that in the middle of that prolonged battle Berlioz should have repeatedly felt it a lost cause. It would do him good just to read the words "High Fidelity," and to see how far the principle they imply can be carried out in the many-sided work of reproducing musical thought. But in one specification of his Euphonia we have not learned from him, and this may still turn out to be a mistake: he advocated moderation in the use of great works. He wanted the listener to be purged and prepared for an unusual experience demanding his fullest resources of intellect, his whole soul. Nowadays the Ninth Symphony is on tap like beer and poured over uncaring heads like shampoo. What effect is this having on our capacity for musical thought and musical enjoyment? Does it account, at least to some extent, for a growing love of the esoteric on the part of the genuinely musical, a growing concentration on detail and nuance to the detriment of substance and meaning? One would like to have a Twenty-sixth Evening from Berlioz on these by-products of the meteoric rise of Music to universal favor and expensive adulation. He might still say, as he did in 1848, though for different reasons, that she acts like a woman of the streets.

Having to deal with these subjects in the daily press, and at a time when cultural analysis was not the common pastime it now is, Berlioz knew that he must first arrest, then amuse his reader. He was well aware—like Shaw half a century later—that the music critic talks mostly to the deaf and must be readable by the nearly blind. His success at overcoming these widespread infirmities of nature leads one to wonder how far his methods were deliberate, how far spontaneous emanations of his exuberant temper. Did he not revel in these fireworks that he set off?

Obviously he had it in him to do the kind of thing he did, for no man can slap his chest and say: "I will now have a sense of humor." Nor do social observation and reasoning power come by internal fiat. But the question of Berlioz's attitude toward his critical work has been raised because in his *Memoirs* he vehemently complains of the journalistic drudgery he bore like the burden of a double life for the whole duration of his creative span. While we follow his orderly analyses or laugh over his ludicrous fancies, we find it hard to imagine that he was not enjoying himself every minute like ourselves. This is the fallacy of inversion: because a man does well the things he likes, we cannot conclude that he likes everything he does well. The conditions of the doing make all the difference, and it is clear that the relentless regularity and dreary occasions of musical journalism must be for a creator the worst kind of slavery. Berlioz wrote the fantastic reviews of *The Lighthouse* and *Diletta* (see the Eighteenth Evening) to relieve his pent-up fury at having to bend over such productions and examine them like jewels. As Ernest Newman has said:

"The composer of the *Symphonie Fantastique*, the *Harold in Italy*, the *Romeo and Juliet*, the *Damnation of Faust*, had to run round night after night reporting the doings of composers who were not fit to black his boots, of conductors who were the merest journeymen in comparison with himself, and of the eternal succession of singers and fiddlers and pianists and all the other small fry of music.

"In addition to all this, notices of operatic revivals, of concerts, of virtuosi, and articles on general subjects! Paris looked calmly on while the best musical brain in the country was prostituted, year in and year out, to trash and futilities and inanities of this kind."

Berlioz's loathing of the trade that gave him his daily bread was complicated by the fact that he never acquired the trick of dashing off his pieces anyhow. His standards (and, it is fair to add, those of the *Journal des Débats* and the *Gazette Musicale*, where all his mature work appeared) were high. And unlike many other great musicians Berlioz was an educated and a traveled man. Shakespeare, Virgil, Goethe, Heine, Cervantes, Molière, Scott, and Cooper were favorite authors, and he read much besides that made him both modest and demanding when he came to his own writings. Precision, clarity, and correctness, as he remarked on revising *The*

Introduction

Evenings and as his manuscripts show, are hard-won virtues in writing French. He insisted moreover on giving each piece a form, each subject a rounded treatment, each article an appropriate tone.

The resulting style bears the marks of his period, but remains individual for all that. We are not surprised to find in it some of the qualities of the author's music: the quick turns of thought akin to abrupt modulations; the care lavished on detail, though never at the expense of the structural members, the development of a theme not in one place but by successive elaborations, and the ability to squeeze poetry or pathos out of apparently unpromising material. At times in the prose one might complain of overdevelopment or again of too great a fondness for the macabre. The second of these period traits was reinforced by Berlioz's experiences as a medical student, but may still pass as a virtue in an age like ours, when sadism itself is felt to have literary charm. If so, one should bear in mind that Berlioz's doctrine and illustration of revenge remained purely fictional. The passion was purged in these very fancies and was never acted out in life. He was too proud for even a vengeful review—which perhaps explains the tale of suicide, which ends in pride and contempt of injury suffered.

However painfully they strike us, these moments of bloodshed in the book are not many, and being but one manifestation of the author's strong presence, they tend to fade from one's memory as one recalls the book as a whole. Its structure is as perfect as its announced intention. Where a less acute artist would have merely balanced Prologue with Epilogue, we have from Berlioz a dramatic Finale, a Beethovenian double coda, in that Second Epilogue which is itself introduced by a new twist in the original idea of the series: no need to wait till André Gide in order to see how an author can make use of his own view of his book in his own book.

As for Berlioz's criticism of life—to use a phrase that will suggest the cogency of his thought on other things than music—it rests on worldly observation that is free from cynicism and a power of irony that is hardly ever mechanical. Take this description of celebrity as it comes to the matinee idol:

"Women whom you do not even know will speak of you as their protégé or very intimate friend. People will dedicate to you their books in prose or verse. Instead of the five francs you give your janitor at Christmas, you will have to give him a hundred. You will be exempted from service in the National Guard; you will get leave [from the Opéra] from time to time so that the provincial towns can fight over your presence and performances. Flowers and sonnets will be heaped around your feet; you will sing at the *soirées* given by the Prefect, and the Mayor's wife will send you apricots."

The passage might come from a novel by Stendhal: he too would have seen and known these things, which were none of his business and trivial in themselves; he too would make them tell a story and define half a dozen types in as many lines; he too would enjoy modulating with the same speed from the dedication of verses to a five-franc tip and from provincial laurels to rural apricots. Though these two fellow countrymen from the region of Grenoble were never much or favorably aware of each other, they have in common the same darting eye serving a penetrating mind, the same thin feasting smile of the ironist at the banquet of life. Berlioz's rapidity of thought may lead him astray now and then, but in the end, like Stendhal, he sees more truly than the rest because his eye is quick and takes in much. This is to say that he is a man of imagination, or —as we knew from his music—a poet-dramatist. *The Evenings* enable us to add that he could also tell a story, judge art, and see around himself.

JACQUES BARZUN

A Note on the Translation

The text is taken from the second edition of *Les Soirées de l'Orchestre*, published in Paris by Michel Lévy Frères in May 1854. I am happy to record the fact that I owe my handsome working copy to the gift of an English Berliozian, Mr. Alan Dent, drama critic of the London *News-Chronicle*.

Except for a few fragments scattered in English and American music journals, no translation of the *Soirées* into English appeared before the complete one by Charles E. Roche, published by Alfred A. Knopf in 1929. That translation had occasional merit and wherever it contained a happy turn of phrase this has been preserved. But as a whole the rendering was inaccurate and unidiomatic —it is, I imagine, the only book in the world that speaks of "the *British* Channel," and tops the error with "the Britannic flag"—and it was virtually unedited. As a consequence, the book teemed with mysteries—some due to failure to understand the French, including ordinary musical terms; the rest due to leaving Berlioz's allusions and references in the dark.

It is hoped that the present version has avoided the worst pitfalls. But a word about method may help to reduce false expectations. The principle I have followed in translating, here and elsewhere, may be described as re-composition. It answers the question: "How would one express precisely this thought in English today?" To those who, in reading a foreign author, like to be continually aware of his foreignness, this book is bound to be disappointing. And the Englishing I have aimed at also annoys certain minds, sharp and pointed like needles (and about as broad), who in a text can see only words. To them, atmosphere and continuity of thought, rhythm and emphasis, allusion and local intent, do not exist. Consequently they are ready to make an outcry when they compare the original "meaning" revealed to their college French with equivalents of the kind I have tried to give. They think that *atroce* should be rendered "atrocious," *séduire* by "seduce," and that wherever *théâtre lyrique* occurs it should invariably read "lyric theater." The meanings actually are: "cruel," "charm," and either "opera house" or "lyric theater," depending on whether the building or the genre is being talked about.

A Note on the Translation

The method just exemplified seems to me indispensable if one is to come close to Berlioz's full message and enjoy it. His puns, parallels, poetic echoes, and ironic emphases must first be understood, then given out again in the nearest words that will do the work. The attempt to do this undoubtedly makes the translator liable to a special kind of error. In trying to cram correspondences into his equivalents he may falsify through misreading or rather, through excessive reading-in. But from their nature these errors can only be occasional, whereas literalism is a continual falsification, doing violence to style in the original and to idiom in the translation.

For my attempts to translate the quoted verse I make no claim whatever. Except in one or two instances, where I have taken care to reproduce the French lines in a footnote, the originals are libretto verses: this may perhaps excuse the shortcomings of their equivalents.

There always remains, of course, the absolutely untranslatable—whether in word, nuance, or even subtler emanations of clustered meanings. The very title *Soirées de l'Orchestre* contains such a cluster, for the words convey the relation of host to guest together with the idea of proffered entertainment. And this is unmanageable in English, unless one were to adopt Sam Weller's admirable but unfamiliar term "swarry." A title is obviously not the place to give this coinage further currency and one must do with "Evenings." For one other term I have chosen literalness: Berlioz and his musicians speak throughout of "our theater," "music in the theater," where we might expect "opera." I wanted to avoid the confusion we tolerate between opera as a work and opera as a place, and I wanted also to recall that nineteenth-century music lived largely in the theater. Berlioz in fact dwells on the evils of this relation and insists on the distinction between dramatic music and theatrical.

I should add that the French second edition of *The Evenings* carries a one-page Postscript which I have not translated. It was meant to serve as an errata list for the first edition. More important, but also outside the scope of *The Evenings* proper, are the half-dozen catalogue pages in that volume which give a list and brief description of Berlioz's musical works up to *The Infant Christ*, part II. They too have been omitted from this translation.

J. B.

Evenings with the Orchestra

PROLOGUE

IN A CERTAIN OPERA HOUSE of northern Europe, it is the custom among the members of the orchestra, several of whom are cultivated men, to spend their time reading books—or even discussing matters literary and musical —whenever they perform any second-rate operas. This is to say that they read and talk a good deal. Next to the score on every music-stand, some book or other is generally to be found, and a performer apparently most absorbed in scanning his part, or most earnestly counting his rests while watching for his cue, may actually be giving all his attention to Balzac's marvelous scenes, to Dickens's enchanting pictures of social life, or even to the study of one of the sciences. I know one who, during the first fifteen performances of a well-known opera, read, re-read, pondered, and mastered the three volumes of Humboldt's *Cosmos*. Another, during the long run of a silly score now forgotten, managed to learn English; while a third, thanks to his exceptional memory, retailed to his neighbors the substance of some ten volumes of tales, romances, anecdotes, and risqué stories.

One man only in this orchestra does not allow himself any such diversion. Wholly intent upon his task, all energy, indefatigable, his eye glued to his notes and his arm in perpetual motion, he would feel dishonored if he were to miss an eighth note or incur censure for his tone quality. By the end of each act he is flushed, perspiring, exhausted; he can hardly breathe, yet he does not dare take advantage of the respite afforded by the cessation of musical hostilities to go for a glass of beer at the nearest bar. The fear of missing the first measures of the next act keeps him rooted at his post. Touched by so much zeal, the manager of the opera house once sent him six bottles of wine, "by way of encouragement." But the artist, "conscious of his responsibilities," was so far from grateful for the gift that he returned it with the proud words: "I have no need of encouragement." The reader will have guessed that I am speaking of the man who plays the bass drum.

His colleagues, contrariwise, hardly interrupt their reading, storytelling, discussing, and chatting, except in behalf of the great masterpieces; or again when in an ordinary opera the composer has assigned a prominent part to one of them, in which case their deliberate inattention would be too noticeable and would discredit them. But even so, since the orchestra is never going full tilt all over, it follows that when the conversations and literary studies trail off on one side, they revive on the other, and the bright wits to the left take up their remarks when those to the right take up their instruments.

The fact that during my annual stay in the town where this club of instrumentalists is to be found I attend its meetings fairly regularly has enabled me to hear a good many anecdotes and novelettes. I have even, I may say, returned the narrators' courtesy by a reading or story of my own. Now the orchestral player is naturally given to repeating himself; when he has held his audience or made it laugh once with a tale or witticism, say on Christmas Day, one may be sure that he will try for a second laugh by the same means without waiting for the end of the year. The result is that, hearing these good stories again and again, I find they now keep running through my head almost as obsessively as the feeble scores to which they served as accompaniment. I have therefore decided to write them down, indeed to publish them, together with the casual dialogue between speakers and listeners, so that I may present a copy to each and not hear another word about it.

It goes without saying that the bass drum will not share in this bibliographical largesse of mine—a man as deep and hard-working as he is scorns the mere play of mind.

DRAMATIS PERSONÆ

THE CONDUCTOR

CORSINO, *concertmaster and composer*

SIEDLER, *leader of the second violins*

DIMSKY, *first double bass*

TURUTH, *second flute*

KLEINER THE ELDER, *timpanist*

KLEINER THE YOUNGER, *first cello*

DERVINCK, *first oboe*

WINTER, *second bassoon*

BACON, *violist (no relation to Friar Bacon,
who invented gunpowder)*

MORAN, *first horn*

SCHMIDT, *third horn*

CARLO, *errand boy*

A GENTLEMAN SUBSCRIBER TO AN ORCHESTRA SEAT

THE AUTHOR

The First Opera

a tale of the past

Vincenza

a sentimental tale

The Vexations of Kleiner the Elder

A VERY DULL modern French opera is being given.

The musicians take their seats with obvious disgust and ill-temper. They do not condescend to tune up, a detail to which the conductor seems not to pay any attention. But when the oboe plays its first A, the violins cannot miss the fact that they are a good quarter tone above the wood wind.

"My!" says one of them, "the orchestra is delightfully dissonant! Let's play the overture just as we are, it will be fun!"

And so the musicians stoutly play their parts, not sparing the audience a single note. I meant to say: not *depriving*, for the audience, enraptured by this dreary rhythmic cacophony, shouts for an encore and the conductor has to begin again. Only, as a matter of policy, he insists that the strings be good enough to take the pitch from the wood winds. He's a busybody.

The men are in tune; the overture is repeated, but this time it makes no impression. The opera begins, and little by little the instruments stop playing.

"Do you know," says Siedler, the leader of the second violins, to his neighbor, "what's happened to our friend Corsino, who's not here tonight?"

"No, what?"

"He's in jail. He is supposed to have insulted the manager upstairs. It seems that this worthy man had commissioned some ballet

9

music from him. Corsino delivered the score, but it was not played and he hasn't been paid for it. He was in a towering rage."

"And why shouldn't he be? Perhaps you think it isn't enough to make a man lose all patience? I'd like to see you diddled that way, so we could test your strength of mind and your spirit of resignation."

"Don't tell *me!* I'm not such a fool; I know only too well that our manager's word is worth as little as his bond. Pfui! But they'll soon let Corsino out. A violinist like him is not so easy to find!"

"So that's the reason he was arrested?" puts in a viola, laying down his bow. "Maybe some day he'll find an opportunity of getting even, like that Italian of the sixteenth century who was the first to attempt dramatic music!"

"What Italian?"

"Alfonso della Viola, a contemporary of the famous goldsmith, sculptor, and engraver Benvenuto Cellini. I have here in my pocket a novel that's just been published, in which those two are the heroes. Shall I read it to you?"

"Let's hear your novel."

"Push back your chair a little, will you? I can't get near enough."

"Don't make such a row with your double bass, Dimsky, or we shan't hear a word. Aren't you tired yet of playing that stupid music?"

"What, a story? Wait a minute, let me in on it." Dimsky hastens to quit his instrument. The whole core of the orchestra gathers around the reader, who flattens out his paperback book, leans one elbow on a horn-case, and begins to read in a low voice.

The First Opera,
A Tale of the Past: 1555 [1]

ALFONSO DELLA VIOLA *to* BENVENUTO CELLINI

FLORENCE, JULY 27, 1555

I am sad, Benvenuto; I am tired, despondent, or rather, to tell the truth, I am sick, I feel myself wasting away, just as you did before

---

[1] The first edition of M. Berlioz's *Voyage musical en Allemagne et en Italie* being out of print, he declined to have the work reissued, because the autobiographical

you had avenged Francesco's death. But you soon were cured, whereas I wonder whether the day of my recovery will ever dawn —God only knows! Yet was ever suffering more worthy of pity than mine? To what other unfortunate could Christ and the Holy Mother do greater justice by granting the sovereign remedy, the precious balm, the most powerful of all to still the bitter pangs of the artist who has been outraged in his art and in his person—revenge? Oh no, Benvenuto, no indeed, without challenging your right to strike down the wretched officer who killed your brother, I cannot help seeing an infinite distance between your grievance and mine. What had that poor devil done, after all? Spilled the blood of your mother's son, it is true. Yet the officer was in command of a night patrol; Francesco was drunk; after insulting the platoon for no reason, and pelting it with stones, he got to the point of trying to disarm the soldiers. They of course made use of their weapons and your brother died. It was a foregone conclusion and, you must admit, a just one.

My case is something else again. Though what I have suffered is worse than killing, I have in no way deserved it. On the contrary it was when I was entitled to reward that I had to endure outrage and insult.

You know how doggedly I have worked for many years to augment the power and multiply the resources of music. Neither the ill will of the older masters, nor the ignorant sneers of their pupils, nor the mistrust of the dilettanti who look upon me as a strange character, closer to madness than to genius, nor the material obstacles of every kind that come with poverty, have managed to stop me, as you know. All this I may say myself, since the credit I claim for it is nil.

The young Montecco named Romeo, whose adventures and tragic death caused so much talk in Verona a few years ago, was surely not able to resist the charms which drew him to the lovely

---

part of that journey is to be included and expanded by him in another work of greater scope on which he is engaged.[2] He therefore felt free to reproduce in the present work excerpts from the earlier book, such as "The First Opera" and some few others, considering the *Voyage musical* as a canceled publication of which he has kept only the substance. [French publisher's note.]

[2] This work of greater scope was the *Memoirs*, which Berlioz began to compose in London after the outbreak of the revolution of 1848. J. B. [From this point on, footnotes not ascribed to Berlioz or his original French publisher are by the present editor.]

Giulietta, daughter to his mortal enemy. Passion was stronger than the insults of the Capuletti's minions, stronger than the poison and cold steel with which he was constantly threatened. Giulietta loved him and he would have braved death a thousand times for an hour spent at her side. Well, music is my Giulietta, and, by heaven, I am her belovèd.

Two years ago I conceived the plan of a theatrical work heretofore unexampled, wherein song, accompanied by divers instruments, was to take the place of the spoken word, and from its union with the drama arouse impressions such as the most elevated poetry has never produced. Unfortunately this project was expensive; only a prince or a Jew could undertake to carry it out.

All the princes of Italy have heard tell of the ineffectiveness of the so-called tragedy in music performed in Rome toward the end of the last century. Again, they know of the meager success accorded the *Orfeo* of Angelo Poliziano, another attempt of the same kind. Nothing would have been more futile than to appeal to them for the support of an undertaking in which the old masters had so completely failed. I should once more have been taxed with arrogance and folly.

As regards the Jews, I never gave them a moment's thought; all I could reasonably expect from them was, on the bare mention of my project, to be turned down without insults or hooting from their menials. Besides, I did not know of any with enough intelligence to let me expect even that much generosity. I therefore gave up my idea, not without regret, you may be sure, and it was with an aching heart that I went back to my obscure labors for a livelihood, labors which are only carried on at the expense of works whose reward might possibly be glory and fortune.

Shortly afterwards another new and disturbing idea occurred to me. Don't laugh at my discoveries, Cellini, and above all don't make the mistake of comparing my new-born art to your own, fully developed long since. You know enough about music to catch my meaning. Tell me honestly, do you really think that our madrigals dragging along in four parts constitute the highest perfection to which composition and performance can reach? Doesn't common sense suggest that in the matter of expression, as in that of musical form, these greatly vaunted works are but childish trifling?

The words express love, anger, jealousy, or courage, but the music is always the same, and too much like the doleful chanting of the mendicant friars. Is this all that melody, harmony, and rhythm can do? Are there not a thousand applications of these elements of art still unknown to us? From an attentive examination of all that is, can we not foresee with certainty what shall be and ought to be? As for our instruments, have they been exploited to the full? What is one to think of our wretched accompaniments, too timid to leave the voice, and trailing after it continually in unison or octaves? Is there such a thing as instrumental music taken by itself? And as regards vocal music, what prejudices, what routine habits! Why forever sing in four parts, even when the song is that of a character lamenting his loneliness? Can anything be more unreasonable to listen to than those *canzonette* recently introduced into tragedy, where an actor, speaking in his own name and holding the stage alone, is none the less accompanied by three other voices in the wings, where they follow his melody as best they can?

Take it from me, Benvenuto, that what our masters, intoxicated with their own works, today style the acme of art is as remote from what will be called music in two or three centuries as the little two-legged monsters made of mud by children are from your sublime *Perseus* or from the *Moses* of Buonarrotti.

All sorts of changes must be brought about in an art that is so little advanced; enormous progress is open to it. And why should I not contribute to forward this achievement?

Without my telling you what my latest invention consists in, let it suffice that it could have been made manifest by ordinary means, without any appeal to the rich and the great. Time was all I needed; and the work once completed, the occasion for producing it would have been easily found in the festivities that were to attract to Florence the cream of the nobility and the friends of art in all nations.

Now here is the subject of the bitter black anger that is gnawing at my heart.

On a certain morning, as I was at work on this unusual composition, the success of which would have made me celebrated throughout Europe, Monsignor Galeazzo, the Grand Duke's chief steward, who had greatly admired my scene about Ugolino last year, came to me and said: "Alfonso, your day has come. It's no longer a question of madrigals, cantatas, or little ditties. Listen to me: the wedding celebration is going to be splendid; nothing is being spared to give it a brilliance worthy of the two illustrious families about to be united; your recent success has inspired confidence; the court now believes in you.

"I knew about your plans for a tragedy in music and spoke of it to His Highness; your idea delights him. Get to work and let your dream become a reality. Write your lyric drama and have no fears about its production. The ablest singers of Rome and Milan shall be summoned to Florence; the leading virtuosos in every kind shall be at your disposal. The Prince is munificent, he will deny you nothing. Live up to my expectations and your triumph is assured, your fortune is made."

I cannot say what I felt at this unexpected speech, but I stood motionless and dumb. Astonishment and joy deprived me of the power of speech; I stood there like an idiot. Galeazzo did not mistake the cause of my confusion; pressing my hand, he said: "Farewell, Alfonso, it's settled, is it not? You promise to put aside any other work and devote yourself exclusively to the one His Highness commissions. Take note of the fact that the wedding takes place in three months' time!" And as I went on signifying my assent by nodding, unable to speak, he added: "Come, now, calm yourself *Vesuvius*, farewell. You will receive your commission tomorrow; it will be signed tonight. It is as good as done. Come, cheer up; we depend on you."

Left to myself, my head reeled: it seemed to me that all the waterfalls of Terni and Tivoli were boiling in it. And it was even worse when I took in the fullness of my good fortune, when I pictured to myself once more the greatness and wonder of my task. I made a dash for my discarded libretto, which had lain yellowing in some corner or other for quite a while; I beheld once more Paolo, Francesca, Dante, Virgil, the shades, and the damned; I heard that exquisite love sighing and lamenting. Tender and graceful melodies, full of abandon, melancholy, and chaste passion, unfolded within me; I heard the outraged husband's awful cry of hatred; I saw the pair of corpses roll entwined at his feet. Next I saw forever united the souls of the two lovers, wandering wind-borne across the depths of the abyss; their plaintive voices mingle with the dull and distant roar of the infernal streams, with the hissing of the fire, with the frenzied screams of the wretched beings it devours, and with all the frightful concert of eternal suffering. . . .

For three days, Cellini, I wandered about aimlessly in unremitting dizziness; for three nights I could not sleep. Not until this prolonged bout of fever had passed did I regain lucidity of mind and a sense of reality. It took me all that time of fierce, desperate struggling to tame my imagination and master my subject. I finally conquered.

In the huge framework of my plan each part of the picture gradually disclosed itself in a simple and logical order, clothed in somber or brilliant colors, in half-tints or strong contrasts. The human forms appeared, some full of life, others under the cold and pallid aspect of death. The poetical idea was always subordinate and never hampered the musical sense. I enlarged, embellished, and intensified the power of the one through the other. In short, I did *what* I willed, *as* I willed, and this so easily that by the end of the second month the entire work was finished.

I must say I felt as if I needed a rest. But when I thought of all the details of preparation to be attended to for the correct execution of my work, my vigor and vigilance returned. I had to supervise the singers, musicians, score-copiers, scene-painters, and stage hands.

Everything went as planned, with the greatest precision, and the huge musical engine was about to get majestically into motion when an unexpected blow fell and smashed its springs, destroying at once the great endeavor itself and the legitimate hopes of your unhappy friend.

The Grand Duke, who of his own accord had bidden me compose this musical drama, and who had made me give up the other work on which I counted in order to make myself known; the Duke, whose golden words had filled an artist's heart and kindled an artist's imagination, now made sport of it all, ordering that imagination to cool off, that heart to be still or to break—it didn't matter which to him! In short, he halts the production of *Francesca*. The Roman and Milanese artists are sent home; my drama is not to be staged; the Grand Duke no longer wants it. *He has changed his mind.* . . .

The crowd that was already gathering in Florence—attracted not so much by the wedding celebration as by the announcement of the musical fête which had excited interest and curiosity throughout Italy—this crowd, eager for fresh sensations and now disappointed in its expectations, seeks the reason that deprives it so brutally of the spectacle it had come for and, unable to discover any reason, does not hesitate to attribute it to the incapacity of the composer. Everyone says: "That touted drama must have been absurd; the Grand Duke, informed just in time, did not want the bootless attempt of an over-ambitious artist to cast ridicule on the ceremony about to take place. There can be no other reason. A prince would never break his word. Della Viola is still the same vain and extravagant fellow we always knew he was; his work was not fit to be shown, but out of courtesy they won't say so."

O Cellini, my noble, proud, and worthy friend! Stop a moment, and from your own experience imagine what my feelings must be at this unheard-of abuse of power, this incredible violation of the most positive promises, this horrible affront which it was impossible to anticipate, this insolent libel against a work of art as yet unknown to everybody except myself.

What can I do? What can I say to that rabble of cowards and fools who laugh when they see me? What explanation can I give to my admirers? Whom can I blame? Who is behind this devilish intrigue? And how am I to counter it? Cellini! Cellini! Why did you go to France? I want to see you, ask your help and advice. By Bacchus, they will drive me mad! Oh, shameful weakness! I have just felt tears in my eyes. Hence, all cowardly thoughts! I must have strength, vigilance, composure, for I am bent on revenge. Benvenuto, I am set upon it. When and how doesn't matter, but I will be revenged, I swear it, and you will approve. Farewell! The fame of your latest triumphs has reached us; I congratulate you and rejoice with my whole soul. May God only grant that the French King will leave you time to reply to your friend grieving and unavenged.

ALFONSO DELLA VIOLA

BENVENUTO *to* ALFONSO

PARIS, AUGUST 20, 1555

I admire, dear Alfonso, the frankness of your indignation. Mine is great too, believe me, but it is more controlled. I have only too often met with similar disappointments to be surprised at yours. The trial of your fledgling valor was, I admit, severe, and the revolt of your soul against an insult so grave and so little deserved is as just as it is natural. But, my poor child, you are hardly at the threshold of your career. Your secluded life, your meditations, your solitary labors were not likely to teach you anything of the intrigues carried on in the higher regions of art, nor of the real character of men in power, who too often hold in their hands our fate as artists.

Some events in my career that I have not told you before will suffice to enlighten you about the condition of us all, and not only your own.

I am not afraid that my story will affect your steadiness of purpose. Your character is my warrent. I know you, I have watched you, you will persevere. You will reach your goal in spite of everything. You are a man of iron mold, and the stones thrown in your face by the low and envious who lie in ambush along your path, far from breaking your head, will strike fire from it. Hear, then, what I have gone through, and may the sad examples of the injustice of the great be a lesson to you.

The Bishop of Salamanca, Ambassador at Rome, had given me an order for a large bowl, on which the extremely fine and delicate work took over two months to do, and for which the large amount of precious metals required almost ruined me. His Excellency was profuse in his praise of the rare beauty of my work. He had it taken to his house and for two whole months said no more about payment than if what he had had from me was an old saucepan or a medal by Fioretti. As luck would have it, the bowl came back to me for a slight repair—and I refused to return it.

The accursed prelate first showered me with abuse as only a priest and a Spaniard can do, then took it into his head to extort from me a receipt for the sum still owing to me. But as I am not a man to fall into so crude a trap, His Excellency went to the lengths of having my shop stormed by his valets. I had suspected the trick, so when the blackguards came to smash in my door, Ascanio, Paolino, and I were armed to the teeth and gave them so warm a welcome that next day, thanks to my gun and my dagger, I was at last paid.[3]

Far worse happened to me later, after I had made the celebrated button for the Pope's cope, a piece of work so wonderful that I cannot resist describing it to you. I had set the big diamond exactly

---

[3] A historic fact. [Berlioz.] Berlioz's reference is to Cellini's *Memoirs* (Chapter iv), which had recently been discovered and translated (1810–30).

in the center of the ornament, and had placed God seated on it in so easy a pose that He did not seem in the least out of place, but the whole formed a very beautiful harmony. God was giving His blessing with upraised right hand. Underneath I had put three tiny angels supporting God on their uplifted arms. One of these angels, the central one, was in high relief, the other two in low. Grouped about them was a number of other small angels, also surrounded by precious stones. God wore a fluttering mantle, out of which flew a quantity of cherubs and a thousand ornaments of the most admirable effect.

Clement VII was full of enthusiasm when he saw the button, and promised me anything I should ask. For all his fair words, nothing happened, and as I refused to make a chalice that he had ordered in addition, though still not giving me any money, this good Pope grew enraged like a wild beast and sent me to jail for six weeks. And that is all I ever received from him.[4]

I had hardly been out a month when I met Pompeo, the wretched goldsmith who had the impertinence to be jealous of me, and against whose persistent plotting I had trouble enough defending my wretched life. I despised him too much to hate him, but on seeing me, his face assumed a mocking expression not usual with him and which this time, embittered as I was, I found I could not bear. As I moved to strike him in the face, fright made him turn his head, and my dagger went in just below the ear. I struck at him only twice, for at the first blow he fell dead in my arms. My intention had not been to kill him, but in the state of mind in which I was, how can one gauge one's blows? And so I had barely come through one odious imprisonment when I found myself compelled to fly for having, in a justifiable fit of anger caused by the dishonesty and the avarice of a Pope, stamped out a scorpion.

Paul III, who showered me with commissions, did not pay me any better than his predecessor. Only, in order to put me in the wrong, he thought up a trick worthy of himself, a piece of deliberate cruelty.

The many enemies I had in the Holy Father's court accused me one day of having stolen jewels from Clement. Well aware that this was not so, Paul III none the less feigned to believe me guilty and had me locked up in the Castel Sant' Angelo, the very fort I had so

---

[4] A historic fact. [Berlioz.] See Cellini's *Memoirs* (Chapter ix).

well defended a few years previously during the siege of Rome: it was from those ramparts that I had fired more cannon than all the other gunners together, and that, to the Pope's intense joy, I myself had killed the High Constable of Bourbon. I succeeded in making my escape, reached the outer walls hanging from a rope above the moat, invoked God, who knew how just was my cause, and cried out to Him as I let myself drop: "Help me, O Lord, since I am helping myself!" God hears me not, and in my fall I break a leg. Exhausted, dying, covered with blood, I manage to drag myself on my hands and knees as far as the palace of my intimate friend Cardinal Cornaro. This base traitor hands me over to the Pope in order to get a bishopric.

Paul condemns me to death; then, as if repenting of putting too quick an end to my torments, he has me thrown into a fetid dungeon full of tarantulas and other venomous insects. Only after six months of such tortures did he, sodden with wine during a night's orgy, grant my pardon to the French Ambassador.[5]

These, my dear Alfonso, are dire sufferings and persecutions hard to bear. Do not suppose that the wound recently inflicted upon your self-esteem can give you any adequate idea of them. Besides, even if an insult to an artist's work and genius does seem to you more galling than an outrage committed on his body, tell me whether I was spared the former at the court of our excellent Grand Duke when I was casting my *Perseus*. I suppose you haven't forgotten the mocking nicknames hurled at me, the insulting sonnets placarded nightly on my door, the secret intrigues by which Cosimo was persuaded that my new casting process would not work and that it was folly to entrust me with the metal.[6] Even here, at the brilliant Court of France where I have made my fortune, where I am powerful and admired, I still must wage a ceaseless battle, if not with my rivals (they are by now in full rout), at least with the King's favorite, Mme d'Étampes, who hates me, God knows why. The malicious bitch speaks all the ill she can of my works,[7] and tries in a thousand ways to ruin me in the eyes of His Majesty. To tell the truth, I am getting so tired of hearing her bark at my heels that if it were not for a great work I have recently begun and from

---

[5] A historic fact. [Berlioz.] See Cellini: *Memoirs* (Chapters xxiii and xxiv).
[6] The incidents surrounding the casting of the Perseus form the subject of Berlioz's opera *Benvenuto Cellini* (1838), for which he framed the libretto.
[7] A historic fact. [Berlioz.] See Cellini: *Memoirs* (Chapters xxxi ff.).

which I expect more glory than from all my previous ones, I should already be on my way back to Italy.

Yes, I tell you, I have endured every sort of buffet that fate can inflict upon an artist. And yet I live. And my living fame is a torment to my enemies. I knew it was to be, so now I am able to bury them in my contempt. This kind of revenge comes slowly, it is true, but for an inspired man who is sure of himself, who is strong and patient, it is a certainty. Consider, Alfonso, that I have been insulted more than a thousand times and that I have killed only seven or eight men. And of what sort—I blush to think of them!

Direct and personal revenge is a rare fruit which it is not given to everyone to pluck. I have not got the better of Clement VII, of Paul III, of Cornaro, of Cosimo, of Mme d'Étampes, nor of a hundred other cowards among the powerful. How, then, could you avenge yourself upon this same Cosimo, this Grand Duke, this fatheaded Mæcenas, who understands your music as little as he does my sculpture, and who has so basely injured us both? Whatever you do, don't think of killing him; it would be sheer lunacy and the consequence would not be in doubt. Become a great musician, make your name illustrious, and if some day his foolish vanity leads him to tender his favors to you, reject them; take nothing from him and do nothing for him. That is my advice to you. That is the promise I ask of you. Trust my experience: what I advise is the only form of revenge within your reach.

I told you just now that the King of France, who is more noble-minded and generous than our Italian princes, had made me rich. It is for me, therefore, as an artist who loves and admires you, to keep the word of the witless and heartless Prince who ignores you. I send you ten thousand crowns. With this sum I hope you can worthily produce your musical drama. Don't waste a minute. Let it be done in Rome, Naples, Milan, Ferrara, anywhere but in Florence; not a ray of your glory must so much as glance upon the Grand Duke.

Farewell, dear child; revenge is a beautiful thing, and a man may be tempted to lay down his life for it; but art is still more beautiful. Never forget that for its sake, in spite of everything, a man must go on living.

Your friend,
BENVENUTO CELLINI

BENVENUTO CELLINI *to* ALFONSO DELLA VIOLA

PARIS, JUNE 10, 1557

Scoundrel! Mountebank! Clown! Pedant! Eunuch! Flute-player! [8] What was the use of screaming as you did, belching fire, babbling of insult and injury, of fury and outrage, and invoking heaven and hell, in order to come to such a trite ending! Man without soul or guts! Why those threats if your resentment was so feeble that less than two years after an insult square in the face you go down on your knees like a coward and kiss the hand that struck you?

Faugh! Neither the promise you gave me, nor the gaze of Europe at present fixed on you, nor your dignity as man and artist has kept you from the seductions of that court where intrigue, avarice, and bad faith reign supreme; that court where you were put to shame, despised, and driven out like a dishonest footman! If what I hear is true, you are composing for the Grand Duke; composing a work which is to be grander and bolder than any you have yet produced. All of musical Italy is to take part in the occasion. The gardens of the Pitti Palace are being prepared for it; five hundred talented virtuosos assembled under your direction in a spacious and beautiful pavilion decorated by Michelangelo will pour out the floods of your splendid harmony on a panting, transported, enthusiastic people. Wonderful! And all this for the Grand Duke, for Florence, for the man and the town that have mistreated you! Oh, what a fool I was when I sought to soothe your childish anger of a day! Oh, what wondrous simple-mindedness made me preach chastity to a eunuch, slowness to a snail! What a fool!

But tell me what strong passion has brought you to your present self-abasement? Is it thirst for gold? But you are today wealthier than I. Love of fame? But no name has been more popular than that of Alfonso, ever since the prodigious success of your tragedy *Francesca* and the three lyric dramas that followed it. Besides, why not select some other capital as the theater of your newest triumph? No other sovereign would have denied you what the *great* Cosimo has just offered you. Everywhere today your songs are loved and admired; they resound from one end of Europe to the other; they are heard in town, at court, in the army, in the churches. King Francis

---

[8] It is well known that Cellini had a singular aversion to the flute. [Berlioz.] See Cellini: *Memoirs* (Chapter i). Berlioz as a young man was an accomplished flutist.

never tires of repeating them; Mme d'Étampes herself finds that *"for an Italian, you are not without talent."* You meet with equal justice in Spain; the women in general and the priests in particular have a genuine cult for your music. If it had been your fancy to offer the Romans the work you are getting ready for the Tuscans, the joy of the Pope, of the cardinals, and of the whole hive of *monsignori* with purple bibs could have been surpassed only by the raptures of their numberless wenches.

Perhaps vanity has trapped you—some bloated dignity—or a resounding title—I can't fathom it.

Whatever it is, bear this in mind: you have failed in nobleness, failed in pride, failed in faith. The man, the artist, the friend, have all fallen equally in my eyes. I cannot bestow my affection and regard but upon men of stout heart who are incapable of shameful acts; you are not one of those; my friendship is yours no longer. I gave you money; you have tried to pay it back: we are quits. I am leaving Paris; in a month I shall be going through Florence. Forget that you ever knew me, and do not try to see me. For even if it were the day when you expect to triumph before the people, the princes, and the (to me) far more imposing assemblage of your five hundred artists, and you accosted me, I should turn my back on you.

Benvenuto Cellini

Alfonso *to* Benvenuto

Florence, June 23, 1557

You are quite right, Cellini. I owe the Grand Duke a humiliation not to be forgiven. To you I owe my fame, my fortune, perhaps my life. I had sworn to take revenge on him and I have not done it. I had solemnly promised you never to accept from him either commissions or honors, and I have not kept my word. It was in Ferrara that, thanks to you, *Francesca* was heard and acclaimed for the first time; and it was in Florence that the work was deemed devoid of meaning and sense. Yet Ferrara, which asked me for my new work, did not secure it, and it is to the Grand Duke that I bring it in homage. Think of it! The Tuscans, formerly so contemptuous of me, rejoice in this token of my preference; they are proud of it; their fanatical devotion to me goes beyond anything you tell me about the French.

A regular exodus is afoot in most of the Tuscan cities. The Pisans and the Sienese themselves, forgetting their old hatreds, are begging Florentine hospitality for the great day. Cosimo, delighted with the success of the man he calls *his* artist, builds great hopes on the results which this renewal of friendly relations among the three rival peoples may have for his power and policies. He overwhelms me with flattery and kind attentions. Yesterday he gave a magnificent banquet in my honor at the Pitti Palace, at which all the noble families of the town were present. The lovely Countess of Vallombrosa lavished on me her sweetest smiles. The Grand Duchess did me the honor of singing a madrigal with me. Della Viola is the man of the hour, the man of Florence, the man of the Grand Duke; there is no one else.

I am utterly guilty, am I not? Utterly vile and despicable? Well, then, Cellini, if you do pass through Florence on the 28th of July next, wait for me between eight and nine o'clock in the evening in front of the door of the Baptistery. I will look for you there. And if from my first words to you I do not clear myself absolutely of all the offenses you reproach me with, if I do not give you an explanation of my conduct that satisfies you completely, then redouble your scorn, treat me as the lowest of mankind, trample me underfoot, strike me with your riding crop, spit in my face: I admit beforehand that I shall have deserved it. Until then keep your friendship for me; you will soon see that I was never more worthy of it.

Yours ever,
ALFONSO DELLA VIOLA

On the evening of the 28th of July a man of high stature, of gloomy and discontented mien, strode through the streets of Florence toward the Grand-ducal piazza. When he reached the bronze statue of Perseus, he stopped to gaze at it awhile with the most profound contemplation. It was Benvenuto. Although Alfonso's answer and protestations had made little impression on his mind, he had long been bound to the young composer by a friendship too genuine and too deep to be wiped out forever overnight. Hence Benvenuto had not had the heart to refuse hearing what Della Viola had to say in vindication of his conduct.

And on his way to the Baptistery, where Alfonso was to meet

him, Cellini had wanted to see once more, after his long absence, the masterpiece which in former days had been the cause of so much toil and vexation to him. The piazza and neighboring streets were deserted; profound silence reigned in the district ordinarily so crowded and noisy. The artist contemplated his immortal work, wondering whether an obscure life and an ordinary mind were not to be preferred to glory and genius.

"Why am I not a drover from Nettuno or Porto d'Anzio?" he mused. "Like the cattle in my care, I should lead a rough, monotonous life, but it would at least be free from the turmoil which since childhood has bedeviled my existence. Treacherous and jealous rivals—unjust or ungrateful princes—relentless critics—brainless flatterers—continual alternations of success and adversity, of splendor and of poverty—overwork without end—never any respite, any comfort, any leisure—wearing out my body like a mercenary and feeling my soul forever chilled or aflame—can that be called living?"

The raucous shouts of three young artisans entering the piazza interrupted his meditation.

"Six florins," one of them was saying; "that's high."

"Maybe," retorted another, "but if he'd asked for ten, we'd have put up with it. Those damned Pisans have taken all the seats. Besides, Antonio, the gardener's cottage is only twenty paces from the pavilion. If we sit on the roof we can hear and see everything; the door of the little underground canal will be left open and we can get through with no trouble."

"Shucks!" added the third, "if only we get there we can afford to tighten the belt for a couple of weeks. You know what they're saying about yesterday's rehearsal? The court alone was allowed in: the Grand Duke and his suite never stopped applauding, the performers carried Della Viola shoulder-high, and in her ecstasy the Countess of Vallombrosa kissed him. It's going to be something beyond belief."

"Just look at these empty streets; the whole town is already in the Palace. We have just time. Let's go."

Only then did Cellini realize that the great musical festival was the subject of their conversation. The day, the hour had come. But this seemed hardly in keeping with Alfonso's fixing on this very evening for their rendezvous. How could the maestro leave the orchestra to itself at such a time, dessert his post on an occasion of such importance to him? It was inconceivable.

Nevertheless Benvenuto proceeded to the Baptistery. He found there his two pupils Paolo and Ascanio with some horses; for he was leaving for Leghorn that same evening, there to embark for Naples on the following day.

He had been waiting but a few minutes when Alfonso stood before him, his eyes burning in his pale face, and with an odd look of affected calmness.

"Cellini, you have come, thank you!"

"What then?"

"This is the night."

"I know it. Say what you have to say. I want that explanation you promised."

"The Pitti Palace, the grounds, the courtyard are packed; the people are jammed against the walls and jostle one another in the half-emptied fountains, on the roofs, in the trees, everywhere."

"I know."

"The Pisans have come; so have the Sienese."

"I know."

"The Grand Duke, the court, and the nobility are all there; the huge orchestra is all there."

"I know."

"But the music isn't there!" shouted Alfonso springing closer; "nor is the maestro there; do you know that too?"

"What! What does it mean?"

"There is no music, don't you understand? I've spirited it away. There is no maestro, for here I am. There will be no musical festival, since the work and the composer have both vanished. A note has just informed the Grand Duke that my work will not be played. '*It no longer suits my convenience*,' as I wrote to him in his own words; I too '*have changed my mind*.' Now can you picture the fury of that crowd, these people balked for the first time in their lives, these people who have left their town, their shops, and spent their money to hear my music, which they are not going to hear? Before I left to join you I was watching them; they were beginning to grow restless; the Grand Duke was being blamed. Do you grasp my plan, Cellini?"

"I think I do."

"Come along; let us get nearer the Palace and see the mine explode. Can you hear the yells, the tumult, the imprecations? Oh, my good Pisans, I can tell it's you by your profanity! Can you see the stones flying about, the branches of trees, the broken vases? None but the Sienese can throw like that! Look out, or we'll be knocked down. How they can run, these Florentines! They are storming the pavilion. Good! There goes a lump of mud into the ducal box. Luckily the great Cosimo has left it. Down goes the grandstand, the music desks, benches, windowpanes; the box and the pavilion crash to the ground. They are wrecking everything, what a magnificent riot! Hail to the Grand Duke! Damn it, Cellini, you took me for a worm: now tell me, are you satisfied? Is this revenge?"

With clenched teeth and dilated nostrils, Cellini stared without a word at the terrible spectacle of the infuriated populace. His eyes, which shone with a sinister glow, his square forehead, furrowed with large drops of sweat, the almost imperceptible tremor of his limbs, sufficiently betrayed the savage intensity of his joy. At last, grasping Alfonso's arm, he said:

"I leave for Naples this very minute; will you come?"

"To the end of the world, now."

"Kiss me, then, and to horse! You are a hero."

SIEDLER: Dear me! Do you want to bet that if Corsino ever found an opportunity to take revenge in the same way, he would pass it up? Of course it's all very well for a famous man who can afford to turn his fame into "fodder for his horses," as the Emperor Napoleon said of himself; but I defy a beginner, or even an artist who is tolerably well known, to indulge in such a luxury. There isn't one lunatic enough or vindictive enough. Still the joke is good. I also admire Benvenuto's moderation in the use of the dagger: "I struck him only twice, for at the first blow he fell dead." That's really touching.

WINTER: Is that cursed opera never going to end? (*The prima donna is uttering heart-rending shrieks.*) Which of you fellows can tell us a funny story to make us forget that creature's yells?

"I can," replied Turuth, the second flute; "I can tell you a little drama I witnessed in Italy, but it's not funny at all."

"Oh, we know you're a sensitive soul, the most sensitive of all the prize winners that the Institute has sent to Rome during the last twenty years to unlearn music—if so be that they knew music when they went."

"Never mind," said Dervinck, "if that's what the French can do, why, let him play on our feelings. I'm game for ten minutes' worth of sentiment. But you guarantee your story is true?"

"As true as it's true that I breathe."

"Observe the purist who won't say like everybody else: 'True as I breathe.'"

"Shush! Begin your yarn."

"Here goes then."

Vincenza

A Sentimental Tale

One of my friends, a talented painter named G., had inspired with a deep love a young peasant girl of Albano, named Vincenza, who occasionally went to Rome to offer her virginal head as model to the pencils of our best artists.[9] The naïve grace of that child of the mountains, and the candor visible in her countenance, had won for her a kind of worship on the part of the painters, which her proper and reserved behavior entirely justified.

From the day that G. seemed to take pleasure in seeing her, Vincenza never left Rome. Albano and its beautiful lake, and its other delightful spots, she exchanged for a dark and dirty little room in the Trastevere in the house of a workman's wife, whose children she took care of. Vincenza did not lack excuses for paying frequent visits to the studio of her *bello Francese*. I found her there one day. G. sat gravely in front of his easel, brush in hand; she, squatting at his feet like a dog at those of his master, watched his every look and drank in his slightest remark. From time to time she leaped up, went and stood in front of G., gazed at him rapturously, flung her arms

---

[9] Presumably at the French Academy in Rome, to which the Paris Institute annually sends the prize winners in the several arts. Berlioz won the music prize in 1830 and spent most of the next two years in Italy.

about his neck, and laughed convulsively without making the least attempt to disguise her frenzied passion.

For several months the happiness of the young Albanese remained cloudless, but jealousy put an end to it. G. was told things that made him doubt the faithfulness of Vincenza, and from then on he closed his door to her, stubbornly refusing to see her. Vincenza, struck to the heart by the separation, fell into a state of fearful despair. She would sometimes wait for whole days on the esplanade of the Pincio, where she hoped to meet G. She rejected all consolation, her remarks became more and more alarming and her manner more and more abrupt.

I had already attempted in vain to bring her obdurate lover back to her. When I would come across her, bathed in tears, a dead look in her eyes, I could only avert my gaze and go my way with a sigh. One day I met her striding in an extraordinary state of agitation along the bank of the Tiber, on a high rocky bluff called Poussin's Walk.

"Where are you going, Vincenza?—You won't talk to me?—I shan't let you go any farther; I foresee some rash act—"

"Please leave me, sir, don't try to stop me."

"But what are you doing here alone?"

"Don't you know that he won't see me any more, he doesn't love me any more, he thinks I am untrue to him? How can I live after that? I came here to drown myself."

Whereupon she began to give forth despairing cries. I watched her rolling on the ground, tearing her hair in fury, and hurling curses at those responsible for her grief. When she was somewhat tired out, I asked her if she would promise to keep calm until the next day, promising her in return that I would make a last plea with G.

"Listen to me, Vincenza. I will see him this evening; I will tell him everything that your unfortunate passion and the pity I feel for you can suggest, and try to make him forgive you. Come to my house tomorrow; I shall tell you the result and what you still have to do to make him yield. If I don't succeed, since nothing really better will offer—why, the Tiber will still be here."

"Oh, sir, you are kind, and I will do as you say."

That evening, accordingly, I saw G. in private, told him the scene I had witnessed, and begged him to grant the poor girl an interview as the only thing that could save her. "Find additional and more accurate information," I said in conclusion; "I wager my right arm that you're punishing her by mistake. Anyhow, even if you think nothing of my arguments, I can assure you that her despair is remarkable; it makes her one of the most dramatic figures you can imagine; take her back as a work of art."

"I must say, dear Mercury, you're a good pleader: I surrender. In a couple of hours I'll be seeing someone who can give me some new light on this ridiculous business. If I've been mistaken, let her come; the key will be in the lock. If, on the contrary, the key is not there, it will mean I have acquired the certainty that my suspicions were well founded. In that case, I beg you, let the matter drop. But let's talk of something else. What do you think of my new studio?"

"Much, much better than your other one, though the view is not so fine. If I'd been you, I'd have kept the garret, if only to see Hadrian's tomb and St. Peter's."

"Just like you, with your head in the clouds! Speaking of clouds, let me light my cigar. . . . Right! . . . And now good-by; I'm off to investigate. Tell your protégée my final decision. I'm really curious to see which of us two has been imposed on."

On the following day Vincenza called on me at an early hour. I was still asleep. At first she didn't dare wake me up; but her anxiety got the better of her, she took my guitar and played three chords, which woke me. Turning over, I saw her at my bedside, dying of emotion. Heavens! but she was lovely! Hope beamed from her enchanting face. In spite of the coppery tint of her skin I could see her flushing with passion; she was trembling in every limb.

"Well, Vincenza, I think he'll receive you. If the key is in his door, it means he forgives you, and—"

The poor girl interrupts me with a joyous cry, seizes my hand and kisses it frantically, wets it with her tears, moans, sobs, and rushes from my room, giving me as thanks a divine smile which shone upon me like a ray from heaven.

A few hours later, just as I had finished dressing, in came G. He was looking very grave and said: "You were right, I found out the truth; but why didn't she come to my place? I waited for her."

"What! She didn't come? She left here this morning half crazy with the hope I held out to her; she must have been at your place in a couple of minutes."

"I never saw her, though the key was certainly in the lock."

"Oh, I forgot to tell her you had changed your studio! She must have gone to the fifth floor, not knowing you're now on the second."

"We must find her! Hurry!"

We rushed to the top floor; the door of the studio was shut. Driven deep into the wood was the silver *spada* that Vincenza wore in her hair. G. recognized it with dismay, he had given it to her. We ran to her place in the Trastevere, to the Tiber, to Poussin's Walk; we inquired of all the passers-by: none had seen her. Finally we heard voices in violent altercation—we reached the spot they came from—two drovers were fighting over the white kerchief which the unhappy Vincenza had torn from her head and thrown on the bank before flinging herself . . .

The first violin was hissing gently between his teeth: "sss, sss, ssst. Pretty short and pretty poor, your story; and not very touching at that. Oh, you sensitive French flute, stick to your rustic tube. I prefer the truly original sensibility of our timpanist, the wild Kleiner, whose one ambition is to be top man in the town for the close tremolo and the breaking in of pipes. One day—"

"But the opera is over, keep your story for tomorrow."

"No, it's quite short; you can swallow it at a gulp. One day, I say, I met Kleiner leaning his elbows on a table at a café, alone as is his wont. He looked gloomier than usual. I go up to him, and say:

" 'Kleiner, what's the matter? You look terribly sad.'

" 'I am—I'm suffering from vexation.'

" 'Have you gone and lost eleven games of billiards again, like last week? Have you broken a new pair of drumsticks or a meerschaum you'd just finished?'

" 'No, I have lost—my mother.'

" 'My dear fellow, I'm sorry I put such questions to you—and then to hear such grievous news.'

"Kleiner (*to the waiter*): 'Waiter, one Bavarian cream.'

" 'Right away, sir.'

" 'Yes, old boy, I am much disturbed, believe me! My mother died last night, after a dreadful agony lasting fourteen hours.'

"The waiter: 'There is no more Bavarian cream, sir.'

"Kleiner (*striking the table with his fist and upsetting two spoons and a cup*): 'Confound it! Another vexation!'

"There you have natural sensibility—and admirably expressed!"

The musicians burst out laughing so loudly that the conductor, who has been listening, is compelled to take notice of it and to reprove them with an angry eye. The other eye smiles.

The Strolling Harpist
a tale of today

The Performance of an Oratorio

The Sleep of the Just

 A CONCERT is being given in the opera house.

The program consists of an enormous oratorio, which the public goes to hear as a matter of religious duty, to which it listens in religious silence, which the artists endure with religious fortitude, and which engenders in everybody a chilling boredom, black and thick as the walls of a Protestant church.

The unfortunate bass-drum player, who has no part in the work, frets anxiously in his corner. He alone has the courage to speak irreverently of the music, which he feels is the work of an inferior mind, so ignorant of the laws of orchestration as not to make use of the king among instruments, the bass drum.

I am seated next to one of the violas, who manages to hold his own during the first hour. But a few minutes later his bow begins to sweep the strings listlessly; then it drops from his hand, and I feel an unusual weight on my left shoulder. It is the martyr's head resting there all unconscious. I move closer so as to afford him a more solid and comfortable support. He is now sound asleep. The devout listeners nearest the orchestra look at us with indignation. It's scandalous! I aid and abet by continuing to serve as pillow for the sleeper. The other musicians are all laughing.

"We'll all fall asleep," says Moran to me, "if you don't keep us awake somehow or other. Come, tell us some anecdote from your recent trip to Germany. It's a country we love even though this fearsome oratorio hails from there. You must have run into a good many unusual adventures. Start talking, quick! the arms of Morpheus are already spreading to enfold us."

"It looks as if my job tonight is to help one of you to sleep and the rest to keep awake. All right, if I must, I must. But when you repeat the story I'm about to tell—it is a little décolleté here and there—don't say where you got it; it would ruin me with the kind of pious folk whose owlish eyes are staring at me this very minute."

"Don't worry," answers Corsino, just released from prison; "I'll take your story on myself." [1]

The Strolling Harpist
A Tale of Today

During one of my trips to Austria, when we were about a third of the way from Vienna to Prague, my train stopped, unable to go farther. Floods had swept away a viaduct, and a great stretch of track was under water, strewn with soil and rubbish. So we the travelers resigned ourselves to going a long way round by coach and thus reach the other section of the broken line. The number of comfortable conveyances was small, and I considered myself lucky to find a peasant's cart with a few bunches of straw. I was worn out and frozen stiff when I got to the spot for rejoining the train.

While I was trying to get thawed in the station waiting-room, there came in one of those strolling harpists so numerous in southern Germany, and whose talent is sometimes much above their lowly condition. Having taken his stand opposite me in one of the corners of the room, he looked at me attentively for a few minutes; then, grasping his harp as if to tune it, he softly repeated several times, by way of prelude, the first four bars of the theme of my *Queen Mab* Scherzo. [2] He scanned me surreptitiously while murmuring the little melodic figure. At first I thought it was chance that had brought these few notes under his fingers, and in order to satisfy myself I replied by humming the next four bars, to which, greatly

---

[1] This is confirmation, if any were needed, that Berlioz makes Corsino his mouthpiece equally with "The Author."
[2] From the *Romeo and Juliet* Symphony (1839). Berlioz performed the work in both Vienna and Prague during the trip referred to here (winter 1845-6).

to my astonishment, he replied quite accurately with the end of the phrase. Thereupon we looked straight at each other and smiled.

"*Dove avete inteso questo pezzo?*" I asked.

My first impulse in countries whose language I do not know is always to speak Italian, imagining that people who do not understand French are bound to know the only foreign tongue of which I know a few words.

But my man said: "I do not know Italian, sir, and do not understand what you have done me the honor of saying."

"You speak French, then. I was asking where you heard that piece."

"In Vienna, at one of your concerts."

"You recognized me?"

"Perfectly."

"But what brought you to that concert? How did you get there?"

"One evening, in a Vienna café where I used to play, I witnessed an argument among the frequenters of the place concerning your music, an argument so violent that for a minute I thought they would use the chairs to drive in their points. The main issue was the symphony *Romeo and Juliet*, and this gave me a strong desire to hear it. I said to myself: 'If I make more than three florins today, I'll spend one on a ticket for tomorrow's concert.' I was lucky enough to make three and a half florins and so was able to gratify my curiosity."

"And my Scherzo stuck in your memory?"

"I know only the first half and the last few bars. The rest I've never been able to remember."

"What impression did it make on you when you heard it? Tell me the truth."

"Oh, a strange impression, very strange! It made me laugh, laugh heartily, so that I couldn't stop. I had never thought that our familiar instruments could produce such sounds, nor that an orchestra of a hundred pieces could go in for such amusing little capers. I was greatly excited and kept on laughing. At the last bars, the quick phrase where the violins come in and shoot up like an arrow, I burst out so loud that one of my neighbors wanted to have me put out, thinking I was laughing at you. But I really wasn't—quite the contrary—but I couldn't control myself."

"You certainly take music in an original way. I am curious to hear how you came to learn it. Since you speak French so well, and the train to Prague doesn't start for a couple of hours, you must have lunch with me and tell me."

"It's a very simple story, sir, and hardly worth your hearing; but if you are willing to listen, I'm at your service."

We sat down to table, the inevitable Rhine wine was brought in, we drank a few bumpers, and here is, very nearly in his own words, what my guest told me of his musical education, or, rather, of the story of his life.

THE STORY OF THE STROLLING HARPIST

"I was born in Styria; my father was a strolling musician, like me today. Having wandered for ten years all over France, where he amassed a little money, he returned to his native country and took a wife. I was born a year after the marriage; eight months after my birth my mother died. My father resolved to stay with me; he looked after me and brought me up with the kind of care which usually only a woman is capable of. Knowing that living as we did in Germany I could not help learning German, he conceived the happy idea of first teaching me French, by using no other language in talking to me. Next, as soon as I was strong enough, he taught me the two instruments with which he was most familiar, the harp and the rifle. You know we are good shots in Styria; I soon became one of the best in our village, and my father was proud of me.

"I had also acquired a fair proficiency on the harp, when my father noticed that the progress I had been making seemed to have suddenly stopped. He asked me the reason. Not wanting to tell him, I assured him that it was no fault of mine and that I was practicing every day as usual, but in the open; feeling that I could not play the harp properly within the walls of our poor dwelling. The truth is that I was not working at all. And this is why: I had a nice youthful voice, strong and of pleasant quality. The pleasure I found in playing the harp in the woods and among the wildest sites of our country had led me also to sing to my own accompaniment. I used to sing with my full voice, using all my lung-power. I would listen rapturously to the sounds as they rolled along and died away in the valleys; it uplifted me to an extraordinary degree. I would impro-

35

vise some words and music, half in German, half in French, in which I tried to express the vague enthusiasm that possessed me. But my harp did not answer to my conception on the right accompaniment for these strange songs. I tried in vain a dozen ways of breaking the chords; the result always seemed to me thin and flat; so that, one day, at the end of a stanza where I wanted a powerful and resounding harmony, I impulsively seized my rifle, which never left my side, and fired a shot in the air to get the final explosion denied me by the harp. It was still worse when I sought after sustained, gently moaning sounds that should both express dreaminess and give rise to it; the harp proved more helpless than ever.

"Finding it impossible to draw from it anything like what I wanted, I stopped one day when I was improvising more sadly than usual, and in my discouragement remained silent, stretched on the heath with my head resting on my imperfect instrument. After a while a strange but sweet, veiled harmony, as mysterious as an echo from the songs of paradise, seemed to rise to my ear. I listened in rapture—and noticed that this harmony, which came from my harp without any apparent vibration of the strings, grew in richness and power, or dwindled, according to the strength of the wind. It was the wind, to be sure, that produced these extraordinary chords which I had never heard spoken of."

"You knew nothing about Æolian harps?"

"No, sir. I thought I had made a real discovery. It took complete hold of my mind; and from then on, instead of practicing my instrument, I did nothing but indulge in experiments that took up my whole time. I tried twenty different ways of tuning so as to avoid the confusion produced by the simultaneous vibration of so many strings; and at last I succeeded, after much trial and error, in tuning the greater number in unison and octaves, doing away with the rest. Then only did I obtain a series of chords truly magical in effect and which fulfilled my ideal aim.

"To these celestial harmonies I sang endless hymns, now bearing me off to crystalline palaces amid a million white-winged, star-crowned angels who sang with me in an unknown tongue; now plunging me in deepest sorrow and causing me to see in the clouds pale young girls with blue eyes, robed in their long, fair hair, more beautiful than the seraphs, and who, smiling through their tears, breathed harmonious moans that were wafted away with them by the gale to the far ends of the horizon. Another time, I dreamed I saw Napoleon, whose amazing history my father had frequently told me. I fancied myself on the island where he died and saw his guard standing motionless around him. Next I would see the Blessed Virgin, St. Magdalen, and our Lord Jesus Christ in a huge church on Easter Sunday. At other times I seemed to be all alone high up in the air while the whole world had vanished away; or else I suffered fearful grief, as if I had lost beings exceedingly dear to me, and I would tear my hair and roll on the ground sobbing.

"I cannot express the hundredth part of what I felt. It was during one of these scenes of poetic despair that I was found one day by a party of local hunters. On seeing my tears, my bewildered looks, my harp partly unstrung, they thought me crazed and brought me home, willy-nilly, to my father. For some time past he had imagined from my manner and my unaccountable excitement that I drank brandy (though I should have had to steal it, having no way to pay for it). Hence he did not share their opinion. Convinced that I had got drunk somewhere, he thrashed me and locked me up for a couple of days on bread and water. I endured this unjust punishment without a word to clear myself; I felt that the truth would not be believed or understood. Besides, I could not bring myself to take anybody into my confidence; I had discovered an ideal and sacred world and did not want to reveal the mystery to anyone. The parish priest, a worthy man whom I haven't yet mentioned, took an altogether different view of my bouts of ecstasy. 'Perhaps,' said he, 'they are visitations of the celestial spirit. This child may be destined to become a great saint.'

"The time of my first communion arrived, and my harmonic visions became both more frequent and more intense. My father gradually lost the bad opinion he had formed of me, and he too began to believe that I was mad. The priest, on the contrary, persisted in his own view and asked me whether I had ever thought of going into the Church.

" 'No, sir,' I replied, 'but I am thinking of it now. I rather think I should be happy to enter into that holy state.'

" 'Well, then, my child, search your heart, think it over, and we shall talk about it again.'

"Thereupon my father died after a short illness. I was fourteen;

I was full of grief, for he had seldom beaten me and I owed him considerable gratitude for having brought me up and taught me three things: French, the harp, and rifle shooting. I was alone in the world. The priest took me into his house, and very soon, on my assuring him of my vocation for the priesthood, he began to teach me what was necessary. Five years passed in learning Latin, and I was on the point of beginning the study of theology when one fine day I fell in love, madly in love, with two girls at the same time. Perhaps you do not think it possible? Do you, sir?"

"Indeed I do; I can quite believe it. Anything is possible to temperaments such as yours."

"It happened just as I said: I loved two girls at once; the one was merry, the other melancholy."

"Like the two cousins in Weber's *Freischütz*?"

"Exactly so. Oh, the *Freischütz*, there's one of my phrases in it! And in the woods, on stormy days, often—"

Here the narrator stopped and stared fixedly into the air, motionless and listening. He seemed to hear his beloved Æolian melodies, blending no doubt with the romantic melody of Weber's that he had just mentioned. His face went pale; tears came to his eyes. I took care not to disturb his ecstatic dream; for I admired, indeed envied him. We stood silent for a while. At last, hastily brushing the tears from his eyes, and emptying his glass, "Forgive me, sir," he resumed, "for having so rudely left you to yourself while I chased my own memories a moment. The fact is that Weber would have understood me, just as I understand him. He would never have taken me for a drunkard, a lunatic, or a saint. He has turned my dreams into realities—or, rather, he has made the common herd feel some of my impressions."

"The common herd, you say," I replied. "Just look around you, comrade, and tell me how many people you think have noticed that phrase, the mere memory of which has moved you so. I am sure I know the phrase you mean: it's in the overture, the clarinet solo above the tremolo? Am I right?"

"Yes, yes, shush!"

"Well, quote that sublime melody to anybody you like, and you'll find that out of a hundred people who have heard the *Freischütz*, not ten perhaps have even noticed it."

"You're probably right. Dear God, what a world! . . . Well,

my two beloveds were precisely the two heroines in Weber, and what's more, one was named Annette and the other Agatha, just as in the *Freischütz*. I never was able to make out which I loved the more, but with the merry one I was always sad, whereas the melancholy one made me merry."

"Naturally: we are all like that."

"If the truth must be told, I was devilishly happy. This double love made me forget my celestial concerts somewhat, and as for my holy vocation, it vanished in the twinkling of an eye. There is nothing like the love of two maids, one merry, the other dreamy, to cure you of the wish to be a priest and to take the bloom off theology. The good father noticed nothing, Agatha did not suspect my love for Annette, nor Annette my passion for Agatha. And I went on being gay and sad alternately, day in and day out."

"The devil! You must possess an inexhaustible fund of sadness and gaiety for such a blissful life to last any length of time."

"I don't know if I was as well provided as you say, for a fresh incident, far more serious than all the previous events of my life, came and tore me away from the arms of my dear girls and the lessons of the priest. I was one day engaged in poeticizing with Annette, who was laughing heartily at what she called my 'look of a house dog in the dumps'; I was singing to my own harp accompaniment one of my most impassioned poems, improvised at a time when neither my heart nor my senses had yet spoken. I stopped singing for an instant, with my head on Annette's shoulder, and tenderly kissed her hand. I asked myself what could be the mysterious faculty that had made me discover in music the expression of love, long before the slightest gleam of that emotion had been disclosed to me, when Annette, restraining with difficulty a new fit of laughter, exclaimed as she kissed me: 'My, but you're a chump! Still it makes no difference, even if you don't amuse me; I love you much more than that queer fellow Franz, Agatha's lover.'

" 'Whose lover . . . ?'

" 'Agatha's, didn't you know? He goes and sees her whenever you and I are together; she told me all about it.'

"You perhaps imagine, sir, that I leaped out of the house with a cry of rage, to go off and exterminate Franz and Agatha. Not a bit of it. I was in one of those cold furies that are far more terrible than frantic rage; I waited for my rival at the door of *our* mistress, and without reflecting that she was deceiving the pair of us—so that he had as much cause to complain of me as I had to complain of him—without even wanting him to know the cause of my aggression, I insulted him in such a fashion that we agreed to fight without witnesses on the following morning. And fight we did, sir, and I—a glass of wine, please, and I—here's your health—and I put his eye out."

"You fought with swords, then?"

"No, sir, with rifles, at fifty paces. I put a bullet in his left eye that left him one-eyed."

"And killed him, no doubt?"

"Oh, very much so; he fell dead on the spot."

"You had aimed at the left eye?"

"Alas, no, sir; I know you will think me very clumsy—at fifty paces—I had aimed at the right eye. But when I took aim, that she-devil Agatha came into my mind and my hand must have shaken, for on any other occasion I swear, without any bragging, that I could not have committed such a blunder.

"Be that as it may, I no sooner saw him sprawling on the ground than my anger and my two loves flew away together. My only thought was also to fly, from the law, which I already imagined on my heels. We had fought without witnesses and I might easily be regarded as a murderer. So I made off into the mountains as fast as possible, giving not a thought to Annette and Agatha. I was cured in a trice of my love for the pair, just as they had cured me of my vocation for theology. Which clearly proved that, in my case at least, the love of women is to the love of God as the love of life is to the love of women. It follows that the best way to forget two mistresses is to put a bullet into the left eye of the first of their lovers you come across. If you ever go in for dual loving as I did, and it gets in your way, I recommend my method."

I noticed that the fellow was getting excited; he kept biting his lower lip while speaking and laughed noiselessly in a strange way.

"You must be tired," I said; "suppose we go outside and smoke a cigar; you'll find it easier by and by to take up and finish your story."

"Very well," he replied.

Whereupon he grasped his harp and played with one hand the entire theme from *Queen Mab*. This seemed to restore his good humor and we went out, I muttering to myself: "What a rum fellow!" and he: "What a rum piece!"

"I lived in the mountains for a few days," resumed my queer companion; "my shooting generally brought me enough to live on, and the peasants never deny a sportsman a piece of bread. I finally got to Vienna, where, much against my will, I sold my faithful rifle in order to buy the harp I so badly needed for earning my livelihood. From that day forth, I followed my father's calling and became a strolling musician.

"I went to all the public places, into the streets, and more especially under the windows of people into whose souls I knew music had never found its way; I pestered them with my wild melodies and they always threw me a few coins to get rid of me. In that way I made a good deal out of Councilor K., Baroness C., Baron S., and twenty more of the Midas types who frequent the Italian opera. A Viennese musician with whom I had become acquainted had given me their names and addresses. As for the professional music-lovers, they listened to me with interest, barring two or three; but it seldom occurred to them to give me anything. I would take up my main collection in the cafés, during the evening, among the students and artists. That is how—as I think I told you—I was a witness to the argument caused by one of your works, which made me want to go and hear the *Queen Mab*. What a strange piece of music! Since then I have often gone through the market towns and villages scattered along your route, and I have gone again and again to Prague the beautiful. Ah, sir, there's a town that's musical!"

"Really?"

"You'll see. But this wandering life gets wearisome after a while I sometimes think of my two loves, and I imagine that it might be very pleasant to forgive Agatha, even if Annette took her turn to deceive me. The truth is, I barely make a living. My harp ruins me; these damnable strings have to be replaced continually; at the slightest shower they either snap or swell in the middle, spoiling the tone or going dead and discordant. You have no idea how much it costs me."

"My dear colleague, do not complain too much. If you only knew! In every opera house there are a good many strings more expensive than yours; some of them cost as high as sixty thousand or even a hundred thousand francs, and they deteriorate and go to

pieces every day, to the desperation of composers and managers!
. . . There are strings of exquisite tone and power which perish,
just like yours, by the merest accident. A little heat, the slightest
moisture, a mere nothing, and that accursed swelling in the middle
of which you speak destroys their whole charm and precision.
Many a fine work then becomes impossible to play. Many a vested
interest is jeopardized. Distracted managers jump into a stagecoach
and fly to Naples, the land of fine strings, but too often in vain. It
takes a long time and much luck to replace a first-class E string." [3]

"That may well be, sir; but your disasters do not make up for my
tribulations; and to escape my present distress, I have decided on a
plan I hope you will think good. During the last two years I have
become really proficient on my instrument; I can now appear as a
serious artist, and I plan to make some money by giving concerts in
Paris and other large towns of France.

"In Paris! Concerts in France! Ha ha! Ha ha! It's my turn to
laugh. Ha ha! What a funny fellow you are! I'm not laughing *at*
you. Ha ha! I can't help it. It's beyond my control, like the blessed
laughter which my Scherzo provoked in you."

"I'm sorry, but what have I said that's so funny?"

"You said—ha, ha, ha!—that you hoped to get rich by giving
concerts in Paris. Oh, that is truly a Styrian idea! See here, it's my
turn to speak, listen to me: to begin with, in France—wait a minute, I'm all out of breath—in France, whoever gives a concert is
taxed. Did you know that?"

"I'll be damned!"

"There are men whose business it is to levy, which is to say, take,
one eighth of the gross receipts of all concerts. They are even allowed the privilege of claiming one fourth if they so choose. This
is the way it goes: you come to Paris, you organize at your own
risk a musical matinee or evening; you have to pay for the hall, the
lighting, the heating, the posters, the score-copiers, and the performers. Your name being unknown, you are lucky if you take in
eight hundred francs. Your expenses, at the lowest, amount to six
hundred. Your profit should therefore be two hundred francs. Actually, you get nothing. The tax-collector takes care of your two

---

[3] Berlioz is punning on the word *chanterelle*, which is derived from *chanter*, to
sing, and which denotes the E string of the violin. Here the "first-class E strings"
are the coloratura sopranos of the opera world.

hundred francs, which the law gives him; he pockets them, with a bow, for he is exceedingly polite.

"If, as is still more likely, you take in no more than the six hundred francs that cover your expenses, the collector none the less takes one eighth of that amount; in effect, you are fined seventy-five francs for your insolence in attempting to make yourself known in Paris and presuming to live there respectably on the returns of your talent."

"But that cannot be!"

"No, it cannot be, you're right, but all the same it is. Besides, it is merely out of courtesy that I assume your receipts to be eight hundred or even six hundred francs. Unknown, poor, and a harpist, you would not get an audience of twenty. What I am telling you is the truth, the whole truth, and nothing but the truth. The greatest, the most famous virtuosos themselves have experienced the fickleness and indifference of the French public. In the lobby of a Marseille theater I was shown a mirror smashed by Paganini in his anger at finding the house empty at one of his concerts."

"Paganini?"

"Paganini. Perhaps they found the weather too warm on that day. For I ought to tell you that in my country there are circumstances which even the most unusual musical genius, the most undisputed, the most astounding, cannot overcome. Neither in Paris nor in the provinces does the public love music enough to face, for its sole sake, either heat, rain, or snow; it will not set back or put forward a few minutes the hour of its dinner; it goes to the Opéra or to a concert only if it can go there without inconvenience, without taking trouble—without much expense, of course—and only if it has absolutely nothing better to do. I am firmly convinced that you could not find one man in a thousand who would consent to go and hear the most remarkable virtuoso or the most sublime masterpiece if he had to listen to it alone and in an unlighted hall. There is not one in a thousand who, while ready to make a gift to a musician to the tune of fifty francs, would be willing to pay half that sum to listen to some prodigy of art unless fashion compelled it; for even masterpieces are occasionally the fashion.

"The public will sacrifice to music neither a dinner, nor a ball, nor even a simple outing, still less a horse-race or a trial in court. People will go to hear an opera if it is a new one, or if the diva or the tenor in vogue is singing. They will go to a concert provided there is something extraneous to excite their curiosity—say, the rivalry or open hostility of two celebrated virtuosos. It is not a matter of admiring their talent, but of finding out which of the two will go under; it is just another kind of foot race or boxing-match.

"Again, people will go and be bored in a theater for four long hours, or at a classical concert will put on the most tiresome show of enthusiasm, because it is the correct thing to have one's own box, and seats in it are sought after. People go especially to certain first nights, and unhesitatingly pay an exorbitant price if on that evening the manager or the authors are gambling their fortune, waging one of those fateful battles that will decide their future. Then the interest runs high. There is no thought of studying the new work, of looking for its fine points and enjoying them; all they want to know is whether it fails or not. And according as chance favors it or not, according as the trend of opinion may be set one way or the other by one of those obscure and inexplicable causes to which the slightest incident may give birth, people will go there and nobly side with the stronger party; crushing the loser if the work is damned, or, if it succeeds, carrying the author in triumph, without having understood any the smallest part of the work. On a night of this sort, hot or cold, windy or snowy, whether it costs a hundred francs or a hundred sous, people *must* see that show: it's a battle—often it's an execution.

"In France, my dear fellow, you must *coach* your public to make it go, just as you coach racehorses; it's a special art. There are enchanting artists who will never master it, while others who are incurably second-rate are irresistible coaches. Fortunate are those who possess both these rare talents! And yet even the most accomplished in this respect occasionally meet their match among the phlegmatic inhabitants of certain cities of antediluvian manners, sleeping cities that have never been awakened, or that have fallen victims, thanks to their indifference about art, to the fanatical passion of thrift.

"All this reminds me of an old story, possibly new to you, in which Liszt and Rubini,[4] seven or eight years ago, cut a rather uncommon figure. They had just gone into partnership for a musical assault upon certain northern towns. Assuredly, if ever two ath-

---

[4] Giovanni Battista Rubini (1795–1854) was a famous tenor.

letic coaches joined forces to break in the public, it was these two incomparable virtuosos. Well, as I say, Rubini and Liszt (you take my meaning: none other than Liszt and Rubini!) come to one of these modern Athenses and announce their opening concert. Nothing is spared, neither elaborate puffing, nor colossal posters, nor a varied and attractive program—nothing. And nothing works: the hour for the concert comes, our two lions enter the hall—not fifty people there! Rubini, indignant, says he will not sing, he is choking with anger. 'On the contrary,' says Liszt, 'you must do your very best. This nuclear public is evidently the elite of the music-lovers in this part of the country, and you must *treat* it as such. Let us do ourselves proud!'

"He sets Rubini the example and plays the first piece magnificently. Then Rubini sings in his most disdainful middle register. Liszt returns and plays the third number; then, stepping to the edge of the platform and bowing graciously to the audience, he says: 'Gentlemen and lady' (there was only one), 'I think you have had enough music. Now I would make so bold as to ask whether you will kindly come and take supper with us.' There was a moment's hesitation among the fifty guests; but since, all things considered, the invitation was enticing, they made a point of not declining it. The supper cost Liszt twelve hundred francs. The two virtuosos did not repeat the experiment. And there they made a mistake, for they would have had a full house at the second concert—for supper's sake.

"That was one of the great feats of coaching, and surely it's within easy reach of any millionaire.

"I met one day one of our leading pianist-composers, who was returning disappointed from a seaport where he had counted on making an appearance. 'I had no chance of giving a concert there,' he said to me with perfect seriousness: 'the herring had come in. The whole town could think of nothing else than this valuable delicacy.' How, indeed, is a man to compete with a school of fish?

"So you see, my dear fellow, that it's no easy matter to coax—I mean coach—one's following, especially in second-class towns.

"But when all is said that can be said against the critical sense of the public at large, one must go on to speak of the many worthless oafs who pester this same public, harass it, beset it without shame, from the soprano to the basso profundo, from the solo flageolet to the euphonium. The meanest guitar-twanger, the heaviest piano-pounder, the most grotesque warbler of inanities, aspires to fame and a competence by giving a concert, were it but on the jew's-harp. Hence the truly pitiful tortures that well-to-do householders have to endure. For the patrons of these virtuosos and the ticket-touts are stinging hornets against whom there is no protection. They use every kind of subterfuge, every trick of diplomacy, to palm off on the poor rich people a dozen of those frightful rectangles of cardboard known as concert tickets. And when a pretty woman has been set the cruel task of disposing of these at second hand, you should see the savage, despotic way she imposes on any man, young or old, who may have the pleasure of meeting her:

" 'Mr. A., here are three tickets which Mrs. G. has asked me to have you take—give me thirty francs. Mr. B., everyone knows you are a great musician; you once knew the tutor of Grétry's nephew; you spent a month in Montmorency next door to the great man himself; here are a couple of tickets for a delightful concert that you dare not miss—twenty francs, please. My dear, last winter I took a thousand francs' worth of tickets for your husband's protégés; he won't object if you ask him to pay for these five orchestra seats—just give me fifty francs. Come now, Mr. C., with your truly artistic nature, you must encourage young talent; I feel sure you will want to hear this entrancing child' (or 'this interesting young girl,' or 'this remarkable wife and mother,' or 'this poor youth who must be snatched from military service'); 'here are two seats, you owe me ten francs, and I'll extend credit till this evening.'

"And so on. I know people who throughout February and March, the months when this scourge is at its worst in Paris, keep away from all drawing-rooms for fear of losing their all in these holdups. I don't dare go into the obvious sequel to these awe-inspiring concerts: the fact that the unfortunate critics have to stand them—it would take too long to paint their woes. But of late the critics are not the only ones who suffer. Since nowadays every virtuoso—jew's-harpist or whatever—who has 'done Paris' (which is trade slang for 'giving some sort of concert' in that city) thinks he must go on tour, he pesters a number of good people who have not had the wit to keep quiet about their foreign connections. The idea is to extort letters of introduction, to get a word sent to some innocent banker, some obliging ambassador, some generous friend of the arts, saying that Miss C. is going to give concerts in Copenhagen or Amsterdam, that she has unusual talent, and begging that she be 'encouraged'—namely, by taking a large quantity of her tickets.

"These efforts generally work harm upon everybody, especially upon the performers who have been thus recommended. Last winter in Russia [5] I was told the story of a singer of romances and her husband who, after 'doing' St. Petersburg and Moscow without much success, considered themselves none the less worthy of recommendation and begged a powerful protector to introduce them at the Sultan's Court. Constantinople had to be 'done.' Nothing less. Liszt himself had not yet dreamed of undertaking the journey. But Russia having been icy to them, this was a further reason for trying their luck under skies proverbially warm, and finding out if, by the merest luck, the best friends of music might not be the Turks.

"So here are our couple armed with good introductions, and like the wise men following a star, which now guides them treacherously toward the East. They reach Pera; their letters of introduction bear fruit; the seraglio is opened to them. Madame is to be admitted to sing her romances before the Lord of the Sublime Porte, before the Commander of the Faithful. But what is the good, may I ask, of being the Sultan if he is exposed to such trials? Anyhow, a concert before the court is allowed; four black slaves bring in a piano. The white slave, the husband, carries the singer's shawl and music. The guileless Sultan, who does not suspect anything like what is in store for him, takes his seat on a heap of cushions, surrounded by his principal officers and flanked by his chief interpreter. His hookah is lit for him, he blows a cloud of fragrant smoke, the singer takes her place and begins with the following romance by M. Panseron: [6]

> *I know it now, I am betrayed,*
> *Another's won your heart away.*
> *But even though your love can fade,*
> *Mine will be true to you for aye.*

---

[5] In 1847, Berlioz's first trip there.
[6] Auguste Panseron (1796–1859), a renowned composer of parlor songs and professor at the Conservatoire.

> *Yes, at that altar you have left,*
> *My passion, vowed to you, will burn.*
> *And should you find yourself bereft,*
> *Just summon me, I will return.*[7]

"At this point the Sultan beckons to his interpreter and says with that Turkish brevity of which Molière has given us such fine examples in *Le Bourgeois Gentilhomme*: '*Naoum!*'

"The interpreter translates: 'Sir, His Highness bids me tell you that the lady would greatly oblige him by shutting up at once.'

" 'But—she has hardly begun—it would be mortifying.'

"During this dialogue the ill-starred songstress, her eyes in frenzy rolling, continues to yelp M. Panseron's romance:

> *If her love too does not abide,*
> *O weak one, waste not your regret:*
> *One word will bring me to your side,*
> *Where I will help you to forget.*[8]

"A fresh sign from the Sultan, who, as he strokes his beard, hisses over his shoulder to the interpreter the single word: '*Zieck!*' The interpreter to the husband (the woman is still proceeding with M. Panseron's romance): 'Sir, the Sultan bids me tell you that if the lady does not stop at once, he will have her thrown into the Bosporus.'

"This time the trembling husband hesitates no longer; he claps his hand over his wife's mouth and abruptly interrupts her tender refrain:

> *Just summon me, I will return,*
> *Just summon me, I—*

"A deep silence, broken only by the noise of the drops of sweat which fall from the husband's forehead to the lid of the humiliated piano. The Sultan sits motionless; our two travelers dare not withdraw. Then a new word: '*Bulak!*' springs from his lips amid a puff

---

[7] *Je le sais, vous m'avez trahie,/Une autre a mieux su vous charmer./Pourtant, quand votre cœur m'oublie,/Moi, je veux toujours vous aimer./*

Oui, je conserverai sans cesse/L'amour que je vous ai voué;/Et si jamais on vous délaisse,/Appelez-moi, je reviendrai.

[8] *Si jamais son amour vous quitte,/Faible, si vous la regrettez,/Dites un mot, un seul, et vite/Vous me verrez à vos côtés.*

of smoke. The interpreter: 'Sir, His Highness bids me tell you that he wishes to see you dance.'

" 'Dance! I?'

" 'Yourself, sir.'

" 'But I am no dancer, I am not even a musician; I accompany my wife on her journeys; I carry her music, her shawl, that is all—and really, I could not—'

" '*Zieck! Bulak!*' repeats the Sultan sharply, blowing a cloud of smoke that speaks louder than threats. Thereupon the interpreter exclaims hurriedly: 'Sir, His Highness bids me tell you that if you do not dance at once, he will have you thrown into the Bosporus.'

"This was no time to argue, so our poor fellow starts gamboling most grotesquely, until such time as the Sultan, stroking his beard for the last time, shouts in a terrible voice: '*Daioum be bulak! Zieck!*' The interpreter: 'Enough, sir. His Highness bids me tell you that you and the lady must withdraw, and leave not later than tomorrow. If you ever return to Constantinople, he will have the pair of you thrown into the Bosporus.'

"Sublime Sultan, admirable critic, what an example you set, and why is the Bosporus not in Paris?

"History does not say whether the unfortunate couple pushed on to China, nor whether the gentle songstress obtained letters of introduction to the Celestial Emperor, supreme ruler of the Middle Kingdom. It is most likely, for she has not been heard of since. The husband, if this surmise is true, will either have come to a wretched end in the Yellow River, or else have been promoted chief dancer to the Son of the Sun."

"This last anecdote, at any rate," broke in the harpist, "doesn't prove anything against Paris."

"Do you mean to say you can't see the obvious implication? It proves that Paris, being in a continual state of fermentation, throws up so many musicians of all sorts, of great merit or little or none, that they either have to devour one another like so many infusoria or to emigrate; and that even the guard keeping watch at the seraglio gates [9] can no longer protect from musicians the Emperor of the Turks."

---

[9] An allusion to Malherbe's lines about death:
"*Et la garde qui veille aux barrières du Louvre/N'en défend point nos rois.*"—
(*Stances à M. du Périer.*)

"It is all very sad," said the harpist with a sigh. "I see I shan't be able to give a concert. All the same, I'm bent on going to Paris."

"Oh, go to Paris; nothing prevents. Indeed, I predict that you will have plenty of windfalls if only you put into practice the system you ingeniously worked out in Vienna for making people who are indifferent to music pay for it. I can be of help to you by pointing out the houses of the rich people who most detest it; though even if you should work by pure chance and play in front of every house of good appearance, you'd win every other time. But to spare yourself fruitless improvising, just take down the following addresses, which I warrant correct and valuable: [1]

"1. Rue Drouot: facing the municipal building;

"2. Rue Favart: opposite the rue d'Amboise;

"3. Place Ventadour: facing the rue Monsigny;

"4. Rue de Rivoli: I forget the number of the house, but anybody will point it out to you;

"5. Place Vendome: all the numbers here are sure-fire.

"There are also many good houses in the rue Caumartin. In addition, find out the addresses of our most celebrated lions, of our popular composers, of most of our writers of opera librettos, of the principal box-holders at the Conservatoire, the Opéra, and the Italian Theater. All these are bound to mean so much coin of the realm to you. Don't forget the rue Drouot, and go there every day—it's the general headquarters of your taxpayers."

I had got as far as this when the bell announced the departure of my train. I shook hands with the strolling harpist, sprang into the carriage, and said: "Colleague, farewell! I'll see you in Paris! With a little method and my advice, you can make your fortune there. Once again I recommend the rue Drouot to you."

"Meanwhile, remember my remedy against dual love."

"Of course! Farewell!"

"Farewell!"

The train for Prague started. For some moments more, I saw that Styrian dreamer leaning on his harp and gazing after me. The rumble of the train prevented me from hearing anything else, but from the motion of the fingers of his left hand I could see that he was playing the *Queen Mab* theme; while from his lips I guessed

---

[1] The first three were those of the Opéra, the Opéra-Comique, and the Italian Theater, respectively.

that at the very instant when I was saying: "What a rum fellow!" he was himself repeating: "What a rum piece!"

Dead quiet. The snores of my viola and of the bass drum, who finally followed the other's example, can be heard interlarding the learned counterpoint of the oratorio. From time to time also, the noise of the pages turned simultaneously by the faithful who are following the sacred libretto makes a pleasant change from the somewhat monotonous effect of the voices and instruments.

"Are you through already?" asks the first trombone turning to me.

"You are most kind. It's the qualities of the oratorio that make you pay me such a compliment. But I am through. My stories are not like this fugue, which will last, I fear, till the Day of Judgment. Drive on, you brute, keep hounding it. That's it, invert the subject now! We can say of it what Mme Jourdain says of her husband: 'As big a fool from the back as from the front.' "

"Be patient," says the trombone, "there are only six more arias and eight little fugues."

"What's to become of us?"

"Be fair now, confess it's irresistible music—let's all go to sleep!"

"All of us? No, that would be risky. Like sailors at sea we must leave a few men on watch. We'll relieve them in a couple of hours."

Three double basses are selected for the first watch, and the rest of the orchestra goes to sleep as one man.

As for me, I gently shift my viola, who seems to have inhaled a phial of chloroform, to the shoulder of the errand boy, and I slip away. It is raining torrents. I hear the gurgling of the spouts, and I drink in avidly this refreshing harmony.

er Freischütz is being performed.

No one in the orchestra speaks. Each musician is intent on his task, which he carries out zealously and lovingly. During the intermission one of them asks me if it is true that at the Paris Opéra a real skeleton was introduced in the infernal scene. I reply in the affirmative, and promise to relate the biography of the poor fellow the next day.

A Debut in *Freischütz*

a necrological tale

Marescot

a study in plastic surgery

A VERY dull Italian opera of the modern school is being given.

Hardly have the musicians arrived when the majority of them put aside their instruments and remind me of the promise I made yesterday. They form a circle around me. The trombones and the bass drum are strenuously at work. Circumstances favor us: we have another hour or two of duets and unison choruses. I cannot decline to tell the wished-for story.

The conductor, who always pretends not to know that we carry on literary diversions, leans back a little, so as to listen more easily. The prima donna has shrieked so fearful a high D that we thought she was in the middle of her confinement. The public stamps with joy; two huge bouquets alight on the stage. The diva bows and goes off. She is recalled, returns, bows a second time, and goes off again. Recalled once more, she hastens to reappear, bows anew, and since we cannot tell when this rigmarole will end, I begin.

"In 1822 I lived in the Latin Quarter, where I was supposed to be studying medicine. When performances of the *Freischütz* were being given at the Odéon under the title of *Robin des bois*, which denoted the adaptation by M. Castil-Blaze,[1] I went nightly, in spite

---

[1] François Henri-Joseph Blaze, known as Castil-Blaze (1784–1857), was a miscellaneous writer and dabbler in music, who wrote music criticism and parlor songs and also "adapted." His adaptation of Weber's *Freischütz* opened in December 1824, not 1822 as Berlioz states.

of my studies, to hear the disfigured masterpiece of Weber. I had by that time all but thrown my scalpel into the bushes. But one of my former fellow students, Dubouchet, who has since risen to be one of the most sought-after doctors in Paris, often accompanied me to the theater, for he shared my musical fanaticism. At the sixth or seventh performance, a big red-haired booby who was sitting beside us took it into his head to hiss Agatha's aria in the second act, alleging that it was Gothic music, and that nothing in the entire opera was any good except the waltz and the hunters' chorus. As you can imagine, he was hustled outside: that was our way of carrying on discussion in those days; and Dubouchet, readjusting his somewhat crumpled cravat, shouted to the crowd: 'What he did is not surprising: I know the fellow—he is a grocer's assistant in the rue Saint-Jacques!' At which the audience applauded wildly.

"Six months later, having done himself too well at his master's wedding breakfast, this poor devil of a grocer's assistant falls ill and has himself carted to the hospital of La Pitié; he is well cared for, dies, and is not buried—as may readily be surmised.

"Our young fellow, well treated and duly dead, comes by chance under the eyes of Dubouchet, who recognizes him. The pitiless medical student of La Pitié, instead of shedding a tear over his vanquished enemy, hastens to purchase the corpse and says, as he hands it to the attendant of the operating-room: 'François, here is a subject for dry preparation; but see that you do it with care; he is an acquaintance of mine.'

"Fifteen years roll by (fifteen years! how long life seems when one is disgusted with it!), the manager of the Opéra entrusts me with the composition of the recitatives in the *Freischütz* [2] and the staging of the masterpiece, the costumes being naturally put in charge of Duponchel."

"Duponchel!" simultaneously exclaim five or six musicians; "do you mean the celebrated inventor of the canopy, the man who introduced the canopy into opera as the principal element of success? The author of the canopy in *La Juive*, in *La Reine de Chypre*, in *The Prophet*,[3] the creator of the floating canopy, the miraculous canopy, the canopy of canopies?"

---

[2] The original calls for spoken dialogue between numbers but the Paris Opéra requires music throughout. Berlioz's recitatives were used in 1841 and thereafter.
[3] Operas by Halévy (the first two) and Meyerbeer.

"The very same, gentlemen. And so, as Duponchel was once more in charge of the costumes, processions, and canopies, I called on him to find out his plans for the properties in the infernal scene, wherein his canopy, unfortunately, could have no place.

" 'By the way,' I said, 'we need a skull for the evocation of Samiel, and skeletons for the apparitions; I hope you are not going to give us a pasteboard skull, or skeletons of painted canvas, like those in *Don Giovanni.*'

" 'My dear fellow, there is no other way of doing it; it is the only method known.'

" 'What do you mean, the only method? Suppose I supply you with something genuine, natural—a real skull, a real man, made of bones, but without flesh on them, what will you say to that?'

" 'Upon my word, I'll say—that it's excellent, perfect—an admirable device.'

" 'Well, then depend on me, you shall have it.'

"Whereupon I jump into a cab and drive in double-quick time to the house of Dr. Vidal, another of my former operating-room comrades. He too has made a fortune; it is only physicians who can afford to live.

" 'Have you a skeleton you can lend me?'

" 'No, but I have a fairly good head, which, I'm told, once belonged to a German physician who died of poverty and grief. Whatever you do, don't spoil it, I value it greatly.'

" 'Don't worry; I'll be responsible for it.'

"I put the doctor's skull in my hat, and off I go.

"On the boulevard fate, which delights in pranks of this kind, brings me face to face with Dubouchet, whom I had lost track of, and the sight of him inspires me with a brilliant idea.

" 'Hello, there!'

" 'How are you?'

" 'Very well, thanks; but never mind me, the question is: how is our music-lover?'

" 'What music-lover?'

" 'Why, the grocer's assistant, of course, the fellow we bundled out of the Odéon for hissing Weber's music, the one who was so carefully "prepared" by François.'

" 'Ah, I get you. Why, he is in the best of health, thank you. He stands clean and neat in my consulting-room, quite proud of being

55

so artistically jointed and built up. Not a bone of him missing, he is a masterpiece. Only the head is damaged a little.'

" 'Well, then give him to me; he is a youth with a future. I want to introduce him at the Opéra; there is a part for him in the next show.'

" 'What do you mean?'

" 'You'll see!'

" 'Oh, well, if it's a theatrical secret—and if you promise to explain later, I won't insist on knowing now. The music-lover shall be delivered to you.'

"No time is lost in conveying the dead man to the Opéra, though in a case far too short for him. I hail the general utility man."

" 'Here, Gattino!'

" 'Ay, Ay, sir.'

" 'Open this case. You see that young man?'

" 'I do, sir.'

" 'He is to make his debut in the opera tomorrow. Make him a nice little box in which he can be comfortable and stretch his legs.'

" 'Yes, sir.'

" 'As for his costume, take an iron rod and stick it in his backbone, so that he may hold himself as straight as M. Petipa when meditating a pirouette.'

" 'Yes, sir.'

" 'You will next fasten four candles together, which you will place in his hands, lighted; he is a grocer, they will be familiar to him.'

" 'Yes, sir.'

" 'But as his head is not in the best of conditions—you can see it has been a bit chipped—we must substitute this other one.'

" 'I follow you, sir.'

" 'It once belonged to a scientist—that doesn't matter—who died of starvation—no need for that to concern us. As for the other skull, that of the grocer, who died of indigestion, you will make a slight slit in the very top (don't be afraid, nothing will come out of it) so that it may receive the point of Caspar's sword in the evocation scene.'

" 'Very good, sir.'

"My orders were carried out and from that time on, at every

56

performance of the *Freischütz*, just as Samiel exclaims: 'I am here!' a thunderclap is heard, a tree crashes to earth, and our grocer, who was once so hostile to Weber's music, appears amid the crimson glow of Bengal lights, enthusiastically brandishing his lighted torch.

"Who could have foreseen the dramatic vocation of the fellow? Who ever would have thought that he might some day make his debut precisely in that opera? He has a better head now, and more good sense: he no longer hisses—*Alas, poor Yorick!*"

"Well, now, that makes me sad," said Corsino simply. "Though he was once a grocer, this beginner, when all is said and done, was almost a human being. I don't like fooling about death like this. Though in his lifetime he hissed Weber's score, I know people who are guilty of worse things, and whose remains have not been dese-crated with such cynical impiety. I too have lived in Paris, and in the Latin Quarter at that; and there I've seen at work one of those wretches who take advantage of the impunity allowed them by French law and practice infamous operations on musical works. There are people of all sorts in this Paris of ours. Some of them beg their bread at street corners. Others earn theirs by night, a lantern in one hand and a hook in the other; some comb out the gutters for their food; others tear posters and sell them to the paper-dealers; a little more useful are the men who kill and skin old horses at Mont-faucon. The fellow I am speaking of killed and skinned the works of celebrated composers.

"Marescot was his name; his trade was to arrange all kinds of music for two flutes, or for one guitar, but especially for two flageolets, and then publish it. Since the music of the *Freischütz* did not belong to him (everyone knows that it 'belonged' to the trans-lator and improver of the libretto, who had labored with such genius to make it worthy of appearing at the Odéon as *Robin des bois*), Marescot did not dare practice his trade on that. This broke his heart, for, as he would say, he had 'an idea' which, applied to a certain part of Weber's opera, would bring him in big money. I occasionally saw this practitioner, and somehow he had taken a liking to me. Our musical tendencies were nevertheless not quite the same, as you can imagine. As a result I almost let him suspect what I thought of him, and on one occasion so far forgot myself as very nearly to tell him my opinion of his musical abattoir. This embroiled us somewhat, and for six months I did not set foot in his workshop.

"Despite his successful raids on the great masters, his appearance was in general rather wretched and his clothing decidedly threadbare. One fine day, however, I met him stepping out briskly under the arcades of the Odéon in a brand-new frock-coat and high boots, and wearing a white tie; I even think that on that day—so greatly had fortune transformed him—his hands were clean.

" 'Heavens!' I exclaimed, absolutely dazzled at the sight of him, 'have you had the misfortune to lose a rich American uncle, or have you become someone's collaborator in a new opera of Weber's? You look so spruce, so furbished, so remarkable!'

" 'I?' he replied, 'a collaborator? What next? I need no collaborator; I elaborate Weber's music without any help, and I thrive pretty well on it. You don't believe me—well, let me tell you that I have at last realized my idea, and I wasn't wrong when I told you that it was worth money, a great deal of money, an immense amount of money. Listen: Schlesinger, the Berlin publisher, owns the *Freischütz* music in Germany; he was fool enough to buy the rights to it, the simpleton. True, he did not pay a high price, but so long as Schlesinger did not publish that Gothic music, it remained, here in France, the sole property of the author of *Robin des bois*, by virtue of the words and the improvements with which he had adorned it. So I could not touch it. But as soon as it was published in Berlin, it became public property here, no French publisher being willing, as you can well believe, to pay the Prussian publisher for the reprint rights to such a work.

" 'I was now free to snap my fingers at the French author's rights, and to publish *my* piece without any words, in accordance with my great idea. I refer to Agatha's prayer in A flat, in the third act of *Robin des bois*. You remember that it is in three-four time, and the pace rather lulling. It is accompanied by syncopated horn chords that are very difficult and as stupid as can be. I thought to myself if I put the song into six-eight time, marking it *allegretto*, and accompanying it intelligibly—that is, with the rhythm proper to that meter (a quarter note followed by an eighth, the rhythm of drums in a quick march)—it would make a very pretty piece, which would be bound to succeed. I therefore wrote out my piece that way, scored for flute and guitar, and I published it, allowing Weber's name to stand on it. Now it has caught on so well that I am selling it, not by the hundreds, but by the thousands. The sales go up daily. It alone will bring me in more than the entire opera brought that blockhead Weber; more even that it brought M. Castil-Blaze, who is a clever fellow just the same. That's what it is to have ideas!'

"What do you say to that, gentlemen? I feel pretty sure that you will take me for a historian and hence not believe me. And yet what I have told you is absolute fact. I may add that for a long time I kept a copy of Weber's prayer thus transfigured by the *idea* which made the *fortune* of M. Marescot, French publisher of music, professor of the flute and guitar, in business rue Saint-Jacques, at the corner of the rue des Mathurins, in Paris."

The opera is over; the musicians file out, looking back at Corsino with an air of mocking disbelief. Some even allow the vulgar word "legpull" to escape their lips.

I can vouch, however, for the authenticity of his story, for I knew Marescot. He has in fact a good many more achievements of the kind to his credit.

The S in *Robert le diable*

a grammatical tale

A VERY dull modern French opera is being given. No one in the orchestra attends to his part; everybody is talking except a first violin, the trombones, and the bass drum. Catching sight of me, Dimsky, the double bass, calls across to me:

"Why, what's become of you? We haven't set eyes on you for nearly a week. You look sad. I hope you haven't had any trouble like our friend Kleiner."

"No, thank heaven; I haven't any loss to mourn in my family; but, as the Catholics say, I have been on a *retreat*. Those are the occasions when the devout prepare themselves without distraction for the performance of some important religious duty by retiring into a convent or seminary, where, for a shorter or a longer time, they fast, pray, and give themselves over to pious meditations. Well, I may tell you that it is my yearly habit to make a *poetical* retreat. I shut myself in at home and read Shakespeare or Virgil, sometimes both. This makes me rather ill at first; next I sleep twenty hours on end, and then I am myself again. The only aftermath is an unconquerable sadness, of which you now see the remains, and which your cheerful talk will soon chase away. What has been said, sung, told, or performed in my absence? Do bring me up to date."

"We have performed *Robert le diable* and *I Puritani*.[1] There has been no singing whatever; all we've done in the orchestra is argue. The last time it was about a passage in the gambling scene in Meyerbeer's opera. Corsino maintains that the Sicilian knights are in league to swindle Robert. I don't believe that the author of the libretto ever meant to brand them all with this shameful deed and that their aside:

'We've got him now! We've got him now!'

is a liberty taken by the translator. We wanted to know from you

---

[1] By Meyerbeer and Bellini respectively.

what the French words are that the chorus sings in the original text."

"They are the same; your translator has no betrayal on his conscience."

"I was sure of it," resumes Corsino; "I've won my bet."

"Yes, and it's another example of M. Meyerbeer's luck—luckiest of composers in this vale of tears. For it's a fact that there is little difference between what is called the theatrical game and other games of chance: the most skillful plotting is no guarantee of success: you win by not losing and you lose by not winning. Those are the only two reasons that can be given for loss or gain, success or failure. Chance, fortune, luck, are merely words for the unknown cause which remains forever unknowable. But this luck, this good fortune, this 'fortune, propitious or the reverse' (as Bertram is simple-minded enough to call it in *Robert le diable*), none the less seems to cling to certain gamblers, to certain authors, with incredible obstinacy. A given composer, for instance, has plotted his game for ten years, has computed all the sequences of the red and the black, has prudently resisted all the snares of ordinary chance and the temptations they held out to him; then at last one fine day he sees the black turn up thirty times in a row and he says to himself: 'My fortune is made; all the operas produced for ever so long have fallen flat; the public wants a success. My score is in a style the exact opposite of my predecessors: I'll stake it on the red.' The wheel goes round, and black comes up for the thirty-first time; his work falls flat.

"Such things happen even to people whose profession it is to write platitudes, a lucrative profession, as everybody knows, and generally successful in all countries. On the other hand, such are the mad whims of the blind goddess, that one sees fine works, masterpieces, new, bold, and grand conceptions succeed effortlessly and brilliantly.

"Thus at the Paris Opéra we have seen these ten years past a fair number of mediocre works reaping mediocre success only; we have heard others entirely worthless whose success has been in keeping, while *The Prophet*,[2] which had held its hand and plotted its game

---

[2] Meyerbeer's opera made its first appearance on April 16, 1849. Thirteen years had elapsed since the composer's previous work, though we now know that *The Prophet* had been ready only since 1843.

alongside the roulette table for twelve, thirteen, or perhaps fourteen years (on the ground that the sequence of defunct operas was never long enough), at last saw the thirty-first black turn up. It was the same calculation as that of the poor devil I referred to just now, with this difference that *The Prophet* staked on red—and red came out! The truth is that the author of *The Prophet* not only has the good luck to have talent, he has also the talent to have good luck. He succeeds as well in small things as in great, in his inspirations, in his skillful strategy, and in his diversions. Take, for instance, the luck he had while composing *Robert le diable*.

In writing the first act of his famous score M. Meyerbeer did not notice, when he came to the scene in which Robert throws dice with the young Sicilian knights, an ill-shaped *s* which was no doubt in M. Scribe's manuscript of the libretto. The result was that when the gambler, infuriated by his previous losses, stakes "both his horses and his suits of armor," the composer took the answer of Robert's opponents to be: 'We've got him now' instead of 'we've got them now,' [3] thus giving the Sicilians' words a mysterious and jeering emphasis appropriate to rascals rejoicing over the haul they are about to make in plucking a gull. When later on M. Scribe attended the first stage rehearsals, he heard the chorus stressing each syllable *sotto voce* in a nonsensical 'We've-got-him-now, we've-got-him-now' instead of the loud boast of gamesters retorting with a 'we've got them now' to Robert's staking his horses and armor.

" 'What on earth is this?' exclaimed M. Scribe (according to report); 'my knights hold the stakes to be sure, but they do not hold Robert; the dice are not loaded, my knights are not knights of the road. I must set that right at once—but let me see—come to think of it—no, let it stand; it adds to the dramatic effect. Yes, yes, "we've got him now," an excellent idea, most amusing, the audience will be moved; the good souls will be touched and say: "Poor Robert! Oh, those cutpurses! The scoundrels! They're in cahoots like thieves at a county fair and are going to strip him clean!" '

"So the *s* was not restored; the misinterpretation enjoyed a wild success, and the Sicilian knights stand charged and convicted of roguery; they are disgraced throughout Europe just because M. Meyerbeer is shortsighted."

---

[3] *"Nous le tenons!"* instead of *"Nous les tenons!"*

Which proves, Q.E.D., that anything even remotely connected with the stage is a matter of luck, good or bad!

The most wondrous part of the whole business is that M. Scribe, who is as jealous as a tiger when it comes to claiming the authorship of a joke on the public, has not allowed his collaborator to take the credit for this find, but has actually erased the *s* from his manuscript: you can read in the printed libretto of *Robert le diable* the "We've got him now," which is so dear to the public, in place of "We've got them now," which is dearer still to good sense. . . .

How a Tenor Revolves around the Public

an astronomical study

The Vexations of Kleiner the Younger

 A VERY DULL modern German opera is being given. General conversation. "My God!" exclaims Kleiner the Younger as he comes into the orchestra; "how can a man stand so many vexations? As if it weren't enough to have to listen to this wretched work, without having it sung by that infernal tenor? What a voice! What a style! What musicianship! What pretensions!"

"Shut up, you misanthrope!" retorts Dervinck, the first oboe; "you'll wind up as brutish as your brother; you have the same tastes, the same ideas. Don't you know that a tenor is a being apart, who holds the power of life and death over the works he sings, over the composers, and consequently over poor devils of players like you and me? He is not a denizen of this world, he is a world in himself. More, he is deified by the dilettanti, and he takes himself so completely for a god that he is forever talking of his 'creations.' Just take a look at this book someone sent me from Paris, and you will see how this celestial body revolves around the public. You who are everlastingly delving into Humboldt's *Cosmos* will readily grasp the phenomenon."

"Read it out to us, Kleinerchen," say the majority of musicians; "if you read properly, you shall have a Bavarian cream."

"You mean it?"

"We certainly do."

"All right, then."

How a Tenor Revolves around the Public

BEFORE DAWN

The as yet unknown tenor is in the hands of an able teacher, who is full of knowledge, patience, feeling, and taste, and who begins by making of him a perfect sight reader and a good harmonist, gives him a broad, pure method, initiates him into the beauties of masterpieces—in a word, trains him in the grand style of singing.

Hardly has the tenor caught a glimpse of the emotional power with which he is endowed before he aspires to the throne. In spite of his teacher he wants to make his debut and rule supreme. But his voice is not yet formed. A second-class theater opens its doors to him; he makes his debut and is hissed. Incensed by this outrage, the tenor obtains permission to break his contract and, his heart full of contempt for his fellow countrymen, hies himself to Italy.

At first he runs into mighty obstacles in the way of a new start, but he ends by overcoming them; he is pretty well received. His voice changes, it becomes full, strong, incisive, fitted to express the violent passions as well as the softest sentiments; its timbre gradually acquires purity, freshness, and a delightful simplicity. These qualities finally make up a talent whose effect is irresistible. He is a success. The Italian managers, who are good businessmen, sell, buy back, and resell the poor tenor, whose paltry salary remains the same even though he brings riches to two or three theaters a year. He is exploited and squeezed dry in a thousand ways, so much and so often that in the end his thoughts revert to his native land. He forgives her and even goes so far as to admit that she was right to be severe at his debut. He knows that the director of the Paris Opéra has his eye on him. He accepts an offer and crosses the Alps again.

SUNRISE

The tenor makes a fresh debut, this time at the Opéra, and before a public predisposed in his favor by his Italian triumphs. Exclamations of pleasure and surprise greet his first melody: from then on, his success is assured. Yet this is but the prelude to the emotions he is to stir before the evening is over. The audience has admired the fusion of feeling and of discipline with an organ of enchanting sweetness; there remain to be heard the dramatic accents, the bursts of passion. A number comes during which the daring artist, stressing each syllable, gives out some high chest notes with a resonant fullness, an expression of heart-rending grief, and a beauty of tone that so far nothing had led one to expect. A petrified silence reigns in the house, people hold their breath, amazement and admiration are blended in a mood akin to fear. There is in fact reason for fear until that extraordinary phrase comes to an end; but when it has done so triumphantly, the wild enthusiasm of the listeners is beyond imagining.

We reach the third act. An orphan returns to his father's thatched cottage; his heart, seared by a hopeless love, and his senses, affected by the blood and slaughter he has just witnessed at the wars, collapse under the shock of the most appalling contrast conceivable: his father is dead; the cottage is empty; all is still and silent; it is peace, it is the grave. Both the bosom on which it would be so sweet to shed tears of filial piety and the heart beside which his own could alone beat with less pain are separated from him by the infinite—*she* will never be his. . . . The situation is poignant and worthily treated by the composer. Here the singer reaches a height no one would have thought him capable of. He is sublime. And from two thousand panting lungs break forth cheers such as an artist hears only twice or thrice in his lifetime, cheers that repay him sufficiently for his long and arduous labors.

It is all bouquets, laurel wreaths, recalls. Two days later the press, overflowing with enthusiasm, broadcasts the name of the radiant tenor to all parts of the world where civilization has penetrated.

It is at this point that, if I were a moralist, I might toy with the idea of addressing a homily to the triumphant hero, somewhat in the style of Don Quixote's speech to Sancho when that worthy squire was about to take possession of the government of Barataria:

"You have reached the summit," I would say. "In a few weeks you will be famous; frantic applause will be yours and likewise endless engagements. Authors will pay court to you; managers will no longer keep you waiting in their anterooms, and if you ever write to them, they will answer you. Women whom you do not even know will speak of you as their protégé or very intimate friend. People will dedicate to you their books in prose or verse. Instead of the five francs you give your janitor at Christmas, you will have to give him a hundred. You will be exempted from service in the National Guard. You will get leave from the Opéra from time to time, so that the provincial towns can fight over your presence and performances. Flowers and sonnets will be heaped around your feet. You will sing at the *soirées* given by the Prefect, and the Mayor's wife will send you apricots. You are on the verge of Olympus at last; for as the Italians call their women singers *dive* (goddesses), it naturally follows that the great men singers are gods. Well, you have now been promoted deity; try to remain a good fellow none the less—and don't look down on people who offer you good advice.

"Remember that the voice is a fragile instrument, which may be spoiled or broken in a minute, often without any discoverable cause; and that such an accident is enough to hurl the greatest of the gods from his high throne and reduce him to mortal rank, and sometimes even lower than that.

"Don't be too hard on the poor composers.

"When from the depths of your elegant carriage you see in the street Meyerbeer, Spontini, Halévy, or Auber going on foot, do not greet them with a slight nod of patronizing friendship. They would laugh at it in pity, and passers-by would look upon it with indignation as supreme impertinence on your part. Do not forget that a number of their works will be admired and full of vitality when the memory of your high C from the chest is sunk in oblivion.

"Should you visit Italy once more, do not become infatuated with some feeble spinner of cavatinas and, on your return, palm him off as a classic, telling us with an impartial air that Beethoven 'was also talented.' For no god can escape ridicule.

"When you accept a new role, do not allow yourself to make any changes in it except by the author's leave. Bear in mind that a single note added, curtailed, or transposed may make a melody commonplace or distort its expression. You have in any case no right to do this at any time. To modify the music one sings, or the book one is translating, without saying a word about it to the man who wrote it only after much thought, is to commit a shocking breach of trust. People who borrow without giving notice are called thieves; unfaithful interpreters are libelers and assassins.

"If by any chance there should arise a rival whose voice has more bite and power than your own, do not, in the midst of a duet, start matching lungs with him. Take it for granted that you must not fight the iron pot, even and especially if you are a piece of Ming china.

"When on tour, beware also of saying to the provincials, by way of reference to the Paris Opéra and its chorus and orchestra: '*My* theater, *my* chorus, *my* orchestra.' Provincials do not enjoy being taken for fools any more than Parisians do. They know full well that you belong to the theater, not the theater to you, and they would find your fatuous conceit the acme of the grotesque.

"And now, friend Sancho, receive my blessing; go and govern Barataria. It is a rather low-lying island, but the most fertile, perhaps, to be found on earth. Your people are but slightly civilized. Therefore encourage public education, so that in a couple of years' time they will no longer suspect of witchcraft those who can read. Do not take too seriously the flattery of those you invite to your table; don't keep repeating your damnable slogans; don't get upset when you have an important speech to deliver; and never break your word. May those who entrust their interests to you feel sure that you will not betray them; and in whatever you do, may you never be accused of being sharp (or flat) anywhere in the world."

THE TENOR AT HIS ZENITH

His salary is one hundred thousand francs, with a month's leave annually. After the first role that brought him dazzling success, the tenor attempts a few others with varied results. He then accepts some which he gives up after three or four performances if he does not excel in them as he did before. In so doing he may spoil the career of a composer, annihilate a masterpiece, ruin a publisher, and do enormous harm to the theater. Considerations of this kind are to him nonexistent. Art for him is nothing but gold coin and laurel wreaths, and the most likely means to obtain both quickly are the only ones he cares to use.

He has noticed that certain melodic formulas, certain vocalizations, certain ornaments, certain *fortissimi*, certain concluding platitudes or vulgar rhythms have the property of immediately drawing applause of a sort. This seems to him reason enough to rely on these devices; indeed, to insist on the composer's supplying them in his roles, regardless of expression, originality, or elevation of style; meanwhile showing hostility toward loftier and more individual productions. He knows the effect of the old methods he is in the habit of using. He is ignorant of the effect of the new methods submitted to his attention, and though an interpreter, he does not regard himself as one who can afford to remain disinterested.[1] When in doubt, he abstains as far as he can.

The timidity of a few composers who have given in to his unreasonable demands has already made him dream of introducing into our theaters the musical practices of Italy. There is no use telling him that *Maestro* means "Master," and that the name has been rightly conferred on the composer; that it is *his* conception that must strike the audience free and unimpaired through the medium of the singer. It is the master who gives out light and casts shadows; it is he who is king and answerable for his acts; he proposes and disposes; his ministers must have no other object, seek no other glory, than that of rightly grasping his plans and, by putting themselves exactly at his point of view, ensuring their realization."

(Here the reader's entire audience shouts "Bravo!" and so far forgets itself as to applaud. The tenor on the stage, who just then was yelling out of tune more than usual, takes the applause for himself and throws a gratified glance at the orchestra.)

The reader continues:

The tenor will not heed. He wants to vociferate in drum-major style. Ten years on the stage south of the Alps have made him an addict to hackneyed themes with pauses during which he can hear himself applauded, or can mop his brow, fix his hair, cough, and swallow a lozenge. Or again he insists on senseless vocalises, interspersed with threatening, angry, or tender accents, and laced with low notes, shrill cries, buzzings of hummingbirds, screechings of guinea-fowl, runs, arpeggios, and trills. Whatever the meaning of the words, the character of the part or the situation, he feels free to accelerate or slacken the tempo, to add scales up and down and ornaments of every species, not to mention ah's and oh's that make the phrase absurd. He dwells on short syllables, gallops through long ones, disregards elisions, introduces aspirate *h's* where none exist, and takes breath in the middle of a word. He no longer has standards; anything goes—provided it helps the emission of one of his favorite notes. Who would notice one absurdity more or less in such good company? The orchestra either keeps its counsel or else humors him. The tenor lords it over everyone and tramples on everything. He struts about the theater with the air of a conqueror;

---

[1] "Disinterested" is used here to mean "just" and "impartial," not "uninterested."

his crest gaily glints above his proud head; he is king, hero, demi-god, god.

Only, it is hard to make out whether he is weeping or laughing, whether he is in love or in anger. There is no melody left, no expression, no common sense, no drama, no music; there is simply an emission of vocal sounds, and this alone matters; this is the great thing. He goes to the theater to hunt down the public as others go to the forest to hunt the stag. Forward boldly! Let us give tongue! Tally-ho! Tally-ho! Let art be our quarry!

Soon the example of this vocal fortune makes the management of the theater impossible. It awakens and fosters mad hopes and ambitions among all the singing mediocrities. "The leading tenor gets one hundred thousand francs; why," asks the second tenor, "shouldn't I get eighty thousand?"—"And I fifty?" puts in the third.

To feed these gaping vanities, to fill up these chasms, the manager vainly cuts down the expenses of the company, reduces and cripples orchestra and chorus by giving the artists who make them up porters' wages. Vain are his efforts, useless his sacrifices—until the day when he tries to find out exactly how he stands, attempts to compare the hugeness of the tenor's salary with the work done, and discovers with a shock the following curious result:

The first tenor, with a salary of a hundred thousand francs, sings approximately seven times a month; he therefore takes part in eighty-four performances a year, and receives a little over eleven hundred francs an evening. Taking a role comprising eleven hundred notes or syllables, this represents one franc a syllable. Thus in *William Tell:*

My (*1 fr.*) presence (*2 frs.*) may well seem to you an outrage (*8 frs.*)

Mathilda (*3 frs.*), my indiscreet steps (*5 frs.*)

Have dared to find their way as far as this, your dwelling (*13 frs.*).

Total, thirty-two francs: your words are golden, my lord.

Given a prima donna receiving a mere pittance of forty thousand francs, Mathilda's answer of course comes cheaper (commercial parlance), each of her syllables averaging a mere eight sous, but even that is not so bad:

It's easy to forgive (*2 frs., 8 sous*) the wrongs (*16 sous*) one has
a part in (*2 frs.*).

Arnold (*16 sous*), I (*8 sous*) expected you (*32 sous*).

Total, eight francs.

So the manager pays, goes on paying, pays again and again, till
the day comes when he can pay no more and is compelled to close
his theater. As his brother managers are in a no more flourishing
condition, some of the immortals have to resign themselves to
teaching sol-fa (those who can) or singing to a guitar in the public
squares, with four candle-ends and a green carpet.

THE SUN SETS—STORMY SKIES

The tenor is on his way out. His voice can neither go up nor
come down. He has to decapitate every phrase and sing only what
lies in his middle register. He wreaks havoc upon the old scores
and clamps an unbearable monotony upon the new as a prerequisite
to their being heard at all. His admirers are disconsolate.

Composers, poets, or painters who have lost their sense of beauty
and truth, those whom vulgarity no longer shocks, who lack the
strength even to follow up their own fugitive ideas, and whose
only pleasure is to set traps under the feet of their active and
flourishing rivals—such men are already dead and buried. And yet
they believe themselves to be still alive; a happy illusion sustains
them, they mistake exhaustion for fatigue, impotence for moderation. But compare with this the loss of an organ! Who could
deceive himself about a loss of that magnitude? Especially when the
loss is that of a voice that was marvelous in range and strength, in
the beauty of its inflections, the nuances of its timbre, its dramatic
expression, its perfect purity?

I have sometimes been moved to deepest pity for these unfortunate singers, and filled with a great indulgence for the whims,
vanities, exactions, immoderate ambitions, exorbitant pretensions,
and infinite absurdities of some of them. They live but a day, and
die once for all. Hardly do the names of a few famous ones survive,
and even these owe their rescue from oblivion to the fame of the
composers whose interpreters they were, all too often unfaithful
interpreters at that. We know of Caffarelli because he sang at
Naples in Gluck's *Tito*. The memory of Mmes Saint-Huberty and

Branchu has been kept in France because they created the roles of Dido, of the Vestal, of Iphigenia in Tauris,[2] and so on. Who among us would ever have heard of the *diva* Faustina were it not for Marcello, who was her teacher, and for Hasse, who married her? Let us therefore forgive these mortal gods for making their Olympus as brilliant as they can, for subjecting the heroes of art to such long and rugged trials, and for being inappeasable except by the sacrifice of ideas.

It is cruel for them to see the star of their fame and fortune sinking moment by moment below the horizon. What an anguishing celebration is that of their farewell appearance! How broken in heart must the great artist be when he last treads the boards and haunts the recesses of the theater of which he was for so long the tutelary spirit, the king, the absolute soverign! Dressing in his room, he soliloquizes: "I shall never be here again; this helmet with its brilliant crest will adorn me no more; never again will this private receptacle open its lid to receive the perfumed notes of fair enthusiasts!"

A knock: it is the call-boy to announce the beginning of the piece. "Poor lad, no more trouble for you from my bad temper; no more abuse or cuffs to fear! Never again will you come to me and say: 'The overture has begun, sir. The curtain is up, sir! The first scene is over, sir! Your turn to go on, sir! They are waiting for you, sir!' Alas, no! It is I who now say to you: 'Santiquet, take off my name, which is still on the door; Santiquet, carry these flowers to Fanny; go at once, she won't care for them tomorrow; Santiquet, drink this glass of Madeira and take away the bottle; you shan't have to drive off the boys of the chorus in order to guard it; Santiquet, just make a parcel of these old wreaths, cart away my little piano, put out the lamp, lock the door; all is over.'"

Under the load of these sad thoughts the virtuoso enters the wings. He meets the second tenor, his closest enemy, his understudy, who outwardly weeps heartily, but inwardly laughs luscious tears.

"And so my dear old chap," says the demigod in a doleful voice, "you're leaving us? But what a triumph is in store for you this evening! It is a great moment!"

"Yes, for you," replies the leading singer gloomily; and turning

---

[2] In the operas, respectively, of Piccinni, Spontini, and Gluck.

his back on him: "Delphine," he says to a pretty little dancer whom he has allowed to worship him, "give me my box of sweets."

"Oh, my box is empty," retorts the wanton creature, spinning on one foot, "I gave them all to Victor."

No matter. He must choke down grief, despair, fury; he must smile and sing. The tenor is on the stage; he is playing for the last time the work which he made a success, the part he *created*. He casts a final glance at the scenery which has reflected his glory, which has so often resounded with his tender accents, his passionate flights. He looks at the lake on whose shore he has waited for Mathilda, at the Grütli, from which he has shouted *Liberty!*—at the pale sun that for so many years he has seen rise at nine o'clock at night.[3]

He would like to cry, to sob his heart out; but he gets his cue, his voice must not tremble, the muscles of his face must express no other emotion than that of the part. The public is there—thousands of hands are prepared to applaud you, my poor old god: should they remain still, you would discover that the private sorrow you have just suffered and stifled is as nothing compared to the lacerating torture of the public's indifference on an occasion such as this. Once your slave, the public is today your master, your emperor. Now then, make your bow, there's the applause. . . . *Moriturus salutat.*

And so he sings, and by a superhuman effort recovers his youthful verve and voice; he arouses transports of enthusiasm beyond any yet seen; the stage is strewn with flowers like a hardly closed grave. His heart throbbing with a thousand conflicting emotions, he walks slowly off. The public wants to see him once more, and loudly calls for him. What sweet and cruel anguish there is for him in that final ovation! It is easy to forgive him for prolonging it a little. It is his last joy, his glory, his love, his genius, his life, shuddering as they die together.

Come, then, poor dear great artist, blazing meteor whose course is run, come forward and hear the ultimate voice of our affectionate admiration, as well as of our gratitude for the many pleasured moments you have given us; come and relish them, be happy and

---

[3] These details refer to Rossini's *William Tell*, whose Paris première Berlioz witnessed in 1829.

proud; you will always remember this hour, though we shall forget it tomorrow.

He comes forward gasping for breath, his heart swollen with tears. Loud cheers greet his appearance; the people clap their hands, call him by the grandest, dearest names; Cæsar crowns him. But the curtain comes down at last, like the cold weighted knife of the guillotine; a chasm yawns between the conqueror and his triumphal chariot, a chasm not to be bridged, a chasm hewed by the years. All is over! The god is no more!

Dark night . . .

    Eternal night . . .

"I think we'd all say that this portrait of the singer-god is not flattering, but marvelously like!" exclaims Corsino. "Has that book an author's name?"

"No."

"Well, the author must be a musician; he is bitter, but truthful, and yet he manages to control his anger."

"Now let's keep our promise. Kleinerchen has done himself credit; he must be hoarse."

"Yes; my throat is dry and I am frozen stiff."

"Carlo!"

"Yes, sir."

"Go get a hot Bavarian cream for Mr. Kleiner."

"Right away, sir." (*The orchestra boy goes out.*)

Dimsky speaks up: "You must give the instrumentalists credit: barring a few exceptions I could name, they're far more faithful than the singers, far more respectful of the masters, better up in their work, and consequently far closer to the truth. What would people say if in a Beethoven quartet the first violin took it into his head to dismember his phrases as a singer does, to change their rhythmic form and accent? They would say quite rightly that the quartet was hopeless or absurd.

And yet that first-violin part is sometimes played by virtuosos of the greatest reputation and talent, who can't help considering themselves supremely capable musicians, and who are in fact much more intelligent than all the gods of song—which is precisely why they do not fall into such errors."

THE ORCHESTRA BOY (*returning*): "Too late, gentlemen, there's no Bavarian left!" (*All laugh.*)

KLEINER (*smashing his cello bow on his music-stand*): "Honestly! That particular vexation was foreordained and reserved for my family! And here I have gone and broken an excellent bow! All right, all right, I'll have a drink of water—don't give it another thought!"

The curtain falls.

The tenor is not recalled; his last note is barely applauded. Backstage is enacted a scene of fury and despair. The demigod tears his hair. As they pass by, the musicians shrug their shoulders.

Historical and Philosophical Studies:
*de viris illustribus urbis Romæ—a Roman woman—
vocabulary of the Roman language*

A VERY dull modern Italian opera is being given. .
A regular subscriber to our orchestra seats, who on previous evenings seemed to show a great interest in the readings and stories of the musicians, leans over the rail of the pit and asks me: "You live in Paris ordinarily, do you not, sir?"

"I do; I even live there extraordinarily, often far more so than I care to."

"That being the case, you are no doubt familiar with the strange tongue spoken there, of which your newspapers also make use at times. Please explain what is meant when in reporting certain incidents, which it would seem occur rather frequently during dramatic performances, they refer to 'the Romans.'"

"Yes," chime in several musicians speaking together, "what do they mean in France by that word?"

"What you're asking for, gentlemen, is nothing less than a course in Roman history."

"What's wrong with that?"

"Only that I'm afraid I haven't the gift of brevity."

"That doesn't matter! The opera is in four acts; we are yours till eleven o'clock."

"Well, then, in order to put you at once in touch with the heroes of my story, I shall not go back as far as the sons of Mars and Numa Pompilius. I shall skip over kings, consuls, and dictators; and yet my first chapter cannot help being called:

DE VIRIS ILLUSTRIBUS URBIS ROMÆ, or
Concerning Rome's Illustrious Men.

Nero—you see how I jump without preamble to the days of the emperors—Nero having set up a guild of men whose business it was to applaud him when he sang in public, the name "Romans" is applied today in France to professional applauders, more commonly known as the *claque*.[1] Also to throwers of bouquets, and generally speaking all promoters of success and enthusiasm. They fall into several species:

the mother who so bravely calls everybody's attention to the wit and beauty of a daughter whose looks are only middling and who is something of a fool; this mother who, in spite of her tender affection for the girl, will nevertheless resign herself to a cruel separation at the earliest possible moment if she can only throw her into the arms of a husband, is a Roman;

the author who foresees the time a year hence when he will need the praises of a critic whom he detests and so starts singing the praises of said critic wherever he goes, is a Roman;

the less than Spartan critic who allows himself to be thus grossly trapped becomes in his turn a Roman;

the husband of the professional singer who lets her—you catch my meaning—

But the common herd of Romans, the mob, the Roman people in short, are made up of such men as Nero was the first to conscript. They go every evening to the theater, and even to other places of entertainment where, under the leadership of a chief and his lieutenants, they applaud the artists and the works he has contracted to support.

Many are the ways of applauding. The first, as you all know, consists in creating as much noise as possible by striking one hand against the other. This first method comprises several varieties and subtle effects. The fingertips of the right hand striking in the hollow of the left produce a sharp and resonant sound favored by the majority of artists. Contrariwise, striking the two hands flat against each other gives but a dull and commonplace sound. Only first-year apprentice *claqueurs* or barbers' assistants applaud like that.

The gloved *claqueur*, dressed like a dandy, stretches his arms out affectedly over the edge of his box and applauds slowly, almost noiselessly, and for the eyes only. He thereby says to the whole house: "Look! I condescend to applaud."

---

[1] Perhaps more likely, the name "Romans" alludes to the populace in the circus who decided the gladiator's fate.

The *claqueur* who is carried away (some do exist) applauds fast, hard, and for a great length of time. During his applause he looks to right and left, and these exhibitions failing to satisfy him, he stamps, he shouts: "Bravo-o-o! Bravo-o-o!" (note the long vowel) or else "Brava-a-a!" (That one is the scholar of the gang; he has kept company with Italians and can distinguish masculine from feminine.) He amplifies his clamor in proportion as the cloud of dust generated by his stamping increases in density.

The *claqueur* disguised as a retired colonel or an old gentleman living on his means gently strikes the floor with the end of his stick, wearing an air of complacent moderation.

The violinist-*claqueur* (for the orchestras of Paris number many who, in order to pay court either to the opera manager, or to the conductor, or to a popular and powerful prima donna, temporarily enlist in the Roman army)—the violinist-*claqueur*, I say, strikes the back of his violin with the back of his bow. This form of applause is less common than the rest and therefore more sought after. Unfortunately, harsh experience has taught the gods and goddesses that it is nearly impossible for them to find out when the applause of the violinists is ironical and when genuine. Hence the perturbed smile of the deities when homage of this kind is rendered them.

The kettledrummer applauds by banging on his drum; this does not happen once in fifteen years.

The Roman ladies occasionally applaud with their gloved hands, but their favor is really effective only when they throw their corsages at the feet of the artist they admire. As this species of applause is rather expensive, it is more commonly the nearest relative, the artist's bosom friend, or the artist himself who pays the cost. The fair flower-throwers are given so much for bouquets and so much for enthusiasm. Moreover, one has to pay for a fellow or young boy quick on his feet to run around backstage after the first avalanche of blooms and retrieve them. They are restored to the Roman dames in the boxes, who then use them a second and even a third time. There is in addition the sensitive Roman woman who weeps, goes into hysterics, faints. A rare species and hard to come upon, being closely akin to the snark.

But to confine ourselves to the study of the Roman people properly so called, I must now take up the questions how and on what terms they work.

Let us suppose a man who acts from an irrestible native urge toward his vocation, or who by long and serious study has acquired a true Roman's talent; such a man calls on a theater manager and addresses him roughly as follows: "Sir, you are at the head of a dramatic concern of which I know the weak and the strong points. So far you have no one in charge of Success: allow me to take it on. I offer you twenty thousand francs cash down and a royalty of ten thousand."

"I want thirty thousand in cash," is usually the manager's reply.

"Ten thousand shouldn't spoil a bargain between us. You'll have them by tomorrow."

"Done; but I want a hundred men for ordinary performances, and at least five hundred for all first nights and important debuts."

"You shall have them—more if you need them."

("What are you talking about?" interrupts one musician; "it's the manager who is paid? I had always thought it was the other way round."

"No indeed; those places are bought, just like seats on the stock exchange or a solicitor's practice.")

Once granted his commission, the chief of the Success Bureau, Emperor of the Romans, easily recruits his troops among hair-dressers' assistants, commercial travelers, grounded cab-drivers,[2] poor students, choristers on the super list, and so on and so on— all of whom are stage-struck. He chooses a meeting-place, generally a low dive or a beershop near the theater of their operations. There he musters them and issues his instructions, together with orchestra or top-gallery tickets, for which these poor wretches pay thirty or forty sous—sometimes less, according to the standing of the theater they are to "work." The lieutenants alone get free passes. On field-days they are paid off by their chief. It may even happen, when it is a matter of thoroughly backing a new work which has cost a large sum to produce, that not only is the chief unable to find sufficient paying Romans, but he is short of faithful soldiers ready to give battle for the love of art. He is compelled to eke out his troops with mercenaries and give each soldier as much as three francs plus a shot of brandy.

---

[2] When a cab-driver has incurred the displeasure of the Prefect of Police, the latter suspends his license for two or three weeks, during which the poor fellow, unable to earn anything, assuredly does not ride about in his vehicle. Being a foot soldier, he frequently joins the ranks of the Roman infantry. [Berlioz.]

But in that case the Emperor does not rake in merely orchestra tickets: bank-notes line his pockets to an incredible amount. One of the performers in the new piece who wants to be unusually "sustained" offers a few tickets to the Emperor. This last, assuming his most freezing look, pulls out a handful of these pasteboards and replies: "You see I don't need any. What I need tonight is men, and to get them I have to pay them." The player takes the hint and gives unto Cæsar a steel engraving worth five hundred francs.

The performer who ranks above the one who has just let himself be bled soon hears about this generous deed, and the fear of not being "taken care of" according to his merit and relatively to the extraordinary care to be lavished upon his inferior induces him to offer the promoter of success an unquestionable thousand-franc note, sometimes more. And so on from the top to the bottom of the whole theatrical personnel. You can now understand why and how the theatrical manager is paid by the chief of the *claque*, and how easily an Emperor gets rich.[3]

The first great Roman I ever met at the Paris Opéra was named Augustus—a lucky name for a Cæsar. I have seen but few majesties more imposing than he. His manner was cool and dignified; he spoke little and was entirely given up to his meditations, his plans, his high strategic calculations. He was nevertheless a generous liege, and as I was at that time an habitué of the pit, I was frequently indebted to him for a kindness. The fervor with which I spontaneously applauded Gluck and Spontini, Mme Branchu and Dérivis, had won me his special regard. I had also just then produced my first work (a Solemn Mass) in the Church of Saint-Roch, and because it passed muster with a few devout old women, the beadles, the pew-opener, the sexton, and the neighborhood loungers, I was naïve enough to believe it was a success. Alackaday! it was at best but a fraction of a success; it did not take me long to find it out.[4]

When he saw me a couple of days after the performance, the Emperor Augustus said to me: "And so you made your bow at Saint-Roch day before yesterday? Why the devil didn't you let me know? We'd have gone in a body."

---

[3] Another brilliant account of this institution may be found in Balzac's *Lost Illusions*.
[4] This Mass of 1825 was largely discarded by Berlioz, who only adapted one portion of it to his later *Requiem* (1837).

"I didn't know you were so fond of sacred music."

"We don't like it at all, what an idea! But we would have warmed up your audience to the Queen's taste."

"How do you mean? You can't applaud in church."

"I know. But you can cough, blow your nose, shift your chair, scrape your feet, hum and haw, lift your eyes to heaven—the whole bag of tricks, don't you know. We could have done a sweet job for you and given you a real success, just as we do for a fashionable preacher."

A couple of years later I again forgot to let him know about my first concert at the Conservatoire,[5] but Augustus came to it none the less, with two of his aides-de-camp; and in the evening, when I took my customary seat at the Opéra, he gave me his powerful hand and said to me in a confident fatherly tone (in French, to be sure): *"Tu Marcellus eris!"*

(Here Bacon nudges his neighbor, and asks him in a whisper what these three words mean.

"I don't know," is the answer.

"They're from Virgil,"[6] volunteers Corsino, who has overheard both question and answer. "It means: 'Thou shalt be Marcellus!' "

"All right, but what *is* it to be Marcellus?"

"Not to be a fool, shut up!")

In general, masters in *claquerie* do not harbor much love for overheated outsiders such as I was. They show a distrust amounting to dislike for such adventurers in enthusiasm, *condottieri*, suicide squads, who rush in among them like fools and applaud without rehearsing first. On the occasion of a certain première, when everybody expected that it was going to be, in Roman parlance, "a tough pull"—that is, a strenuous job for the troops of Augustus to win the public over—I had by chance sat on a downstairs bench that the Emperor had marked on his military map as reserved for his own. I had been there a good half-hour, a target for the hard looks of my neighbors, who seemed to be wondering how to get rid of me, while I was wondering in turn (with some dismay though my conscience was clear) what I had done to incur these officers' displeasure, when the Emperor himself sprang at me surrounded by

---

[5] On May 26, 1828.
[6] In the *Æneid* (VI, 883), the prophecy of future imperial greatness to the nephew of Augustus.

his staff. He made matters clear by saying sharply, yet not angrily (for as I have said, I was a protégé of his): "My dear sir, I must disturb you; you cannot stay where you are."

"Why not?"

"I cannot let you: you are in the very center of my front line, you *intercept* me."

You may be sure I hastened to abandon the field to this great tactician.

Another outsider, not seeing the exigencies of the position, might have resisted the Emperor and compromised the success of his plans. From which follows a proposition that scholarly investigation has fully proved, and that Augustus with his whole army makes no secret of: namely, that *the public is of absolutely no use in the theater*. It is not only of no use, but it spoils everything. As long as the public is allowed at the Opéra, the Opéra will not get along. When Augustus first uttered those bold words, the managers of the day called him a lunatic. Great Augustus! He could hardly foresee that only a few years after his death his doctrine would receive a triumphant vindication. But it is the fate of genius to be misunderstood by its contemporaries and exploited by its descendants.

Beyond cavil, no more ingenious, no more daring dispenser of glory than Augustus ever held absolute sway under a theater chandelier. Compared to Augustus, the reigning monarch at the Opéra today is a mere Vespasian, a Claudius. His name is David—how can one call him Emperor? Nobody tries. The most his flatterers can do is to style him King, in deference to his name.

At the Opéra-Comique the famous and skillful chief of the Romans is named Albert, and like his medieval namesake he is called Albert the Great. He was the first to put into practice Augustus's bold theory of ruthlessly excluding the public from first performances. At the present time, if one excepts the critics who for the greater part also belong in some way or other to the *viris illustribus urbis Romæ*, the house on a first night is filled from floor to ceiling with *claqueurs* only.

Again, it is to Albert the Great that we owe the touching custom of recalling all the actors at the end of every new work. King David promptly followed his lead, and the success of this experiment emboldened him to add another, that of recalling the tenor to the front of the curtain as many as three times in the course of an evening. A god who in a gala performance should be recalled only once at the end of the work, like an ordinary mortal, would be, in technical language, a flop. It follows that whenever, in spite of all his efforts, David has only secured this very slim result for some free-handed tenor, his rivals of the Théâtre-Français and the Opéra-Comique sneer at him the next day, and say: "Last night David 'warmed up a dead duck.' " (I shall give in a moment the explanation of these Roman words.)

Unfortunately Albert the Great, probably weary of power, has seen fit to lay down his scepter. In handing it over to his obscure successor he could have said, like Sulla in M. de Jouy's tragedy:

I governed fearlessly and abdicate the same [7]

—if only the line had been a better one. But Albert is a man of parts, he detests second-rate literature, which, come to think of it, might explain his eagerness to leave the Opéra-Comique.

Another great man, whom I never knew but who enjoys great renown in Paris, ruled, and I believe still rules, over the Gymnase Dramatique. His name is Sauton. To him is due the advance of his art into a new and fertile field. By promoting friendly relations, he has established equality and fraternity between the Romans and the authors, a system which David, the plagiarist, hastened to adopt. Nowadays one sees a *claque*-leader sitting casually at table not only with Melpomene, Thalia, or Terpsichore, but even with Apollo and Orpheus. He goes bail for the boys as well as the girls, helps them with his purse in their private difficulties, defends them and loves them with all his heart.

An admirable gesture is attributed to Emperor Sauton in his relations with one of our quickest-witted but least solvent writers. Toward the end of a cordial luncheon at which cordials had not been spared, Sauton, flushed with excitement and twisting his napkin, finally worked up his nerve to saying to his host with only a little hemming and hawing: "My dear D., I have a favor to ask you—"

"Certainly. Out with it!"

"I wonder if—would you let me—could I call you by your first name?—and you by mine?"

"Why of course! And apropos of names, George, can you lend me a thousand?"

---

[7] "*J'ai gouverné sans peur et j'abdique sans crainte.*"

"Oh, my dear Charles, you make me so happy!" And pulling out his pocketbook: "Here you are!"

I cannot, gentlemen, sketch for you the portraits of all the illustrious men of the city of Rome. I lack both time and biographical information. Let me only add a word more about the three heroes whom it has been my privilege to describe. Though rivals, Augustus, Albert, and Sauton always remained friends. During their triumvirate, they did not go in for the wars and treacheries which disgraced the historic triumvirate of Antony, Octavius, and Lepidus. Far from it. Whenever the Opéra waged one of those dreadful encounters where a brilliant, overwhelming, and epic victory absolutely must be won—one that would leave Pindar and Homer tongue-tied—Augustus would disdain raw recruits and call upon his triumvirs. Proud to lend a hand to so great a man, they would readily acknowledge him as their chief and bring him, Albert his indomitable phalanx and Sauton his light infantry, all fired with the irrestible energy that performs miracles.

The three crack corps would be merged into one army on the ground floor of the Opéra on the day preceding that of the first night. His plan of campaign, libretto, and notes in hand, Augustus would put his troops through a strenuous rehearsal, occasionally adopting the suggestions of Antony and Lepidus, who had but few to make, so quick and perceptive was Augustus, so sharp at guessing the schemes of the enemy, great in genius to thwart them, and wise in refraining from the impossible. And on the morrow what ovations, what cheers, what heaps of rich spoils, not indeed offered to, but by, Jupiter Stator and twenty of his fellow gods!

Such are the priceless services rendered to art and artists by the Roman nation.

Would you believe it possible, gentlemen, that there is some talk of driving the Romans out of the Opéra? Several newspapers have announced this reform, which we will not credit even if we see it with our own eyes. For the *claque* has become a necessity of our time. In whatever shape or disguise, with whatever excuse, it has won its way everywhere. It reigns and governs in the theater, at concerts, in the National Assembly, in clubs, churches, and corporations, in the press and even in the salons. Wherever twenty people are gathered together to pronounce judgment on the sayings or doings or ideas of anyone standing before them, you may rest assured that at least one fourth of this jury has been planted among the other three fourths for the purpose of sparking them if they can catch fire; or if not, at least to make a noise and a flash.

In the latter case, which is common enough, this minor show of prearranged enthusiasm is still sufficient to flatter the self-esteem of most performers. Some manage to fool themselves as to the real value of the approval so obtained; others are not fooled but like the result just the same. They have sunk so low that if the living could not be hired to applaud them, they would make do with the applause of a set of dummies, not to say of a clapping machine: they would not be above turning the crank themselves.

The *claque* at our theaters have become experts. Their profession has risen to be an art. People have often admired, but never adequately in my opinion, the wonderful talent with which Augustus *directed* the great works of the modern repertory, and the high quality of the advice he could give to authors on many occasions. Hidden in a lower-tier box, he would attend all the musicians' rehearsals before rehearsing his own army. Then when the maestro came and told him: "Here you give three rounds of applause; there you shout "encore," he would with perfect self-confidence reply, according to cases: "Sir, that's dangerous," or "It shall be done," or "I must think it over, my mind is not yet made up. Have a few free-lances go over the top. If they make it, I'll follow."

It might happen that Augustus would sternly resist some author who wanted to draw "dangerous" applause from him. He would say: "I can't do it, sir. It would compromise me in the eyes of the public, of the artists, and of my colleagues who know perfectly well that *it isn't done*. I have my reputation to maintain; I too have self-respect. Your work is very difficult to direct, and I'll do my best for you; but I cannot allow myself to be hissed."

Alongside the professionals, who are educated, shrewd, cautious, inspired—artists, in short—there are the occasional *claqueurs* who applaud out of friendship or for their own ends. These will never be banished from the Opéra. They include:

the naïve friends who sincerely admire whatever they're about to hear on the stage, "even before the candles have been lit" [8] (it

---

[8] Quoted from Molière's *Précieuses ridicules*, Scene x.

must be added that this species of friends is daily becoming scarcer; those who disparage everything, before, during, and after, have increased enormously);

the relatives, or the *claque* that Nature supplies;

the publishers—fierce *claqueurs* all;

and finally, the lovers and husbands.

These last are the reason why women, besides the many other advantages they possess over men, have an additional chance of success. In a theater or concert hall a woman can hardly applaud her husband or lover to any purpose. Anyway, she is always busy about something else; whereas the men, given the slightest native gift for the art, or even an elementary notion of it, can by sudden, well-placed, and vigorous attack bring about success in less than three minutes and "milk the audience for a renewal"—that is to say, stimulate enough applause to make the manager renew an engagement.

For this type of operation husbands are even better than lovers. The latter are usually afraid of ridicule; they are also secretly afraid that too marked a success will add to the number of their rivals. Besides, they are not interested financially in the triumphs of their mistress; but the husband, who holds the purse-strings, who knows what a bouquet tossed at the right moment will bring in, and likewise the value of a nicely protracted salvo, of a contagiously contrived excitement, of a recall timed just right—for these the husband alone dares to avail himself of his aptitudes.

He has the gifts of ventriloquism and ubiquity. One moment he is clapping from the balcony and shouting: "Brava!" in the chest notes of a tenor. Next he has leaped to the corridor behind the first boxes and, thrusting his head through a peep-hole, he exclaims: "Wonderful!" in a bass voice as he runs by; only to fly panting to the top gallery, where he makes the house ring with his ejaculations of "Delightful! Exquisite! Ye gods, what a talent! It hurts!"—this in a soprano voice, the choked tones of feminine emotion. There you have the model husband, the hard-working, competent head of a family.

As for the husband who is a man of taste, who is undemonstrative, and who remains quietly in his seat during an entire act, who does not even applaud the finest efforts of his better half, it can be said of him without fear of contradiction that as a husband he does not exist—unless his wife has the fidelity of an angel.

Was it not a husband who invented the *hissing success?* I refer to the hissing bid for enthusiasm or pressurizing hiss, which is used in the following manner: If the public has had enough of the talent of a woman who is heard every day, and the audience lapses into indifference and apathy, a man with devotion but not known to the public is planted in the hall to wake up the crowd. Just as the diva gives unmistakable proof of her talent, and the professional ensemble of the *claque* is doing its best in the middle of the floor, a strident and insulting noise bursts forth from some dark corner. The whole house rises in a fit of indignation, and a furious storm of avenging plaudits breaks loose. Cries of "Outrageous!" are heard from every part of the house. "It's a foul cabal! *Brava, bravissima!* Enchanting! Maddening!" and so on and so on. But this daring device calls for very delicate handling, and very few women will submit to the fictitious affront of a hiss, however rewarding it may prove in the sequel.

For such is the amazing effect of approving or disapproving noises on musicians, even when these noises actually express neither praise nor blame. Habit, imagination, and weakness of mind have made them feel joy or pain according to the manner in which the air vibrates in an auditorium. The physical phenomenon, apart from any notion of glory or displeasure, is quite enough. I am sure there are actors childish enough to be annoyed, when traveling, by the whistle of the locomotive.

The art of the *claque* has affected even musical composition. It is the many kinds of Italian *claque*, whether amateurs or artists, that have led composers to end their pieces with the redundant, trivial, absurd, and invariable formula called *cabaletta*, the little cabal, which calls forth applause. When the *cabaletta* no longer worked, they introduced the bass drum into the orchestra, a big cabal now destroying both music and singers. Tired at last of the bass drum, and unable to take applause by storm with the old devices, the poor maestri have finally been forced to resort to duets, trios, and choruses in unison. In some instances composers have even been compelled to write for voices and orchestra in unison, thus producing an ensemble number in only one part, preferring this enormous weight of sound, it would seem, to any harmony, instrumentation, or musical idea, in the hope of rushing the public and making it think it is electrified.[9]

Corresponding examples are plentiful in the literary trade.

As regards dancers, the business is very simple: it is settled with the impresario: "You will give me so many thousand francs a month, so many passes,[1] and the *claque* will give me an *entrance*, an *exit*, and two rounds at each of my *echoes*." [2]

By means of the *claque*, the managers make or unmake at will what people continue to call a "success." A single word to the leader enables them to destroy an artist whose talent is not top notch. I remember hearing Augustus say one night at the Opéra, as he was reviewing the ranks of his army before the curtain: "Nothing for Dérivis.[3] Nothing!" The order went round and, to be sure, Dérivis did not get a single hand. The manager who wants to get rid of someone for whatever reason has recourse to this ingenious means, and after two or three performances in which "there has been nothing" for M. —— or for Mme —— he tells the performer: "You must see that I can't keep you on. Your work isn't congenial to the public."

It sometimes happens, however, that these tactics fail with a virtuoso of the first rank. "Nothing for him" has been decreed in official circles. But the public, at first amazed by the silence of the Romans, soon guesses what is behind it, goes into action unofficially, and all the more warmly because there is a hostile cabal to thwart. The singer then obtains an unusual success, a *peripheral* success, the center of the orchestra taking no part in it. But I should not like to say whether he is prouder of this spontaneous enthusiasm than irritated by the inaction of the *claque*.

To imagine that such an institution, rooted in the greatest of our theaters, can be suddenly uprooted seems to me as impossible and as insane as to try to abolish a religion between noon and night.

Can one imagine the confusion at the Opéra; the despair, melancholy, and depression to which its dancing, singing, walking, rhym-

---

[9] In the overture to *Robert Bruce* (1847), a hodgepodge of Rossini's music made by Niedermeyer, the public heard, in addition to saxhorns, eight trumpets in four different keys.
[1] Free tickets for the days when the artist is performing. [Berlioz.]
[2] "Echoes" are the dancer's solos within the ensemble work. [Berlioz.]
[3] Henri Étienne Dérivis (1780–1856), a powerful bass whose voice spoiled early.

ing, painting, and composing population would succumb? the death wish that would overtake the gods and demigods when a *cabaletta* sung or danced in less than faultless style was succeeded by a frightful silence? Has a thought been given to the fury of the mediocrities on seeing real talents occasionally applauded, while they themselves, who formerly were always applauded, get not a single hand? It would be tantamount to conceding the principle of inequality and demonstrating it in public; whereas we live under a republic and the word "Equality" is inscribed on the pediment of the Opéra.[4]

Furthermore, who would see to it that the leading man or lady was recalled after the third and fifth acts? Who would shout: "The Company!" at the end of the show? Who would laugh when one of the characters says something silly? Who would drown out with kindly applause the wrong note of a bass or a tenor, and keep the public from hearing it? The mere thought is enough to make one shudder. And besides, the doings of the *claque* are a part of the fun; it is a pleasure to see it maneuver. This is so true that were the *claqueurs* excluded from certain performances there would not be a soul in the house.

No, the suppression of the Romans in France is happily a madman's dream. Heaven and earth shall pass away, but Rome is immortal and the *claque* shall stand.

Listen!—here is our prima donna, who has taken it into her head to sing soulfully, and with tasteful simplicity, the only melody of distinction in this wretched opera. You'll see she will not get a hand. . . . Ha! I was mistaken; they are applauding, but notice the lack of style in that clapping—what an abortive round, a poor attack and a worse reprise. The public is full of goodwill, but it has no technique, no ensemble, and hence no power. If Augustus had had that woman in his care, he would have carried the house from the word go, and you, my friends, who wouldn't dream of applauding, would chime in willy-nilly.

So far, gentlemen, I have not given you a full-length portrait of the Roman female. I shall for this purpose make use of our opera's last act, which will shortly begin. Meanwhile let us have an intermission. I feel rather tired.

The musicians move about a little, exchanging ideas in a low

---

[4] This article was written in 1851, during the Second French Republic.

voice while the curtain is down. But the three raps of the conductor's baton on the stand indicate the resumption of the performance, and my audience gathers around me again in an attentive attitude.

Mme Rosenhain
Another Fragment of Roman History [5]

Some years ago a five-act opera was ordered by M. Duponchel from a French composer whom you do not know. While the final rehearsals were taking place, I sat by my fireside thinking of the pangs that the unfortunate author was busy feeling. I mused over the recurring torments of all kinds which no opera-composer in Paris can escape, neither the great nor the small, the patient, the irritable, the modest, the proud, the German, the Frenchman—not even the Italian.

I pictured to myself the excruciating slowness of the preliminaries, during which one and all waste their time in tomfooleries, though every hour lost may mean wrecking the work; the witticisms of the tenor and the prima donna, at which the poor composer feels bound to shriek with laughter, though death grips his soul; the inane quips to which he retorts with the dullest jokes he can find, the better to set off those of his singers and make them look like wits. I could hear the manager's voice finding fault with the work, treating him scornfully, reminding him of the extreme honor done to him in giving so much time to his score, and threatening to throw the whole thing over if everything is not ready on the appointed day. I could see the poor slave shiver and flush at the lunatic views of his overlord (the manager) upon music and musicians, at his fantastic theories concerning melody, rhythm, instrumentation, and style; in the course of uttering which, the dear man treats the great masters as blockheads, and the blockheads as great masters, and mistakes Piræus for a man.

Next comes the announcement that the mezzo-soprano has left

---

[5] The first part of this tale is a paraphrase of Berlioz's own experiences during the production of *Benvenuto Cellini* in 1838 and '39. For the sequel see pp. 110–12.

and that the bass is ill. It is proposed to fill the latter's place with a beginner, and have the leading role rehearsed by a member of the chorus. The composer feels he is being garrotted but is careful not to complain. . . . Oh, how pleasant to dream at home of rain, snow, icy winds, dark squalls, barren woods wailing under the north wind's blast, quagmires, deep ditches hidden under a treacherous crust, the growing obsession of fatigue, the gnawings of hunger, the terrors of solitude and of the night; how pleasant when safe in one's retreat (though it be as small as that of the hare in the fable),[6] in the cozy quietude of idleness, to feel one's repose increased two-fold by the distant noises of the storm, and to repeat, while ruffling one's beard and shutting one's eyes sanctimoniously, like a parson's cat, the prayer of the German poet, Heinrich Heine,[7] a prayer so seldom granted: "Oh God, Thou knowest my heart is good, my feelings lively and deep, I am full of pity and sympathy for the sufferings of others, so pray let my neighbor bear my ills; I will surround him with such care, show him such delicate attentions; my compassion will be so thoughtful, so active, that he will bless Your right hand, O Lord, for so much solace and sweet consolation. But to crush me under the load of my own pains, to make me suffer personally, how frightful that would be! From my lips, O merciful God, take away this cup of bitterness!"

I was thus sunk in pious meditation when I heard a slight knock at the door of my study. My man being on a mission to a foreign court, I asked myself whether I was visible, and on my affirmative answer, I showed the caller in. A very well-dressed lady, and I may add none too young, came forward. She was in the bloom of her forty-fifth year. I saw at once that I was in the presence of a performing artist; there are infallible signs for detecting these unhappy victims of inspiration.

"Sir," said she, "you recently conducted a grand concert at Versailles,[8] and I had hoped, up to the very last day, to have a part in it —but what's done is done."

"Madam, the program was drawn up by the committee of the Musical Association; I was not responsible for it. Moreover, Mme Dorus-Gras and Mme Widemann—"[9]

---

[6] La Fontaine's "The Hare and the Frogs."
[7] He and Berlioz were good friends.
[8] On October 29, 1848, for the benefit of the musicians' union.
[9] Two singers who frequently performed under Berlioz's direction.

"Oh, those two ladies may not have said anything, but it's a fact none the less that they were greatly displeased."

"On what account, if you please?"

"Because I was not engaged."

"Do you think so?"

"I am sure of it, but let's not hark back to that. I came to ask you, sir, for a recommendation to Messrs Roqueplan and Duponchel. I should like to join the Opéra. I belonged to the Italian Theater until last season, and I was certainly very happy under M. Vatel's direction, but ever since the February Revolution [1]—you must see that a theater like that cannot suit me."

"Madam, I dare say you have excellent reasons for being particular in the choice of your colleagues; if I might venture an opinion—"

"It's no use, sir; my mind is made up; I cannot remain at the Italian Theater on any terms whatsoever. Everything connected with it rubs me the wrong way—the players, the public that goes to it, the public that keeps away. And though the present condition of the Opéra is hardly flourishing, still, as my son and two daughters were engaged last year by the new management—on very flattering terms, I may say—it would please me greatly to be engaged, and I shan't haggle about salary."

"But you forget that the managers of the Opéra are only superficially acquainted with music and possess only the weakest knowledge or sense of it. Consequently they entertain very set ideas concerning our art and do not take much stock in recommendations, especially mine. Even so, be good enough to tell me what your voice is."

"I do not sing."

"Ah, if you're a dancer, my influence is virtually nil."

"I am not a dancer."

"Then it is merely a walk-on part that you want?"

"I do not walk on, sir. You mistake me completely. (*With a somewhat ironic smile*) I am Mme Rosenhain."

"Related to the pianist?" [2]

"No, but Mmes Persiani, Grisi, Alboni, and Messrs Mario and

---

[1] The first revolution of 1848.
[2] Jakob Rosenhain (1813–94). His brother Edward (1818–61), though less well known, was also an excellent pianist.

Tamburini[3] have surely spoken to you about me. During the last six years I have had a great deal to do with their success. For a while I thought of going and giving lessons in London, where I hear they are somewhat behind the times. But as I told you, my children being at the Opéra—and then, the size of the house is an opportunity which—"

"Please forgive my ignorance and stupidity, madam, and kindly tell me what your talent actually consists in."

"I, sir, am the artist who caused M. Vatel to make more money than Rubini himself, and I flatter myself I can similarly improve receipts at the Opéra, provided my two daughters, who have already distinguished themselves there, follow my example. I, sir, am a flower-thrower."

"Now I understand. You are in the Enthusiasm Department?"

"Precisely. This branch of musical art is only just beginning to flourish. Formerly it was the great society ladies who attended to it, gratis, or very nearly so. You remember the concerts of M. Liszt, and the debut of M. Duprez? What volleys of bouquets! What applause! Young girls and even married women waxed shamelessly enthusiastic; a number of them more than once compromised themselves. Such uproar, such confusion, such a waste of beautiful flowers! It was pathetic. We have changed all that. The public no longer meddles in anything whatever, thanks be to God and the artists, and everything in the way of ovations is regulated according to my system.

"True, under the previous management at the Opéra our profession became nearly extinct, or at least it suffered a setback. The Enthusiasm Department was entrusted to four inexperienced young ballet girls, who—worse yet—were personally known to all the subscribers. These innocent babes (what can you expect at their age?) always sat in the same seats and everlastingly threw the same bouquets to the same singers at the same moment. In the end the language of their flowers became a subject of derision. My daughters, who learned from me, have reformed all that and I think the management is now fully satisfied."

"Is your son likewise in the flower squad?"

"Oh, as for my son, he has other ways of arousing enthusiasm; he has a magnificent voice."

---

[3] All singers.

"How is it that I don't know his name?"

"It doesn't appear on the program."

"And yet he sings, you say?"

"No, sir, he shouts."

"That is what I meant."

"Yes, he shouts, and in critical moments his voice has often been enough to stir the most stolid masses; my son, sir, works at the recall."

"Are you perhaps kinsmen of Daniel O'Connell's?" [4]

"I do not know any actor of that name. My son goes in for the recall of leading men when the public is cold and doesn't want them back again. You can see that his job is no sinecure and that he earns his pay. He was lucky, when he made his debut at the Théâtre-Français, to find there a tragic actress whose name began with a very good syllable, the syllable *Ra*.[5] It's no secret how much can be done with a *Ra*. I should have felt anxious about him at the Opéra, after the retirement of the famous prima donna whose solitary *O* resounded so well, in spite of the five Germanic consonants that hemmed it in,[6] had there not arisen another prima donna with a still more favorable syllable, the syllable *Ma*,[7] which raised my son to the pinnacle at one bound. And so my boy, who is rather witty, says (no pun intended) that she's been a second mother to him. Now you know the whole story."

"I do indeed, and I say to you that your talent itself is the best of introductions, and that the management of the Opéra will recognize its worth. You should go there at once; the Opéra is looking for just such talent. For the last week they have been composing a great enthusiasm in behalf of a third act which they are taking an interest in."

"Ever so many thanks, kind sir. I am off this very minute."

The dainty bacchante was gone. I have not heard from her since, but I have had proof that she made a good contract with the Opéra management. At the première of the new work, the one ordered by M. Duponchel, a veritable cascade of flowers kept dropping on the stage at the close of the third act. Anyone could tell they dropped

---

[4] The pun that brings in the name of the Irish politician is untranslatable.

[5] Obviously Rachel.

[6] Rosina Stoltz, who withdrew after a scandal in 1847.

[7] Mlle Masson.

from a practiced hand. Unfortunately this graceful ovation did not keep the show from doing the same."

"From doing what?" asks Bacon, always the naïve questioner.

"From being dropped, you idiot," retorts Corsino brutally. "Confound it, your wits are even slower than usual this evening. Go to bed, Basile." [8]

Gentlemen, it remains for me to give you the meaning of the terms most frequently used in the Roman language, terms which only the Parisians thoroughly understand:

Faire four [9] (to flop) means to produce no effect, to fall flat before the indifference of the public.

Chauffer un four (to warm up a dead duck, bolster up a failure) is to applaud in vain a performer whose talent will not rouse the public; this idiom is the counterpart of the proverbial expression "a stab in the water"—labor lost.

Avoir de l'agrément (to get a lift, a boost) consists in being applauded by the *claque* plus a portion of the public. On the day of his debut in *William Tell*, Duprez got an extraordinary lift.

Égayer (to enliven, to barrack) someone is to hiss him. This irony is cruel enough, but it conceals a secondary meaning, which makes it still more galling. The unfortunate actor who is hissed can hardly be said to feel more lively on that account, but his rival does feel enlivened at hearing him hissed, while others also laugh in secret at his mishap. Taking all in all, whenever one is hissed, another is enlivened.

Tirage (pulling teeth, a tough pull) is used in the Roman language for difficulty, painful effort. The Romans are apt to say: "It is a fine piece, but it will be like pulling teeth to get it going." This means that despite some good qualities the work is boring and will require the strenuous efforts of the *claque* to secure a semblance of success.

Faire une entrée (to give an entrance round) is to applaud an actor on his appearance, even before he has opened his mouth.

Faire une sortie (to give an exit round) is to pursue him with

---

[8] An allusion to Beaumarchais's *Barber of Seville*, where all the characters try to get the old pedant out of the way by persuading him that he is ill and ought to be in bed.

[9] These and the following expressions are left in French both because some of them have no English equivalents, and because together they constitute a small glossary which may be of use to those who read French critical writings.

plaudits and bravos as he goes off into the wings, regardless of his last gesture, word, or exclamation.

Mettre à couvert (to supply cover to) a singer is to applaud and cheer him vigorously the instant he lets out a wrong or cracked note; the noise of the *claque* protects him by preventing the public from hearing.

Avoir des égards (show consideration) for a performer is to give him some applause, even when he has not furnished tickets to the *claque*. It is encouragement *d'amitié* or *à l'œil* (out of friendship, or "for free"). These words are equivalent to gratis.

Faire mousser solidement, or *à fond* (to do a job, dent the lid), is to applaud frantically, with hands, feet, voice, and word. During the intermissions the *claque* will then "crack up" the work or the performer in the lobbies and corridors, in the neighboring bars and cafés, at the tobacconist's—everywhere. It is their duty to say: "A masterpiece, amazing talent; hair-raising; a miraculous voice; there has never been anything like it." On great occasions the management of the Paris Opéra always summons from abroad a well-known professor who knows how to do a job on the big works by "firing" the lobbies and corridors in masterly fashion. The genius of this Roman master is serious; his seriousness is genius.

The foregoing operations taken together are referred to as *soins* (attentions) and *soigner* (to nurse or care for).

Faire empoigner (to give the bounce) is to applaud a feeble passage or inferior artist, which often rouses the public to retaliation. For it sometimes happens that the creature who rules the heart of the manager sings in lamentable fashion. In the center of the orchestra, gloomy and crushed, the Emperor sits with bowed head, thus telling his prætorian guard that they must keep quiet and not give any sign whatever of satisfaction, must in fact conform to his melancholy thoughts. But the diva finds such prudent reserve little to her taste and rushes full of indignation into the wings. She complains to the manager about the incompetence or treachery of the leader of the *claque*. Whereupon the director orders the Roman army into action for the next act. Regretfully Cæsar is compelled to obey. The second act begins, the angered goddess sings more out of tune than ever, and as three hundred pairs of devoted hands clap all the same, the enraged public retorts with a symphony of hissing and whistling orchestrated in the modern manner, fit to pierce the ear-drum. The diva asked for it: she has been "bounced."

I believe the use of this expression goes back no farther than the reign of Charles X, when at a memorable sitting of the Chamber of Deputies, Manuel ventured to say that France had accepted the return of the Bourbons with repugnance. This let loose a parliamentary storm and M. de Foucault called out his bodyguard, pointed to Manuel, and said in parliamentary language: "Bounce this man!"

To denote a disastrous provocation of hissing, one can also use the words "*faire appeler Azor* (calling to Fido)," an expression derived from the habit old ladies have of whistling for their dog, which is always named Azor.

After one of those catastrophes I have seen Augustus in despair, ready to take his life, just like Brutus at Philippi. One thought alone held him back: his art and his country; both needed him, and he managed to live for them.

Conduire (to direct) a work consists in organizing the operations of the Roman army during rehearsals.

Brrrrrr!!—when this sound comes from the lips of the Emperor as he directs certain troop movements, it is a signal to all his lieutenants that the hand-clapping must be executed with great speed and accompanied by stamping. It is the order to "dent the lid."

When the Imperial head, lit up with a smile, is turned from right to left and from left to right, it is a signal for moderate laughter.

Cæsar's two hands brought together in one vigorous slap, then raised in the air for the space of a second, give the order for a sudden burst of laughter.

If the two hands remain in the air longer than usual, the laughter is to be prolonged and followed by a round of applause.

Hum! uttered in a particular way should stir tender emotion in Cæsar's soldiers; on hearing it they are to melt, shed a few tears, and murmur their approbation.

This is all I can tell you, gentlemen, about the illustrious men and women of the city of Rome. I did not live among them long enough to learn more. Please excuse the historian's errors.

The subscriber to our orchestra seats thanks me warmly; he has hung on every word of my narrative, and I saw him surreptitiously taking notes. The lights are dimmed and we go out. On our way downstairs, Dimsky asks me with a quizzical look:

"Do you know who that was asking you about the Romans?"

"No, I don't."

"He's the manager of the theater at ———; you can bet he's going to make use of what you told him; he will set up a *claque* in his own theater, just as in Paris."

"In that case, I'm sorry I didn't mention one important fact. The managers of the Opéra, the Opéra-Comique, and the Théâtre-Français in Paris have gone into partnership to found a Conservatoire of Claque. Our inquisitive friend, if he wants to get a practical man as chief, a tactician, a real Cæsar—or at least a young Octavius —should be sure to hire the Conservatoire student who has just won the first prize."

"I'll write and tell him that; I know who he is."

"You'll be doing him a good turn, my dear Dimsky. Let us *nurse* our art, and watch over the welfare of the empire. Good night!"

Romans of the New World

Mr. Barnum

Jenny Lind's Trip to America

A MODERN Italian opera is being given, etc.

The regular subscriber who was identified by Dimsky as being manager of the theater at —— is not here. He must have left with the intention of putting to use his new knowledge of Roman history.

"With that ingenious system," says Corsino to me, "the practical details of which you explained to us yesterday, and with the exclusion of the public from first performances, every theatrical production in Paris must succeed."

"The fact is, they do. Ancient or modern, good, bad, or indifferent, and even excellent plays and scores, are equally successful nowadays. The trouble is—anybody could see it coming—this persistent applause detracts somewhat from the value of our large theatrical output. The management makes a little money and helps authors and composers to earn their living, but it's hardly flattering to succeed when no one fails, and as a result everybody goes rather indifferently to work. The literary and musical movements in Paris get neither a forward nor a backward push from so many journeymen.

By the same token, no genuine success is possible for singers or actors. By dint of getting themselves recalled invariably and all together, ovations have become trite and valueless. Indeed, they are beginning to arouse contemptuous laughter. The one-eyed men, who are kings in the land of the blind, no longer rule when everyone is king. Seeing the results of this steady stream of enthusiasm bottled under pressure, one is inclined to doubt the modern maxim:

"Everything in excess and excess in everything." Excess might after all turn out to be a defect, not to say a most repellent vice. Nowadays, when in doubt, no one abstains: Who cares? And yet, as it's a sure way to come to a bad end, perhaps the experiment is worth seeing through. Still, no matter what we do in Europe, we shall always be outstripped by the enthusiasts of the New World; compared to ours they are as the Mississippi is to the Seine."

"How is that?" breaks in Winter, the American, who plays the second bassoon, though no one knows exactly how he got into the orchestra. "Have my fellow countrymen suddenly become dilettanti?"

"They are unquestionably dilettanti, and fierce ones too, if we can believe Mr. Barnum's newspapers about Jenny Lind's triumphs, which he is responsible for. Look at what they were saying two years ago on her arrival in the new continent: [1]

"When she landed in New York, the crowd rushed at her so frantically that large numbers of persons were crushed. The survivors, however, were numerous enough to keep her horses from making headway. It was at that point that, seeing her coachman raise his arm to strike these enthusiasts with his whip, Jenny Lind uttered the sublime words so oft repeated from upper Canada right down to Mexico, words that bring tears to the eyes of all who hear them quoted: 'Don't hit them, don't hit them! They are my friends, they've come to see me.'

"One hardly knows what to admire most in this never-to-be-forgotten sentence—the heartfelt impulse that dictated the thought, or the genius that cast it in a form so beautiful and poetic. Frenzied hurrahs naturally greeted it. The manager of the steamship line, Mr. Colini, was waiting for Jenny Lind on the landing stage, armed with a huge bouquet. In the center of the dock stood a triumphal arch made of foliage and crowned with a stuffed eagle who seemed to be waiting to greet her too. At midnight the orchestra of the Philharmonic Society serenaded Mlle Lind, and for two hours the famous singer had to stay at her window, despite the coolness of the

---

[1] On September 1, 1850. Berlioz's comic narrative is, needless to say, exaggerated, but only in spots; and the details of his extravaganza are usually based on fact; for example, the crush at the boat landing did catapult one man into the water, which upset the tenderhearted Miss Lind. For a full account see Barnum's *Recollections;* and for a large extract, my *Pleasures of Music* (New York, 1951).

night. The next day Mr. Barnum, the clever bird-catcher who managed to cage the Swedish nightingale for a few months, accompanied her to his Museum, and showed her all the curiosities, including the cockatoo and the orang-outang. Finally, holding up a mirror to the goddess, he said, with exquisite gallantry: 'And this, madam, is the rarest and most enchanting thing we have to show you right now.'

"As she left the Museum, a choir of pretty young girls gowned in white formed a virginal escort, singing songs of praise, and scattering flowers on her path. Farther on, a striking scene of quite a novel kind deeply affected the celebrated visitor: the dolphins and whales that had for more than twenty-five hundred miles (some say twenty-six hundred) shared in the triumphal progress of this new Galatea, convoying her ship while spouting scented jets, were twisting and turning outside the port, in despair at their inability to accompany her ashore. Sea lions shedding salt tears could be heard bellowing their lamentations. There followed a spectacle even more endearing to her tender heart—gulls, frigate-birds, loons, ond other wild inhabitants of the solitary ocean wastes, luckier than the seals, circled fearlessly about the adorable creature, perched on her pure shoulders, and hovered over her Olympian head, bearing in their bills abnormally large pearls, which they presented to her most courteously, cooing gently the while. The guns thundered, the bells pealed *Hosanna!* and at intervals magnificent claps of thunder resounded through a cloudless sky of unbroken radiance.

"All this, which is as unquestionably true as the marvels accomplished in the past by Amphion and Orpheus, are doubted only by us old Europeans, effete as we are, blasé, without faith or love of art.

"Yet Mr. Barnum did not consider this spontaneous behavior of the wild things of heaven, earth, and the waters under the earth sufficient, and wanting to enhance it through a little innocent charlatanry, he is said to have used a form of promotion that might be called—but for the vulgarity of the expression—'dead man's *claque.*' The master promoter of excitement was aware of the great poverty of a number of families in New York and decided to come to their aid so as to connect the arrival of Jenny Lind with the record of benefactions worthy of note. He took aside the heads of these families, and said to them:

> '*When everything is lost and every hope is gone*
> '*Tis shameful to survive—*

you know the rest.[2] Well, I'm giving you an opportunity of doing the right thing in a way that will benefit your poor children and unfortunate wives, who will be eternally grateful to you. *She* has arrived!'

" 'She, who?'

" 'She herself. I therefore guarantee your heirs the sum of two thousand dollars, to be punctually paid on the day you carry out the deed you must by now have in mind, but which you must carry out in the way I am about to tell you. The idea is to pay particular homage to *her*. This can be done with your help as follows: some of you will climb to the topmost story of the houses next to the concert hall and fling yourselves into the street when *she* passes, shouting: "Long live Jenny Lind!" Others will throw themselves under the hoofs of her horses or the wheels of her carriage, but without any disorderly display or shouting—solemnly, gracefully if possible. The rest of you will be admitted to the entertainment free and will have to hear part of the concert.'

" 'We will have to?'

" 'Yes, part. At the end of her second cavatina, you will cry aloud that after such bliss you cannot endure your prosaic existence any longer, and will thereupon stab yourselves through the heart with the daggers I will provide. Not pistols, please note, for they are instruments devoid of nobility and the report might be distasteful to her.'

"The bargain was struck and would no doubt have been faithfully carried out by all parties, had not the American police—as interfering and stupid a body as is to be met with—taken a hand to prevent it. Which proves that even among artistic nations there are always a certain number of narrow-minded, cold-hearted, uncouth —in a word, envious—men. Thus it was that dead man's *claque* could not be put into effect, and a number of the destitute were denied a fresh opportunity to make good.

"Nor is this all. It was generally believed in New York (why doubt it?) that on the day of *her* landing, a *Te deam laudamus*

---

[2] Quoted from Voltaire's *Mérope* (Act II, Scene vii). The rest of the line is: "—and death becomes a duty."

would be sung in all the Catholic churches. But after a long confer-
ence the several parish authorities came to the conclusion that such
a demonstration would hardly be compatible with the dignity of religion. They even thought that the slight change in the text which
would be necessary was blasphemous. Hence not a single *Te deAm*
was intoned in the churches of the Union. I give you the bare brutal
fact without comment.

"Another great mistake, I was told by a music-lover, was per-
petrated by the Department of Public Works of that strange country. Everybody knew, from reading the newspapers, of the huge
railroad being built to span the continent between the Atlantic
Ocean and California. We simple-minded Europeans thought it had
been undertaken merely to facilitate travel for the explorers of the
new El Dorado.[3] We were wrong. The object, on the contrary, was
an artistic event more than a philanthropic or commercial one.
Those hundreds of miles of track were voted by the States to allow
the pioneers wandering among the Rocky Mountains and on the
banks of the Sacramento to come and hear Jenny Lind. They must
not waste too much time making this indispensable pilgrimage.

"But owing to some sinister plot, the work, far from being finished, had hardly been begun when *she* arrived. No words are bad
enough for such carelessness on the part of the American Government, and it is easy to see why *she*, who is so kind and so human,
complained bitterly about it. As a result, the poor seekers-after-gold
of every age and sex were forced to undertake their long and dangerous transcontinental journey on foot, on mule-back, and with
great hardships, when they were already exhausted by their arduous
labors. Claims were abandoned, diggings left yawning, buildings in
San Francisco stood unfinished, and heaven knows when work will
be resumed. This may upset the entire world trade."

"Come now," said Bacon, "do you expect us to believe all that?"

"I shan't say another word: you might think I was giving Mr.
Barnum a retroactive boost when in the simplicity of my heart I
was merely translating into lowly prose the poetic rumors that have
come to us from our all too happy America."

"Why do you say *retroactive* boost? Does Mr. Barnum no longer
function?"

"I can't tell you for sure, though it's hardly likely that such a man

---

[3] That is, the rush for gold following its discovery in California in 1849.

would remain inactive. But he no longer promotes Jenny Lind. You know, of course, that our wonderful virtuoso (I'm altogether serious now) weary, no doubt, of being mixed up in the fantastic doings of all the Romans who exploited her, suddenly retired from the world to get married, and now lives happily out of the reach of any promoting. She was just married in Boston to Mr. Goldschmidt, a young pianist and composer from Hamburg, whom we had the pleasure of applauding in Paris some years ago. This marriage, clearly an artistic one, called forth the following pretty compliment from a French grammarian in Philadelphia: 'She had at her feet princes and archbishops, but declined to be one.'

"Her retirement is a blow to opera managers in both hemispheres. It accounts for the speed with which London impresarios have sent expert scouts on the road throughout Italy and Germany with orders to capture all the sopranos or contraltos of any merit they come across. Unfortunately, in this sort of privateering, quantity can never replace quality. Even if it were true, there aren't enough mediocre singers in the world to make one Jenny Lind."

"She is through, then," said Winter mournfully as he put away the bassoon, from which not a note had issued the whole evening; "we'll never hear her again! . . ."

"I am afraid not. Emperor Barnum is to blame, and that is proof positive of the rightness of the maxim: 'Nothing in Excess.'"

The Paris Opéra and London's Opera Houses

a moral study

THEY are giving a French comic opera, etc., followed by an Italian ballet, also etc.

The musicians are still pondering the course of Roman history we surveyed together the other evening, and are making the oddest comments about it. And Dimsky, who is more eager than his colleagues to learn everything concerning the musical life of Paris, puts a further question to me:

"Now that you have described the habits of the Romans, please tell us about their principal theater of operations. You must have a good many curious revelations to make about that."

"Revelations? You are perhaps the only person for whom the word would hold good. The mysteries of the Paris Opéra, I can assure you, have long since been revealed."

"Well, we in this town are hardly abreast with what you say everybody else knows, so please go on."

"Yes, tell us all you know about the Opéra," say the other musicians.

"*Si tantus amor casus cognoscere nostros . . .*"[1]

"What is he saying?" asks Bacon while his colleagues form a circle about me.

"He says," replies Corsino, "that if we really want to hear about the misfortunes of the Parisians, we must hold our tongues, and tell the bass drum to go easy."

"It's another line from Virgil, isn't it?"

"Right."

"Why does he throw in this Greek all the time?"

---

[1] *Sed si tantus*, etc.: "But if you are so eager to know about our misfortunes . . ." Æneas's reply to Dido's request for the story of Troy's downfall. Virgil's *Æneid* (II, 10).

"Because it makes him seem learned and superior. It's a little foible we must overlook. Quiet! he's started."

"Gentlemen, do you know a fable by La Fontaine that begins with the two lines:

> *One day on stilt-like legs the heron wended*
> *His way, long beak on longer neck extended.*" [2]

"Of course; who doesn't? Do you take us for Zulus?" [3]

"Well, the Opéra, that big theater with its big orchestra, big choruses, big subsidy from the government; with its numerous staff and acres of scenery, resembles in many ways the pathetic bird in the fable. Now it stands motionless, sleeping on one leg; now it strides along full of agitation, going nobody knows where, seeking food in the tiniest streams, not turning up its nose at the gudgeon, which it usually scorns, and whose name alone is enough to fret its gastronomic pride.

"But the wretched bird has been wounded in the wing; unable to fly, it walks; and its strides, however bustling, are all the less likely to take it to its goal that it does not itself know where this lies. Like all other theaters, the Opéra is after money and prestige; it wants wealth and glory. A big success brings both; fine works sometimes earn a big success, but great composers and competent writers alone create fine works. And these works, which glow with the intellect of genius, come alive and are beautiful only through a performance that is equally living and beautiful; that is to say, inspired, delicate, faithful, lofty, brilliant, animated.

"The quality of a performance naturally depends not only on the choice of performers, but on the spirit that pervades them. Now, this spirit might be just right if they had not all long ago found out something which has discouraged them, made them indifferent and, in the end, bored and disgusted. They found out that one master passion controls all the purposes, fetters all the ambitions, and absorbs all the thoughts of the Opéra: the Opéra is madly in love with mediocrity. In order to possess mediocrity, do honor to it, give it a home, pet it and cherish it and glorify it, it will stop at nothing, shrink from no sacrifice, and accept any hard labor with enthusiasm.

---

[2] *Un jour sur ses longs pieds allait je ne sais où/Le héron au long bec emmanché d'un long cou.*—La Fontaine's "The Heron."
[3] In the original: Botocudos, Indians of Brazil.

With the best of intentions, the utmost goodwill, it works itself up to ecstasy over platitude, shows a raging appetite for the insipid, and burns with the fever of love for what is lukewarm. It would turn poet in order to sing the praises of prose.

"Moreover, having noticed that the public has slipped from boredom into indifference and has long since resigned itself to accepting whatever is set before it without praise or blame, the Opéra has rightly concluded that it is master in its own house and that it can without fear give free rein to all the transports of its fiery passion and, putting mediocrity on a pedestal, worship it with myrrh and frankincense.

"To achieve this fine result, in partnership with those of its servants whose natural inclination is the same and who love being left to their own devices, the Opéra has so effectively worn out, disillusioned, shackled, and besmeared its performers that many of them have given up, hung their harps on the willows by the river-bank, and wept. 'What else could we do?' they now keep saying; '*Illic stetimus et flevimus.*' [4]

"Others grew indignant and came to loathe their duties, and the rest simply went to sleep. These are the philosophers; they draw their salaries, and parody Mazarin's mot: 'The Opéra does not sing, but it pays.' [5]

"Only the orchestra causes the management any trouble by putting up resistance. Most of its members being virtuosos of the first rank, they also belong to the Conservatoire's famous orchestra, which keeps them in touch with art in its purest form, and with a choice public. Hence their maintenance of standards and their opposition to the efforts made to enslave them. But given time and bad music, there is no band of men whose spirit cannot be broken, whose fire cannot be put out, whose vigor cannot be undermined, whose proud mien cannot be humbled.

" 'And so,' says the Opéra to them again and again, 'you scoff at my singers, you make fun of my new scores? Just wait! I know the way to make you highbrows come around. Here is an opera in numberless acts, the beauties of which you are going to relish. Three full rehearsals would suffice to get it ready—it's dinner music —you will therefore do twelve or fifteen; Make Haste Slowly is

---

[4] "There we sat down and wept." (Psalm cxxxvi, 1.)
[5] Mazarin's saying apropos of a new tax was: "If they still sing, they'll pay."

my motto. You'll play the work a dozen times or so; which means until nobody comes; then we'll pass on to another of the same kind and merit. Ah, you thought it dull, did you? common, frigid, and flat? I have the honor to present to you an opera full of galops which was written at just that speed, and which you will be good enough to learn with the same devotion as its predecessor. And in a little while you will have another from the pen of a composer who has never composed anything, which I hope you will dislike even more.

" 'You complain that the singers sing out of tune and cannot keep time; they, on the other hand, complain that your accompaniments are too strict; hereafter you will relax your rhythm and wait on any given note until they have finished swelling out their chest on their favorite sound, or until they have had time to take a breath. And now here is a ballet which is to last from nine o'clock until midnight. The bass drum is to be heard throughout. I expect you to struggle against it and make yourselves heard all the same. By God, gentlemen, you're not to think of *accompanying* this time and I'm not paying you to count rests.' And so on and so on until I'm afraid that noble but humbled orchestra will become despondent, then fall into a sickly torpor, into a comatose depression, and finally into mediocrity—the abyss into which the Opéra drives everyone under its sway.

"As for the choruses, they are handled differently. To avoid the arduous system applied to the orchestra with so little success so far, the Opéra tries to replace its old choristers by choristers 'already trained,' which is to say, 'already bad.' But here it overreaches itself, for in a very short time these newcomers get worse and thus lose the special quality for which they had been engaged. Hence the divine cacophony so frequently heard, especially in the scores of Meyerbeer. Nothing less than this has the power of rousing the public from its lethargy; it calls forth yells of disapproval, gestures of horrified indignation, which in themselves are quite impressive and as such ought to greatly displease the Opéra.

"And yet the poor public has been utterly tamed, as I have said; its teeth have been pulled; it is as submissive and gentle as a well-behaved child. In the old days the public was served with masterpieces whole, with operas in which every part was beautiful, in which admirable recitatives rang true and the dance tunes were exquisite. There was nothing to brutalize the ear; even the language was respected—yet the public was bored.[6] Drastic methods followed in hopes of shaking it into wakefulness: high C's from every type of chest, bass drums, snare drums, organs, military bands, antique trumpets, tubas as big as locomotive smokestacks, bells, cannon, horses, cardinals under a canopy, emperors covered with gold, queens wearing tiaras, funerals, fêtes, weddings, and again the canopy, always the canopy, the canopy beplumed and splendiferous, borne by four officers as in *Malbrouck*,[7] jugglers, skaters, choirboys, censers, monstrances, crosses, banners, processions, orgies of priests and naked women, the bull Apis, and masses of oxen, screech-owls, bats, the five hundred fiends of hell, and what have you—the rocking of the heavens and the end of the world, interspersed with a few dull cavatinas here and there and a large *claque* thrown in.[8]

"The poor bewildered public caught in this cataclysm finally opened its eyes wide and its mouth still wider and stayed awake, to be sure, but silent, acknowledging defeat, powerless to retaliate, forced to unconditional surrender.

"And so the public, dog-tired, broken-backed, done for in this scrimmage like Sancho after the siege of Barataria, brightens up with joy as soon as anyone offers it some quiet enjoyment. It takes in with relish any refreshing bit of music, revels in it, drinks it in. For it has been cowed to the point where it does not dare complain of the diet. You could feed it on tallow soup, live crayfish, roasted crows, or ginger custard, and if amid these repellent messes it could find just a little bit of barley sugar to suck, it would be in the seventh heaven, and smacking its lips would say: 'What a generous host! Three cheers! I am more than content!'

"And now comes the good side of the whole business. The submissiveness of the public having become obvious, and its errors of judgment no longer having to be feared (since it no longer passes judgment), all the composers have decided, as they say, to go the whole hog and produce nothing but masterpieces."

---

[6] Berlioz is harking back to his first decade in Paris, 1821–30, when the tradition of Gluck and his followers still held the stage, and so did some great singers. The change he deplores came with their retirement and the triumph of Meyerbeer with *Robert le diable* in 1831.

[7] A reference to the French popular song: *"Malbrouck s'en va-t-en guerre,"* which antedates, and has nothing to do with, the Duke of Marlborough.

[8] This catalogue, which could be documented almost completely, summarizes the spectacular, "realistic" features of the then new genre known as grand opera.

"What a good idea!" exclaims Corsino, "that's the revolution we've all been waiting for."

"Still, it would be too bad to put on too many masterpieces at the Opéra. Let us hope that composers will be reasonable and set a limit to their inspired fertility. Enough fine scores have already been spoiled in that place. As soon as the composer's influence no longer controls his interpreters, two or three nights after the première, the performances go from bad to worse, especially in works of uncommon finish. Nor is the trouble, in general, that insufficient time is allowed to rehearse them, for this is the way the preparations are organized:

"At first there is no thought of preparation. Then, when it begins to dawn that it might not be a bad idea to think about it a little, everybody takes a rest. This is sound. After all, it won't do to overwork and risk a premature exhaustion of the managerial intellect. By a series of such wise calculations, the point is reached where a rehearsal may safely be announced. On that day the manager rises early, shaves close, repeatedly scolds his servants for their sloth, hastily swallows a cup of coffee—and goes off to the country.

"Several actors are good enough to attend the rehearsal; as many as five drop in one by one. The hour set to begin being twelve thirty, they pleasantly talk politics, business, railroad-building, fashions, the money market, dancing, and philosophy until two o'clock. Then the accompanist ventures to point out to the ladies and gentlemen that he has been waiting quite a while and would they be good enough to open their parts and look at them. At this suggestion, each performer asks for his, riffles through the leaves, shakes off the sand while cursing the copyist,[9] and they all begin—to chatter a little less.

" 'How are we going to sing this? The first piece is a sextet, and we are only five; that is, we were five a moment ago, but L. has just left; his lawyer sent for him on important business. Four can't rehearse a sextet. Suppose we put it off to another time.' Whereupon they depart as gradually as they came.

"No rehearsal can be held on the following day, for it is Sunday, nor the day after that, for it is Monday, and there is a performance. Usually on such days no one works, not even the actors who do not

---

[9] Sand was used to blot the handwritten parts.

appear in the particular show: they are resting with all their might, thinking of the hard work their colleagues are facing. Till Tuesday, then. The clock strikes one. The two who failed to turn up at the first rehearsal walk in, but none of the others. This is only fair: they waited in vain the first day, the absentees made them waste their time, they owe it to their dignity to retaliate.

"At a quarter to three all are present except the second tenor and the first bass. The charming ladies being in an adorable mood, one of them suggests trying the sextet without the bass. 'What does it matter? We shall at least see what our separate parts are like.'

" 'One moment, please, gentlemen,' says the accompanist, 'I am trying to make out this chord; I find it hard to read the notes. You know how difficult it is to play a twenty-part score at sight.'

" 'What?' says Mme S., who is used to speaking her mind, 'You don't know the score, and you come here to teach us our parts! Why don't you study it a little at home before coming here?'

" 'Since that's more than you could ever do with your own part, madam, I can't invite you to go and do likewise.'

" 'Now, now, don't get personal!'

" 'Let's begin!' says D., impatiently. 'First, the *ritornello*, then D.'s recitative, and all together on the F-major chord. Ouch! An A flat! That was you, M.'

" 'I! How could I have sung A flat when I haven't even opened my mouth? I am a sick man; I can't stand this much longer. I must get to bed.'

" 'So now our sextet of four is reduced to a trio, but a real trio, a trio of three. Better than nothing. Let's go on: Greece expects—'

" 'Greasy specks—ha, ha! [1] you stole that from Odry! [2] It's a good one, isn't it? Ha, ha, ha! Greasy specks, ha! ha! ha!—'

" 'My word, how that woman giggles!' says Mme G., breaking a needle in the pocket-handkerchief she is embroidering.

" 'At least, we who are gay don't cast gloom on others. You look pained, madam. You mustn't drop a stitch over a pun—or get a stitch trying not to laugh. Ha, ha, ha! Another pun!'

" '*Buona sera a tutti.* Good night, all,' says D., rising. 'You're all

---

[1] In French: *La Grèce doit* and *la graisse doit* (goosefat). The pun was also used by Offenbach in *La Belle Hélène.*

[2] Jacques Charles Odry (1781–1853), a comedian of international reputation who created the now legendary character of Bilboquet and published some of his quips and puns in *Odryana.*

very witty, darlings, but much too hard-working. It's now a quarter past three; we are never supposed to rehearse after three. Today is Tuesday and I may have to sing *The Huguenots* on Friday, so I have to take it easy. Besides, I'm hoarse, and it's only because I am always conscientious that I turned up today—arrrhum!'

"They all leave. The eight or ten sessions that follow more or less resemble the first two. A whole month passes by that way, after which the rehearsing goes on almost seriously for a whole hour three times a week, or twelve hours' work in a month. The manager continues to stimulate his performers by keeping away, and if a small one-act opera, announced for the first of May, can finally be produced by the end of August, he's entitled to throw out his chest and say: 'Oh, that? A mere trifle—we put that on in forty-eight hours!'

"The London impresarios, now, those are the men to get the most out of time! It's the English who have brought the art of speeded-up rehearsing to a degree of splendor unknown to other nations. I cannot praise their method more highly than by saying that it is the exact opposite of the one adopted in Paris. On one side of the English Channel it takes ten months to learn and stage a five-act opera; on the other, ten days. In London the great thing for an impresario is the placard. If he can plaster it with celebrated names, announce celebrated works, or describe as celebrated the obscure works of celebrated composers, driving in this epithet with all the power of the press, he's turned the trick.

"But as the public thirst for novelty is insatiable and curiosity is its ruling passion, the gambler who wants to win every trick must shuffle the cards as often as possible. It therefore becomes imperative to move fast rather than with care, very fast—to the point of folly. The manager knows that the audience will not see defects in performance if they are cleverly concealed; that it will never even suspect the ravages caused in a new work by the lack of ensemble and the hesitations of the chorus, by its coldness and its neglect of delicate nuances, by the wrong tempi, the fine strokes that are muffed and the intentions that are turned upside down. He counts on the self-esteem of those who sing the main parts. Being in a conspicuous position, they surely will make superhuman efforts to do themselves justice in the public eye despite the paucity of rehearsals. This is indeed the fact and it gets by.

"Nevertheless there are occasions when, with the best will in the world, the most zealous performers cannot pull it off. People will long remember the first performance of *The Prophet* at Covent Garden, when Mario "dried up" several times for not having had enough time to learn his role. It wouldn't be of any use to say as the first night of a new work approaches: 'It's not ready, it's all wrong, it needs another three weeks!'

" 'Three weeks!' the impresario would cry, 'you shan't get three days; it goes on tomorrow.'

" 'But, my dear sir, there is a big ensemble, the biggest in the opera, of which the chorus hasn't yet seen a note; they can't guess their way, improvise the music on the stage!'

" 'Never mind, just cut out the ensemble; there's always enough music left.'

" 'There's also a small part, sir, that they've forgotten to cast, and we have nobody to take it.'

" 'Then give it to Mme X. and let her learn it tonight.'

" 'But Mme X. is already singing another part.'

" 'That's all right; she can change costumes and do both. You don't suppose I am going to hold things up for trifles like that?'

" 'The orchestra, sir, hasn't yet gone over the ballet music.'

" 'They can read it at sight! Enough now, leave me alone. The opera is announced for tomorrow; the seats are sold and all is well.'

"It is the fear of being outdone by their rivals, coupled with the necessity of meeting an enormous overhead, that causes this fever, this *delirium furens* among managers. Art and artists bear the brunt of it. The manager of a London opera house is a man who carries about a barrel of gunpowder and cannot put it down because he's pursued with flaming torches. The poor devil runs as fast as his legs will carry him, falls down, gets up again, leaps over ditches, palings, streams, and bogs, knocks down everything he meets, and would trample on the bodies of his father or his children if they got in his way.

"All this I admit is the sad result of circumstance. But what is still more deplorable is that this necessity for wild hurry in the preparation of operatic performances in England should have turned into a habit and come to be regarded by some as a special talent worthy of admiration. 'We produced that opera in a fortnight,' says one. 'And we in ten days,' retorts another. 'And a pretty mess you've made of it,' is what the author would say if he were there.

"The upshot of proudly citing certain examples of this sort of success is brashness unlimited. As a result the contempt for all the qualities that make a performance worthy, the contempt even for the exigencies of art, goes on increasing. During the brief life of the English Grand Opera Company at Drury Lane in 1848, the manager, who had exhausted his repertory and was at his wits' end, one day told his conductor [3] in all seriousness: 'There is only one thing left for me to do, and that is produce *Robert le diable* next Wednesday. That gives us six days to get it up.'

" 'That's fine!' was the reply, 'and we will rest on the seventh. But have you the English version of the opera?'

" 'No, but it can be made in a jiffy.'

" 'The score?'

" 'No, but . . .'

" 'The costumes?'

" 'Oh, no!'

" 'Do the singers know the music of their roles, and the chorus theirs?'

" 'No—no—no. Nobody knows anything, I haven't got anything, but it must be done.'

"The conductor kept a straight face; he saw that the poor fellow was losing his mind, or rather that he had lost it already. Would that were all he had lost! [4]

"On another occasion this same impresario having conceived the idea of staging Donizetti's *Linda di Chamouni* (the translation of which he had this time taken care to procure), and the actors and chorus having most extraordinarily had the time to study it, a full rehearsal was called. The orchestra was seated, singers and chorus were on stage, and everyone waited. 'Well, why don't you begin?' asked the stage director.

" 'I should like nothing better,' replied the conductor, 'but there is no music on the stands.'

" 'What! Incredible! I'll have it brought.' He sends for the head of the copying staff and says: 'Here, put the music on the stands.'

---

[3] Berlioz himself. The manager was Antoine Jullien (1812–60), whose earlier and later doings may be read about in Berlioz's *Memoirs*.

[4] Jullien went bankrupt.

" 'What music?'

" 'Good Lord, why, the music of *Linda di Chamouni.*'

" 'There isn't any. No one told me to copy the orchestral parts of that work.'

"Thereupon the musicians rise from their seats with shouts of laughter and ask permission to leave. The only thing forgotten in connection with the opera was merely *the music.*

"Forgive me, gentlemen, if I break off a moment. This anecdote depresses me, humiliates me, awakens sad recollections. Besides, just listen to that delightful dance tune that has strayed among the rubbish of your Italian ballet."

"Right you are! Here we go!" exclaim the violinists, grasping their bows, "we must play it like masters, for it is masterly." And indeed the whole orchestra performs with irreproachable ensemble, expression, and delicate shading the admirable Andante that breathes the voluptuous poetry of the *Arabian Nights.* It is hardly finished before most of the musicians quit their stands, leaving two violins, a double bass, the trombones, and the bass drum to deal with the remainder of the ballet.

"We'd noticed that bit," says Winter, "and we'd planned to perform it *con amore;* it's you who nearly made us miss it."

"But where does it come from, who wrote it, where have you heard it before?" asks Corsino.

"It comes from Paris; I heard it in a ballet called *La Péri,* music by Burgmüller, a German composer whose talent is equal to his modesty." [5]

"It is very beautiful, it lingers divinely."

"It makes one dream of Mohammed's houris. That music, gentlemen, accompanies the entry of the Peri. If you could hear it with the stage effects for which the composer conceived it, you would admire it even more. It is simply a masterpiece."

The musicians with but one thought go back to their desks, and pencil in, where the Andante appears on the orchestral score, the name of Burgmüller.

"But to resume my sad narrative.

"The managers of our Paris Opéra, some of whom have been

---

[5] Friedrich Burgmüller (1806–74), a popular composer known chiefly for his unpretentious piano pieces.

men of brains and ability, have from time immemorial been chosen from among men with the least interest in and knowledge of music. There have even been some who absolutely loathed it. One of them told me to my face that any score over twenty years old was only fit to be thrown into the fire; that Beethoven was 'an old fool,' whose works a handful of lunatics affected to admire, but who as a matter of fact had 'never composed anything tolerable.' "

The musicians blow up: ! ! ! . . . ! ! ! . . . (and other exclamations not fit to print).

" 'Good music,' another director was wont to say, is music which 'doesn't interfere' with the rest of the opera. Little wonder that such managers do not know how to get their huge musical engine under way, or that they take every opportunity to treat cavalierly the composers they do not think they need or are likely to need. Spontini whose two masterpieces, *La Vestale* and *Cortez*, 'fed' the Opéra for twenty-five years, was at the end of his life put on the index of that institution and could not even get an audience from the manager. Rossini, if he were to return to France, would have the pleasure of seeing the score of his *William Tell* completely garbled and cut by a third. For many years one half of the fourth act of his *Moses in Egypt* was played to his face as a curtain-raiser before a ballet! Whence the delightful repartee attributed to him. Meeting by chance the manager of the Opéra, he is greeted with the words: 'Well, my dear maestro, we are playing the fourth act of your *Moses* tomorrow.'

" 'You don't say! All of it?'

"The interpretation and mutilation inflicted from time to time at the Opéra on *Der Freischütz* provoke general indignation, if not in Paris, which nothing can make indignant, at least in the rest of Europe, where Weber's masterpiece is admired.[6]

"Everybody knows the insolent contempt with which, toward the end of the last century, Mozart was treated by the great men who were then at the head of the *Académie royale de musique*.[7] Having quickly sent about his business the little harpsichord-player who had had the audacity to offer to write for their theater, they nevertheless promised by way of compensation, and as a special favor, to give a short orchestral piece of his at one of the Opéra's

---

[6] For confirmation see my *New Letters of Berlioz*, pp. 113 ff.
[7] The official title of the Paris Opéra.

concerts of sacred music, and urged him to write such a piece. Mozart soon completed it and hastened to submit it to the manager.

"Some days later, the concert in question having been advertised and Mozart not seeing his name on the program, he returned full of anxiety to see the management. As usual he is kept waiting a long time in an anteroom, where rummaging idly among a heap of papers lying on the table, he finds—what do you suppose?—his manuscript, tossed there by the manager. On seeing his patron, Mozart quickly asks him for an explanation. 'Your little symphony?' replies the manager, 'yes, that is it. There is no time now to give it to the copyist. *I had forgotten it*.'

"Ten or twelve years later, when Mozart was with the immortal dead, the Paris Opéra felt it a duty to put on *Don Giovanni* and *The Magic Flute*. But for the occasion the works were mutilated, soiled, disfigured, vilely travestied by wretches whose names it should be forbidden to pronounce. Such is our Opéra, such it was, and such it will be."

A Few Words about the Present State of Music, Its Faults, Its Misfortunes, and Its Sorrows

The Tradition of *Tack*

A Victim of *Tack*

a downstage story

A FRENCH opera is being given, etc., etc.

As I enter the orchestra after the overture, I find the musicians (the bass-drum player and the snare-drummers excepted) listening to the reading of a pamphlet that excites their risibilities.

"We made you feel depressed yesterday by getting you on the subject of the Paris and London operas," says Dimsky, holding out his hand; "now here is something that will revive your good humor. Just listen to the critical fun that one of your compatriots, who remains anonymous, pokes at the present state of music in France. His ideas resemble your own and confirm everything you have told us on the subject. Start again from the beginning, Winter."

"No, our guest would laugh at my English accent."

"Your American accent you mean, you Yankee!"

"You read it, Corsino."

"I have an Italian accent."

"Then you, Kleiner."

"I have a German accent; read it yourself, Dimsky."

"I have a Polish accent."

"I see it is a conspiracy to make me read the pamphlet just because I am French. Give it here."

Winter hands me the pamphlet, and during the performance of a long trio, which is sung precisely as it deserves, I read what follows:

A Few Words about the Present State of Music, Its Faults, Its Misfortunes, and Its Sorrows

The times, as everybody knows, are hardly favorable to any movement in the arts. Music, for one, hardly stirs. It is asleep. It could be pronounced dead if it were not for the feverish motions of its hands, which open wide and then close convulsively during its sleep, as if they sought to grasp something. Then, too, it dreams, and talks in its dream. Its brain is full of strange visions: it challenges the Minister of the Interior, it threatens, it complains. "Give me money," it cries out in a choked guttural tone, "give me a lot of money or I shall close my houses, give my singers unlimited leave, and—take it from me—Paris, France, Europe, the world, and the government can get on thereafter as best they can. The paying public does not come to me—is that my fault? It doesn't even want to come without paying. Is that my fault? What if I haven't enough money to pay it to come, is *that* my fault? Oh, if I had money to buy an audience, you'd soon see crowds at my festivals, trade and the arts would flourish once more, the universe would be born again to joy and health, and we could all of us snap our fingers at the insolent virtuosos and the haughty composers who allege that there is nothing artistic or musical about me, and that the name I go by is a fraud."

What nonsense! The Minister heeds Music's threats as little as its complaints. He stuffs the key of his safe into the deepest recesses of his pocket and calmly replies with overwhelming good sense: "My poor dear Music, I appreciate your arguments. You want to be indemnified for your losses, on the understanding that if you ever make a profit, you'll keep it. That's a convenient, delightful, excellent system for you; I envy it, but I must refrain from putting it into practice. Proposals like yours can be made to royal brigands, rascally emperors, dreadful absolute monarchs rolling in gold, gorged with the sweat of the people, but not to the ministers of a young republic plagued from birth by certain constitutional defects that force it to think of its health before anything else. In these days of cholera, physicians come high. And surely those other heads of state without liberty, equality, or paternity, those kings—to call them by their right names—would themselves not surrender at the first words of your disrespectful summons.

"Most of these idlers have devoted much time to the arts and literature; some of them know you well, Music, old thing, and would show no mercy to any of your faults. They might even say: 'If persons of good repute give you a wide berth, young lady, it may be because the repute of those you go with is bad. If your purse is empty, it is because you spend too much on knick-knacks, ornaments in doubtful taste, tinsel of various kinds, costly and useless accessories suitable only for tight-rope walkers. If today your finances are in poor shape, if your ventures fail, if you are made fun of, if you are headed for ruin, blame only the detestable advice you choose to listen to, as well as your own stubbornness in rejecting the sensible warnings that fortune occasionally puts in your way.'

" 'Where have you gone for your advisers, anyhow? your trustees, your father confessors? Silly creature that you are! Isn't it obvious that those about you are your worst enemies? Some of them, who cannot love anything in the wide world, hate you all the more because they have to look as if they loved you. Others detest you because they know nothing about what concerns you, and feel inside how ridiculous they are in performing functions for which they are totally unfit. Others again, who used to worship you, now hate and despise you because they know you too well. Shame on you! You are a brainless harlot, a real Opéra wench, a business slut—as Voltaire used to say—yet with no business sense: foolish in choosing her stewards, and gullible about them to a degree next door to stupidity. What would you say if a nation like England, for instance, should entrust the command of its navy to a Parisian dancer who had never seen any other maneuvers than those of the ropes and spars of a theater, or to a Burgundian peasant incapable of steering a barge on the Saône?

" 'Away with you! Don't bother us; your entreaties are a bore; if you were what you ought to be—sensitive, intelligent, passionate, devoted, enthusiastic, proud, and courageous; if you had energetically put all those people in their place, and kept to your own; if you had preserved something of your noble origin; if the born princess still showed in you, kings might still come to your rescue and receive you at their courts. But courts are not the sanctuary provided for creatures of your kind. You no longer possess even the seductiveness of vulgar charms. Pale and wrinkled, you have come down to painting your face blue, white, and red, like female savages. Very soon you will be staining your eyelids black and wearing gold rings in your nose.

" 'Your talent has undergone a similar metamorphosis. You no longer vocalize: you vociferate. What do you mean by forcing your voice on every note, pausing with a yell on the next-to-last beat of every melodic phrase, regardless of the syllable under that beat or the meaning of the piece, or the movement of the parts, or the intention of the composer? What of the liberties you take with the finest texts, omitting the high and low notes so as to make the melody shuttle between the five or six notes of your middle register, notes which you then blow up till you lose breath, producing effects akin to the singing of night-prowlers, the wine-sodden bellowing of tavern Orpheuses?

" 'Tell me, you triple-plated little fool, where you got the idea that you were free to chop up a melody and make verses of fourteen syllables by omitting the elisions and taking more frequent breaths? What language do you speak, anyway? Is it the patois of Auvergne or of lower Brittany? The people of Clermont and Quimper would disown it. You must be in that last stage of consumption if you must always take extra beats to bring forth from your chest the shortest melody in quick time, which continually delays the entrances, spoils the attack, destroys all balance and regularity, and painfully asphyxiates your hearers while the contrast with the precision of the orchestra creates that hideous hullabaloo of contrary rhythms one associates with ailing timepieces in a watchmaker's hospital.

" 'You care so little about the imperative ensemble between

voices and instruments, O miserable and degenerate Muse, that to please the opera-producers (who laugh behind your back) you put the chorus at such a distance from the orchestra that the two cannot possibly work together rhythmically. What are you about when you attempt to make an ensemble of the four parts of a chorus, the upper parts of which are downstage, the basses upstage, forty feet away, while the altos and the tenors, half-hidden in the wings and surrounded by groups of marchers and dancers, cannot catch even a glimpse of the concertmaster's bow on the horizon of the footlights? But to say that you are trying to get a four-part ensemble in this way is singularly to flatter you. You make no such attempt. On the contrary, the atrocious muddle and cacophony that result leave you utterly unconcerned; trifles of that sort don't bother you. And yet this nonchalance of yours revolts a good many people, and their number is swelled by all the malcontents whom you merely bore, and together they form the huge public that has acquired the firm habit of never setting foot in your house.

" 'I am speaking now of your misdeeds in the theater only. It would take too long to remind you of all your misdemeanors elsewhere. Go, you are a pitiful sight, and we save our gold for worthier folk than you. What! You threaten? You disgusting crone! Go, no one holds you back. The country will be none the worse for your absence. Regrets? Not a bit, my dear; you are

'*Somewhat too full of jaw, and much too impudent.*' [1]

"Such is the pretty compliment, unhappy Muse, with which pitiless monarchs might show you the door. As for us republicans, we are hardened by patriotic songs, proof against singing out of tune, and we shan't treat you rough. We shan't drive you out of our beautiful France; you'll be free to die a natural death there when you've lost hearth and home."

To which, Music, opening eyes dimmed with tears, replies: "Yes, I shall die a slow and ignominious death. I know it. You thought I was sleeping, but I heard all too plainly the horrible things you have been saying. Still is it quite just, Your Excellency, Minister of State, to blame me for the associations to which I am condemned, the false friends I am forced to frequent and who treat

---

[1] "*Un peu trop forte en gueule et trop impertinente*"; a description of the servant girl Dorine in Molière's *Tartufe*, Act I, Scene i.

me like a slave, give me orders against which I rebel, and impose on me their craziest whims? Was I the one who chose such awful associates? Are they friends of my own making, or of your predecessors', who handed me over to them shackled and defenseless? You know perfectly well that on that score at least I am innocent.

"I am aware that my threats of closing down are absurd; force of habit made me repeat them just now. Alas! just recently I learned the bitter truth! I closed my theaters under pretense of repairs, and the Parisians took about as much notice of it as they would about repairs to the Great Wall of China. You throw in my face my vocal excesses; you are right, I feel it in my soul, but for the last ten years I have managed to exist in Italy only with their aid. In France, where the theatrical public is represented by hired delegates occupying the center seats of the parterre, I can exist only by flattering these gentry, and my vocal debauch delights them. If I don't call forth their applause, I get no other, and then people say that I am not successful. The conclusion follows that I have no talent; the public hears this, believes it, and stays away—hence my poverty and despair. You do not and never will know, sir, what it is to cry out in the desert.

"For the least of your speeches there is an audience which is highly paid by the nation. I should be content with the listeners left to you on days when the Assembly can barely make up a quorum. There, even if you are repeatedly interrupted, challenged, insulted, you have at least a proof that you are listened to. The tumult shows that your audience is passionately for or against your ideas; this may be painful, but it spells life. In my theaters my heart is broken by the utter contempt, the lordly indifference of a public concerned about everything except me; a public which thinks itself sophisticated, though it has never felt anything; which, like the marquesses in Molière, knows everything without having learned anything; a public which is smart enough at raillery, but not enough to hiss my errors, because that would be in bad taste, or too much trouble, or perhaps—the very thought gives me a turn—because it does not notice them.

"I know you will tell me that these reasons do not justify the shameless vices to which I admit I have surrendered; you will quote the famous dictum of the greatest of poets about vulgarity, and say that 'though it make the unskilful laugh, cannot but make the judicious grieve; the censure of the which one must in your allowance o'erweigh a whole theater of others.'[2] Alas! The poet placed this noble sentence in the mouth of a youthful Prince to whom the shocks of hunger, cold, and poverty were unknown; and I could answer him as the actors to whom he gave this advice would have done had they dared: 'Who suffers more than I from the degradation to which I am reduced?' But necessity compels me: I must live, and I could hardly obtain the approval of that single 'one' of the 'judicious' if I didn't exist at all. Guarantee my existence, even if it is less luxurious than that of the Danish Prince, and I shall think as he did, and put into practice his admirable precepts.

"There are in Europe, sir, states where I am free, not to say protected. In France, on the contrary, although more or less sufficient subsidies are granted to some of my theaters, it seems as if everything conspired to paralyze the disinterested efforts I attempt outside the theatrical genres. Instead of help I run into a thousand hurdles. I am gagged. I struggle against prejudices worthy of the Middle Ages. Now it is the clergy who prevent my singing the praises of God in their churches by forbidding women to take part in my most serious works. Now it is the municipal government of Paris that decrees a musical education for working-class children and youths, on the express condition that they must not make use of it. They learn for the sake of learning, and not to practice what they know when they know it. It is like the workmen of the first national workshops, who were made to dig holes in the ground, remove the soil, and bring it back the next day to fill up the holes previously dug.

"When I appeal to the public with the production of a long-pondered work, a work written for the judicious few whom the poet speaks of, without any commercial intention, and solely with the object of bringing to light something that strikes me as beautiful, I am despoiled in the name of the law, smitten with an exorbitant tax. And while I am half slain in this way, I am brazenly told, in a spirit of cynical mockery: 'You are wrong to complain, for the law authorizes us to slay you outright.' To be exact, of the gross receipts that might just cover the expenses I incur, one eighth is taken from me, though one quarter could be legally demanded.

---

[2] *Hamlet* (Act III, Scene ii).

They have the right to break both my legs; they break only one, I must show my gratitude.

"What I say is true, sir, I am not exaggerating. At the coming of liberty, equality, and fraternity I believed for a moment in my coming liberation; but I was mistaken. When the hour of Negro emancipation struck, I indulged in fresh hopes; I was again mistaken. It is settled that in France, under the monarchy as under the Republic, I remain a slave, condemned to hard labor. When I have worked seven days I may not rest on the eighth, for I owe this eighth to the tax-collector, my master, who might require one more day's work. No one has ever dreamed of saying to the shoemaker: 'You have just made eight pairs of shoes; you owe two of them to the state, which is gracious enough to take but one.' Tell me why, sir, why is the art of music not equal to the shoemaker's? [3] What have I, Music, done to France? In what way have I offended? How have I deserved such stern and persistent oppression?

"What makes this oppression still harder to bear and to explain is that, in the eyes of the rest of Europe, France has the reputation of surrounding me with care and affection. She has indeed founded institutions, such as our noble Conservatoire and the annual prize for composition awarded by the Academy of Fine Arts, which continually supply me with zealous disciples, not to say evangelists. But hardly is their education begun, barely has a sense of the beautiful shed its twilight upon their souls, when contrary institutions come and nullify these happy results, thus imparting to the favors I receive the character of a malicious hoax.

"Charlet, the satirical painter, must have had some such thought when he made his delightful drawing *The Marauding Hussars.* Two hussars are shown standing at the door of a hencoop; one of them holds a bag of feed which he scatters in front of the narrow exit, while he calls in falsetto tones: 'Here, chickie, chickie, chick.' The other, with a saber, chops off the heads of the poor birds as fast as they come out. Take another look at that lithograph, sir, and ponder a few moments on the meaning of the allegory. It is only too clear: the feed is the prizes of the Conservatoire and of the Academy; the blows of the chopper—you know who deals those

---

[3] "The American Federation of Musicians today declared a 'war of survival' against the Federal amusement tax, which in some fields amounts to 20 per cent." *New York Times,* June 9, 1955.

out; and my children it is who stick out their necks like stupid fowl. Were they eagles they would perish just the same."

Somewhat moved, the Minister replies: "My child, you may be right; I was ignorant of most of the details you have just told me. I am going to give some thought to them and see if I can't make you at least the equal of the shoemaker in future. It seems only fair, though it disposes only of the material side of the difficulty. As to the other, the moral or æsthetic side, as your dear Germans say, bear this in mind: the time may come when foolish orders and absurd whims will no longer be imposed on you; when your stewards will truly understand your interests and devote themselves to their defense; when your father confessors will not inflict humiliating and ridiculous penances upon you; when you will no longer have to cohabit with your mortal enemies; when in theaters hired men will not usurp the functions of the public; when the public whom at present you tire out and possibly disgust will give you the warmest welcome.

"But before that time you must mend your ways, change your company as far as you can, and your language and your manners absolutely. Do not forget that it is a gross blunder to believe that only uncouth exertions, shouts, violent motions, rhythmical anarchy, vagueness of form, inaccurate design, assaults on expressiveness and idiom, excess of ornaments, senseless din, bombast, or affectation will move an audience—even an audience of vulgarians. These, it is true, are frequently carried away by means that taste and common sense reprove. But it is equally true that they seldom resist a true inspiration when it manifests itself in all its simplicity, with grandeur and energy: they will not hold it against you if you are sublime. They may possibly be disappointed on the first day, but they will be surprised on the second, charmed on the third, and they will end by being infinitely grateful to you. Have we not often seen, do we not even still see on rare occasions, the public—which is, after all, not exclusively composed of those so despised by our poet—applaud, with all its might and all its heart, compositions that are truly beautiful as well as virtuosos whose talent is truly marvelous?

"No, from that quarter you have nothing to fear; the education of the regular patrons of your theaters is now rather advanced; use no artifice, just be sublime, and I warrant you that all will be well.

You invite me to ponder one of Charlet's clever drawings. Let me recommend to you the fable of the 'Wagoner in the Mud' by La Fontaine. Reread the end specially:

> *Says Hercules: 'Bestir yourself*
> *And help will come. But seek, inquire*
> *Why you are stuck, and what the rub*
> *That keeps your wheels from turning. Scrape*
> *The wretched mud off, cursèd mire*
> *Smeared solidly up to the hub.*
> *Now use your pickax on this clod,*
> *And with it fill the holes that gape.*
> *You're done?'—'Yes,' says the man.—'Your whip?'*
> *'I have it—why, what's this? It moved!*
> *Praise Hercules!' To which the voice: 'You've proved*
> *Horses can pull if they can get a grip.*
> *Who helps himself is helped by God.' "* [4]

"Well, what do you think of it?" asks Winter laughingly.

"I think the pamphlet, however full of ludicrous and sad truths, must have made as little impact on Paris as would my 'revelations' of last night if they were printed. In Paris you can say anything you like, because nobody pays attention to anything. Criticism blows over, the abuse remains. Pungent words, sound reasoning, just complaints, glide off the minds of people like water off a duck's back."

"But, gentlemen, what's the matter with your Kapellmeister, rapping on his desk like that?"

"The tenor wants to slow up the tempo of the duet, but the conductor won't have it. There's lots to be said for our conductor."

"So I see. But do you know that the raps which he has indulged

---

[4] *Hercule veut qu'on se remue,/Puis il aide les gens. Regarde d'où provient/ L'achoppement qui te retient,/Ote d'autour de chaque roue/Ce malheureux mortier, cette maudite boue/Qui, jusqu'à l'essieu, les enduit,/Prends ton pic et me romps ce caillou qui te nuit,/Comble-moi cette ornière. As-tu fait?—Oui, dit l'homme./Or bien, je vais t'aider, dit la voix, prends ton fouet./Je l'ai pris. . . . Qu'est ceci? Mon char marche à souhait!/Hercule en soit loué! Lors la voix: Tu vois comme/Tes chevaux aisément se sont tirés de là,/Aide-toi, le ciel t'aidera.*

in from time to time this evening are a continual feature of the Paris Opéra?"

"Is that so?"

"Yes indeed, and their effect is even more deplorable because the conductors rap, not on their desk, but on the top of the prompter's box just in front of them. This gives each rap more resonance and acts like torture on the unfortunate prompter. One of them died as a result of this ordeal."

"You're joking!"

"Not at all. Habeneck [5] noticed some twenty years ago that the people on the stage paid little attention to his gestures, hardly ever looked at him, and consequently often missed their cues. Since he could not speak to their eyes, he conceived the idea of warning their ears, by rapping with the end of the bow he uses to conduct, thus: *tack!*—a smart rap of wood on wood, which can be heard through all the more or less harmonious emissions of the other instruments. This beat preceding the beat that opens the phrase has today become the one necessity of all performers at the Opéra. It is the sign for any of them to begin and it indicates the principal effects to be produced, even to the shades of expression. If the sopranos are to come in, *tack!* meaning: your turn, ladies! Are the tenors supposed to take up the same theme a couple of bars later—*tack!* it's up to you, gentlemen. Are the choirboys gathered at center stage for a hymn?—*tack!* come on, children! Is more warmth required from a singer? *tack!* Sentiment? *tack!* Dreaminess? *tack!* Gaiety? *tack!* Precision, verve? *tack! tack!* The leading male dancer would not venture to 'soar' from an 'echo' without a *tack!* The prima ballerina would feel she had neither legs nor bounce, and her smile would be more like a grimace without her *tack!* All await this pretty little signal, failing which nothing could move or be heard on the boards. The singers and dancers would stand there mute, motionless, aghast, like the courtiers in *The Sleeping Beauty*. Yet the noise remains most distasteful to the audience, and scarcely fitting in an institution that aspires to high rank among the musical and choreographic establishments of Europe. But as it once caused the death of a worthy man, it will surely not be given up."

---

[5] François Habeneck (1781–1849) conducted both the Conservatoire and the Opéra orchestras in Paris. He belonged to the old school and used, not a baton, but a violin bow.

A Victim of *Tack*
A Downstage Story

The victim of *tack* was named Moreau. An honest prompter, he fulfilled, with exemplary accuracy and good conscience, duties that are more difficult than is generally supposed. And thus it stood when Habeneck, in order to make up for the inadequacy of his telegraphic signals, invented the telephonic signal that we know.

On the day when, intoxicated with his discovery, he made use of it for the first time, Moreau jumped in his cave at each rap of the learned bow. But he was more surprised than angry. He imagined that a series of accidents in the performance had made Habeneck impatient in an unusual way which took its toll on the prompter, but which would doubtless be only a temporary inconvenience he must endure without complaint.

At the next performances, though, the *tack* continued; in fact it increased, so delighted was the inventor with its efficacy. Each rap concussed the brain of the wretched prompter, who, cowering in his shelter, leaped from left to right, put his head forward, drew it back, twisted his neck, and broke down in the middle of his lines, like a blackbird shot in full song.

"You are my son no longer. Go, my hatred is too (*tack!*) . . ."

"In my lacerated soul, Nature, I say (*tack!*) . . ."

"The rights Eteocles and you (*tack!*) . . ."

And so forth. For a whole night the poor man suffered martyrdom, an ordeal that defies description but that people who are afflicted like him with a nervous constitution will readily understand. He took good care not to complain, so great was the fear in which Habeneck was held. Yet seeing plainly that here was no whim or fit of bad temper, but a new tradition being founded at the Opéra, Moreau felt that his poise and presence of mind, as well as the close attention needed for his duties, would give way if he were to work forever under this bow of Damocles. He went to the head carpenter and, having unbosomed himself of his troubles, said to him: "If you can't find some way to protect me against that infernal *tack*, I'm done for; it shatters me to the marrow of my bones; it trepans me; it unhinges my cerebellum!"

"I'll be hanged if I don't think you're right," replied the carpenter, "you won't be able to stand it. Wait! I have an idea; bring me your lid."

Moreau removes the roof of his little nook and takes it into the carpenter shop. The two close the door carefully and go to work padding and lining and stuffing the thing with a quantity of small tufts of cotton wool, making it as impervious to sound as an eiderdown quilt. Behold our prompter reassured, cheered up, in the seventh heaven. He goes home and sleeps the clock round, a thing that had not happened to him for a long while. On the evening of the next performance he goes to the theater with that serenity which marks a modest satisfaction devoid of irony. He was such a good man, so completely harmless, was poor Moreau!

The opera on that night was *Robert le diable*, still quite a novelty and hence admirably performed. Consequently the conductor did not have to resort so often to the new device against which the prompter had just protected himself. For the entire first half of the first act Habeneck conducted for the eye and nothing more. Moreau breathed relief and prompted with incomparable verve and delight. He was almost beginning to regret as unworthy the precautions he had taken when, in the middle of the gambling scene, the chorus not having come in at the right time, Habeneck stretches out his arm and strikes a violent blow on the padded roof of the bungalow. *Pouf!* no sound whatever, no *tack*, nothing. Moreau smiles quietly to himself, and continues to recite the words to the absent-minded choristers:

We've got him now! We've got him now!

Habeneck, astounded, gives another *pouf!* "What's this?" he thinks. "The board is soundproof. Has the rascal by any chance padded his shell? The wretch! But this is my chance: just watch! Whereupon, leaning over, he strikes the side wall of Moreau's little crib, which the latter had incautiously neglected to pad. The wood promptly gives out a *tack!* more distinct, sharper, more triumphant than the top had ever done, a *tack* all the more dreadful for the prompter since the blows fell right against his ear. Habeneck, with a Mephistophelean smile, avenged his own temporary discomfiture by redoubling his energy during the entire evening. He made his victim suffer tortures compared with which the Persians' drop of water on the skull must be mere child's play. To crown it all, the performance once done, and with no appearance of having grasped why the prompter had had his apartment upholstered, Habeneck calmly instructed the carpenter to remove the lining of the cover and restore the box to its former state.

Moreau then saw that resistance was henceforth vain and that he was approaching his end. He went home so resigned to his fate that once again he slept. It was to be his last sleep but one. From that day on, *tack* grew by leaps and bounds—on the top, on the side, on the front, on the back of his box; the executioner left no spot unbruised. Moreau was flayed, broken, narcotized, and soon ceased to writhe. He counted the *tacks*, not like a Mucius Scævola holding his hand over the flame without flinching, but rather like an Austrian soldier receiving the hundred and twelfth stroke of the lash on his back. Habeneck had conquered, and the tradition of *tack*, shaken for a moment, was reaffirmed.

Moreau became sad and taciturn; his hair, which had been fair, turned white and soon after began to fall out. His memory went with his hair; his eyes grew weak. The prompter began to make enormous blunders. In the revival of *Iphigenia in Aulis*, instead of prompting: "What grace, what majesty!" he cried out: "Your grace, what cruelty!" In another work, instead of "Extremity of bliss!" he let slip: "Extremity of pain!" From that particular lapse he came to be known as Prompter Pain, "the counterpart," said some heartless joker, of the quack advertisements' "prompt relief." Then he fell ill and ceased to speak. He rapidly grew worse; no physician could extract from him an account of his symptoms. But during his long moments of drowsiness he would occasionally give a slight jerk of the head, as if struck on the skull. Finally one evening, having been quite calm for some hours, just as his friends began to regain hope of his improvement, he again gave a little jerk of the head, breathed the one word "*tack!*" and gave up the ghost.

A long silence. Sighs. Then simultaneous exclamations break out:

WINTER: The poor devil!

CORSINO: *Ohí me! povero!*

DIMSKY: *Pauvre diable!*
KLEINER THE YOUNGER: What vexation of spirit!

The conductor, heartless man, who was often unable to refrain from silent laughter during my sad tale (as I could see from the bouncing of his pot-belly) resumes his solemn face and says as he comes off his stand:

"Silence, gentlemen, the performance is over."

Tonight the musicians have come in dress suits and white ties. Their faces show a most uncommon kind of excitement. Their hearts are full of respect and admiration. They are playing admirably. No one says a word.

After the finale of the second act, the first trombone says to Corsino: "Why, you're crying, old man! I don't mind telling you I thought I'd never manage to get through my part; my lips kept twitching, and toward the end I could hardly get a sound out of my tube."

"Ye gods! What music!" exclaims one of the double basses. "I feel weak in the knees; if I hadn't been able to sit down I couldn't have played a note of the coda."

The third act is played with the same religious fervor as the first two. The conductor, whose understanding, precision, and verve have been perfection itself, bites hard on his handkerchief to control his emotion; he leaves his desk with face aflame, and presses my hand as he goes by.

Suicide from Enthusiasm

a true tale

An ITALIAN opera is being given, etc., etc.

Everybody in the orchestra is talking. Corsino, especially, speaks very loud, gesticulates, and moves about restlessly. He turns to me: "Weren't we worked up last night, though! But once in Paris I heard tell of a Frenchman who was still more impressionable than we were. He worshipped *La Vestale* to the point of taking his own life on account of it. That's history, not a tale, and it shows that musical enthusiasm is a passion just like love. I must tell you about it."

"Please do."

"We are all ears."

"Now be quiet, Moran."

Moran, the first horn, puts his instrument back into its case, and Corsino begins:

I shall call my story *Suicide from Enthusiasm*. In 1808 a young musician had for three years been serving, with obvious distaste, as first violin in a theater in southern France. The boredom he carried with him every evening to the orchestra, where he had to play *The Barrel-Maker, The King and the Farmer, The Betrothed*,[1] or some such score of the kind, meant that he was looked upon by his colleagues as a stuck-up prig. "He thinks," said they, "that he alone in all the world has learning and taste; he scorns the opinion of the public, whose applause makes him shrug his shoulders, and also the opinion of other musicians, whom he affects to consider mere babes." His contemptuous laugh and impatient gestures every time that he had to play some platitude had repeatedly brought down on

---

[1] Operas by, respectively: Isouard, who used the name Nicolo (1799); Monsigny (1762); and Lemoyne (1780).

him severe reprimands from the conductor, and he would long ago have sent in his resignation if poverty, which always seems to choose for its victims temperaments of this sort, had not hopelessly nailed him to his post in front of a greasy and grimy old music-stand.

Adolphe D. obviously was one of those artists predestined to suffering; men who carry within themselves an ideal of the beautiful, pursue it unremittingly, and feel intense hatred for everything alien to it. Gluck, whose scores he knew by heart (for he had copied them in order to be better acquainted with them), was his idol.[2] He read him, played him, and sang him night and day. A misguided amateur to whom he was giving lessons in solfeggio was once incautious enough to tell him that Gluck's operas were merely shouting and plainsong. D. flushed with indignation, yanked open the drawer of his desk, took from it the ten vouchers for the fees due him by this particular pupil, and flung them in his face, roaring: "Get out of here! I don't want you or your money, and if you ever step inside this door again, I will throw you out the window!"

It is easy to see that with so much tolerance for his pupils' tastes, D. hardly made a fortune giving lessons. Spontini was just then in all his glory. The dazzling success of *La Vestale*, proclaimed by the thousand tongues of the press, made all the provincial dilettanti anxious to hear a score so touted by the Parisians. Accordingly the unfortunate theater managers strained themselves to circumvent, if not to overcome, the difficulties of staging and performing the new work.

Not wanting to lag behind, D.'s manager, like the rest, shortly announced that *La Vestale* was in preparation. D., as is true of all fiery spirits whom a sound education has not taught to reason out their judgments, was an exclusivist in taste. He was at the outset full of prejudice against Spontini's opera, of which he knew not a single note: "They say it is in a new style, more melodic than Gluck's. So much the worse for the new style! Gluck's melody is good enough for me; the better is the enemy of the good. I bet it is detestable."

It was in this frame of mind that he took his seat in the orchestra on the day of the first stage rehearsal. As concertmaster he had not

---

[2] This sentence applies in every detail to the young Berlioz.

had to attend the earlier partial rehearsals. The other players, though they admired Lemoyne,[3] found merit just the same in Spontini's score, and on seeing D. said among themselves: "Let's see what the great Adolphe's verdict about it is!" The latter went through the rehearsal without a word or a sign of either praise or blame. His ideas were undergoing a curious transformation. He realized fully from the very first scene that this was a noble and powerful work and that Spontini was a genius whose greatness he could not Ignore. But not conceiving clearly what the composer's methods were, for they were new to him and the poor provincial performance made them still more difficult to grasp, D. borrowed the score, began by reading the words attentively, studied the spirit and character of the persons in the drama, then gave his whole mind to the analysis of the music, thus following a path that could not but lead him to a real and complete understanding of the opera as a perfect whole.

From that time forward it was noticed that he was becoming more and more sulky and taciturn; he evaded any questions put to him, or laughed sardonically when he heard his colleagues vent their admiration of Spontini. "Fools," he seemed to be saying, "how can you understand his work when you admire *The Betrothed*?"

Noticing the ironic expression on D.'s features, the players were sure that he judged Spontini as severely as he had Lemoyne, and that he bracketed both composers in one and the same reprobation. But one day when the performance was a trifle less execrable than usual, it was seen that the finale of the second act had moved him to tears, and they no longer knew what to think. "He is mad," said some; "he is play-acting," said others. And all together: "He is a second-rate musician."

Motionless in his chair, sunk in deep abstraction, and furtively wiping his eyes, D. said not a word to all this impertinence, but was hoarding a treasure of contempt and fury in his heart. The inadequacy of the orchestra, the even greater incompetence of the chorus, the lack of intelligence and feeling in the actors, the vocal ornaments added by the prima donna, the mutilation of every phrase and rhythm, the arrogant cuts—in short, the relentless beating and torturing he saw inflicted on the score which had become

---

[3] See above, note 1, for his popular opera *The Betrothed*. The composer's real name was Jean-Baptiste Moyne (1751–96).

the object of his deepest worship and of which he knew every detail, caused him torments with which I am well acquainted, but which I am unable to describe.

One night after the second act, the whole house having risen to its feet with cries of enthusiasm, D. felt fury overwhelm him; and as an enraptured habitué asked him the commonplace question: "Well, M. Adolphe, what do you say?"

"I say," shouted D., pale with anger, "that you and all the others who are carrying on like lunatics in this theater are fools, asses, louts fit only to hear Lemoyne's music. If you weren't, you would break in the skulls of the manager, the singers, and the musicians, instead of condoning by your applause the most shameful profanation that genius can endure."

This time the insult was too great, and despite the fiery artist's performing talent, which made him invaluable; despite, also, the dreadful poverty which dismissal would entail, the manager could not avoid placating the public for the insult by relieving him of his duties.

Unlike the generality of men of his caliber, D. was not given to expensive tastes. He had some savings from his salary and from the lessons he had been giving, and was secure for three months at least. This cushioned the blow of his dismissal and even made him look upon it as likely to be useful for his artistic career by restoring his freedom. But the chief appeal of his unexpected liberation lay in the possibility of a journey which D. had been vaguely planning ever since the genius of Spontini had been revealed to him. To hear *La Vestale* in Paris had become the fixed goal of his ambition.

The hour of reaching this goal was at hand, when an incident that our enthusiast could not foresee threw a hurdle in his path. Though born with a fiery character and unconquerable passions, Adolphe was nevertheless shy in the presence of women, and apart from some less than poetic affairs with the princesses of his theater, love, all-devouring love, frantic love, the only love that could seem genuine to him, had not yet dug a crater in his heart. On returning home one evening, he found the following note:

Sir,

If you should find it possible to devote a few hours to the musical education of a pupil who is already sufficiently advanced not to put too great a strain on your patience, I should be glad if you would place them at my disposal. Your talents are better known and better appreciated than perhaps you yourself suspect, so you must not be surprised if immediately on her arrival in your city, a Parisian woman hastens to charge you with the direction of her studies in the great art which you honor and so thoroughly understand.

HORTENSE N.

This blend of flattery and self-conceit, the tone at once detached and engaging, aroused D.'s curiosity so that instead of answering the letter, he decided to call on the Parisian lady herself, thank her for her expression of confidence, assure her that she in no way "surprised" him, and inform her that, being on the point of leaving for Paris, he could not undertake the unquestionably agreeable task that she proposed.

This little speech, rehearsed beforehand with the appropriate irony, expired on his lips the moment he entered the stranger's sitting-room. The unusual and challenging grace of Hortense, her deftly fashionable mode of dress, the something indefinable that is so fascinating in the gait and carriage and all the movements of a beauty from the Chaussée d'Antin, made their impact on Adolphe. Instead of irony, he began to utter regrets at his approaching departure. The tone of his voice, the dismay visible in his features gave proof of his sincerity, but Mme N., like a clever woman, interrupted him:

"You are leaving? Then I was well advised to lose no time. You are going to Paris, but let us begin our lessons during the few days that remain. As soon as the cure season in your city is over, I am going back to the capital, where I shall be charmed to see you again and to take further advantage of your instruction."

Adolphe, secretly happy to see his arguments for refusing so easily disposed of, promised to begin the next day and left the house in a dream. That day he did not give one thought to *La Vestale.*

Mme N. was one of those adorable women (as they say at the Café de Paris, Tortoni's, and three or four of the other resorts of dandyism) who find their slightest whims "delightfully novel," and feel that it would be tantamount to murder not to gratify them.

They profess a species of respect for their own fancies, however absurd they are.

"My dear Fr—" said one of these charming creatures to a celebrated dilettante a few years ago, "you know Rossini: tell him from me that his *William Tell* is a deadly thing, it is enough to bore one to extinction; he must *not* take it into his head to write a second opera in that vein—otherwise Mme M. and I, who have always given him our support, will abandon him to his fate." And on another occasion: "Who on earth is this new Polish pianist whom all you artists are so crazy about and whose music is so *queer*? I want to see him; bring him around tomorrow."

"Madam, I will do my best, but I must confess that I am but slightly acquainted with him and that he is not mine to command."

"No, no, of course not; you can't issue an order, but he will obey mine, so I count on his coming."

This strange invitation not having been accepted, the queen told her subjects that M. Chopin was "an odd little body," who played the piano "passably well," but that his music was simply "one long riddle, a ridiculous acrostic."

A fancy of this sort was the main motive behind the rather impertinent note that Adolphe had received from Mme N. as he was preparing to leave for Paris. The beautiful Hortense was a most accomplished pianist and gifted with a magnificent voice which she used as well as it is possible to do when the soul is not in it. She therefore stood in no need of the lessons of the Provençal musician. But his shouting defiance to the public in the theater had had reverberations throughout the town, and our Parisian lady, hearing them talked about on all sides, obtained particulars about the hero of an adventure which to her seemed full of piquancy.

She too "wanted to have him brought around," fully intending, after she had ascertained at leisure what sort of "odd little body" he was, and after she had played with him and upon him as on a new instrument, to send him about his business for good.

But matters turned out quite differently, much to the annoyance of the pretty *Simia parisiensis*.[4] Adolphe was very handsome. Great black eyes full of flame, regular features, which a habitual pallor invested with a slight tinge of melancholy, but into which the

---

[4] Parisian she-ape.

warmest color came from time to time as enthusiasm or indignation quickened his pulse; a distinguished bearing, and manners rather different from what might have been expected from someone who had seen almost nothing of the world except through the curtain-hole of his theater; a character at once passionate and reserved, with the most singular mixture of stiffness and grace, brusqueness and forbearance, sudden gaiety and deep abstraction—such traits made him, by their unexpectedness, the man most capable of catching a coquette in her own net.

And that is just what happened, though without premeditation on Adolphe's part, for he was smitten before she was. From the very first lesson Mme N.'s musical mastery shone forth in all its splendor. Far from needing advice, she was in a position to give some to her new teacher. The sonatas of Steibelt—the Hummel of the day—the arias of Paisiello and Cimarosa, which she smothered with ornaments that were often original and daring, gave her an opportunity to make each facet of her talent sparkle in turn. Adolphe, to whom such a woman and so fine an execution were something new, soon fell completely under her spell. After Steibelt's grand fantasia, "The Storm," in which Hortense seemed to him to display all the powers of musical art,[5] he said to her, trembling with emotion: "Madam, you were making fun of me when you asked me to give you lessons. But how could I take it amiss when your hoax has opened to my unsuspecting eyes the portals of the world of poetry, the artistic paradise of my dreams, turning these dreams into a dazzling reality? Please prolong the hoax, madam, I implore you—tomorrow, next day, every day. I shall be indebted to you for the most intoxicating joys it has ever been given me to know."

The tone in which these words were spoken, the tears which welled up in his eyes, the nervous spasm which shook his frame, astonished Hortense even more than her talent had surprised the young artist. If, on the one hand, the arpeggios, the turns, the showy harmonies, the finely chopped melodies, that rippled from the hands of the graceful fairy caused, so to speak, a paralysis of

---

[5] This reference to Steibelt's "Storm" confirms the likely supposition that Hortense is a portrait of Camille Moke (Mme Pleyel) at a time when Berlioz himself bore a great resemblance to Adolphe D. But differences of more than detail should not be overlooked. See my *Berlioz and the Romantic Century*, Chapters v and vi.

amazement in Adolphe; on the other, his impressionable nature, his lively sensibility, the picturesque expressions he used, their very exaggeration, affected Hortense no less powerfully.

His impassioned praise, springing from true artistic bliss, was such a far cry from the lukewarm and studied approval of the dandies of Paris that self-esteem alone would have sufficed to make her look indulgently upon a man less outwardly favored than our hero. Art and enthusiasm were face to face for the first time; the result of the encounter was easy to foresee: Adolphe, drunk with love, seeking neither to conceal nor to moderate the impetus of his altogether southern passion, disconcerted Hortense completely, and thus unwittingly upset the plan of defense prepared by the coquette. It was all so new to her! Though not actually feeling anything like the devouring ardor of her lover, she nevertheless understood that here was a whole world of sensations (not to say emotions) that the insipidity of her earlier affairs had never disclosed.

They were thus both happy, each in his own way, for a few weeks. The departure for Paris, as may be imagined, was postponed indefinitely. Music was to Adolphe an echo of his profound happiness, the mirror in which were reflected the rays of his frenzied passion, whence they returned more scorching to his heart. To Hortense, on the contrary, music was but a relaxation about which she had long been blasé. It procured her some agreeable diversions, and the pleasure of shining in the eyes of her lover was often the only motive that could bring her to the piano.

Wholly given over to his rage for loving, Adolphe had during the first few days partly forgotten the fanaticism that had filled his life until then. Though far from sharing Mme N.'s sometimes strange opinions about the merits of the various works in her repertory, he none the less made extraordinary concessions to her, avoiding in their conversations, without quite knowing why, the broaching of musical doctrine. A vague instinct warned him that the divergence between them would have been too great. Nothing less than some frightful blasphemy, such as the one that had made him show the door to one of his pupils, could have upset the balance in Adolphe's heart between his violent love and his despotically impassioned artistic convictions. And this blasphemy, one day, did escape Hortense's pretty lips.

It was on a fine morning in the autumn. Adolphe, lying at his mistress's feet, was reveling in the melancholy happiness, the delightful dejection, that follows the great climaxes of voluptuous bliss. The atheist himself, in such moments, hears within himself a hymn of gratitude rising toward the unknown cause that gave him life. And at the same moment, death—a death "dreamy and calm as night," in Moore's beautiful words—is the goal earnestly desired, the only fitting one that our eyes, dimmed with celestial tears, can glimpse as the gift to crown that superhuman intoxication. The common life, life devoid of poetry and love, *prose* life, in which one walks instead of flying, speaks instead of singing, in which so many bright-colored flowers lack perfume and grace, in which genius is worshipped for a day or done glacial homage to, in which art is too often the partner of a misalliance, *this* life, in short, shows itself under so gloomy an aspect, feels so empty, that death, even stripped of the real charm it holds for a man drowned in happiness, would still seem desirable to him, by offering him an assured refuge from the insipid existence he above all things dreads.

Lost in thoughts of this kind, Adolphe was holding one of the delicate hands of his lady-love, imprinting on every finger slight nibbles which he effaced with endless kisses, while Hortense with her free hand, humming the while, ruffled the black locks of her lover. Hearing that voice, so pure, so full of seduction, he felt an irresistible impulse to ask: "Oh, do sing me the elegy in *La Vestale,* my love; you know the one I mean:

> *Thou whom I leave on earth,*
> *Mortal I dare not name.*

Sung by you, that inspired melody will be incredibly sublime. I can't imagine why I haven't asked you before. Sing, sing Spontini to me; let me enjoy every kind of happiness all at once."

"Really? Is that what you would like?" replied Mme **N.**, with a slight pout she thought charming. "You *enjoy* that long, monotonous dirge? It's the most boring thing—like monks chanting! Still, if you insist—"

The cold blade of a dagger plunging into Adolphe's heart would not have lacerated it more cruelly than her words. Starting up like a man who discovers an unclean animal in the grass he has been sitting on, he first riveted on Hortense a dark glance full of threatening fire. Then, striding restlessly about the room, fists clenched, teeth convulsively set, he seemed to be taking counsel with himself about the way in which he should speak to signify their breaking off. To forgive such a remark was impossible. Love and admiration had fled, the angel had become an ordinary woman; the superior artist had fallen to the level of the ignorant and superficial amateurs who want art to "amuse them," never suspecting that it has a nobler mission. Hortense was now but a graceful form without mind or soul; the musician had nimble fingers and a warbler's throat, nothing more.

In spite of the torments Adolphe felt at his discovery, in spite of the horror of so abrupt a disenchantment, he would not have been likely to fail in consideration and tact when breaking off with a woman whose sole crime, after all, was to have perceptions inferior to his own and to love the pretty without understanding the beautiful. But as Hortense was not able to credit the violence of the storm she had just raised, the sudden contraction of Adolphe's features, his excited striding about the sitting-room, his barely controlled indignation—all this seemed to her so comical that she could not restrain a burst of mad merriment and she let out a peal of strident laughter.

Have you ever noticed how hateful a high cackling laugh can be in certain women? To me it seems the sure sign of a withered heart, selfishness, and coquetry. Just as the expression of great joy is in some women marked by charm and modesty, so in others it takes on a tone of indecent sarcasm. Their voice becomes harsh, impudent, and shameless, which is all the more odious the younger and prettier the woman is. At such times I can understand the pleasure of murdering, and I absent-mindedly reach for Othello's pillow. Adolphe no doubt had the same feelings in the matter. A moment before, he was already out of love with Mme N., but he had pity for her and her limited faculties; he would have left her coldly, but without insulting her. The stupid noise of her laughter, at the very instant when the wretched man felt his heart torn, exasperated him. A flash of hatred and unutterable contempt suddenly darted from his eyes. Wiping the cold perspiration from his brow with an angry gesture, he said in a voice she had never heard him use: "Madam, you are a fool."

That same evening he was on his way to Paris.

No one knows what the modern Ariadne thought on finding herself thus forsaken. At all events Bacchus, who was to console her and heal the cruel wound inflicted on her self-esteem, was probably not slow in making his appearance. Hortense was not the woman to stay moping. "Her mind and heart required sustenance." Such is the usual phrase with which such women poetize and try to justify their most prosaic lapses from grace.

Be that as it may, from the second day of his journey, Adolphe had completely broken the spell and was all wrapped up in the joy of seeing his darling hope, his obsessive dream, on the verge of realization. At last he was to see Paris, to be in the center of the musical world. He was about to hear the magnificent orchestra of the Paris Opéra, with its large and powerful chorus, he would see Mme Branchu in *La Vestale*. A review by Geoffroy,[6] which he read on reaching Lyon, further increased his impatience. Contrary to custom, the famous critic had uttered nothing but praise.

"Never," he wrote, "has Spontini's beautiful score been given with such fine ensemble by orchestra and chorus, nor with such passionate inspiration by the principal actors. Mme Branchu, among others, soared to the highest pitch of tragedy; a finished singer, gifted with an incomparable voice, a consummate actress, she is perhaps the most valuable member that the Opéra has been able to boast of since the day of its foundation—be it said with due deference to the admirers of Mme Saint-Huberty.[7] Mme Branchu is, unfortunately, small in stature; but the naturalness of her attitudes, the energetic truth of her gestures, and the fire in her eyes make this lack of stature pass unnoticed. In her exchanges with the priests of Jupiter her acting is so expressive that she seems to tower a full head above Dérivis, who is a colossus.

"Last night a very long intermission preceded the third act. The reason for this unusual pause in the performance was the violent state of excitement into which the part of Julia and Spontini's music had thrown the singer. In the prayer ('O ye unfortunates') her tremulous voice already betrayed an emotion she could scarcely control, but in the finale ('Of this temple priestess lost in sin'), her part being all pantomime and not requiring her to restrain so completely the transports that agitated her, tears flooded her cheeks, her

[6] Louis Geoffroy (1743–1814) was a critic of drama and opera, whose opinions carried weight throughout the Continent during the Napoleonic period.

[7] See above, pp. 71–2.

144

gestures became disordered, incoherent, wild; and when the pontiff threw over her head the huge black veil which covers her like a shroud, instead of fleeing distracted, as she had always done before, Mme Branchu dropped fainting at the feet of the Grand Vestal. The public, mistaking this for a new invention by the actress, covered with applause the peroration of this magnificent finale. Chorus, orchestra, Dérivis, the gong—all was drowned out by the shouts of the audience. The house was in a state of frenzy."

"My kingdom for a horse!" exclaimed Richard III. Adolphe would have given the whole world to have been able to gallop from Lyon to Paris then and there. He could hardly breathe as he read Geoffroy's words. The blood throbbed in his head and made him deaf, he was in a fever. Perforce he had to wait till the starting-time of the lumbering coach, so inappropriately called a diligence, in which he had reserved a seat for the next day.

During his few hours in Lyon, Adolphe took good care not to enter a theater. On any other occasion he would have been eager to do so; but feeling sure as he now did that he would soon hear Spontini's masterpiece worthily performed, he wished to remain until then virginally pure of all contact with the provincial Muses.

At last they were off. Ensconced in a corner of the carriage, buried in thought, D. maintained an unsociable silence and took no part in the cackling of three ladies who were taking pains to keep up a steady conversation with a couple of soldiers. The talk, as usual, ran on every conceivable subject, and when the turn of music came, the thousand and one absurdities retailed barely drew from Adolphe the laconic aside: "Old hens!" But the next day he was forced to answer the questions that the eldest of the women was determined to ask him. All three of them had lost patience with his persistent silence and the sardonic smile that played from time to time on his features. They made up their minds that he should speak and tell them the object of his journey.

"You are no doubt going to Paris?"

"Yes, madam."

"To study law?"

"No, madam."

"Ah, then, you are a medical student?"

"Not at all, madam."

The questioning had come to an end for the time being. It was resumed the next day with an importunity fit to make the most forbearing man lose patience.

"Can it be that our young friend is about to enter the Polytechnic School?"

"No, madam."

"Some business firm, then?"

"Heavens, no, madam."

"As a matter of fact, nothing is nicer than to travel for pleasure, as you appear to be doing."

"That may have been my object in setting out, madam, but I am doomed to miss it altogether, if the future is anything like the present."

This rejoinder, dryly uttered, had the effect of silencing the impertinent questioner at last, and Adolphe was able to take up the thread of his thoughts. How was he going to manage in Paris? His whole fortune consisted of his violin and a purse containing two hundred francs. By what means could he put the former to use and save the contents of the latter? Would he find a way to make something of his talent? But what matter all these worries about trifles and fears about the future? Was he not going to hear *La Vestale*? Was he not on the point of enjoying to its fullest the happiness so long dreamed of? Even if he should die the moment after, he would have no complaint. It was in truth perfectly fair that life should come to an end when the sum of the possible joys that fill a human existence is spent at one stroke.

In this state of exaltation our Provençal reached Paris. Hardly out of the carriage, he rushed to look at the playbills. But what does he see on the Opéra's: *The Betrothed*! "A barefaced fraud!" he exclaims; "what was the use of getting myself expelled from my theater and flying from Lemoyne's music as from plague and leprosy, only to find it again at the Paris Opéra?"

The fact is that this mongrel work, this archetype of the powdered, embroidered, gold-laced rococo style, which seems to have been composed expressly for the Viscount Jodelet and the Marquis de Mascarille,[8] was then in high favor. Lemoyne shared the programs in alternation with Gluck and Spontini. In Adolphe's eyes the putting of these names cheek by jowl was a desecration. It

---

[8] The lackeys masquerading as noblemen in Molière's *Précieuses Ridicules*.

seemed to him that a stage adorned by the finest geniuses of Europe should not be open to such pallid mediocrities; that the noble orchestra, still vibrating with the virile tones of *Iphigenia in Tauris* or *Alcestis*, should not be debased by having to accompany the twitterings of Mondor and la Dandinière. As for the comparison between *La Vestale* and those ghastly and stale potpourris, he tried to drive the thought from his mind. Such an abomination curdled his blood, and to this day there still exist a few ardent or *extravagant* minds (you may call them either way) who take exactly the same view of the matter.

Swallowing his disappointment, Adolphe was glumly going home when chance made him meet a fellow countryman to whom he had formerly given lessons. The latter, a wealthy amateur and well known in musical circles, readily told his former teacher all he knew about what was going on, and reported that the performances of *La Vestale*, which had been suspended because of Mme Branchu's indisposition, would in all probability not be resumed for some weeks to come. As for Gluck's works, which ordinarily formed the core of the Opéra's repertory, they were not scheduled during the first days of Adolphe's stay in Paris. This circumstance made it easier for him to fulfill the vow he had made of preserving his musical virginity for Spontini. He did not set foot in any theater and abstained from every kind of music.

Meanwhile he sought a position that would give him his daily bread without condemning him anew to the humiliating role he had so long occupied in the provinces. He played to Persuis, at that time conductor at the Opéra.[9] Persuis saw that he had talent, invited him to come and see him again, and promised him the first opening among the violins of the Opéra. Thus reassured, and banking for his livelihood on a couple of pupils whom his patron had found for him, the worshipper at Spontini's shrine felt increasing impatience to hear the magic score. Every day he ran out to scan the playbills, only to have his hopes dashed to the ground.

On the morning of the 22nd of March, reaching the corner of the rue Richelieu just as the billposter was climbing up his ladder, and seeing the placard of, successively, the Vaudeville, the Opéra-

---

[9] Luc Loiseau de Persuis (1769–1839) was a violinist and composer who rose to the musical direction of the Opéra in 1817 and made his management notable. He also wrote some two dozen operas, ballets, and oratorios.

Comique, the Italian Theater, and the Porte-Saint-Martin, finally saw the slow unfolding of the large brown sheet bearing as headline the words "*Académie impériale de Musique.*" He nearly collapsed in the street on reading at last the title so greatly desired: *La Vestale.*

Hardly had Adolphe seen this promise of *La Vestale* for the next day when he was seized by a sort of delirium. He rushed madly through the streets, bumping into the jutting angles of houses, elbowing passers-by, laughing at their insults, talking, singing, gesticulating like an escaped lunatic.

Dead with fatigue, spattered with mud, he finally entered a café, ordered dinner, wolfed down without noticing what the waiter set before him, and lapsed into a strange fit of melancholy. Suddenly a prey to anxiety without quite discerning what could be causing it, and overawed by the nearness of the stupendous event which was to come into his life, he listened awhile to the violent thumping of his heart, he wept, and letting his poor, emaciated head drop to the table, he fell into a deep sleep.

The following day he was calmer. A call on Persuis shortened his wait. The manager, on receiving Adolphe, handed him a letter bearing the official stamp of the Opéra: it was his appointment as second violin. Adolphe thanked him, though without much alacrity. This favor, which at any other time would have overwhelmed him with joy, had become to him hardly more than a secondary matter of little interest. A few minutes later he had forgotten it. He avoided speaking to Persuis of the performance that was to take place that evening; the subject would have shaken him to the core. He dreaded it. Persuis, not knowing what to think of the young man's strange looks and incoherent speech, was about to ask the cause of the trouble, when Adolphe noticed this, rose, and left.

He strolled awhile in front of the Opéra, looked again at the bill to make sure there was no change in the program or in the cast. All this helped him to wait till the close of that interminable day. At last the clock struck six. Twenty minutes later Adolphe was in his box, for in order to be undisturbed in his ecstatic admiration, and to enhance the solemnity of his happiness, he had taken, regardless of the extravagant expenditure, an entire box for himself alone.

We shall now let our enthusiast give his own account of that memorable evening. A few lines that he wrote on reaching home, as a sequel to the sort of diary from which I have culled the fore-going particulars, show but too well the state of his mind and the inconceivable frenzy which formed the groundwork of his tem-perament. I give them here without alteration.

"March 23rd, midnight

"This, then, is life! I gaze upon it from the pinnacle of my hap-piness . . . it is impossible to go further. . . . I have reached the summit. . . . Come down again? Go back? . . . Certainly not! I prefer making my exit before nauseating tastes poison that of the delicious fruit I have just plucked. What would my life be if it were to go on?—that of the thousands of insects I hear buzzing about me. Chained once more to a music-stand, forced to play in alternation masterpieces and filthy platitudes, I should end like the rest and become hardened. The exquisite sensibility that enables me to enjoy so many sensations and gives me access to so many emo-tions unknown to the common herd would gradually become blunted, and my enthusiasm would cool, even supposing it did not die out altogether under the ashes of habit. I might perhaps come to speak of geniuses as if they were ordinary beings; I might utter the names of Gluck and Spontini without raising my hat. I am fairly sure that I should always hate with all my soul anything I now hate; but is it not a cruel necessity to husband one's energy only for the purposes of hatred?

"Music occupies too large a place in my life. My passion for it has killed and absorbed all the rest. My last experience of love has disillusioned me only too harshly. Could I ever find a woman whose being would be tuned to the same high pitch as mine? No, I'm afraid they are all more or less like Hortense. I had forgotten her name—Hortense—odd how a single word from her mouth broke the spell! Oh, the humiliation of having loved with the most ardent and poetic love, with all the strength of my heart and soul, a woman possessed of neither, and radically incapable of understanding the meaning of the words "love" and "poetry." Fool, thrice-silly fool, of whom I still cannot think without a blush.

"Yesterday I thought of writing to Spontini and begging him to let me pay a call. But even if my request had been granted, the great man would never have believed me capable of understanding his work as I do understand it. I should probably appear to him merely as an excited young man, childishly infatuated with a work miles above his grasp. He would think of me what he must necessarily think of the public. He might even attribute my transports of admiration to shameful self-interest, thus confusing the most sincere enthusiasm with the meanest flattery. Horrible! No, no, better make an end of it. I am alone in the world, an orphan from childhood; my death will grieve no one. A few will say: 'He was crazy.' That will be my epitaph.

"I shall die day after tomorrow. *La Vestale* is to be performed again, I want to hear it a second time. What a work! How love is pictured in it! as well as fanaticism! All those mastiff-priests barking at their wretched victim! And what harmonies in that gigantic finale! What melody even in the recitatives! What an orchestra! It moves so majestically; the basses swell and sink like the waves of the ocean. The instruments are actors whose language is as expressive as that spoken on the stage. Dérivis was superb in his recitative of the second act: he was *Jupiter Tonans*. In the aria 'Unrelenting gods,' Mme Branchu tore my heart out; I nearly fainted. That woman is lyric tragedy incarnate; she would reconcile me to her sex. Yes! I shall see her again . . . once . . . this *Vestale* . . . a superhuman work, which could have come to birth only in an age of miracles like Napoleon's. I shall focus into three hours the life force of twenty years' existence. Afterwards, I shall go . . . and ponder over my happiness in eternity."

Two days later, at ten o'clock at night, a report was heard at the corner of the rue Rameau, opposite the entrance to the Opéra. Some footmen in gorgeous liveries rushed to the spot on hearing the noise, and raised the body of a man bathed in blood who showed no signs of life. At that instant a lady who was leaving the theater came by to find her carriage and recognizing the blood-bespattered face of Adolphe, said: "Oh, mercy! It's that unhappy young man who's been following me all the way from Marseille!"

Hortense (for it was she) had then and there seen the way to make her vanity benefit from the death of the man who had vexed her by his humiliating departure. The next day the talk in the Club in the rue de Choiseul was: "That Mme N. is really a captivating woman! When she went south some time ago, a Provençal fell so madly in love with her that he followed her all the way to Paris and blew his brains out at her feet last night, just outside the Opéra. That's success, as you might say; it will make her absolutely irresistible."

Poor Adolphe! . . .

"I'll be hanged," remarked Moran, "if in depicting his Provençal, Corsino hasn't painted his own portrait!"

"That's what I was thinking awhile ago, when he was reading Adolphe's letter."

I turn and say to Corsino: "You're his twin, my dear fellow."

Corsino gives us an odd glance, looks away, and goes off without replying.

Spontini

a biographical sketch

A FRENCH opéra-comique is being given; it is very etc.

Everybody is talking, no one is playing, barring the faithful four—the four Catos—who tonight are assisted by a snare drum. The hideous row that the five of them make seriously interferes with conversation. Fortunately, the snare drum soon gets tired, the bass drum is seized with a cramp in his right arm which completely nullifies his zeal, and we are at last free to enjoy a chat.

"Do you really believe such fanaticism possible?" Dimsky asks, after giving me his opinion of the story told the previous evening.

"I don't believe it, but I've experienced it—often."

"You got the answer you deserved, you chump," says Corsino, who then asks me: "Did you ever know Spontini?"

"I knew him very well indeed, and out of my immediate admiration for his genius grew a genuine personal affection on my part."

"They say his severity toward performers was beyond belief."

"In one respect you've been told wrong; I have often heard him compliment indifferent singers. But he was pitiless toward conductors, and nothing infuriated him more than to have his tempi misinterpreted. Once in a German town that shall be nameless, he attended a performance of *Cortez* under an incompetent conductor. In the middle of the second act the torture he suffered was such that he had a nervous seizure and had to be carried out."

"Be a good chap and give us a biographical sketch of him. His life must have been full of adventure and very instructive."

"I won't say no to you, gentlemen, but the master's life, though it was certainly full of turmoil, is nothing like a romance. You can judge for yourselves.

On the 14th of November 1779 there was born at Majolati, near Jesi, in the March of Ancona, a child named Gasparo Spontini. I shall not say of him what biographers never tire of repeating when telling the lives of famous artists: "He showed at a very early age an extraordinary aptitude for his art. When hardly six years old he was producing remarkable—and so on and so forth." My admiration for his genius is too real and rational for me to use the commonplaces of vulgar praise. Everyone knows what those "masterpieces" by infant prodigies are really like, and how much better it would have been for the reputation of those who subsequently became *men* to have destroyed on their first appearance the foolish botches of their overpraised childhood. All I know of Spontini's early years from having heard him tell about them is limited to the few facts I shall mention, and I do not attach to them more importance than they deserve.

He was twelve or thirteen years old when he went to Naples, in order to enter the Conservatory Della Pietà. Was it at the child's own wish that his parents opened to him the doors of this famous music school, or did his father, who perhaps was a man of small means, hope that by giving his son this opportunity he was putting him in the way of a career at once modest and easy? Or was it the father's intention merely to make Gasparo choirmaster of some small church or monastery? I do not know. I lean toward the second possibility, in view of the penchant for the religious life shown by all the other members of the Spontini family. One of his brothers was a village priest near Rome; [1] the other (Anselmo Spontini) died, if I am not mistaken, a monk in a Venetian monastery a few years ago; and his sister also ended her days in the convent where she had taken the veil.

Whatever the truth of the matter, Gasparo's studies at La Pietà bore sufficient fruit to enable him to compose, very nearly like anybody else, one of those absurdities dignified in Italy as elsewhere with the pompous name of opera. His was entitled *Honor among Women*.[2] I do not know whether this first essay was performed or not. But it gave its author enough confidence in his powers and spurred his ambition sufficiently to make him run away from the Conservatory and go to Rome, where he hoped to have his theatrical works more easily produced than in Naples.

---

[1] When Berlioz went to Italy as Rome Prize winner, he carried with him a very warm letter of introduction from Spontini to this brother.

[2] *I Puntigli delle donne.*

The fugitive was soon caught and, under pain of being taken back to Naples as a vagabond, was ordered to justify his escape and the pretensions that had inspired it by writing an opera for the Carnival. He was given a libretto entitled *The Lovers in Peril,*[3] which he promptly set to music. It was almost immediately produced with success. The public indulged in the transports usual among the Romans on such occasions: the maestro's youth and the story of his flight had predisposed the dilettanti in his favor. Spontini was applauded, cheered, recalled, carried in triumph, and—forgotten at the end of a fortnight. But this short-lived success at least brought him his freedom, to begin with (he was exempted from returning to the Conservatory); and second, a rather profitable engagement to go and, as they say in Italy, *write* in Venice.

So there he was, emancipated and left to himself after what does not seem to have been a very long stay in the classes of the Naples Conservatory. Here one would like to be able to throw light on the question that naturally arises: who was his teacher? Some say Padre Martini, who had died before Spontini entered the Conservatory, even I think before he was born; others say one Baroni, whom he might have known in Rome, though these people have also attributed the honor of his musical education to Sala, Traetta, and even to Cimarosa.

I was never inquisitive enough to question Spontini on this point and he never saw fit to talk to me about it. But I did definitely gather from his remarks the practical admission that the real teachers of the composer of *La Vestale, Cortez,* and *Olympia* were the masterpieces of Gluck, with which he became acquainted for the first time on his arrival in Paris in 1803, and which he at once studied with a passion. As for the composer of the numerous Italian operas I shall shortly list, I do not think it greatly matters to know who the professor was who taught him the method of manufacturing them. The usages and customs of the Italian opera houses of his day are faithfully observed in these scores, and any one of the musicasters of his native country could easily have supplied him with the formula which, even at that time, constituted the open secret of the theater. To confine myself to Spontini the Great, I think that not only Gluck, but also Méhul, who had already written

---

[3] *Gli Amanti in cimento,*

his admirable *Euphrosine*, and Cherubini, with his first French operas, must have developed in him the latent germ of his dramatic faculties and hastened their magnificent expansion.

On the other hand, I do not find in his works any trace of the influence that might have been exercised over him, from a purely musical point of view, by the German masters, Haydn, Mozart, and Beethoven. The last-named was hardly known in France even by reputation when Spontini arrived there, and *La Vestale* and *Cortez* were successful on the boards of the Paris Opéra long before their author visited Germany for the first time. It was Spontini's instinct alone that guided him and made him suddenly discover in the use of vocal and instrumental masses, and the linking of modulations, so many treasures unknown to or at least unexploited by his predecessors in opera. We shall soon see the result of his innovations, and the hatred they drew upon him from his compatriots, as well as from the French musicians.

To take up the thread of my biographical narrative, I must confess my ignorance of the thoughts and deeds of young Spontini in Italy after the production of his third opera in Venice. I am not even sure about the theaters where he produced the works that followed this. They must have brought him as little money as fame, since he resolved to try his fortunes in France without being summoned there either by public demand or by a powerful patron.

We know the titles of the thirteen or fourteen Italian scores composed by Spontini during the seven years following his first ephemeral success in Rome. They are: *Loving in Secret, The Deserted Isle, Heroism Misplaced, Theseus Acknowledged, The Fake Bluestocking, The Masked Fugitive, The Speaking Portraits, The Fake Painter, Elysium Beguiled, The Jealous and the Bold, Pascal's Transformations, The Harder You Look, the Less You Can See, The Princess of Amalfi*, and *Berenice*.[4] He preserved in his library the manuscripts and even the printed librettos of all these colorless works and occasionally showed them to his friends with a contemptuous smile, as playthings of his musical childhood.

In his early Paris days, Spontini had, I believe, a very hard time;

---

[4] *L'Amor secreto, L'Isola disabitata, L'Eroismo ridicolo, Teseo riconosciuto, La Finta Filosofa, La Fuga in Maschera, I Quadri parlanti, Il Finto Pittore, Gli Elisi delusi, Il Geloso e l'Audace, Le Metamorfosi di Pasquale, Chi più guarda meno vede, La Principessa d'Amalfi*, and *Berenice*.
All these seem to have been composed between 1796 and 1802.

he just managed to make both ends meet by giving lessons. He succeeded in getting *The Fake Bluestocking* produced at the Italian Theater, where it met with some favor. Whatever the majority of his biographers may say, there is good reason to believe that the opera *Milton* (text by M. de Jouy)[5] was Spontini's first attempt to set French words to music, and that it came before the insignificant trifle entitled *Julie, or The Flowerpot*. For we can see on the title-pages of these two engraved scores that *Milton* was performed at the Opéra-Comique on November 27, 1804, whereas *Julie* was not given at the same theater until March 12, 1805.

Milton was quite well received. *Julie*, on the contrary, fell under the weight of public indifference, like a thousand other productions of the same kind, which are born and die the same day without anyone's condescending to notice them. One number from it has been preserved by the comic-opera stage; it is the aria "And so, for reputation's sake." The famous singer Elleviou[6] had taken a liking to Spontini, and wanting to give him an opportunity of bettering himself, he procured for him a comic-opera libretto in three acts: *The Little House*, which was very likely no better than *Julie*, and which the incautious composer was foolish enough to accept. *The Little House* collapsed so completely and with such a crash that not a trace of it remains. The piece could not even be played to the end. Elleviou had a main part in it; indignant at some scattered hisses, he so far forgot himself as to make a gesture of scorn. A fearful row ensued, the pit invaded the orchestra, drove out the musicians, and smashed everything it could lay its hands on.

After this twofold defeat, every door would inevitably be closed to the young composer, but a high-placed patron remained to him: the Empress Josephine. She did not fail him, and it is unquestionably owing to her alone that Spontini's genius, which was being dimmed before it could even shine, was able two years later to make its radiant ascension in the artistic heavens. M. de Jouy had had on hand for a long time a grand-opera libretto, *La Vestale*, which had been refused by both Méhul and Cherubini. Spontini begged it

---

[5] Étienne de Jouy (1764–1846), soldier of fortune, then prolific writer, was a successful dramatist and unfailing best seller in his own day. He is remembered now for the librettos he supplied to Spontini and Rossini (*William Tell*).
[6] Jean Elleviou (1769–1842), the matinee idol of the Opéra-Comique during Napoleon's reign.

from him so pressingly that the author finally decided to entrust it to him.

Still very poor, much decried and hated by the rabble of Paris musicians, Spontini put all this from his mind and swooped like an eagle on his rich prey. He shut himself up in his wretched lodgings, neglected his pupils, and with no thought even of the bare necessities of life, plunged into his work with that feverish ardor, that trembling passion, which in him were the sure signs that his musical volcano was about to erupt.

The score once completed, the Empress had it immediately put in rehearsal at the Opéra. Then began for Josephine's protégé the tortures of rehearsing—a frightful ordeal for an innovator as yet without authority, and to whom the whole performing staff was naturally and systematically hostile. It was a continuous struggle against ill will, a heart-rending effort to widen old boundaries, to put heat into icicles, to reason with fools, to preach love to eunuchs, imagination to idiots, art to mechanics, truth to liars, enthusiasm to cynics, and courage to cowards. Everybody was up in arms against the alleged difficulties of the new work, the novel forms of this grand style, the impetuosity of this incandescent passion lit by the purest rays of the Italian sun. Everybody wanted to shorten something, to cut, prune, and flatten out this proud music, which demanded so much of its interpreters and tired them out by its need of unflagging attention, vigor, and scrupulous fidelity.

Mme Branchu herself, the inspired woman who created in so admirable a fashion the part of Julia, confessed to me later, not without remorse over her culpable discouragement, that she once told Spontini she would never be able to learn to sing his "unsingable recitatives." The revising of the instrumentation, the cutting and restoring of phrases, the transpositions, had already caused the Opéra enormous expense for copying. Without the tireless good nature of Josephine and the orders of Napoleon, who willed that the *impossible* should be done, there is no doubt whatever that the score of *La Vestale*, deemed absurd and unperformable, would never have seen the light of day.

But while the poor great artist writhed under the torments inflicted on him with such cruel persistence at the Opéra, the Conservatoire was melting the lead which on the great day of the première it meant to pour into his live wounds. The whole swarm of counterpoint crammers kept swearing, on their professors' say-so, that Spontini did not know the first thing about harmony and that his melody lay on the accompaniment like a handful of hair on a bowl of soup—for more than ten years I myself heard this elegant simile applied to Spontini's works in the classes of the Conservatoire. All these young note-spinners, who were about as capable of grasping and feeling greatness in music as the janitors, their fathers, were of judging literature and philosophy, banded together to bring about *La Vestale's* downfall. The hissing system was ruled out. That of yawning and laughing was substituted, in keeping with which everyone of these whippersnappers was to don a nightcap at the close of the second act and pretend to go to sleep. I owe this detail to the leader of the gang of sleepers himself. He had chosen as his assistant sleep manager a young singer of parlor songs who later became one of our most celebrated composers of comic operas.

The first act went by without interference, and the cabal, which had to admit the effectiveness of this superb music—though to hear them talk it was very badly written—were reduced to saying with naïve astonishment devoid of any trace of hostility: "It sounds all right." Twenty-two years later, when Boieldieu attended the final rehearsal of Beethoven's Symphony in C minor, he was also to say with the same feeling of surprise: "It sounds all right!" The Scherzo had seemed to him so "oddly written" that in his opinion "it wouldn't sound." Poor fellow! A good many other things have sounded, are still sounding, and will continue to sound, despite the professors of that sort of counterpoint and the composers of comic operas.

When the second act of *La Vestale* came, the breathless interest of the temple scene kept the conspirators from thinking even for a moment that they might carry out the wretched prank they had planned. And the finale drew from them, just as it did from the impartial public, wholehearted applause—for which no doubt they had to do penance the next day by continuing to run down in their classes the ignorant Italian who had all the same moved them so deeply.

Time is a great teacher! The saying is not new, but the revolution that has come about during these past twelve or fifteen years in the ideas of our Conservatoire is a striking demonstration of its truth. One can hardly find in that institution today any prejudice against, or hostile opposition to, what is new. The attitude of the school is excellent. I rather think that the Société des Concerts,[7] by familiarizing young musicians with a host of masterpieces by great composers whose bold and independent genius never acknowledged any of our scholastic fictions, is to a large extent responsible for this result. Hence it is that the performances of fragments of *La Vestale* by the concert society and the pupils of the Conservatoire are always a great success. Marked by protracted applause, shouts, and tears, they unman performers and public so much that it is sometimes impossible to continue the concert for a whole half-hour.

One day, on an occasion of this kind, when Spontini was concealed at the back of a box and philosophically taking in this storm of enthusiasm, he doubtless asked himself, in the face of this tumultuous exhibition by the orchestra and the chorus, what had become of all the young hoodlums, the little counterpointers and baby-faced nitwits of the year 1807. Just then the audience, having caught sight of him, rose in a body and turned toward him, the house once more resounding with shouts of gratitude and admiration. Sublime is the clamor with which souls deeply moved salute true genius, whose most noble recompense it is. Was there not something providential in this ovation awarded the great artist in the very bosom of the school where for over thirty years the hatred of his person and the contempt for his work were regularly taught?

And yet how greatly does the music of *La Vestale* lose when deprived of the impressiveness of the stage, especially for those hearers (and their number is great) who have never heard it at the Opéra! It is impossible at a concert to guess in how many effects of various kinds the composer's dramatic inspiration has been abundantly and magnificently displayed. What hearers do grasp is the truth of expression manifested from the very opening bars of each role, the intensity of passion that makes this music luminous from the burning flame focused in it—*sunt lacrimæ rerum* [8]—and the purely musical value of the melodies and chord progressions. But there are ideas that cannot be perceived except in a stage performance. A

---

[7] The Conservatoire orchestra, made up of students and former students of the school, was founded in 1828 to give public performances at regular intervals.
[8] "There are tears in such things"—Virgil: *Æneid* (I, 462).

particularly beautiful example among many others occurs in Julia's aria "Unrelenting gods!" in the second act. The melody is in a minor key and charged with the restlessness of despair; then comes a phrase of heart-rending abandon and sorrowful tenderness, "Let the blessing of his presence cast its charm upon this place awhile." After the end of the aria and the recitative "Come, belovèd mortal, I give my life to you," while Julia goes up-stage to open the door to Licinius, the orchestra takes up again a fragment of the preceding aria, in which the distraught accents of the Vestal's passion still predominate; but at the very moment when the door opens and lets in the friendly rays of the moon, the phrase "Let the blessing of his presence" re-enters *pianissimo* in the orchestra, this time with a little added ornament in the wood wind. It is as if a balmy breeze pervaded the temple, an exhalation of the fragrance of love, the blossoming of the flower of life, the opening of heaven's gates. And one can see why Licinius' belovèd, worn down by the struggle against her heart, totters to the altar steps, where she sinks to the ground, ready to give her life for a moment of ecstasy. I have never witnessed that scene without being moved by it to the point of dizziness.

From then on, the musical and dramatic interest increases steadily. One might almost say that the second act of *La Vestale* taken as a whole is just one gigantic crescendo, the *forte* of which does not come till the final scene with the veil.

You do not expect me, gentlemen, to analyse here the beauties of the immortal score that you admire as much as I do. But I cannot refrain from pointing out in passing such marvels of expressiveness as are found at the beginning of the lovers' duet:

LICINIUS: *I behold you!*
JULIA: *But on forbidden ground!*
LICINIUS: *The god who brings us together*
Keeps watch without and will protect our lives.
JULIA: *My fear is for you alone!*

How different the accents of these two characters! The words of Licinius rush to his burning lips; Julia, on the contrary, has now hardly any inflections in her voice, her strength is failing, she is dying.

The character of Licinius is still further developed in his cavatina, the melodic beauty of which cannot be too much admired.[9] At first he is tender, then he consoles, he worships, but toward the end, at the words:

> *Yes, the gods themselves should envy us,*

a kind of pride betrays itself in his accents, he gazes at his lovely conquest, the joy of possession becomes greater than bliss itself and his passion is tinged with pride. As for the duet, and especially the peroration

> *For you alone I mean to live,*
> *Yes, for you alone I mean to live!*

there are in it indescribable things, heart-throbs, cries, gestures of distracted passion unknown to you, pale lovers of the north. It is Italian love in all its fury and volcanic ardor. In the finale, at the entrance of the priests and people into the temple, the rhythmic forms become hugely magnified, the storm-swept orchestra swells and moves with a terrible majesty. Religious fanaticism is at work:

> *Oh murder! Oh despair! Oh dire distress!—*
> *The sacred flame put out, the priestess dying:*
> *The gods will slay, and for their laws' defying*
> *Reduce the universe to nothingness.*

This recitative is awe-inspiring and true in its melodic unfolding, its modulations, and its instrumentation; it is monumental and grandiose; the threatening power of a priest of Jupiter Tonans is manifest throughout. And among Julia's utterances, which successively express despondency, resignation, revolt, and recklessness, there are accents so natural that it seems no others were possible, and yet so uncommon that the finest scores seldom contain their like. Such are:

> *Is it true? Do I still live?*
> *Let me now meet my death. . . .*
> *Death makes me free of your authority. . . .*
> *Priests of Jupiter, I do confess my love. . . .*
> *Is any law enough to vanquish nature? . . .*
> *You shall not know. . . .*

---

[9] "Too much" is used here in its ancient sense of "excessive." It does not mean "very much," which would convey the exact opposite.

At this last answer of Julia's to the pontiff's question, the orchestral thunders break out and crash around her. Everyone feels that she is lost, and that the touching prayer she has just addressed to Latona will not save her. The measured recitative "Time ends for me" is a masterpiece of modulation, considering what precedes and what follows. The high priest has ended his phrase in the key of E major, which will later recur as that of the final chorus. The Vestal's song, moving gradually away from that tonality, dwells awhile on the dominant of C minor. Then the altos alone begin a sort of tremolo on the B, which the ear takes for the leading note of the key lately established; and bring about, by means of this same B, which will suddenly reappear once more as the dominant, an explosion of the brass and kettledrums in the key of E major, which resounds anew with redoubled power, like illuminations by night, which seem more dazzling after they have been cut off from view by some intervening body.

As for the anathema with which the pontiff now overwhelms his victim, as well as about the *stretta*, description is meaningless and of no use to anyone who has not heard them. Here especially one discovers the power of Spontini's orchestra, which in spite of the many developments of modern instrumentation remains unshaken, majestic, marked by beauty of form, draped in the antique style, and as brilliant as on the day when it sprang fully armed from the brain of its author. One is racked with anguish under the incessant percussion of the pitiless rhythm in which the priests sing their syllabic double chorus, contrasting with the moaning melody of the weeping vestals. But the divine distress of the hearer reaches its height only at the point where the hurtling rhythm stops and the instruments and voices, the former in held notes, the latter in tremolo, pour out a steady torrent of strident harmonies for the peroration.

This is the culminating point of the crescendo that has been working up intensity and breadth during the whole of the second half of the second act, and which, in my opinion, is beyond comparison with any other in scale and in the formidable deliberateness of its onward march. During the great performances of this Olympian scene at the Conservatoire or at the Opéra, the tremor is universal—in the public, the performers, and the building itself, whose metallic parts from top to bottom seem to turn it into a colossal gong emitting sinister vibrations. The means at the disposal of small theaters like your own, gentlemen, are insufficient to produce this strange phenomenon.

Please note in the arrangement of the men's voices in this incomparable *stretta* that, far from being a "clumsy blunder" and a "poor thing," as some have maintained, the subdivision of the vocal forces is beautifully calculated. At the beginning the tenors and basses are divided into six parts, of which three only are heard at any one time: it is a double choir in dialogue. The first chorus sings three notes, which are immediately repeated by the second, thus producing a continuous repercussion on each beat of the bar, without ever using more than half the men's voices at any given instant. It is only as the *fortissimo* nears that the entire mass is fused into a single chorus. This occurs when the melodic interest and the impassioned expressiveness are at their acme and the panting rhythm needs new strength to launch the heart-rending harmonies that accompany the song of the women.

All this follows logically from the composer's great plan for his crescendo, the ultimate term of which is found (as I have already said) in the dissonant chord that bursts forth when the pontiff throws the fatal black veil over Julia's head. The scheme is admirable, no matter what anyone has said against it; it is beyond praise, and only a semi-demi-fraction of a musician, such as the one who censured it, could fail to acknowledge its worth. But it is usual for criticism that is launched from below upward against the superior men whom it permits itself to rebuke, to blame them for the very qualities that make them what they are, and to see weakness and error in the most obvious proofs of their knowledge and strength. Will the time ever come when the Paganinis of composition will no longer have to go to school to the blind fiddlers who squat on the Pont-Neuf?

The success of *La Vestale* was striking and complete. One hundred performances did not suffice to damp the enthusiasm of the Parisians. *La Vestale* was given, somehow and anyhow, in all the provincial theaters; it was produced in Germany; it even held the boards for a whole season at the San Carlos in Naples, where Mme Colbran, later Mme Rossini, sang Julia. The composer did not hear of this particular success until long afterwards, when it gave him deep joy.

This masterpiece, so much admired all over France for twenty-five years, would be almost unknown to the present musical generation if it were not for the excerpts given at big concerts, which bring it back into the limelight from time to time.[1] The opera houses have not kept it in their repertory: this is a boon upon which Spontini's admirers should congratulate themselves. For its proper execution requires qualities that are daily becoming scarcer. Great voices trained in the grand style are indispensable, as well as acting singers—especially women—possessed of something more than talent. To give works of this kind adequately also requires choruses that know how to sing and act, a powerful orchestra, and a leader of great ability to conduct and inspire it. Above all, the entire company must be imbued with a feeling for expression, a feeling nowadays almost extinct in Europe, where the most egregious absurdities become easily popular and where the most trivial, indeed the falsest, style is the one that, in the theater, has the greatest chance of succeeding.

Hence the extreme difficulty of finding for these models of pure art any audiences and some worthy interpreters. The stultification of the majority of the public, its lack of understanding in matters of imagination and the heart, its love of brilliant platitudes, the vulgarity of all its melodic and rhythmic instincts, have of necessity driven the performers along the road they now follow. It would seem the most ordinary common sense that the public's taste should be formed by the artists, but unfortunately it is contrariwise and the artists' taste is actually deformed and corrupted by the public's.

One need not consider it to the public's credit that from time to time it takes some fine work to its bosom and accords it an ovation. This merely shows that though "the smallest millet-seed would have been more his dish,"[2] it has unknowingly swallowed a pearl, and that its palate is less delicate than that of the rooster in the fable who made no mistake about it. For if it is on account of their beauty that the public applauds certain great works, that same public should on the contrary occasions display violent indignation and

---

[1] Berlioz himself was responsible for a good many of these concerts, including the one he gave the Londoners in April 1852. He conducted large parts of *La Vestale* with Spontini's baton, which his widow presented to Berlioz for the occasion. The biographical sketch here reproduced had been written as an obituary the year before.

[2] From La Fontaine's "The Rooster and the Pearl."

deal out strict justice to the productions of those men who repeatedly and publicly give art and common sense a slap in the face. But the public is very far from so acting. One can only conclude that some circumstance foreign to the merit of the masterpiece causes its success. Like a big noise-making toy, it amuses these overgrown children, or its performance carries them away by its verve or fascinates them by its unusual lavishness. In Paris, at least, by taking the public unawares before it has had time to have an opinion manufactured for it, one can make it swallow anything with the aid of a performance exceptional and "amazing" as regards externals.

One can understand, then, why we should congratulate ourselves that the French opera houses neglect the monumental scores as they do: the obliteration of the public's sense of expression being patent and proved, there is no chance of success for such miracles of expressiveness as *La Vestale* and *Cortez* except through performances now beyond our reach.

When Spontini first came to France, the art of florid singing among women professionals was perhaps not so advanced as it is today, but unquestionably the broad dramatic impassioned style existed pure, unalloyed. It existed at least at the Opéra. There was then a Julia, an Armida, an Iphigenia, an Alcestis, a Hypermnestra. There was Mme Branchu, the archetype of the full yet resonant, gentle yet powerful soprano capable of dominating the orchestral choirs, yet also able to sink to the feeblest murmur of timid passion, fear, or reverie. No one has ever taken her place. Everyone had long since forgotten the superb way in which she declaimed recitatives and sang slow and sorrowful melodies, when Duprez made his debut in *William Tell* and recalled that same art and showed its power when carried to high perfection.

But Mme Branchu added to these eminent qualities an irresistible impetuosity in scenes of action and an ease of voice production such that she never had to slow up a passage for no good reason, or to add beats to a bar as is continually done nowadays. Mme Branchu was moreover a tragic actress of the first rank, a talent which is indispensable for playing the great female roles in Gluck and Spontini. She was as naturally energetic as her sensibility was genuine, and she never had to study tricks to supply their imitation. I never saw her in the part of Julia, which had been written for her.

When I heard her at the Opéra, she had already given up playing it. But what she displayed in *Alcestis, Iphigenia in Aulis*, the *Danaïdes*, and *Olympia*[3] enabled me to judge what she must have been in *La Vestale* fifteen years earlier.

Spontini had the further good fortune, when he first staged his work, to find an actor out of the common for the part of the high priest; this was the elder Dérivis,[4] with his tremendous voice, his high stature, his dramatic delivery, his elaborate and majestic gestures. He was young at the time and practically unknown. The part of the pontiff had been assigned to another singer, who was struggling with it and who naturally kept grumbling at the rehearsals about the supposed difficulties of this new music which he could not understand. One day when his incompetence and impudence were being shown more openly than usual, the outraged Spontini snatched the part from him and threw it into the fire. Dérivis, who was present, rushed to the fireplace, plunged his hand into the flames, and rescued the part, exclaiming: "I've saved it, I keep it!"

"It is yours," replied the composer, "I know you'll be worthy of it."

The prediction came true; the part was one of Dérivis's best creations; indeed, it was possibly the only one that allowed the lack of flexibility of his rough voice to appear without disadvantage.

This score of *La Vestale* is, to my mind, in entirely different a style from that which had been adopted in France by the composers of that period. Neither Méhul, Cherubini, Berton, nor Lesueur wrote thus. It has been said that Spontini derived from Gluck. As regards dramatic inspiration, character portrayal, accuracy and vehemence of expression, this is true. But as regards melodic and harmonic style, scoring, and musical coloring, Spontini proceeds from himself alone. His music has an individual look which it is impossible to mistake. Some instances of harmonic carelessness (they are few and far between) have been made the pretext for a thousand ridiculous charges of incorrectness formerly leveled against him by the professors, charges which in fact grew out of the new and beautiful harmonies that this great master had discovered and used felicitously, long before the pedants of the day had even dreamed of their existence or found reasons for them. That was

---

[3] Operas respectively by Gluck (the first two), Salieri, and Spontini.
[4] See above, note 3, p. 88.

his great crime. What did he mean by it?—writing chords and modulations that usage had not yet made commonplace, and before the learned doctors had decided whether it was permissible to use them?

To tell the truth, there was another reason for this onslaught by the Conservatoire en masse. If one excepts Lesueur, whose opera *The Bards* enjoyed a large number of performances, none of the composers of the period had met with success at the Opéra. The *Jerusalem* and the *Triumph of Trajan* of Persuis [5] were given the sort of transient approval that does not count in the history of art. It was attributable to the lavishness of the staging and to political parallels which the circumstances of the time established between the heroes of these works and the hero of the great drama that was then thrilling the entire world. The Opéra's grand repertory was consequently sustained for a long run of years almost exclusively by Spontini's two operas, *La Vestale* and *Cortez*, and by Gluck's five scores. The ancient glory of the German composer had no other rival on our leading lyric stage than the youthful fame of the Italian master. And this was the motive of the hatred shown him by the School: its teachers were musicians who had failed in their attempts to share his reign at the Opéra.

La Vestale, they said, could not have been produced without the corrections that learned men had been good enough to supply in that monstrous score in order to make it "performable"—and so on, and so on. Hence the ridiculous pretensions of a host of people to the merit of having revised, corrected, and purified the work of Spontini. I personally know four composers who are reputed to have had a hand in it. Once the success of *La Vestale* was fully assured, irresistible, unquestionable, these people went even further. It was no longer a mere matter of corrections, but of whole numbers that had been contributed: this one laid claim to the duet in the second act, another to the funeral march in the third, and so forth. What is rather odd is that among the large number of duets and marches written by these illustrious masters it is impossible to find pieces of that quality or fulness of inspiration. Can these gentlemen have carried their devotion so far as to make Spontini a present of their finest ideas? Such self-sacrifice is beyond the bounds of the sublime!

---

[5] See above, note 9, p. 147.

The final version of the story accepted for a long time in the musical purlieus of France and Italy was this: Spontini was not the author of *La Vestale* at all. The score supposedly written in defiance of common sense, corrected and revised by everybody, the score against which scholastic and academic anathemas had been incessantly hurled for so long, this crude and confused work, Spontini was actually incapable of writing it: he had bought it ready-made at a grocery; it came from the pen of a German composer who had died of want in Paris. All Spontini had to do was to "adapt" the melodies of this unfortunate musician to the words of M. de Jouy and add a few bars to join up the scenes.

It must be admitted that the "adaptation" is skillful: one could swear that each note had been written for the word to which it is set. M. Castil-Blaze [6] himself never rose as high as this. In vain would one ask at whose grocery Spontini had later purchased the score of *Fernando Cortez*, which, as everybody knows, is not without merit. No one has ever been able to find out. Yet how many composers there must be to whom the address of this inestimable merchant would have been a priceless bit of information, and who would have rushed to his shop and laid in a stock! He is undoubtedly the same who sold Gluck his score of *Orpheus*, and Jean-Jacques Rousseau his *Devin du Village*. (The authorship of these two works, though of disproportionate merit, has been similarly denied to their composers.)

But a truce to this arrant nonsense. We all know that raging envy can produce in its unfortunate victims a state verging on total imbecility.

Master of a position so hotly contested, and knowing his strength at last, Spontini was about to undertake another composition in the antique style; it was to be an *Electra*. But the Emperor let it be known that he would be pleased to see him take as the subject of his new work the conquest of Mexico by Hernando Cortez. This command the composer hastened to obey, though the tragedy of *Electra* had made a deep impression on him and setting it to music was one of his dearest wishes. I have often heard him express regret at having had to give it up.

None the less, I think that the Emperor's choice was a fortunate

---

[6] See above, note 1, p. 53.

one for the author of *La Vestale* in that it drew him away from composing a second time in the antique style, and compelled him to discover, for scenes just as moving but more varied and less solemn, the strange and charming color, the proud and tender expressiveness, and the happy audacities that make the score of *Cortez* the worthy rival of its elder sister. The success of the new opera was triumphant. From that day forward, Spontini was the undisputed master of our leading opera house. Like his hero he must have exclaimed:

This land belongs to me: I'll never give it up!

I have often been asked which of the first two great operas of Spontini I prefer, and I must confess that I have never been able to decide. *Cortez* resembles *La Vestale* only in the unvarying truth and beauty of its expression. In all other qualities of style the two are entirely different. The scene of the soldiers' mutiny in *Cortez* is one of those miracles practically undiscoverable in the thousands of operas hitherto composed, a miracle of which the finale of the second act of *La Vestale* can alone, I'm afraid, be called the counterpart. In *Cortez* all is energetic, imperious, brilliant, passionate, and full of grace; its inspiration burns and overflows, yet is governed by reason. All the characters are undeniably true. Amazily is tender and devoted; Cortez hot-tempered and fiery, but with tender moments; Telasco gloomy, but noble in his savage patriotism. One soars again and again on mighty wings, such as eagles alone possess, to see lightning flashes of a brightness to illuminate a whole world.

Don't talk to me of the painful seeking after effects, the supposedly faulty harmony, or any of the other defects still imputed to Spontini. Even were these things true, the impression produced by his work, the emotion aroused in me and in thousands of other musicians who are not easily dazzled, would remain equally true. If the rejoinder is that in our excitement we have lost the power of reasoning, that in itself is the greatest praise that could be conferred on this music. By heaven, I should like to see any of those who deny the superiority of such a power try their hands at it! I should say to them: "You don't really maintain that dramatic music shall have as its sole aim that of discoursing to the listener's reasoning faculty, leaving him absolutely calm and cold in the midst of his orderly contemplation? Well then, if you grant that art can also, without excessive degradation, seek to produce in certain temperaments the emotions they prefer, here is a large and well-trained chorus, a first-rate orchestra, chosen singers, a poem strewn with striking situations, lines well adapted to music—buckle down and get to work! Try to move us. Try to make us, as you put it, *lose our power of reasoning.* It should be easy, according to you, since after one act of *Cortez* you find us in this state of fever and trepidation. Don't spare us, we surrender completely to you; take advantage of our impressionable selves; we'll bring smelling-salts and see to it there are doctors in the house; they can decide to what point musical intoxication can be carried without danger to life."

Alas, poor fellows, I'm afraid we'd soon show you that your efforts are futile, that our reason stays put, and that our hand stays calm as it travels over your whole work with a scalpel, in a vain effort to discover a beating heart.

After one of the last performances of *Cortez* in Paris [7] I wrote Spontini the following letter, the reading of which caused him to stir a little from the seeming coldness that was habitual with him:

DEAR MASTER,

Your work is noble and beautiful, and it is perhaps the *duty* of an artist able to appreciate its magnificence to tell you this again today. Whatever may be your vexations in these days, the consciousness of your genius and of the infinite worth of what it has created should make it easier for you to forget them.

You have provoked violent hatred, and because of it some of your admirers seem afraid to confess their admiration. They are cowards. I prefer your enemies.

Cortez was given last night at the Opéra. I am still shattered by the overwhelming effect of the mutiny scene, and I cry out to you: Glory! Glory to the artist and profoundest respect to the man whose powerful mind, warmed by his heart, has created that immortal scene! When has indignation ever found such accents in a work of art? When has martial enthusiasm been more ardent and poetic? Where have daring and will, those proud daughters of genius, been painted in such colors and exhibited so brightly? Nowhere. Never. And we all know it.

---

[7] In August 1841. Spontini was known to be nursing his injured pride at the loss of his pre-eminence in opera.

Your work is beautiful, it is true, it is new, it is sublime. If music were not left to the tender mercies of public charity, there would exist somewhere in Europe a stage, a lyric pantheon exclusively devoted to the production of monumental masterpieces. They would be given at wide intervals, and with the care and dignity which they deserve by musical *artists*, and they would be listened to on the solemn festal days of art by musically sensitive and intelligent hearers.

But almost everywhere music has lost its birthright and forgotten its noble origin; it is a waif whom the world, it seems, wants to turn into a prostitute.

Farewell, dear master; there is such a thing as the religion of the beautiful, and that is the one I profess. If it is a duty to admire great things and honor great men, I feel, as I press your hand, that it is also a joy.

One year after the first appearance of *Fernand Cortez*, Spontini was appointed director of the Italian Theater. He had gathered together an excellent company and it was owing to him that Mozart's *Don Giovanni* was heard in Paris for the first time. The cast was as follows: Don Giovanni was sung by Tacchinardi; Leporello by Barilli; Masetto by Porto; Ottavio by Crivelli; Donna Anna by Mme Festa; Zerlina by Mme Barilli.[8]

In spite of the distinguished services Spontini was rendering to art in his management of the Italian Theater, a rather low intrigue soon compelled him to relinquish his post. Moreover Paer,[9] who was at that time managing the little Italian theater at the court, and who was anything but pleased with his rival's success on the great stage of the Opéra, affected to belittle him, styled him a renegade, and to emphasize his French ways called him M. *Spontin*. On more than one occasion Paer made him fall into the traps that Signor Astucio, as we all know, is so adept at setting.[1]

Free once again, Spontini wrote an occasional opera, *Pelagius, or the King and Peace*, which is now forgotten. He followed this

---

[8] The year was 1811. Berlioz omits Elvira, who was sung by Mme Benelli.
[9] Ferdinando Paer (1771–1839), Italian composer, settled in Paris in 1807.
[1] A caricature of Paer, Astucio was a character in Auber's opera *A Concert at Court* (1824). Berlioz often refers to this nickname for an intriguer, from *astus*, a ruse.

by *The Rival Gods*, an opera-ballet, composed in collaboration with Persuis, Berton, and Kreutzer. When *Les Danaïdes* was revived, Salieri, who was too old to leave Vienna, entrusted Spontini with the task of directing the rehearsals and authorized him to make such changes and additions as he might consider necessary. Spontini confined himself to touching up, in his fellow countryman's score, the end of Hypermnestra's aria "By your daughter's tears," adding to it a coda full of dramatic vigor. And he composed in addition several delightful dance tunes, including a bacchanal that will remain a model of fiery energy, not to say the archetype of sinister and orgiastic frenzy.

These works were succeeded by the composition of *Olympia*, a grand opera in three acts. Neither on its first production nor when it was revived in 1827 did it meet with the success which, in my opinion, it deserved. Various causes combined by mere chance to check its career. Even political feeling was against it. The Abbé Grégoire was just then in everybody's mind,[2] and people thought they detected a premeditated allusion to the notorious regicide in the scene where Statira exclaims:

> *I brand in all men's eyes,*
> *And to their vengeance bring*
> *The murderer of his king.*

The whole liberal party was henceforth hostile to *Olympia*. Shortly afterwards the assassination of the Duc de Berri led to the closing of the opera house in the rue de Richelieu[3] and the run of the work had to be interrupted. This was the death blow to a success not yet firmly established, the public's attention having been violently wrenched away from matters of art. When eight years later *Olympia* was staged again, Spontini, who had meanwhile been appointed musical director to the King of Prussia, found on his return from Berlin a marked change in the tastes and ideas of the Parisians. Rossini, strongly supported by M. de la Rochefoucauld[4] and the whole directorate of the Fine Arts Departments, had

---

[2] Henri Grégoire (1750–1831), a leader of the French Revolution, who subsequently launched bombshells, in print or deed, from his retirement.
[3] The Duke died of his wounds in the lobby, which could not be cleared in time. By royal edict the house was closed and torn down.
[4] Sosthènes de la Rochefoucauld (1785–1864) was Superintendent of Fine Arts under Charles X.

just arrived from Italy. The sect of the pure dillettanti would turn delirious at the mere name of the composer of the *Barbiere* and would have torn all others limb from limb. The music of *Olympia* was called plainsong. M. de la Rochefoucauld refused to prolong for a few weeks Mme Branchu's stay at the Opéra, and as she alone could carry the part of Statira, which she had sung at the première solely for her retirement benefit, that was the end of the matter. Spontini, feeling lacerated by other hostile acts which it would take too long to relate here, returned to Berlin, where in all respects his position was worthy of his genius and of the monarch who appreciated it.

On his return to Prussia he wrote for some court festivities an opera-ballet, *Nurmahal*, the subject of which was taken from Thomas Moore's *Lalla Rookh*. In this graceful score he inserted—developing it and introducing a chorus—his awesome bacchanal of the *Danaïdes*. He next rewrote the end of the last act of *Cortez*. This new denouement, which the Paris Opéra did not condescend to use when *Cortez* was revived six or seven years ago, but which I saw in Berlin, is magnificent, and much superior to the one we know in France.

In 1825 Spontini produced in Berlin the opera-pantomine *Alcidor*, which the composer's enemies made much fun of, because (they said) of the noisy instrumentation and an orchestra of anvils that accompanied a blacksmiths' chorus. This work I do not know at all. But I have had the opportunity of going over the score of *Agnes von Hohenstaufen*, which followed *Alcidor* after a lapse of twelve years. This so-called romantic subject is treated in a style entirely different from any that Spontini previously used. He has introduced into the ensemble numbers some very curious and difficult combinations such as, among others, an orchestral storm which goes on while five of the characters sing a quintet on the stage and a chorus of nuns is heard in the distance, to the accompaniment of a supposititious organ. That instrument is imitated to perfection by means of a small number of wind instruments and double basses in the wings. Nowadays when organs are to be found in theaters as readily as in churches, this imitation, however interesting as an instance of difficulty overcome, seems rather pointless. To complete the list of Spontini's productions it remains to mention his *Song of the Prussian People* and several pieces for military bands.

The new King, Frederick William IV, continued his predecessor's kindness and generosity toward Spontini, in spite of the unfortunate notoriety given to a no doubt incautious letter of the composer's, a letter which drew upon him a trial followed by a conviction.[5] The King not only pardoned him, but consented to Spontini's return to France when his election as a member of the Institute compelled him to take up his residence there. The King gave him further proof of his affection by allowing him to retain the title and the salary of Kapellmeister to the Prussian Court, although he had resigned the duties of the post.

Spontini had begun to yearn for rest and academic leisure, both because of the persecutions and enmities that were being set afoot in Berlin, and because of a strange disease of the ear, from the cruel attacks of which he repeatedly suffered over a long period. In these bouts affecting an organ he had made such great use of, Spontini could scarcely hear at all, though every single sound that he could distinguish seemed to him an accumulation of discords. Hence it became absolutely impossible for him to endure music, and he had to give it up until the morbid condition passed.

His election to the Institute was carried out in a worthy manner which, it must be said, did honor to all French musicians. Those who could have come forward as rival candidates felt they should give way before a glorious name, and by declining to compete added in effect their votes to those of the entire Academy of Fine Arts.

In 1811 Spontini had married the sister of Érard, the famous piano-manufacturer. The constant care she lavished on him contributed not a little toward soothing the irritability and allaying the grievances to which his nervous nature and circumstances all too real had made him a prey during the last years of his life. In 1842 he made a pilgrimage to the land of his birth, where he endowed several charitable institutions.

Not long ago, to chase away the sad thoughts that obsessed him, he decided to undertake a second journey to Majolati. On arriving there, he went to the deserted house where he had been born seventy-two years before. There he stopped for a few weeks' rest, meditating on the many vicissitudes of his brilliant but stormy

---

[5] The culmination of a series of disputes, Spontini's open letter in the Leipzig *Allgemeine Zeitung* of January 20, 1841, gave grounds for a charge of *lèse-majesté*.

career, and there he died suddenly, rich in glory and in the blessings of his compatriots. The cycle was completed; his task was done.

Despite the honorable inflexibility of his artistic convictions and the strength of his reasons in passing judgment, Spontini, whatever has been said to the contrary, would allow discussion up to a certain point. He brought to it the warmth that is found in all he wrote, and yet he would give up, at times philosophically enough, when he had no further arguments to offer. One day as he was blaming me for admiring a modern work of which he did not think much, I succeeded in giving him fairly good reasons for valuing something by a great master whom he did not like. He listened to me with surprise; then, with a sigh, replied in Latin: "*Hei mihi, qualis est! Sed de gustibus et coloribus non est disputandum.*" [6] He wrote and spoke Latin with ease; it was a language he often used in his correspondence with the King of Prussia.

He has been accused of selfishness, brutality, and hardness of heart. But when one considers the unremitting hatred to which he was exposed, the obstacles he had to overcome, the barriers he had to break through, and the tension that this continual state of war must have produced in his mind, one may allow oneself rather to feel surprised that he remained as sociable as he was; especially if one takes into account the great worth of his creations and his awareness of this, in contrast with the worthlessness of most of his enemies and their lack of any high-minded motives.

Spontini was first and foremost a dramatic composer whose inspirations grew and kept pace with the importance of the situations and the strength of the passions that he had to depict. Hence the pale coloring of his earlier scores, written to infantile or commonplace Italian librettos, the insignificance of the music he provided for the dull, trivial, false, and frigid genre of which the comic opera *Julie* is so perfect a model, and the upward movement of his musical thought in the two beautiful scenes of *Milton*—the one in which the blind poet laments the misfortune that keeps him forever from witnessing the wonders of nature, and the one where he dictates to his daughter the lines on the creation of Eve and her appearance amid the peaceful splendor of the Garden of Eden. Hence, finally, the prodigious and sudden explosion of Spontini's genius in *La*

---

[6] "Ah, dear me! So it goes! But then, there's no arguing about colors and tastes."

Vestale, that burning shower of ideas, those heart-wrung tears, that pelting stream of noble, touching, proud, or threatening melodies, those warm-colored harmonies, those modulations never before heard in any theater, that youthfully vigorous orchestration, that depth and truthfulness of expression (I keep harping on this), and that luxuriance of great musical images, so naturally presented, set forth with such masterly authority, and wedded to the poet's thought so closely, that one cannot imagine the words they fit ever to have existed apart.

In *Cortez* there are not so much unwitting errors as a few purposeful instances of harmonic harshness. In *Olympia* I can find only some magnificent audacities in that kind. But the orchestration, which is of a sober richness in *La Vestale*, grows complicated in *Cortez* and is overdrawn with a number of useless lines in *Olympia*, to the point of occasionally making the instrumentation heavy and confused.

Spontini had a certain number of melodic ideas for each type of noble expression. Once this cycle of ideas had been run through and the melodies applied to their predestined sentiments, the wellspring became less abundant—which is why we find less originality in the melodic [7] style of the works, at once passionate and heroic, that followed *La Vestale* and *Cortez*. But what are such casual repetitions compared to the practice of certain Italian masters who cynically reproduce the same cadences, the same phrases, and the same numbers in their innumerable scores?

Spontini's orchestration, the germ and method of which can already be seen in *Milton* and *Julie*, was his own invention; it is in no way derivative from anyone. Its special coloring is due to the use of the wind instruments, which, if just short of very adroit from a technical point of view, is at least most competent in its contrast with the body of strings. The important as well as novel role assigned by the composer to the violas, now massed together, now divided like the violins into firsts and seconds, is likewise characteristic of his orchestration. The frequent accenting of the off beats in the bar; the resolution of dissonances in another part than the one in which they have occurred; the use of broadly spread arpeggios taking various forms in the bass and undulating with majesty

---

[7] In the French text, *méthodique*, which I take to be a misprint.

beneath the orchestral mass; the moderate but exceedingly ingenious use of trombones, trumpets, horns, and kettledrums; the almost total omission of the shrill high notes of the piccolos, oboes, and clarinets—all impart to the orchestration of Spontini's masterpieces a tone of grandeur, an incomparable energy and power, and often a mood of poetic melancholy.

As for modulations, Spontini was the first to introduce boldly into dramatic music those known as foreign to the key, as well as enharmonic modulations. Though they occur rather frequently in his works, they are always motivated and brought about with enviable skill. He never modulates without good reason, unlike those restless and uninspired musicians who, when they weary of vainly tormenting a key without finding anything in it, shift to another in hopes of being luckier in that. As against this, some of Spontini's eccentric modulations are flashes of genius. In the first rank among these is the abrupt passing from the key of E flat to that of D flat in the chorus of soldiers in *Cortez:* "Let us desert these shores: Spain is calling us." At this sudden overturn in tonality the listener is struck in such a way that his imagination clears an immense distance at a bound; he flies, so to speak, from one hemisphere to the other and, forgetting Mexico, follows to Spain the mutinous soldiers' thoughts. I may cite another example in the prisoners' trio in the same opera, where at the words: "Inglorious death will close our days," the voices go from G minor to A flat major; and still another: the wonderful exclamation of the high priest in *La Vestale*, where the voice drops abruptly from the tonality of D flat major to that of C major on the line

Reduce the universe to nothingness.

Once more, it was Spontini who invented the colossal crescendo, which his imitators later gave us again in diminutive, microscopic replicas. Genuine is the one in the second act of *La Vestale*, when Julia, mad with love and no longer struggling against her passion, feels terror blending and growing with it in her distracted soul:

> *My steps are leading—where? O Heaven! What fire*
> *Is coursing through my veins! I am undone;*
> *Against me greater powers all conspire,*
> *I am enslaved—oh, stop! My time has run—*

This progression of wailing harmonies broken by muffled pulsations which grow stronger and stronger is an amazing invention, the full impact of which can be felt only in the theater, not in the concert hall. So it is again with the crescendo of the first-act finale in *Cortez*, where the Mexican women, distraught with terror, throw themselves at Montezuma's feet:

> *Hark the fearful crying*
> *Of our children dying!*

I have already referred to the crescendo of the finale in *La Vestale*. Need I mention the duet between Telasco and Amazily in *Cortez*, which begins with what is possibly the most admirable recitative in existence; or the one between Amazily and Cortez, in which the martial fanfares of the Spanish army blend in so dramatic a fashion with the passionate farewells of the two lovers; or the grandiose aria of Telasco: "O native land, O well-loved countryside!" or Julia's in *La Vestale*: "Unrelenting gods!" or the funeral march; or the aria at the tomb in the same opera; or the duet between Licinius and the high priest, a duet that Weber declared to be one of the most wonderful known to him? Should I recall the triumphal religious march in *Olympia*, or the chorus of Diana's priests in their dismay when the statue veils itself; or the extraordinary scene and aria when Statira, sobbing with indignation, reproaches the officiating priest with having foisted on her as son-in-law the murderer of Alexander; or the choral march of Telasco's attendant suite, also in *Cortez* ("What novel sounds"), the first and only one of its kind ever written in triple time; or the bacchanal in *Nurmahal;* or the numberless recitatives, as beautiful as the most beautiful melodies, and of an accent so truthful as to make the ablest masters despair; or those slow dance-movements whose soft and dreamy melodic curve at once calls up the feeling of voluptuousness and turns it to poetry? I wander about this great temple of Expressive Music and lose myself in its winding ways, in the thousand details of its rich architecture, in the dazzling profusion of its ornaments.

The vulgar herd, frivolous or stupid, forsakes the temple in these days and refuses or neglects to sacrifice at the shrine. But for a few artists and connoisseurs, who are possibly more numerous than is commonly believed, the goddess to whom Spontini erected this vast monument is still so beautiful that their fervor does not cool. And I, like them, prostrate myself and worship her.

"And so do we," say the musicians, rising to go, "we worship her, all of us."

"I know it, gentlemen. It is because I am convinced of it that I gave myself up in front of you to my passionate admiration. One can express such ideas and such deep emotions only before an audience that shares them. Good night, gentlemen."

Operas off the Assembly Line

The Problem of Beauty

Schiller's *Mary Stuart*

A Visit to Tom Thumb
an improbable tale

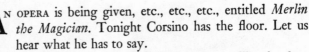

AN OPERA is being given, etc., etc., etc., entitled *Merlin the Magician*. Tonight Corsino has the floor. Let us hear what he has to say.

CORSINO: It is often said that operas are like the days of the week: they come single file and all alike. It might be more accurate to say, keeping to the analogy, that they come single file but quite unlike. Surely we have fine summer days that are glorious, calm, radiant with harmony and light, during which the whole creation seems to be all happiness and love; the nightingale is hidden in the bush, the lark lost in the blue of the sky, the cricket in the grass; the bee is gathering honey, the countryman at his plow, the child playing in the dooryard of the farm, the elegant silhouette of the aristocratic beauty outlined in white on the dark green of a park full of shadow and mystery. On days such as this, to breathe, to see, to hear, is to be happy.

The next day the sun rises grim and clouded; a thick mist weighs on the atmosphere; everything droops on the mountain and the plain; the songbirds are silent; nothing is heard save the silly notes of the cuckoo and the harsh, stupid cries of the geese, peacocks, and turkeys. The frog croaks, the dog howls, the child whines, the weather vane creaks on the roof. Then an irritating wind rolls in on itself, and at last, in the evening, dies away under a silent, tepid rain, malodorous as marsh water.

And are there not also days of sublime storm, when the thunder and the winds, the crash of torrents, the tumult of the forest crying out under the onslaught of storm, flood, and fire, fill the soul with great and terrible emotions? How, then, are the days all alike? Is it in their length, the degrees of heat and cold, the beauty of the twilight that precedes the rising or setting of the great luminary? Not at all! We see days and operas that are deathly cold follow upon days and operas of a burning heat; a production that has shone brilliantly during the life of the composer is abruptly extinguished when he dies, as light is at sundown in equinoctial lands. Another, which at first gave off but the palest rays, is lit up after the composer's death with lasting radiance and takes on a marvelous glow like a gorgeous sunset, or like the aurora borealis, which makes certain polar nights more beautiful than the day.

I therefore stick to my comparison: operas, like the days, follow single file but are not at all alike. Astronomers and critics come along afterwards and give us a host of more or less valid explanations of the facts. Some say: here is why hail fell yesterday and why tomorrow will be fine. Others say: this is why the latest opera failed, and why the next one will succeed. Still others are willing to admit that they know nothing certain, and that after studying the fickleness of the wind and the public, the endless variability of taste and temperature, the infinite whims of nature and the human mind, they have come to acknowledge the vast extent of their ignorance. They are unable to assign causes, even the most immediate, for the good reason that they are unknown.

MYSELF: You are right, my dear Corsino, and I must confess that I am one of those learned men. I have sometimes thought that I descried a new star in the heavens, the size and brilliancy of which seemed to me considerable, only to have everybody refute me and deny not only the size, but the very existence of Neptune. Then when I said: "The moon, surely, is one of the lesser celestial bodies; it is only its close proximity to the earth that makes us ascribe to it a size it does not possess; Sirius, on the contrary, is a huge star," I met with the rejoinder: "Why on earth do you talk about Sirius? It occupies no more space in the sky than the head of a pin! We far prefer our majestic moon."

Tracking this argument to its source, I ended up with people who preferred a street lamp to the moon, and a ragpicker's lantern to the street lamp.

And that is why there is not a single production of the human mind, not one, you understand, that can command—I will not say the approval of all humanity, but even that of the infinitesimal fraction of humanity to which it is addressed. How many people does our largest theater seat today? Barely two thousand, and most theaters far fewer. Very well. Now, given an excellent performance, has it ever happened that even five hundred persons assembled together in a theater have agreed about the merits of Shakespeare, Molière, Mozart, Beethoven, Gluck, or Weber? I have heard students hiss *Le Bourgeois Gentilhomme* at the Odéon. We all know what riots took place at the Comédie Française over Alfred de Vigny's translation of Shakespeare's *Othello,* and the hooting that greeted Rossini's *Barber of Seville* in Rome and *Der Freischütz* in Paris.[1] I have never yet attended a first night at the Opéra without finding among the judges in the lobby a large majority hostile to the new work, however beautiful and great it may have been. Nor is there a single score, however flat and empty, null and void, that does not gather a few votes of approval or that fails to number sincere admirers, as if to justify the proverb that says there is no pot without a lid.

This or that opinion is heatedly maintained behind the curtain which is no less warmly denounced in the orchestra pit. Take four listeners occupying the same box at the same performance; the first is bored, the second entertained, the third is idignant, and the fourth enthusiastic. Voltaire told France that Shakespeare was a Huron, a drunken Iroquois; and France believed Voltaire. And yet the most fervent disciple of the Sage of Ferney, however convinced of the absolute truth of the sentence pronounced on the author of *Hamlet,* had only to cross the Channel to find the contrary opinion current. On one side of the Channel, Shakespeare was a beast and a barbarian; on the other, a god. In France today, should Voltaire return and again express his opinion, no

---

[1] Respectively in 1829, 1816, and 1825.

matter how great a Voltaire he was, is, and will remain, people would laugh in his face. Some that I know might even do worse. The question of what is beautiful would therefore seem to be a question of time and place. A sad conclusion, but true.

For unless absolute beauty is that which at all times, in all places, and by all men must be acknowledged as beautiful, I cannot imagine what it means or where it might reside. And that kind of beauty I am sure does not exist. I believe only that there exist artistic beauties of which the appreciation has become inherent in certain civilizations and which will last, thanks to a minority, as long as those civilizations themselves.

"Why," asks Corsino, after a pause and as if trying to break off a conversation he finds painful, "why didn't you go to Schiller's *Mary Stuart* day before yesterday? Our best actors were in it, and the masterpiece, I assure you, was not badly done at all."

"You won't, I hope, fail to number me among Schiller's most sincere admirers, even if I was absent, but I must confess to an insuperable aversion for dramas in which the block, the ax, and the headsman appear. I cannot bear them. That form of death and the preparations for it have something about them I find particularly hideous. Nothing inspires me with deeper repugnance for the multitude, for the mob of whatever rank or class, than the horrible lust with which one sees it rush off on certain days to the place of execution. When I picture to myself this eager populace gaping about a scaffold, I always think of the bliss it would be to have at hand a battery of eight or ten guns loaded with grapeshot, so as to annihilate at a stroke this fearful rabble without having to lay a hand on them. For I imagine that when one spills blood in this way, with fire and thunder from a distance, it expresses anger, and I would rather pour grapeshot into forty of my enemies than see a single one of them guillotined."

Corsino nods approval: "You have artistic tastes."

"As for that poor and lovely Queen Mary," says Winter, "I agree with you that they could have disposed of her without going and spoiling her beautiful neck."

"Maybe," rejoins Dimsky, "it was precisely that beautiful neck Elizabeth had a grudge against. Anyhow 'disposed of her' is neat; I like the expression."

"But gentlemen, how can you joke and make fun of such a ghastly event, such a dreadful crime?"

"Moran is right," replies Corsino. "And since our friends are so gay tonight, why don't you, Schmidt, spin them some silly yarn. It's been a long time since the last one; you must have been saving up and can afford it."

Schmidt, the third horn, has a queer countenance that incites to mirth. He is reputed to be witty, and since he is usually taciturn, his stories seem more comical than they actually are. But he can mimic like a professional comedian. Schmidt responds to the invitation, blows his nose, takes an enormous pinch of snuff, and without preamble begins in his cracked voice the story of

A Visit to Tom Thumb

The scene shows an absurdly simple-minded French provincial who thinks he is a great lover of music, and who is therefore in despair because he has not been able to attend the *soirées* given by the dwarf Tom Thumb. He knows that this Lilliputian wonder has utterly delighted the Parisian public for any number of months past. Our man has undertaken the trip to Paris for the sole purpose of admiring the little General, who is reputed to be so witty, so graceful, and so courtly. But as bad luck will have it, the performances of the prodigy have stopped for the time being. What is he to do?

A letter of introduction with which our provincial has been provided opens to him the door of an artist renowned for his talent as a practical joker. Having heard Tom Thumb's admirer recount his disappointment, the artist says to him: "I can fully understand, my dear sir, that for a friend of the arts like yourself this is indeed a cruel blow.— You are from Quimper, I believe?"

"Yes, sir, from Quimper-Corentin." [2]

"To think you have taken such a long trip in vain! Let me see,

---

[2] In Brittany; traditional for "the depths of the provinces"; an equivalent would be Kalamazoo or Peoria.

I have an idea. It's true that Tom Thumb isn't performing any more, but he's still in Paris. Why don't you go and call on him; he is a perfect gentleman, he'll receive you cordially."

"Oh, I'd be deeply indebted to you if I could get to see him! I'm so fond of music!"

"It's a fact, he doesn't sing at all badly. This is his address: rue Saint-Lazare at the corner of the rue de la Rochefoucauld. You'll see a long alleyway and at the very end is the house where Tom Thumb has his being. It is a sacred abode inhabited in turn by Talma, Mlle Mars, Mlle Duchesnois, Horace Vernet, and Thalberg.[3] Tom Thumb now shares it with the celebrated pianist. Not a word to the janitor, but just stroll to the end of the alley and follow the advice of the gospel—knock, and it shall be opened unto you."

"My dear sir, I'm on my way—it's as if I were seeing him already, already hearing him. I am all atremble at the thought. You have no idea of the depth of my passion for music!"

And so our amateur runs panting to the address given him, walks in and up, knocks with a trembling hand, and—a colossus opens the door. It so happens that Lablache,[4] who lives there with Thalberg, his son-in-law, was just going out.

"Whom are you looking for, sir?" asks the famous singer.

"I wanted to see General Tom Thumb."

"I am he," replies Lablache with impressive self-assurance and in his most thunderous voice.

"But—how can—they told me the General stood no higher than my knee, and that his charming voice—was something—like—a—cricket's. I don't see—that is—recognize—"

"You do not recognize Tom Thumb? And yet it is I, sir, who have the honor of being that justly celebrated artist. My stature and my voice are exactly as you were told—that is to say, *in public* —but you can understand that in my own house *I make myself at home.*"

Whereupon Lablache strides away majestically, while the music-lover stands lost in amazement, flushed with pride and joy at having seen General Tom Thumb in private and life-size.

---

[3] Respectively: three actors, a painter, and a virtuoso pianist.
[4] A famous Italian singer (1794–1858), and a man of huge stature. See Henry F. Chorley's *Thirty Years' Musical Recollections* for a description of his size.

Evenings with the Orchestra

> *To Merlin's magic equal,*
> *This gentleman's the sequel*
> *—And easier to believe!*

Corsino rises. "I knew he'd end up with a *mot*. One verse more, and we'd have had a quatrain full in the face. No doubt about it, Schmidt, you were born to write musical comedies—in German."

Another Vexation of Kleiner the Elder's

BEETHOVEN's *Fidelio* is being performed.

Not a word is spoken in the orchestra. The eyes of all true artists are aglow, those of ordinary musicians remain open, those of the blockheads are shut from time to time. Tamberlik [1] has been engaged by our manager for a few performances and sings Florestan. He electrifies the house with his prison song. The pistol quartet drives the audience wild with enthusiasm.

After the grand finale Kleiner the Elder exclaims: "That music sets your insides on fire. I feel as if I'd swallowed fifteen glasses of brandy. I'm going to the café and get a —"

"There aren't any left," breaks in Dimsky; "I just saw Tamberlik getting the last one; he's certainly earned it."

Kleiner goes off muttering.

---

[1] Enrico Tamberlik (1820–89), a famous Italian tenor.

Musical and Phrenological Studies

Nightmares

The Puritans of Sacred Music

Paganini

a biographical sketch

A CONCERT made up of mediocre and bad music is being given at the theater. The program is one mass of Italian cavatinas, fantasias for piano, excerpts from Masses, flute concertos, lieder with solo trombone obbligato, bassoon duets, and the like. In consequence, conversation flourishes in every corner of the orchestra. A few musicians are sketching. For a contest is under way for the best pencil drawing of the scene in which Lablache standing on his doorstep says to the provincial who asks for Tom Thumb: "I am he, sir!" Kleiner the Elder wins the prize, which is something of a solace to him for his previous day's vexation. When I join the group I take a look at the program.

"The devil! We certainly are in for a staggering bunch of nightmares tonight!"

"Nightmares! That's another of your Parisian terms that we don't understand," says Winter. "Please explain."

"Look out, young man from America, you're on the way to becoming one yourself."

"One what?"

"A nightmare, you simple-minded musico!" retorts Corsino. "I'll prove it to you. Here's what we European musicians mean by that term:

"—Not, of course, one of those frightful dreams in which one feels a crushing weight on one's chest, or is pursued by a monster which is always ready to catch up, or feels oneself dropping down, down, down into a bottomless pit, in thick darkness and silence more terrifying than the clamors of hell. No, it isn't that, and yet it almost is. A musical nightmare is one of those indescribable realities that you hate and despise, which haunt you, infuriate you, and give you a pain in the midriff akin to indigestion. It is the sort of work that carries an infectious germ and that in spite of every sanitary precaution finds its way somehow or other into the heart of all that is finest and most beautiful in music. And yet it's endured with a wry face and not hissed—sometimes because such works are put together with a low sort of talent, sometimes because the composer is a nice fellow whose feelings you would not want to hurt, or again because the work bears some relation to a doctrine dear to a friend, or yet again because the connection is with some idiot who has had the conceit to pose as your enemy, and you don't want to appear to concern yourself with him by treating him as he deserves.

"When the damnable piece begins you leave (if you can) the hall where it is strutting. You go into the street and watch a trained dog do his tricks, or a Punch-and-Judy show, or you listen to the big aria from *La Favorita*[1] wailed by a barrel-organ which breaks off on the leading note because a coin tossed out of a window has interrupted the virtuoso in the midst of his melody. Next you read all the posters, then you look at your watch and compute that the nightmare of that concert is no longer to be feared, so you venture to come back to your seat. But that is precisely the moment the nightmare will sometimes choose to pounce on the poor musician who tried to escape it. He re-enters the hall; the nightmare has said its say, to be sure, but what is this racket going on? What's this applause? For whom? These tokens of pleasure come from the public and are addressed to the nightmare in person. There he is, cooing and pouting and ruffling his feathers like a pigeon. He bows modestly. By heaven, it's true: the public has found the animal charming and lovable and is giving it thanks for the pleasure it has received.

"That is when you go berserk and wish yourself at the antipodes, among savages, in the midst of a tribe of apes on Borneo, or even

---

[1] Donizetti's opera (1840).

among the ruthless gold-diggers of California. It is then that one realizes the futility of fame, the insignificance of the success obtained by masterpieces at the hands of judges who are equally capable of applauding nightmares. And you appreciate how right the ancient orator was who, turning anxiously to his friend after the multitude had warmly approved one of his speeches, said: 'The people applaud: can it be that I have said something foolish?'

"In addition to the nightmare-works, most of which are written in a style that can only be called the stupid style, there are the nightmare-men. We have the nightmare-orator who buttonholes you at the street corner or clamps you to the drawing-room mantelpiece in order to saturate you with his doctrine; the nightmare who proves to all comers the superiority of Oriental music over ours; the old theorist who finds mistakes in harmony wherever he looks; the discoverer of ancient manuscripts that make him fall into ecstasy; the defender of the rules of the fugue; the man who worships exclusively the 'limpid' style, the 'sense-of-form' style, the good-and-dead style, the enemy of expression and life; the admirer of organ music, of the *Missa Papæ Marcelli*, of the *Missa l'Homme-Armé*, of the *chansons de gestes*. All these people are the *greatest nightmares you could name.*

"And then we have the fond mothers who introduce their infant prodigies to you, and the composers who willy-nilly try to get you to read their scores, and all the good burghers who talk about music, and all the crashing bores—not forgetting the inquisitive simpletons. Which is why, my dear Winter, our friend has the right to say to you: 'You're another!'

"Listen to this, gentlemen!" (The *O salutaris* of a great master is being sung.) "Notice this example of the stupid style which is just now put before us! The author has the words *Da robur, fer auxilium* sung to an energetic phrase symbolic of strength (*robur*). Of the hundred composers who have treated this subject since Gossec, there are perhaps not two who have steered clear of the nonsense sanctified by our old master as a model."

"What nonsense?" asks Bacon.

"The *O salutaris* is a prayer, isn't it? In it the Christian prays God for *strength*, he implores His *help*; but if he begs for them he obviously does not possess them, he feels the lack of them. Hence he who prays is a weak creature, whose voice, when pronouncing the *Da robur*, should be as humble as possible, instead of breaking out in accents far more suggestive of a threat than a supplication. And they call this type of thing masterpieces of sacred music! Masterpieces of stupidity. Nightmares. And those who admire them, supernightmares!

"Compositions in which sacred texts are treated in the would-be expressive style are overrun with similar nonsense. It is this nonsense, undoubtedly, that has given pretext for the founding of a new sect of the strangest kind, which keeps alive in its conventicles a delightful proposition on the agenda. According to this innocent heresy, the object is to preserve a truly Catholic music; actually, it tends to the total suppression of music in the divine service. These Anabaptists of art would not tolerate violins in the churches, because violins suggest the music of the theater—as if the double basses, the violas, and the other instruments, together with the voices, were not in exactly the same position. Still, according to this doctrine, the new organs have been provided with too many stops and are too expressive. They conclude next that melody, rhythm, and modern tonality are damnable. The moderates will still accept Palestrina; but the perfervid ones, the Balfours of Burleigh [2] of this new Puritanism, will have nothing but plainsong, raw.

"One of them, the Macbriar of the sect,[2] goes even farther; he has reached in one leap the goal toward which the rest are moving more slowly; the goal being, as I have said, the abolition of sacred music. The way I came to know the full intent of the leading zealot's mind is this. Shortly after the death of the Duc d'Orléans, I attended the funeral service held in the Church of Notre-Dame for this noble prince, so deeply and rightly lamented. The Puritan sect was victorious on that occasion, having had it decreed that Mass should be sung in plainsong altogether, and that the accursed modern tonality, which is dramatic, passionate, and expressive, should be entirely prohibited. The choirmaster of Notre-Dame considered, however, that he should compromise a little with the corruption of the age by adding four-part harmony to the funeral plainsong. He had not felt strong enough to make a clean break with the impious world. Grace sufficient had apparently proved insufficient.

"Anyhow, I found myself seated in the nave next to our fiery

---

[2] These Scottish names allude to Scott's novel *Old Mortality*.

Macbriar. While abominating modern music, 'which excites the passions,' he was comically passionate about plainsong, which, I must admit, is far from possessing that grave defect. He managed to control his feelings fairly well until the middle of the ceremony. A rather long pause having occurred and the congregation being sunk in deep and solemn meditation, the organist inadvertently let a key drop on the keyboard, in consequence of which accidental pressure a flute-stop A was heard for a couple of seconds. This solitary note rose in the midst of silence and re-echoed from the vault of the cathedral like a soft mysterious wail. At this my man sprang to his feet in transport, and without respect for the true devotional absorption of his neighbors exclaimed: 'Wonderful! Sublime! There is your genuinely religious music! That is pure art in its divine simplicity! All the rest is shamelessly profane!'

"He was at any rate a good logician. Since according to him sacred music must contain neither melody, nor harmony, nor rhythm, nor instrumentation, nor expression, nor modern tonality, nor ancient modes (for these recall the music of the Greeks, who were pagans), all he needed was an A, a mere A, sustained for an instant in the midst of the silence of the crowd—a crowd, to be sure, that was humbled and moved. One might of course disturb his ecstasy by assuring him that theaters make a habitual and frequent use of his celestial A. But one must admit that his system of *monotonous* music (none has ever deserved the name better) can easily be put into practice, and at a very low cost. From that point of view it is truly superior.

"There is a brain disease that the Italian physicians call *pazzia*, and the English "madness"; it is clearly this that reigns and rages among the sectaries of the new musical creed. I could name several who are as completely mad at this moment as the admirer of the solitary A. They have sometimes tried to draw me into a formal discussion of the doctrine engendered by their malady, but I knew better and contented myself with saying to these Gregorians, Ambrosians, Palestrinians, Presbyterians, Puritans, Shakers, Anabaptists, and Unitarians—all more or less touched with madness or *pazzia*: 'Away!' adding only: 'Hence ye nightmares!'

"The majority of these people, I suspect, believe that once melody, harmony, rhythm, instrumentation, and expression have been banished from the religious genre, they will be able to write

the most beautiful sacred music. And indeed, as soon as these qualities are no longer needed in that genre, they will have all the
requisites to succeed."

"Good Lord!" breaks in Corsino, "here is Racloski, who is trying
to tackle with piano accompaniment the Paganini Rondo in B
minor!"

"The Rondo of the Bells? What a nerve! He's crazy; he won't
get through two bars of it decently."

"Does he at least play in tune?"

"Yes, it's only fair to say that in the course of a long piece like
that he repeatedly manages to play in tune."

"Thanks, I'm off."

"For God's sake, don't desert in the face of the enemy! We
know you were quite intimate with Paganini; tell us something
about him. Then we won't have to hear his work mangled by that
catgut-scraper. Hurry up, he's beginning."

"Really, you'll turn me into a rhapsodist. I comply; but don't
you think that some performers should be forbidden under severe
penalties to *tackle* (as you rightly say) certain compositions? Don't
you think that masterpieces should be protected against vandalism?"

"No question about it, and the time will come, I hope, when it
will be so. Of all the artists in Greece, Alexander the Great considered only one worthy of depicting his features and forbade the
rest to attempt it. The most gifted virtuosos should alone have the
right to transmit to the public the thought of the great masters,
those Alexanders of art!"

BACON: "Now, that's not a bad idea! That Greek composer was no
fool. Where the deuce did Corsino find out about him?"

"Quiet, please!"

Paganini

A very intelligent man, Choron,[3] used to say of Weber: "He is a meteor." One might with equal justice say of Paganini: "He is a comet," for never did a flaming body appear so unexpectedly in the heavens of art, or excite in the course of his long orbit greater amazement mixed with a sort of terror, before it disappeared forever.[4]

The comets of the physical world, if poets and popular tradition are to be believed, appear only as harbingers of the terrible storms that upheave the human ocean. Certainly, neither our age nor the emergence of Paganini will give the lie to this tradition. Paganini's extraordinary genius, unique in its kind, was maturing in Italy at the beginning of the greatest events that history records: his career began at the court of one of Napoleon's sisters, at the most solemn hour of the Empire; he was making a triumphant tour through Germany just as the giant was going to his grave; he made his first appearance in France to the noise of a crumbling dynasty, and he entered Paris at the same time as the cholera.[5]

The fear of infection by this dread disease was unable to restrain either the widespread curiosity or the enthusiasm that made the masses everywhere follow in Paganini's wake. It is difficult to credit such feelings for a virtuoso in such a time, but the fact remains: Paganini had so forcibly struck the imagination and heart of the Parisians that he made them forget death hovering over them.

Everything conspired, moreover, to increase his prestige—his strange and hypnotic appearance, the mystery surrounding his life, the tales told concerning him, even the crimes his enemies had had the stupid audacity to impute to him, not to speak of the miracles performed by a talent which upset all accepted ideas, brushed aside all known methods, announced the impossible and accomplished it.

---

[3] Alexandre Choron (1771–1834), theorist and teacher, founded a music school which greatly influenced the composers and singers who studied there from 1824 to 1830.

[4] Part of this essay written as an obituary notice in 1840.

[5] These dates are, respectively: 1806, 1821, 1830, 1831.

This irresistible influence of Paganini's made itself felt not only in the world of amateurs and artists; the sovereigns of art themselves succumbed to it. It is said that Rossini, that great scoffer at enthusiasm, felt for him a sort of devotion mingled with fear. Meyerbeer, during Paganini's travels in northern Europe, followed him around, each day more eager to hear him, and vainly seeking to understand the mystery of his incredible talent.

Unfortunately, Paganini's superhuman musical powers are known to me only through the accounts I have heard of them. A fateful series of circumstances brought it about that he never performed publicly in France when I was there; and I must admit to my sorrow that in spite of the close relations I was fortunate enough to have with him during the last years of his life, I never heard him play. Only once after my return from Italy did he play at the Opéra. But I was then confined to my room by a severe ailment and I could not attend the concert, the last, if I am not mistaken, that he ever gave.

From that time on, the throat disease he was to die of,[6] coupled with a nervous malady that gave him no respite, grew more and more serious and he was forced to give up entirely the exercise of his art. But as he loved music passionately, finding it indeed an absolute necessity, he would occasionally, in one of his rare moments of surcease from pain, take up his violin again to play with friends the trios and quartets of Beethoven. These performances were impromptu, strictly among friends, and the players themselves were the only audience.

At other times, when playing the violin tired him too much, he would take from his music case a collection of duets he had composed for the violin and guitar (pieces still unknown to the world), and choosing as his partner a worthy German violinist, M. Sina, who still teaches in Paris, he would take the guitar part and draw incredible effects from that instrument.[7] And these two, Sina, the unassuming violinist, and Paganini, the incomparable guitarist, would thus spend together long evenings to which no one, even the worthiest, ever won admittance.

After a time his laryngeal tuberculosis made such inroads that

---

[6] Tuberculosis of the larynx.
[7] Paganini bequeathed his guitar to Berlioz. It may be seen in the Library of the Paris Conservatoire, bearing the signatures of the two owners.

he entirely lost his voice and he was compelled to give up virtually all social relations. One could barely make out a few words by bringing one's ear close to his lips. When I used to stroll about with him in Paris, on days when the sun gave him the desire to go out, I carried a notebook and a pencil. Paganini would write down in a few words the subject to which he wished to direct the conversation; I would develop it as best I could, and from time to time, taking the pencil, he would interrupt me with reflections that were often highly original in their laconic brevity. The deaf Beethoven used a notebook to take in his friends' ideas; the mute Paganini used it to convey his own. One of those do-or-die collectors of autographs who haunt the drawing-rooms of artists no doubt "borrowed," without letting me know, the notebook used by my illustrious interlocutor. What is certain is that I could not find it one day when Spontini wanted to see it, and that from that day to this I have been unable to lay my hands on it.

I have often been asked to tell in full detail the incident in Paganini's life in which he acted with such cordial magnificence toward me. The various events that preceded and followed the main occurrence, which is now common property [8]—events of a kind so remote from the ordinary course of artistic life—would, I feel sure, be of lively interest to you, but you can readily understand how embarrassing such a recital would be to me, and you will excuse me if I say no more. I do not even consider it necessary to take notice of the stupid insinuations, the crazy counter-statements, and the erroneous affirmations to which Paganini's noble act gave rise on the occasion I speak of. To make up for these, I may say that never did certain critics find more handsome expressions of praise; never, in particular, was the prose of Jules Janin [9] stirred by a nobler emotion than on this occasion. Some time later, the Italian poet Romani also wrote for a Piedmont newspaper some eloquent pages that deeply moved Paganini when he read them in Marseille.

For he had been compelled to flee the Paris climate. Once in Marseille, that of Provence soon seemed to him too severe also, and he settled for the winter in Nice, where he was fittingly re-

---

[8] Paganini, having attended a performance of Berlioz's *Harold in Italy* and *Fantastique* in December 1838, made him a present of 20,000 francs to free him for further composition. The full story is given in Berlioz's *Memoirs*, Ch. xlix.

[9] The literary critic of the *Journal des Débats*.

ceived and surrounded with the most affectionate care by a wealthy patron of music, himself a virtuoso, the Conte di Césole. None the less his sufferings kept increasing (though he did not as yet consider himself in danger of death), and his letters breathed a deep sadness. "If God permits," he wrote to me, "I shall see you next spring. I am hoping the state of my health will improve here; it is the last remaining hope. Farewell; love me as I love you."

I did not see him again. A few years later, when I was myself compelled to pray in aid from the balmy breezes of the Sardinian Sea after the severe fatigues of a harrowing musical season in Paris,[1] I was one day returning in a boat from Villafranca to Nice when the young fisherman who was rowing me back suddenly dropped his oars and pointed out on the shore a small isolated villa of somewhat strange aspect, saying: "Did you ever hear of a gentleman named Paganini, who sounded the violin very good?"

"Yes, my lad, I've heard tell of him."

"Well, sir, that's where he stayed for three weeks after his death."

It seems, indeed, that his body was laid in that tiny villa during the protracted dispute between his son and the Bishop of Genoa, a dispute which ought not, for the honor of the Genoese and Piedmontese clergy, to have lasted so long, and the reasons for which, even from the point of view of the most rigid orthodoxy, were by no means so serious as has been made out, for Paganini died quite suddenly.[2]

On the night following my excursion to Villafranca I was sleeping in the tower of Ponchettes, which is stuck like a swallow's nest against a rock two hundred feet above the sea, when the sounds of a violin playing Paganini's variations on *The Carnival of Venice* rose to my retreat as if emerging from the waves. Just at that moment I was dreaming of the man whose mortuary villa the young fisherman had pointed out to me during the day. I woke up with a start and listened for some time with a dull throbbing in my chest. My mind, instead of growing clearer, became more and more confused—*The Venetian Carnival*! Who but Paganini himself

---

[1] In August 1844, after the anxieties of the music festival for the great exhibition. (*Memoirs*, Ch. lxiii).
[2] The difficulty was to obtain Christian burial for an infidel popularly suspected of dealings with the devil, and who had not received the last rites of the Church.

could know those variations? Was it another farewell to me from beyond the grave? Imagine E. T. A. Hoffmann in my place and what a touching, elegiac fantasy he would have written around this strange incident!

It was M. de Césole who, alone at the foot of the tower, was giving me this graceful serenade.

The famous variations on the Venetian air form part of the works of Paganini that the firm of Schonenberger has recently published in Paris; and here I may say in passing that those by Ernst [3] on the same theme, which he has frequently been accused of plagiarizing from Paganini, do not resemble them in the least.

Among the other works of the master that the French publisher has just disclosed to the eager curiosity of artists, one notes with regret the absence of the fantasia on the prayer in *Moses*,[4] one of the pieces, it is said, in which Paganini produced the most gripping effects. No doubt M. Achille Paganini is reserving it for a complete edition of his father's works, an edition which in one respect he has been right to withhold from premature publication. For in spite of the rapid strides which, thanks to Paganini, the technique of the violin has been making, compositions such as these are still beyond the majority of violinists. Reading the scores one can hardly understand how their author could ever have played them. It would take a book to enumerate all the new effects that Paganini has introduced into his works, the ingenious devices, the grand and noble forms, the orchestral combinations never before employed or dreamed of. His melody is in the great Italian tradition, but it generally moves with a more passionate life than the melody met with in even the finest pages of the dramatic composers among his compatriots. His harmony is always clear, simple, and of extraordinary sonority.

He found the way to make the solo violin predominate by tuning his four strings a semitone higher than those of the violins in the orchestra. He could thus play in the brilliant keys of D and A, while the orchestra accompanied him in the less sonorous E flat and B flat. It is past belief how much he discovered in the use of simple and double harmonics, in the handling of notes plucked with the left hand; in the forming of arpeggios, in bowings, in

---

[3] Heinrich Ernst (1814–65), violin virtuoso.
[4] Rossini's oratorio-opera (1818).

passages on three strings—all the more unbelievable that his predecessors did not so much as give a hint of such effects. Paganini is
one of those artists of whom it must be said that they are because
they are, not because others were before them.

What he unfortunately could not hand down to his successors
was the fire that animated him and made his astounding feats of
technique congenial. An idea can be set down, a form outlined,
but the performing instinct cannot be transfixed; it is impossible
to grasp; it is genius, soul, the flame of life; and when it passes
away, it leaves behind a darkness all the more profound because
its brilliance has been more dazzling. That is the reason not only
why the works of the great virtuoso inventors suffer more or less
from not being played by their composers, but also why those of
original and expressive composers retain only a part of their power
when the author does not preside over their performance.

Paganini's orchestra is brilliant and energetic without being
noisy. He made use of the bass drum in his *tutti*, often with uncommon intelligence. In the prayer from *Moses*, Rossini, as elsewhere, simply lets it thump on the strong beats. Paganini when he
composed his fantasia on the same theme took good care not to
imitate him on that point. At the opening of the melody "From
thy starry throne," Rossini bangs on the next-to-last syllable,
which falls on the strong beat. But Paganini thought the melodic
accent of the next syllable incomparably more important, and he
brings in the drum on the weak beat; the effect resulting from this
change being, in my opinion, both novel and preferable. One day,
after complimenting Paganini on this piece, someone added: "You
must admit that Rossini supplied you with a grand theme." Paganini retorted: "That may be, but he never hit upon my drumbeat!"

It would be difficult for me to go farther into the analysis of the
scores of this artistic miracle-worker, scores that are wholly inspired and in which we may see chiefly the written exemplifica-
tion of his marvelous powers as a virtuoso. Besides, tonight—these
recollections—

"And so you never heard him?" asks Corsino.

"Never. Good night, gentlemen."

R OSSINI's *Barber of Seville* is being given.

Not a word is spoken in the orchestra. Corsino contents himself with remarking at the close of the opera that the actor *burdened* with the role of Alma-viva in that dazzling masterpiece was born to be an alderman, and that the Figaro would have made an accomplished beadle.

Charges Leveled against the Author's Criticism

his defense—the district attorney's rejoinder—

documents in evidence

Analysis of *The Lighthouse*

the submarine congress

Analysis of *Diletta*

an idyll

The Piano Possessed

 A GERMAN opera is being given for the first time, which is very etc.

During the first act, the orchestra does its duty. During the second, discouragement seems to overtake the musicians. One after the other they put their instruments down, and conversation begins.

"Now there's a work," says Corsino to me, "on which, if you had to write a notice, you could exercise your great talent for saying nothing. And that, you must admit, is the most shameful kind of criticism there is."

"What do you mean? I certainly always try to say something in my wretched *feuilletons*. Only I also try for variety of form. What you call saying nothing is often a way of speaking very plainly."

"Yes, it's one of those fiendishly wicked things that only Frenchmen can devise. I am going to let our friends here judge for themselves. I have the complete collection of bouquets for Chloris [1] that you've produced so far. I'll get it and let the others enjoy the fragrance of your flowers." (*Exit Corsino.*)

---

[1] That is, birthday or other presentation verses.

Dervinck then turns to me: "I don't quite get what he means by your 'bouquets for Chloris.' We Germans also indulge in criticism, but our way of doing it is quite simple: when a new work appears, we go to hear it, and if after we've listened to it attentively, it seems to us beautiful, original, and great, why, we write—"

"—that it is dreadful," puts in Winter, who has composed a pretty poor ballet.

CORSINO (*carrying a bundle of newspapers*): Here, gentlemen, are our guest's masterpieces of courtesy and kindliness. Let us study them. You will note first of all that if he wants to jeer at the author of a libretto without uttering the slightest word about his lyrics, he has recourse to the cruel method of telling the story in verse that runs along like prose. Observe the compliment implied. I choose a scene at random—a band of Arabs who march in time and sing, according to custom: "Hush, hush! Not a word while we go and hide." This is the way the critic describes the scene:

"Silently they steal away in the dark that follows day, but another group's behind. The Cadi, a fat old gent, with a hump and nearly blind, all in all not very bent on asserting sovereignty, is afraid that on his rounds he will meet the enemy, who are roaming out of bounds. Now if these unfeeling men have a mind his head to crack—there and then—they will put him in a sack and toss him from the walls like a beggar or a barber, and he'll find his resting-place in the waters of the harbor.

"He's not covered twenty paces ere his shoulders form the basis of a dozen cudgel-blows. He breaks out in ah's and oh's as he's beaten to the ground. 'Murder! Help! They're killing me!' Here a gallant fellow comes to see, drives the Cadi's muggers off, and calls the neighbors round. One of them's a bit of fluff, with a countenance that slays and a negligee that shows her stays. The victim, as he tells his tale, gives a moan and then a wail: 'I shall die, I've lost a tooth, and they also broke my back.' It's the truth—oh, what a whack!"

Here is another review in which verses by the author of the foregoing libretto come before and after some false prose by our critic, which creates the most grotesque mixture. The subject is a young man whom someone is trying to hold as security for debt:

"Albert: Good heavens!

"Rudolph: Yes, 'tis fair: The law ordains
          That here our live collateral remains.[2]

"Zila is crying and Albert replying but time is flying. Oh!
What will befall? Rudolph then offers to take him in hall.
Quick, Albert, just trust to *my* door and *my* lock. Come, you
old Shylock; open your coffers and lend him a sum: he swears
he will come and pledges his life. He has signed, this will bind,
are you glad? Yes. Here's the gold, now I hold him and go.

"No! not so! Cruel host, I don't owe you a bean! You are
mad! Come, my love, my sweet! Now the Count steps between:
"What a cheat!" says the Count. "Here I mount my high horse,
of course, or my name it is mud. You sucker of blood, open
your pouch, give me back the boy's note. Not without discount,
Count? Yes, without—Ouch!—You've made a profit off it of a
hundred per centum: don't you dare torment him!

"Rudolph: *That was a lucky hit*—(pointing to Albert)
          This note should do the rest,
          For if I use my wit,
          Whatever comes is best:
          The girl will be for me,
          Or else I'll set him free!"

MYSELF: You think this cruel, my dear Corsino; but there is not
the slightest malicious intent behind it. It's the swing of the
author's rhythm that made me write like that. I'm the counterpart of Molière's Bourgeois: I wrote poetry without knowing
it. When you've heard a barrel-organ grind out the same tune
for an hour, don't you end by singing that tune in spite of yourself, no matter how awful? It's quite natural that when I give
an account of operas into which verses like these have crept,
they should also creep into my prose. I have to make an effort
later on in order to disenrhyme myself.

Besides, why suppose me capable of irony toward operatic
poets? Their faults, if any, are out of my line. I am not a literary
man. That literary men should issue rules about music, well and
good, it's their privilege. But never, I swear to you, will it enter
my head to venture on literary criticism. You slander me. It's

---

[2] The substance of the plot that follows is, happily, beyond recovery.

merely the fear of being too dull, too monotonous, too boring, that makes me—as I said just now—try to vary a little the turn of my poor sentences.

Especially at certain times of year, when nothing one does comes off; when it seems wrong for artists and critics to be alive; when none of their efforts can either attract the public or arouse its sympathy; when the public seems to say: "What do all these fellows want with me? What possesses them? A new opera? To begin with, *is* there such a thing as a new opera? Isn't the form worn out, played out, squeezed dry? Can it hold novelty at this late date? But all this aside, what are to me the inventions of poets and musicians anyway? Or the opinions of any critic? Let me snooze, good people, and go to sleep yourselves. We are bored, bored by you."

On such days, while you imagine that critics are preoccupied with malicious and bitter jokes, the poor devils are really in the deepest dejection; twenty times they take up their pen, and twenty times it drops from their fingers, and in the bitterness of their hearts they say to themselves: "Oh, why are we so far from Tahiti, and why has that delightful island not kept to its primitive semi-nude beauty, instead of dressing itself up in sackcloth and learning to chant the Bible with a nasal twang to old English tunes? We might at least go there and find refuge from European boredom, philosophize under the coconut trees with young Tahitian girls, fish for pearls, drink kava, dance the pyrrhic, and ingratiate ourselves with Queen Pomare. Instead of these innocent overseas diversions under the finest skies in the world, we must sweat out a report of how they went about it the other day in Paris to keep us five mortal hours in a stuffy theater!"

For it isn't just a matter of listening to a three-act opera (dress rehearsal included); of eating only half a dinner on the opening night so as not to miss a single note of the overture; of being called down by his lordship's doorman for staying out till one in the morning, the time when at last all the actors were recalled and the ultimate bouquet fell at the feet of the prima donna. It is not just a matter of spending part of the night running over in your mind the various incidents of the piece, the form of the numbers, the names of the characters; of dreaming about it—

supposing one can fall asleep—and pondering it when one awakes. Alas, no, that isn't the end of it; we critics must also give an intelligible account (or nearly) of what very often we haven't understood; make an amusing story of what bored us; give the whys and wherefores, the too much and too little, the strong and weak points, the mush and the grit, of a work taken on the wing, a work that did not sit quiet before its depicters for as long as it would take to make a good daguerreotype.

For my part, I must say I'd rather write the whole opera than tell the story of a single act of it. For the composer, no matter how much he hates to set one cavatina after another like beads on a chain—when you are harnessed to the score of a Parisian opera, don't forget, you mustn't waste time stringing pearls—the composer at least can work when he likes. But the reporter is condemned to a deadline; he must write just when he would rather not. He has had a bad night; he gets up not knowing what his mood is; he says to himself: "At this precise moment Halévy, Scribe, and Saint-Georges [3] are enjoying the deep restorative sleep of women after confinement, while here am I with their child on my hands, obliged to wheedle its nurse into suckling it, and having to wash it and primp it, and tell everybody how pretty it is, how much it looks like its fathers, and drawing its horoscope so I can predict it will have a long life."

I should really like to know, my dear Corsino, what you would do if in addition to these torments of theatrical criticism you also had to review concerts; if you faced a crowd of talented men, remarkable virtuosos, and first-rate composers whom you had to praise; if your friends came to you and said: "Here are nine violinists, eleven pianists, seven cellists, twenty singers, one symphony, two symphonies, a mystery, and a Mass about which you haven't yet said anything: come on, say something! Show a little spirit! Give the boys a hand! And take care to vary your expressions. Don't keep saying: 'Sublime! inimitable! marvelous! unheard of!' Give praise, but do it delicately; don't lay it on with a trowel. Let them all see that they are gods, yet nothing more. Above all, don't be crude when you say it: you might offend their modesty. You can't tickle a man with a pitchfork, and you are dealing with very worthy people who will be in-

---

[3] One composer and two librettists. See below note 6, p. 241.

finitely grateful to you for any home truths you may kindly tell them. Composers and artists no longer resemble the Archbishop of Granada.[4] However great you may suppose their vanity, not one of them nowadays would be capable of acting like Gil Blas's patron and telling his too outspoken critic: 'Go to my treasurer and tell him to pay you five hundred ducats—' you know the rest.

"Most of our celebrities would content themselves with repeating the remark of a member of the Academy under the Empire, a *mot* the modesty and profundity of which cannot be too often held up to admiration. A banquet was being given in honor of this Immortal. After dessert a youthful enthusiast said to his right-hand neighbor: 'Let us propose a toast—To M. D. J., who has surpassed Voltaire!'

" 'You should be ashamed!' retorted the other; 'that's a wild exaggeration; let's stay within the truth, and say: To M. D. J., who has equaled Voltaire.'

"M. D. J., who had overhead the exchange, warmly grasped the objector's hand and said to him: 'Young man, I admire your blunt frankness!'

"That is how criticism is received these days, and why it has become so easy to perform this sacred ministry. We know there are free-spoken Franks who would perform it even better if the Archbishop's five hundred ducats were added to the splendid eulogy of the Academician. But such people are too demanding. Most of your colleagues are content to enjoy the gentle satisfaction that comes from the thought of duty well done—which proves at least that they have a sense of duty. Whereas seeing your stubborn silence, one wonders about yours."

What would you say, Corsino, to people who preach at you that way? You would no doubt reply as I have done on such occasions: "Dear friends, you go too far. I have never given anybody cause to believe that I am without a conscience. I have one, I too, no doubt about it. But it is very weak, very puny, very ailing as a result of the poor treatment it endures every day. At times people want to shut it up, deny it exercise in the open air, condemn it to silence. At other times they force it to appear in public half naked despite the cold weather, compel it to

---

[4] In Le Sage's *Gil Blas*, a prelate who asks for and punishes frankness.

harangue the crowd, pretend to be courageous and face the rude jeers of idlers, the hoots of street urchins, and a thousand other affronts. It was easy to foresee the result: a ruined constitution, a consumption now in the second stage, with blood-spitting, giddiness, uneven temper, bouts of weeping, outbursts of rage, a persistent cough—in short all the symptoms that betoken the end. Once dead, it will be embalmed according to the method Ruisch used to preserve the appearance of life in his daughter's corpse.[5] I shall preserve my conscience with care. It will be on view in my library, and then, I really and truly hope, it will suffer no more."

CORSINO: My dear sir, forgive me if I remark that for the last fifteen minutes you have been off the point. What is worse, you use irony in the midst of proving that you never use it. But I have evidence, and if after I've put it in the record my colleagues do not agree that I am right twice over, I undertake to apologize to you most humbly in their presence, and to acknowledge that I have slandered you. Oyez, oyez, all of you.

The Lighthouse[6]
An Opera in Two Acts

THURSDAY, DECEMBER 27, 1849

The scene represents a square in the village of Pornic. Breton fishermen are about to go to sea with Valentine, the pilot. They sing in chorus:

> *Hooray! Valentine!*
> *Yours be all the cash—a-ash,*
> *Yours be all the loot—toot-oot!*
> *Master of the brine!*
> *When you cut a dash—a-ash,*
> *You can press your suit—toot-oot!*

---

[5] This allusion has defied identification.
[6] Adolphe Adam's opera *Le Fanal* (*The Beacon*) was reviewed by Berlioz in the *Journal des Débats* on December 27, 1849.

> *No girl will decline.*
> *If a roll you flash—a-ash,*
> *You can have, to boot—toot-oot,*
> *A whole tun of wine—*
> *Hooray! Valentine!*

Just then a gun fires an S O S. (-ess -ess) there is a lightning flash (-a—ash) which sets the whole horizon aflame, and Valentine leaps into his boat to try to save a ship in distress, telling his friend Martial to tend his light carefully, for if it goes out, ship and pilot are doomed. Tremendous noise, storm, prayers, and so on and so on.

I should be afraid of wearying the reader if I went into further detail about the music and words of this work. I shall content myself with a remark on the stage production. At the first performance, while the chorus was singing downstage, another drama was being enacted upstage, under the very eyes of the spectators though they had no notion of it.

The background represented a stormy sea, the waves heaving and tossing furiously; and this effect, you must know, is produced by means of a flat piece of painted canvas stretched across the back of the stage and beneath which rise and squat in alternation a number of small boys. Their heads lift the canvas and produce the crest of the wave. Can you imagine the torture of these poor little chaps, who for an hour and a half must agitate this heavy sea with their backbones, who dare not sit down, can't stand upright, are half-smothered, and leap about like monkeys without rest or respite till the end of an interminable act? The famous cage invented by Louis XI, in which prisoners could not stretch their limbs, was nothing in comparison. The only difference is that the Tritons of the Opéra, who are numerous under their blue canvas, enjoy the pleasures of conversation, and often abuse the privilege. For example, at the first night of *The Lighthouse*, a terrific argument stirred the sea off Brittany to its very depths. The waves had at first talked together reasonably enough, and if Neptune had chosen to listen, he would have had no cause to shout his *quos ego*,[7] for he would have heard nothing but harmless remarks, interspersed with

---

[7] The god's interrupted exclamation of anger against the winds in Virgil's *Æneid* (I, 135).

sounds like hiccups whenever the unfortunate boys bobbed up or waved around beneath the canvas—remarks such as:

"See here, Moniquet, you're not working; you make me carry this who-o-o-le co-co-corner of the sea. Get a move on and do-oo-oo your sha-a-are!"

"You poor sap, it's because I'm ha-a-all in!"

"Shut up, you lousy bum. D'you think they p-p-p-ay you to make the sea look like the river Seine? . . ."

"Weh-eh-eh-ll, if that f-f-fellow can do a river scene," puts in a huge wave that works with a will, "don't thwa-a-art his vocation. We're not doing so bad tonight. Listen to that applause; we're a suc-suc-success! What if the house gives us a curtain call, do we ap-ap-pear?"

"Why, of co-ourse!"

"Not me, I wouldn't dare. You should see how I'm sweat-eatting; I'm not presentable."

"Who cares, you sno-o-hob? Think the public's going to mind when it's us hartists? I say, you chaps, will you come out in ca-a-ase you get a call?"

"No-o-o!"

"Ye-e-es!"

"Let's vote on it."

"Let's take a rising vote."

"Stand up all those in favor—the others sit."

"Hell! we've been voting like that for an hour. I'm sick of it."

"Peter," whispers a wave that has quit work, "you can stop, I won't tell on you. Don't tell and I'll stop."

"The others can't see. My back is breaking, let's sit and have a pipe. Have you a match?"

"You mustn't—you'll start a fire."

"Nonsense! M. Ruggieri [8] makes fire enough, and yet this old barn hasn't caught yet. Look out! There goes thunder—bzz!" (*A stage rocket goes off but doesn't explode.*)

"Hallo, the thunder went phut! What a dump! That's what M. Ruggieri was planning the other day when he had a tiff with the manager. I heard him. He says: 'The crowd's welcome to my

---

[8] Claude Ruggieri (*fl.* 1830) was descended from a large family of pyrotechnic experts who came to France under Louis XV and maintained their specialty through the ensuing regimes.

hide,' he says, 'if I don't give it thunderbolts that fizzle.' He's kept his word, we get nothing but bolts that fizzle. He's saving powder."

"True enough, but we haven't had applause since we stopped working. Back to work, or no curtain for us."

"Right, then, here we go-o-ho."

All is quiet among the Tritons; they toil conscientiously; the storm is superb, the seas bound like rams, the waves like lambs (*sicut agni ovium*). Suddenly an angry wave, who so far hadn't said a word, rises to his full height, stands motionless, and shouts: "He sure is right, Citizen Proudhon, when he says that if we in France were the least bit equal, those good-for-nothing bourgeois who look down on us all chesty in their boxes would be down here jiggling their carcasses while we'd be up there looking down at them."

"But, you poor boob," retorts a wavelet, tripping up the ground swell and flattening it out, "can't you see that that wouldn't be no Equality—just inequality turned around?"

"That's not true!"

"He's right!"

"Aristocrat!"

"Reactionary!"

"Let's make him hop!"

Whereupon the storm becomes a fearful hurricane, a tidal wave; the breakers roll on top of one another with unbelievable force, unprecedented roar; it's a waterspout, a typhoon. And the public admires this magnificent disturbance, political in origin, for which it praises to the skies the stage managers of the Opéra. Happily, the act is over and the curtain falls. But it is with great difficulty that the session of the submarine congress is adjourned, by rolling up the sea on a long pole.

"Now! Really!" exclaim all the musicians laughing, "is that what you call analyzing an opera?"

"That's not all, gentlemen," replies Corsino. "Just wait; the next is a stronger dose—still our kindly critic at work:

Analysis of *Diletta*[9]
A Comic Opera in Three Acts

MONDAY, JULY 22, 1850

It is depressing to have to bother about comic operas on a Monday, if only because Monday comes right after Sunday. Now on Sunday one goes to the Northern Railway, finds a seat in a carriage and says to the train: "Take me to Enghien." [1]

On getting out of the obedient vehicle you run across some old friends, real friends, the kind whose names you don't exactly know, but who do not couple too insulting an epithet with your name when your back is turned and someone asks them who you are. And conversation begins in the customary way: "Hello, you here?"

"Pretty well, and you?"

"I? Oh, I'm going to hire a boat and fish in the lake. What about you?"

"Well, I'm only a fisher of souls, and I'm going to vespers. I was at the Opéra-Comique yesterday. What about you?"

"I go in for virtue and I was afraid that if I didn't deprive myself of the show you speak of, I wouldn't wake up early enough to see the sunrise. I just heard that fat gentleman who carried a pumpkin say it was very good. What did *you* think of it?"

"I never speak ill of bumpkins and lovers of comic operas. What about you?"

No answer. You've just rounded the corner of a field full of gooseberry bushes; you've taken one path, your friend, the other; he is eating gooseberries and has forgotten you. What about you? The same.

That is true friendship, akin to republican brotherhood. Delighted with the freedom it affords, you tramp across the plain of Enghien. All is quiet. A shy little breeze would like to spring up,

---

[9] *Diletta* is undoubtedly Adolphe Adam's *Giralda*, which Berlioz reviewed in the *Débats* on July 30, 1850.
[1] Countryfied suburb of Paris, noted for its lake, park, and woods.

but does not dare, and the sun gilds at his leisure the motionless crops. Two cracked bells send their discordant notes from the top of the adjoining hill; it is the call to vespers at the Montmorency church. You stop, you listen, you look into the distance, toward the west; you think of America, of the new worlds springing up there, of the virgin solitudes, the vanished civilizations, the greatness and fall of primitive cultures. Then to the east: recollections of Asia beset you—you muse on Homer, his heroes, Troy, Greece, Egypt, Memphis, the Pyramids, the Court of the Pharaohs, the great temples of Isis, the mystery of India, its sad inhabitants, decrepit China, and all those mad ancient peoples—or at least obsessed. You congratulate yourself on not worshipping either Brahma or Vishnu and on going quietly, like a good Christian, to vespers at Montmorency.

A playful warbler suddenly darts from a bush, rises perpendicularly, flinging skyward its joyous song, zigzags whimsically and erratically in the air, snaps up a gnat and carries it off, giving thanks to God, whose goodness, says the bird, extends over the whole of nature, since He does not disdain to feed the fledgling birds [2]—a naïve gratitude probably not shared by the gnat. All this gives one a good deal to ponder, so one ponders.

Two young women from Paris, dressed with great simplicity in white, walk past with the consummate grace that only Parisian women possess. Four little feet well shod, well arched, well everything . . . four large, velvety eyes, well-eyebrowed—in a word, more food for further pondering. They disappear into a field where the wheat is almost as high, as straight, and as flexible as their waists are high, flexible, and straight. You ponder enormously, you ponder like mad. But the two discordant bells ring out a second and final call, and you say to yourself: "Nonsense! Let us go to vespers." At last you reach a round hill. At the top, picturesquely perched, is a charming Gothic church, not too new, yet not too dilapidated either, with a very beautiful stained-glass window. All around the grass-plot isn't badly torn up; it is clear that the vulgar herd seldom comes by: no mess, no obscene markings, but just three words discretely written in a corner: "*Lucien, Louise, forever!*"

---

[2] Embedded in this last clause are two verses from Racine's *Athalie* (Act II, Scene vii).

You are moved, upset: this church out of the pages of a novel—
its isolation—the peace that envelops it—the wonderful landscape
unrolled all about it—you feel stirring in you again your first
love, so long dormant in the depths of your heart. Your eighteenth
year rises up again before you. You seek in empty space a vanished
form. . . . The organ plays; a simple melody comes to your ears
through the church walls. You wipe your right eye, and once
more say to yourself: "Nonsense! Let us go to vespers," and you
enter the church.

Some thirty women and children in their Sunday clothes, the
parish priest, the curate, the choristers in the choir. All sing out of
tune fit to give a toothache to a hippopotamus. The organist knows
nothing of harmony; he mixes with every phrase little worm-like
ornaments in the most hideous style. Nevertheless you endure for
a time the barbarous rendering of the psalm *In exitu Israel de
Ægypto,*[3] and the persistence of this melancholy psalmody in the
minor mode, which recurs always the same in each stanza, ends
by lulling the pain in your ears and restores you to your reverie.
This time the daydream turns to art. You think how lovely it
would be to have this charming church to yourself, where music
could make its home and show its sweetest enchantments, where
it could blissfully sing its hymns, idyls, and poems of love; where
it could pray, meditate, call up the past, weep and smile, and
preserve its virginal pride from being profaned by the herd, living
forever pure and angelic for herself and a few friends.

Now the organist plays a little dance tune from an old operatic
ballet, and the ludicrous contrast between this and the choir's
ancient narrative irritates you so much that you walk out. You
step once more on the grass; the murmur of voices from the sacred
edifice still reaches you. The organ pursues its little vagaries. You
curse like a trooper. Two balloons go up in the distance; a column
of smoke rises from a locomotive. You are about to fall a prey to
prose. So you quickly pull a book out of your pocket, and seeing
in the humble cemetery adjoining the church a tombstone leaning
in a certain way, you find that you can stretch comfortably upon
it and read the twelfth book of the *Æneid* for the two hundredth
time.

---

[3] "When Israel came out of Egypt," a chant always associated for Berlioz with the
emotions of youthful love and melancholy.

You are just settling down when you are stopped by sobs that come from the sunken road alongside the cemetery. A little girl on crutches who carries a basket in her hand is climbing up the hill and crying bitterly. You ask: "What's the matter, dear?" . . . (No reply.) "Come, tell me what happened." (Her tears redouble.) "Shall I give you some money to buy gingerbread with?"

"A lot I care for your gingerbread!"

"But what have they done to you? Tell me, and don't be cross, don't be rude to me. I'm not making fun of you, don't worry: I don't come from Paris."

"It was grandmother. She told me it would bring me luck, and my leg would get well the same day as hers, and I took good care of her, and gave her all the flies I could catch for her to eat!"

"What are you talking about? Your grandmother eats flies?"

"No, sir, my swallow did. I didn't tell you—you see, the swallow got her leg tangled in some horsehair and feathers, I don't know how, but her leg was broken, and then there was a big lump of mud from her nest that hung from the horsehair on her foot, kept her from flying. I caught her last week and grandmother said: 'That's the kind of bird brings good luck, mind you take care of her, and if she gets well, so will you, you'll be able to do without your crutches the very same day.' I hate it so like this, not being able to jump around, I did what grandmother told me; I cleaned her leg all up, and tied it together with matchsticks. And all the time she didn't feel any better she stayed quiet in her basket and looked at me with her big eyes as if she knew me. And I gave her nice flies all the time, and I only pulled off their heads so's they wouldn't fly away. And grandmother kept on saying: 'That's right, you must be good to animals if you want them to get well. Only a few days more and you'll be well yourself.' And just now she hears that flock of other swallows squalling up there in the steeple, and the mean thing pushes up the lid of her basket, and while I'm busy getting more flies ready for her, she—hee-hee! she —hoo-hoo! she hooked it."

"I know how you feel, my child; you loved your swallow very much."

"Me? What an idea! But she wasn't quite well yet, and now I won't be well myself at all. The others she's gone off with are going to break her leg for her again, I know they will."

"What makes you think the others will do that?"

"Because they're wicked, o' course, like all the birds are. I saw it all right this winter, when it was so cold; I plucked the feathers off a sparrow somebody gave me; I left only his wing and tail feathers; then I let him loose in front of some others. He flew to them, and they all pounced and pecked him to death. I saw it I tell you" (crying) "I never laughed so—hee-hee! And now you see my leg will never get well. Nice for me, isn't it? Oh, if I'd known—boo-hoo! I'd have wrung her neck proper the minute I found her."

You put back into your pocket the book you were holding. Poetry is no longer apropos. You feel angry. You light a cigar and stroll along smoking desperately. You have hardly gone thirty yards before the little girl with the crutches hails you with a "Sir! what about the money for the gingerbread you promised?"

"But you said you didn't like gingerbread!"

"No, but give me the money anyhow."

"I'm sorry; I see I have only a little bit of change—here you are."

You toss the coin to her, she picks it up, waits till you have gone a few steps farther, and then shouts at you: "Go 'long, you old crook! you aristocrat!"

You smoke furiously fast and cross the plain once more, feeling like a fool. You find a seat in the train back to Paris, saying to yourself: "If she'd only called me a crook, or an aristocrat—but *old!* Really! You won't catch me again going to vespers at Montmorency."

And that is why I feel so little inclined, today being Monday, to talk to you about the new comic opera. Yesterday's idyllic excursion has made me groggy. Perhaps tomorrow—"Old crook!" That's what she said. She is only a child.

TUESDAY, JULY 23

It is always depressing to have to bother about comic operas on a Tuesday, if only because Tuesday is the day after Monday. As we decided that the days follow one another but are not alike, it is obvious that if you felt melancholy on Monday, some sort of cheerfulness ought to break in on Tuesday. And we know there is no worse kill-joy, for a writer, than to have to analyze one of these works, unless it be, for a reader, to read that same analysis. And the truth is, I haven't stopped laughing since this morning when I heard what happened last Friday to M. Érard—something the entire district around the Conservatoire is still talking about. You can see it must be something extraordinary to engross public attention for all that length of time. In fact, it is a miracle I am about to relate, a miracle which has meant the undoing of a famous man; but even so, I can't consider it anything but most entertaining. It is bad of me, I know. Can it be that hobnobbing with the children of Montmorency has corrupted me already?

And now for the event in all its inexplicable and terrifying simplicity.

The Conservatoire competition began last week. M. Auber having decided, as the saying goes, to take the bull by the horns, the first day began with the piano students. The dauntless jury summoned to hear the candidates discovered without visible dismay that these numbered thirty-one—eighteen women and thirteen men. The piece chosen for the audition was Mendelssohn's Concerto in G minor; so that unless one of the candidates is struck down with apoplexy during the session, that concerto is going to be played thirty-one times in a row—anybody can see that.

What you perhaps cannot see as yet, and what I myself did not know until a few hours ago, not being intrepid enough to attend the affair, is the thing I was told this morning by one of the attendants at the Conservatoire when I was walking across the courtyard.

"Poor M. Érard!" he said. "What a calamity!"

"Érard—what's happened to him?"

"Why, weren't you at the piano contest?"

"I should say not, tell me about it."

"Well, M. Érard had been very kind and had lent us for that day a superb new piano he'd just finished, one he was going to send to London for the Great Exhibition of 1851. You can tell from this how proud he was of the instrument. A powerful tone —diabolical, in fact; a bass like nothing you have ever heard—an amazing instrument. Its only fault was that the action was a little stiff, but that was one reason he had lent it to us. M. Érard is no fool; he said to himself: 'Those thirty-one students pounding out their concerto will liven up the action; it can't do my piano any harm, it will only improve it.' True enough. But the poor man couldn't foresee the way his keyboard would be livened up. Just think! the same concerto, thirty-one times in succession all on one day! And yet nobody could possibly have foreseen the consequences of all that repetition.

"Well, the first candidate comes forward and, finding the piano a little stiff, puts his back into it to get the tone he wants out of it. The second, ditto. To the third, the piano offers less resistance and still less to the fifth. I can't tell you how the sixth found it, because just as he came on I had to get spirits of ammonia for a gentleman of the jury who had fainted. By the time I was back, the seventh had finished, and I heard him say, as he passed me in the wings: 'That piano isn't as stiff as they say; it seems to me just right.' The next ten or twelve performers were of the same opinion; the last few of them even declared that far from being too stiff to the touch it was too soft.

"At a quarter to three or thereabouts we had reached No. 26, having begun at ten o'clock. It was Mlle Hermance Lévy's turn and she hates a stiff action. Circumstances could not have favored her more, for by this time everybody was complaining that the keyboard hardly needed touching to make it sound. So she whisked through the concerto with such lightness that she won first prize then and there. When I say she won it, I am not being exact: she shared it with Mlle Vidal and Mlle Roux. These two young ladies also benefited from the softness of the action—so soft a softness that the keyboard moved if you merely breathed on it. Who ever saw a piano like that? Well, just as they were about to hear No. 29 I had to go out again and get a doctor: another of our jurymen had become very red in the face and had to be bled at once. A piano competition is no joke; when the doctor arrived it was only just in time.

"As I was crossing the lobby of the hall, I saw No. 29, young Planté, leaving the platform. He was very pale and trembling from head to foot; he said: 'I don't know what's wrong with the piano, but the keys go down all by themselves; you'd think there was someone inside moving the hammers. I'm scared.'

" 'Come, come, young fellow, you're daft,' replied young Cohen, who is three years older than Planté. 'Let me by: I'm not afraid!'

"Cohen (No. 30) comes on, sits down to the piano without looking at the keyboard, and plays his concerto very well. But after the final chord, just as he was leaving his seat, the piano without a word begins the concerto all over again by itself. The poor young chap thought he wasn't scared of anything, but after one petrified moment of staring he bolted out as fast as his legs could carry him.

"From that time on, the piano gets into stride by the minute, plays louder and louder, turning out scales, trills, and arpeggios. Not seeing anyone at the instrument and hearing it make ten times the noise it did before, the public gets really upset; some laugh, others begin to get frightened. All are flabbergasted as you can imagine. One member of the jury who sat at the back of the box and could not see the platform, thought that M. Cohen was playing the concerto a second time, and shouted at the top of his voice: 'That's enough! Be quiet! Send for No. 31, that's the last.' We had to shout to him from the stage: 'Nobody's playing, sir! It's the piano! It's formed the habit of Mendelssohn's concerto and is playing it on its own, to suit itself. Just look and see.'

" 'But this is most improper! Send for M. Érard. Hurry! Perhaps he can control his dreadful instrument!'

"We go after M. Érard. Meanwhile that lawbreaker of a piano, having finished its concerto, starts it again without losing a minute, and with ever-increasing volume. You would have thought it was four dozen pianos in unison, flinging out turns and trills like rockets, tremolos, runs of sixths and thirds in octaves, chords of ten notes, triple trills, a cascade of sound, the loud pedal, the devil and all his train.

"M. Érard arrives; but try as he will, the piano, which is out of its mind, has no intention of minding him either. He sends for holy water and sprinkles the keyboard with it—in vain: proof that it wasn't witchcraft, but the natural result of thirty performances of one concerto. They take the instrument and remove the keyboard, still moving up and down, and throw it into the middle of the courtyard next to the Warehouse.[4] There M. Érard in a fury has it chopped up with an ax. You think that did it? It made matters worse: each piece danced, jumped, frisked about separately—on the paving stones, between our legs, against the wall, in all direc-

---

[4] A state repository for government property.

tions, until the locksmith of the Warehouse picked up this bedeviled mechanism in one armful and flung it into the fire of his
forge to put an end to it. Poor M. Érard! Such a fine instrument!
We were heartbroken, but what could we do? There was no other
way to loose its grip. But after all, how can a piano hear a concerto
thirty times in the same hall on the same day without contracting
the habit of it? M. Mendelssohn won't be able to complain that his
music isn't being played. But think of the damage!"

I shan't add anything to the story you have just heard; it has
all the earmarks of a fantastic tale. Perhaps you won't believe a
word of it; you may even say it is absurd. Now, it is precisely because it is absurd that I believe it, for no Conservatoire attendant
could have invented anything so extravagant.

And now to come to the main topic of this article. Let us not
put off important business till the morrow: it is always very depressing to have to bother about comic operas on a Wednesday:

Diletta ....
.... but .... very .... the music ....
always .... colorless .... platitude.

{ (The author's manuscript is here so illegible that none of our compositors
could read more than this. We therefore have to give in this somewhat incomplete form his criticism of the charming opera *Diletta*.—Note by the
editors.) }

All the musicians in unison: "Outrageous! Unspeakable! Corsino
is right. It is inhuman to be so cruelly reticent. How can a man do
such a thing!"

"But, gentlemen, please! Do you know any of the operas I have
thus struggled not to write about?"

"No."

"No one here knows them?"

"No, no!"

"All right. If I proved to you that they are nonentities more
complete, more absolute, than the one you are so cavalierly per-
mitting yourselves to underplay this evening with a demi-orchestra,
would you still think me too severe?"

"No indeed."

"Then I've made out my case, and Corsino is wrong. For I
solemnly assert that compared with those two scores your new
opera is a masterpiece. After all, before you give a decision from

the bench you must hear both sides. However ailing my critical conscience may be, I do have one, as I said, and it is still alive. But it would surely have died if I had expressed a reasoned opinion, even a severe, ruthless opinion of things of this sort, about which there is artistically nothing to be said, absolutely nothing. Your promptness to condemn me upsets me and hurts my feelings. I thought you felt more kindly toward me. Permit me to go."

"Now, now," says Kleiner the elder, trying to hold me back, "you mustn't let a little thing like that vex you. I have had much worse—"

"No, good-by, gentlemen."

I leave in the middle of the third act.

Don *Giovanni* is being played.

I appear again in the orchestra after several days' absence. I had not intended to come back this evening, but Corsino and a few of his colleagues called on me to express their regret at having hurt my feelings by taxing my criticism with cruelty. They were disarming; I laughed, and followed them to the theater.

The musicians greet me with the utmost cordiality; they want to make me forget my displeasure, which they thought cut deep. But the moment the overture begins, they all stop talking. Mozart's masterpiece, worthily performed by both chorus and orchestra, is listened to religiously.

At the end of the first act Bacon asks me, with nationalistic pride: "What do you think of our baritone Don Giovanni?"

"I think he deserves the Montyon prize." [1]

"And what may that be?" he inquires, turning to Corsino.

CORSINO: It's the prize for virtue.

BACON (*at first taken aback, then feeling much flattered, finally with an air of quiet satisfaction*): Why not? M. K. is a thoroughly good man.

---

[1] Baron Jean Montyon (1733–1820) founded several prizes awarded yearly by the French Academy. One of these, for virtuous behavior, has given his name notoriety and overshadowed his other bequests.

Historical Gleanings:

Napoleon's odd susceptibility—his musical judgment—
Napoleon and Lesueur—Napoleon and the Republic of
San Marino

 A<small>N OPERA</small> is being given, etc., etc., etc.

Everyone is talking. Corsino is telling stories. I turn up just as he begins the following:

On the 9th of February 1807 a grand concert was given at the court of Napoleon. It was a brilliant gathering; Crescentini [1] was to sing. At the appointed time the Emperor is announced. He enters, takes his seat, and is given a program. The music begins, the overture is done, he opens the program, reads it, and, while the first song is being sung, calls out loud for Marshal Duroc, to whom he whispers a few words. The marshal crosses the room, goes up to M. Grégoire who as musical secretary to the Emperor drew up the programs, and says to him with severity: "Monsieur Grégoire, the Emperor bids me tell you that you must not hereafter exercise your wit in your programs."

The unfortunate secretary is dumbfounded, having not the slightest notion of what the marshal means. He hardly dares raise his eyes. In the intermissions, people ask him in a low voice what the rumpus is all about, and the wretched Grégoire, more and more upset, can only repeat again and again: "I don't know any more about it than you do. I don't understand." He expects to be dismissed the next day and is already steeling himself against a disgrace which he thinks inevitable but cannot account for.

The concert over, the Emperor as he goes out leaves his program

---

[1] Girolamo Crescentini (1766–1846), a mezzo-soprano and the last great castrato. Napoleon attached him to his court in 1806, where he remained till 1812. The Emperor's award of the Iron Crown to the singer caused great uproar.

on the chair. Grégoire rushes over to it, seizes it, and reads it through half a dozen times without discovering anything untoward in it. He gives it to Messrs Lesueur, Rigel, Kreutzer, and Baillot [2] to read, but they can find nothing in it either, except what is proper and harmless. The sneers of the musicians were beginning to pour in on the unlucky secretary when a sudden idea gave him the clue to the riddle and redoubled his fears. The program (hand-written according to custom) began with the words:

THE EMPEROR'S MUSIC

Instead of drawing the usual straight line under this title, some whim or other of Grégoire's had led him to draw a series of stars, increasing in size as far as the middle of the page, and decreasing to the other margin. No one could fail to see that Napoleon, then at the height of his glory, would be sure to find in this innocuous ornament an allusion to his past, present, and future fortunes, an allusion as distasteful to him as insolent on the part of any prophet of doom who might make it with design, since it implied, by means of the two tiny stars at each end and the huge one in the center, that the Imperial star, till then so brilliant, was to decline by degrees, diminish, and be blotted out in the reverse manner of its rise to the present. Time has shown all too well that it was to be so. But had the great man's genius already revealed to him what was in store? This odd susceptibility of his would lead one to believe so.

Here, gentlemen, is the copy of the program that nearly brought about the ruin of the worthy musical secretary. Grégoire himself, when he told me his adventure, made me a present of it. You will note incidentally that the secretary of the Emperor's Music did not know how to spell Guglielmi.[3]

---

[2] Composers and performers of the Imperial Chapel. Rigel was court pianist, and Baillot a virtuoso violinist. See below, p. 244 and note.

[3] Pietro Guglielmi (1727–1804), prolific composer of operas, which were produced chiefly in Italy in competition with Paisiello and Cimarosa.

THE EMPEROR'S MUSIC

*   *   *   *   ✸   *   *   *   *

GRAND CONCERT
French and Italian

———◆●◆———

MONDAY, FEBRUARY 9, 1807

OVERTURE TO *The Twins*	Guillelmi
1. ARIA FROM *Romeo and Juliet* MME DURET	Zingarelli
2. ARIA FROM *The Horatii*	Cimarosa
3. ARIA MME BARILLI	Crescentini
4. DUET FROM *Cleopatra* MME BARILLI AND M. CRESCENTINI	Nazolini
5. ARIA, WITH CHORUS M. LAYS	Jadin
6. DUET FROM *The Rustic Prima Donnas* MME AND M. BARILLI	Fioravanti
7. GRAND FINALE FROM *King Theodore in Venice*	Paisiello

"You can readily guess that Grégoire, who gradually got over his fear of being dismissed, took care not to ornament the programs of later concerts with the slightest design or symbolic vignette. It was as much as he dared to put the dots on the *i's*. The lesson had been rough: he was scared of being witty unwittingly.

On another occasion Napoleon showed a feeling for music that he was perhaps not generally credited with. A concert had been arranged for a *soirée* at the Tuileries. Of the six numbers on the program, No. 3 was by Paisiello. The singer of this aria felt indisposed at the rehearsal and was unable to perform at the concert. It became necessary to substitute another aria by the same composer, the Emperor having always shown a marked preference for Paisiello's music. This being no easy matter, Grégoire conceived the idea of substituting an aria by Generali and boldly attributing it to Paisiello. Between ourselves, Mr. Secretary, you were taking a very great liberty—nothing more nor less than hoaxing the Emperor. But perhaps this time it was daring that you showed unwittingly. Be this as it may, the illustrious dilettante, greatly to the surprise of the musicians, was not taken in by this bit of deception. No. 3 had hardly begun when the Emperor, making the usual sign with his hand, stopped the concert.

"M. Lesueur, this piece is not by Paisiello."

"I beg Your Majesty's pardon; it is by him, is it not so, Grégoire?"

"Yes, Your Majesty, certainly."

"Gentlemen, there is some mistake here. Be good enough to begin again."

At the end of twenty bars the Emperor interrupts the singer a second time: "No, no, it is impossible, Paisiello has more brains than that."

Grégoire, with a meek holier-than-thou expression, says: "It is likely a work of his youth, a mere essay."

"My dear sirs," rejoins Napoleon sharply, "the essays of a great master like Paisiello always bear the stamp of genius and are never below mediocrity like the piece you have just made me listen to."

We have had in France since that time many managers, directors, and patrons of the fine arts, but I doubt whether they have ever shown this purity of taste in the musical doings with which, for the sins of artists and composers, they have been concerned. Many of them, on the contrary, have furnished endless proof of their ability to take the music of Mozart and Beethoven for that of Pucita and Gaveaux, and vice versa.

And yet it remains a fact that Napoleon had never learned music.

MYSELF: Since we are telling stories about the great Emperor this evening, here is another which shows that he knew exceedingly well how to honor the artists whose works appealed to him. Lesueur, whose name Corsino mentioned awhile ago, and who was for a long time Superintendent of the Imperial Chapel, had just produced his opera *The Bards*. In such a subject the strange melodies, antique coloring, and solemn harmonies of Lesueur were thoroughly justified.

Napoleon's predilection for the poems of Macpherson (attributed to Ossian) is common knowledge, and the musician who had just given them a new life was therefore bound to reap his reward. At one of the early performances of *The Bards* the delighted Emperor summoned him to his box after the third act and said to him: "Lesueur, this music is entirely new to me, and very fine it is; your second act especially is *unapproachable*."

Deeply touched by this approval and by the shouts and applause that came from all over the house, Lesueur was about to withdraw; but Napoleon, taking him by the hand, led him to the front of the box and, placing himself beside him, said: "No, no, stay; enjoy your triumph; one doesn't often have the chance."

Surely, in doing him justice in so glorious a fashion, Napoleon did not make an ungrateful subject. Never did the admiring devotion of any Imperial Guardsman surpass the worship that the composer professed for the Emperor to the end of his days. He could not speak of him with composure.[4] I recollect that one day, returning from the Academy, where he had heard Victor Hugo's famous *Orientale* entiled "He" violently criticized, he begged me to recite it to him. His agitation and amazement on hearing those beautiful lines are not to be described; at the following stanza:

> *What greatness in him when, his power gone,*
> *The sport of English jailers, he again*
> *Keeps the earth breathless at his step, renews*
> *His virtue in the sacrament of pain,*
> *And from the rocky cage his captors use,*
> *Sees death creep upward like an island dawn!* [5]

---

[4] Berlioz knew this at first hand. He had been a student of Lesueur's and remained his grateful disciple.

[5] *Qu'il est grand là surtout, quand, puissance brisée,/Des porte-clefs anglais misérable risée,/Au sacre du malheur il retrempe ses droits,/Tient au bruit de ses pas deux mondes en haleine,/Et mourant de l'exil, gêné dans Sainte-Hélène,/Manque d'air dans la cage où l'exposent les rois.—Les Orientales*, No. 40, December 1828.

he could not bear it any longer; he asked me to stop, he was sobbing.

DIMSKY: Wasn't it for this opera that Napoleon sent Lesueur a gold box with an inscription? I've heard something to that effect.

MYSELF: Yes, the costly box, which I was shown, bears the inscription:

THE EMPEROR OF THE FRENCH TO THE AUTHOR
OF THE BARDS

CORSINO: Enough to make any artist dizzy! What a man! That was in the grand manner. But how graciously delicate he could also be on occasion, and how well he knew how to blend banter with kindness! My brother, who served in the French army during the first Italian campaign, told me how Bonaparte "recognized," without a smile, the independence of the Republic of San Marino. On seeing, perched on its rock, the capital of that Free State, he asked: "What village is that?"

"General, it is the Republic of San Marino."

"Indeed? Well, let no one trouble these good republicans. Go and tell them from me that France recognizes their independence and begs them to accept two field guns as a token of friendship —and that I wish them good-day."

The Study of Music

The Charity Children at St. Paul's in London
a chorus of 6,500 voices

The Crystal Palace at Seven in the Morning
the Chapel of the Emperor of Russia

England's Musical Institutions
the Chinese singers and instrumentalists in London—the Hindus; the Highlanders—the blackamoors of the streets

 THERE is being given etc., etc., etc.

On seeing me, four or five musicians question me about what I must have seen in England last year—the Charity Children, the Hindus, the Highlanders, the blackamoors singing in the streets, the Chinese at the Albert Gate and those aboard the junk.

"None of us here," says Moran, "has come across any earwitness of these musical oddities of which we've heard so much. We know you were in London in 1851 by order of the French Government, acting as juryman at the Great Exhibition;[1] you must have seen and heard everything. Tell us the long and the short of it; we are all ears."

"Very kind of you, gentlemen, but it's a long story, and—"

"We have four acts tonight."

"Four acts!—"

---

[1] To pass upon the merits of musical instruments. Part of Berlioz's report is reprinted in his book *Les Grotesques de la musique* (1859).

"Not counting the ballet."
"Lord help us! In that case, I'll begin.

I was in London during the early part of June last year, when a scrap of newspaper that came accidentally into my hands informed me that the *Anniversary Meeting of the Charity Children* was about to take place in St. Paul's. I went at once in search of a ticket, which, after many applications and letters, I ended by securing through the courtesy of Mr. Goss,[2] chief organist of that cathedral. By ten o'clock in the morning the crowd had blocked the approach to the church. I managed, with some little trouble, to force my way through it. On reaching the organ loft reserved for the regular choir of seventy men and boys, I was given a bass part, which I was requested to sing with them, and a surplice, which I had to put on in order not to destroy, with my black frock-coat, the harmony of the other choristers' white garb.

Thus disguised as a churchman, I awaited what I was to hear with a certain vague emotion brought on by what I saw. Nine very steep stands, each numbering sixteen rows of benches, had been erected for the children in the center of the building, under the dome and under the eastern vaulting in front of the choir stalls. The six stands under the dome formed together a sort of six-sided enclosure, with openings to the east and west only. From the latter opening rose a broad ramp of seats extending to the top of the principal entrance door, and already occupied by a huge crowd, which could thus, even from the most distant benches, hear and see everything perfectly.

To the left of the gallery where we stood in front of the organ, a platform was in readiness for seven or eight trumpeters and kettledrummers. On this platform a large mirror had been placed, so as to show the musicians the movements of the precentor beating time far away in his corner, under the dome but over the entire choral mass. This mirror also served the organist, whose back was turned to the choir. Banners affixed all round the vast amphitheater, whose sixteenth and last row almost touched the capitals of the columns, marked the places to be occupied by the various schools,

---

[2] Later Sir John (1800–80). The meetings of the Charity Children began in 1704, and first took place in St. Paul's in 1789.

and bore the names of the parishes or districts of London to which these schools belonged.

As the groups of children filed in, the compartments filling up successively from top to bottom presented an unusual spectacle which suggested what occurs in the micoscropic world during the phenomenon of crystallization. The shafts of this crystal made up of human molecules that continually proceeded from the circumference to the center, were of two colors: the dark-blue coats of the small boys on the upper tiers, and the white gowns and caps of the little girls in the lower rows. Moreover, as the boys wore on their jackets, some a plaque of polished copper, others a silver medal, their motions made the light reflected from these metallic ornaments glitter in such a way as to produce the effect of a thousand sparks flashing and blotted out every moment on the dark background of the picture. The appearance of the stands occupied by the girls was still more strange; the green and pink ribbons adorning the head and neck of these little maids in white made that part of the amphitheaters look like a mountain covered with snow, but streaked with blades of grass and flowers here and there.

Add to this the variegated tints melting in the distant chiaroscuro of the sloping platform on which the audience sat, the red-hung pulpit of the Archbishop of Canterbury, the richly ornamented benches of the Lord Mayor and the British peerage on the floor below the dome, then at the farther end, high up, the gilded pipes of the great organ—imagine this magnificent church of St. Paul's, the largest in the world after St. Peter's, framing the entire scene, and you will still have but a poor idea of this incomparable spectacle. And everywhere perfect order, quiet, and calm, which enhanced still farther the magic of the scene. The most wonderful stage-setting imaginable could never approach this reality which, as it now seems to me, I must have seen in a dream.

As the children, dressed in their new clothes, gradually took their seats with a sober joy devoid of any turbulence, but in which, rather, some little pride was discernible, I could hear my English neighbors say among themselves: "What a sight! What a sight!" And deep was my emotion when the six thousand five hundred little singers were at last seated and the ceremony began.

After a chord on the organ, there arose in a gigantic unison the first psalm sung by this incredible choir:

All people that on earth do dwell,
Sing to the Lord with cheerful voice.

It would be useless for me to try to give you an idea of the musical effect; the strength and beauty were to those of the best choirs you have ever heard as St. Paul's itself is to a village church, and then a hundred times more. I must add that this broad and grand hymn is set to superb harmonies, with which the organ flooded it without ever succeeding in drowning it out. I was agreeably surprised to learn that the melody, long attributed to Luther, is by Claude Goudimel, a choirmaster at Lyon in the sixteenth century.[3]

In spite of the feeling of oppression and the tremor I was experiencing, I managed to control them sufficiently to be able to take a part in the "reading psalms," which the regular St. Paul's choir had to perform next. Boyce's *Te Deum*, written in 1760, a featureless work also sung by the choir, finally restored my equanimity. In the Coronation Anthem the children joined the small organ choir from time to time, but only with solemn ejaculations such as "God save the King!" "Long live the King!" "May the King live for ever!" "Amen, hallelujah!" and again I was electrified. I had to count many rests, in spite of the kind attentions of my neighbor, who kept pointing out to me in his part the bar we had reached, in the belief that I had lost my place. But when we came to the psalm in triple time by Joseph Ganthony, an old English master (1774) sung by all the voices to the accompaniment of trumpets, kettledrums, and organ—nature, under the shattering effect of this inspired and glowing hymn, so grand in its harmony and of an expression as noble as it is touching—nature reasserted her right to be weak, and I had to make use of my vocal score as Agamemnon did of his toga, to veil my face.

Following this sublime piece, and while the Archbishop of Canterbury was delivering his sermon—which the distance prevented me from hearing—one of the masters of ceremonies sought me out and led me, my face wet with tears, to various places of the church, so that I might gaze upon all aspects of a scene which the eye could not take in from any single point of vantage nor ap-

---

[3] The "Old Hundred" (or "Hundredth") is a tune from the Genevan Psalter, and its authorship has long been in dispute. Goudimel's claims now seem finally disallowed.

preciate in all its grandeur. He then left me alone below, near the pulpit, among the fashionable world—that is to say, at the bottom of the crater of the vocal volcano; so that when the eruption began again for the final psalm, I had to admit that here its power was twice as great as in any other part of the church. In going out I met old Cramer,[4] who in his enthusiasm forgot that he knows French to perfection and began shouting at me in Italian: *"Cosa stupenda! stupenda! la gloria dell'Inghilterra!"*

And then Duprez,[5] the great artist who in the course of his brilliant career has moved the hearts of so many, found many outstanding debts paid back to him that day—debts owed him by France and paid him by these English children.[6] I have never seen Duprez in such a state; he stammered, wept, and rambled, the while the Turkish Ambassador and a handsome young Hindu passed close by us, cold and sad, as if they had just heard their dancing dervishes howling in a mosque. O sons of the East, you lack one of the senses of man. Will you ever acquire it? . . .

Now for a few technical particulars. This institution of the Charity Children was founded by George III in 1764. It is supported by the voluntary donations or subscriptions of the rich or even ordinary well-to-do classes of the capital. The profits derived from the Anniversary Meeting in St. Paul's, tickets for which are sold at half a crown and half a guinea, belong to it also. Although all the seats reserved to the public on this occasion are sold out a long time ahead, the space taken up by so many children means that a large part of the church has to be sacrificed to the admirable arrangements I have described, and this naturally cuts into the financial returns of the ceremony. The expenses, moreover, are quite high: the erection of the nine amphitheaters and of the ramp alone costs £450 ($2,250). The receipts generally amount to £800 ($4,000). Hence there remain at most but £350 ($1,750)

---

[4] J. B. Cramer (1771–1858), the famous pianist admired by Beethoven, and senior partner in the music-publishing firm of Cramer and Beale, who strongly supported all Berlioz's musical activities in London. Cramer's words below read: "A stupendous thing! stupendous! the glory of England!"

[5] Gilbert Duprez (1806–96), a famous French tenor.

[6] In the recently published letters of George Eliot, one hears a delayed echo of this event, a year later: "On Thursday morning I went to St. Paul's to see the Charity Children assembled and hear their singing. Berlioz says it is the finest thing he has heard in England and this opinion of his induced me to go. I was not disappointed—it is worth doing once, especially as we got out before the sermon." —To Mr. and Mrs. Charles Bray, June 5, 1852.

for the 6,500 poor youngsters who give such a festival to their mother city. The voluntary donations, however, always amount to a considerable sum.

The children have no knowledge of music; they have never seen a note in their lives. Every year they are made to parrot, by ceaseless repetition on the violin for three whole months, the hymns and anthems they are to sing at the Meeting. They thus learn them by heart, and consequently bring to the church no notes or anything else to guide their singing, which is why they sing only in unison. Their voices are beautiful, but of narrow range. Hence they are generally given only phrases that lie within the interval of an eleventh, from the lower B to the E on the fourth space (G clef). All these notes, which are virtually common to the soprano, mezzosoprano, and contralto, and are consequently to be found in all the children, have a marvelous sonority. It is doubtful whether the children could be made to sing in several parts. In spite of the extreme simplicity and breadth of the melodies there is, to the musical ear, nothing like a faultless ensemble in the attacks after the pauses. This is due to the fact that the children do not know the meaning of beats in a bar and do not dream of counting them. Besides, their sole conductor stands high above the choir, where he can readily be seen only by the higher ranks of the three tiers facing him; he does hardly more than indicate the beginning of each piece, the majority of the singers being unable to see him, and the rest seldom deigning to look at him.

The amazing effect of the unison is due, in my opinion, to two causes: to the enormous number and good quality of the voices in the first instance, and secondly to the disposition of the singers in very high tiers. The reflectors and producers of sound are thus nicely balanced. The air within the church is struck from so many points at once, in surface and in depth, that it vibrates as a whole and its disturbance develops a power and majesty of action on the human nervous system which the most learned efforts of musical art under ordinary conditions have so far not given us any notion of. I may add, as a mere conjecture, that under exceptional circumstances such as these there must occur a good many as yet uncharted phenomena having to do with the mysterious laws of electricity.

I wonder also whether the cause of the notable difference between the voices of the children reared by charity in London and those of our poor children in Paris may not be due to the good and plentiful food given to the former, while the food the latter get is insufficient and of low quality. This seems very likely. These English children are strong, with solid muscle, and not in the least like the sickly and debilitated young of the working classes in Paris, who are themselves run down by malnutrition, hard work, and privations. It is quite natural that the vocal organs of our children should reflect the weakness of the rest of the organism, and that even their intelligence is affected by it.

At any rate it is not the voices alone that would be lacking today to reveal to Paris, with the same amazing effect, the sublimity of *monumental* music. What would be lacking in the first place is the cathedral of gigantic proportions (the Church of Notre-Dame itself would not be suitable); next, alas, would be the artistic faith, a direct and passionate drive toward art; then the patience and calm discipline of pupils and artists; the conscious will, if not of the government, at least of the wealthy classes, to attain the goal after having perceived the beauty of it; and as a consequence, finally, the money would not be forthcoming and the undertaking would totter on its base. We need only recall—to compare small things with great—the sad end of Choron,[7] who with his slender resources had already obtained such important results in his school for choral music, and who died of grief when, *for the sake of economy*, the July Monarchy cut off his subsidy.

And yet by means of three or four institutions which could easily be established in France, nothing would prevent our giving in Paris after a certain number of years a parallel to the English music festival, on a small but perfected scale. We have no St. Paul's, true; but we have the Pantheon, which affords, if not the size, at least a similar internal structure. The number of performers and audience would be less huge; but the edifice being also less vast the effect might still be most unusual.

Supposing that the ramp from the top of the central door of the Pantheon could hold no more than five thousand, it would still make a respectable gathering, and would, as I think, suffice to seat all those in Paris who possess an understanding of, and a feeling

---

[7] See above note 3, p. 194.

for, art. Suppose next that instead of 6,500 ignorant children, we had in the amphitheater 1,500 young *musicians*, 500 musical women with real voices, and 2,000 men singers sufficiently equipped by nature and training. Suppose further that instead of allotting the central space of the hexagon under the dome to the public, we placed there a little orchestra of three or four hundred instrumentalists, and entrusted to that well-trained mass of 4,300 musicians the performance of a fine work, written in a style suited to such means, on a subject in which grandeur blends with nobility, and in which one is stirred by the expression of all the elevated thoughts that can move the heart of man: I believe that such a manifestation of the most powerful of the arts, aided by the magic of poetry and architecture, would be truly worthy of a nation like ours and would leave far behind the vaunted festivals of antiquity.

With exclusively French resources such a festival would be possible within ten years; Paris has only to will it so. Meanwhile, relying solely on the first rudiments of music, the English do will it and do do it. A great people, which still has an instinct for what is great! The soul of Shakespeare survives in it!

On leaving St. Paul's for the first time after witnessing this function, and being in a state of semi-intoxication which you can now conceive, I let myself be led, without quite knowing why, to a Thames boat, where for twenty minutes I was pelted by a driving rain. Returning home on foot and soaked through from Chelsea, where I had no business to keep me, I tried to go to sleep. But on nights that follow days like that one I am a stranger to sleep. I kept hearing in my mind the harmonious clamor of "All people that on earth do dwell." I saw St. Paul's spinning around me; I was again inside it and saw it now weirdly transformed into a pandemonium; the scene was that of Martin's famous painting.[8] Instead of the Archbishop in his pulpit, I saw Satan on his throne; instead of the thousands of worshippers and children grouped about him, hosts of demons and damned souls darted their fiery glances from the bosom of a visible darkness; and the iron amphitheater in which these millions sat vibrated as one mass in a terrible fashion, emitting hideous harmonies.

Worn out at last by the persistence of these hallucinations, I

---

[8] Presumably John Martin (1789–1854), who illustrated Milton and painted apocalyptic scenes.

made up my mind, though it was hardly daybreak, to go out and stroll toward the palace of the Exhibition, where my duties as juryman required my presence in a few hours. London was still asleep; none of the Sarahs, Marys, and Kates who wash the door-steps every morning were as yet on hand with their mops. A gin-soaked old Irishwoman was squatting by herself in a corner of Manchester Square, smoking her pipe. Cows lying in the thick grass of Hyde Park were leisurely chewing the cud. The little three-master, the plaything of that nation of mariners, was swaying sleepily on the waters of the Serpentine. A few fan-shaped rays were already beginning to shine, reflected from the upper panes of the palace that is open to all people that on earth do dwell.

The guard that keeps watch at the gates of this Louvre,[9] accustomed to seeing me at all sorts of unearthly hours, let me pass and I went in. The deserted interior of this crystal palace was an unusual sight and not without grandeur, even at seven in the morning: a vast solitude, soft gleams of light falling from the transparent top, stilled fountains, silent organs, motionless trees, and a harmonious display of rich products brought there from all corners of the globe by a hundred rival nations. All this ingenious handi-work, the fruits of peace, and the instruments of destruction recalling war, all these causes of movement and noise seemed, in the absence of man, to talk mysteriously among themselves in the unknown tongue heard by the mind's ear.

I was getting ready to listen to their secret dialogue, thinking myself alone in the palace, but actually there were three of us—a Chinaman, a sparrow, and myself. The strung lids of the Asiatic had opened betimes, it would seem; or perhaps, like mine, they had not closed. With a feather duster he was carefully dusting his beautiful china vases, his hideous idols, his lacquers and silks. Next I saw him take a watering-pot, fill it with water from the basin of the glass fountain, and return to quench tenderly the thirst of a poor flower, no doubt Chinese, that was drooping in a mean European vase.

After this he went and sat down a few steps from his shop, looked at the gongs hanging inside, and he sketched a motion as if about to strike them. But he reflected that he had neither friends nor brothers to awaken, and he let drop the hand that would have

---

[9] For this allusion, see above, note 9, p. 49.

held the hammer and sighed. "*Dulces reminiscitur Argos*," [1] said I to myself. Assuming my most courteous manner, I go up to him, and presuming that he knows English, I wish him a "Good morning, sir," so full of good nature that he could not mistake it. My man's only answer is to rise, turn his back on me, open a cupboard, and take out some sandwiches, which he proceeds to munch without glancing at me, though with a certain air of contempt for such barbarian food. Then he sighs once more—he is evidently thinking of the succulent sharks' fins fried in castor oil to which he used to treat himself in his own country, of the swallows'-nest soup, and the famous wood-louse jam they make so well in Canton. Ugh! The thoughts of this uncivil epicure give me a turn and I walk off.

Passing close to a big 48-gun, cast in Seville, that seemed, when looking at Sax's [2] counter adjoining it, to defy him to make a brass instrument of equal bore and volume, I scare a sparrow hidden in the mouth of the Spanish monster. "Poor little survivor of the massacre of the innocents, don't be alarmed, I am not going to tell on you. On the contrary, take this—" and drawing from my pocket a bit of cracker that the master of ceremonies at St. Paul's had pressed upon me the previous day, I crumble it on the floor. While the Crystal Palace was being built, a tribe of sparrows had taken up its residence in one of the big trees that now adorn the transept. It insisted on remaining there in spite of the threatening progress of the workmen's efforts. How indeed should the birds believe that they could be caught in such a huge glass cage and its iron framework? When they discovered that it could happen their surprise was great. They sought a way out, fluttering in every direction. Since it was feared that they might cause damage to some of the delicate objects on exhibit, their extermination was decided upon and carried out with pea-shooters, twenty kinds of traps, and the deadly nux vomica. The sparrow whose retreat I had discovered, and which took care not to betray, was the sole survivor. He is, I said to myself, the Joash of his people, [3]

And saved by me from Athaliah's wrath.

---

[1] "He recalls his sweet homeland."—*Æneid* (X, 782).
[2] Adolphe Sax (1814–94), the famous manufacturer of wind instruments, inventor of the saxophone, saxhorns, etc.
[3] An allusion to the plot of Racine's *Athalie*.

As I uttered this remarkable verse, improvised (also by me) on the spot, a noise rather like that of rain spread through the huge galleries; it was the fountains just let loose by their keepers. The crystal castles and artificial rocks rang under the shower of liquid pearls. The policemen, those unarmed gendarmes whom all respect so justly, were returning to their posts. M. Ducroquet's young helper was making his way to his master's organ, thinking over the new polka to which he was about to treat us; the ingenious manufacturers of Lyon were giving the last touches to their admirable display; the diamonds, wisely hidden during the night, once more sparkled in their showcases; the big Irish bell in D-flat minor, enthroned in the east gallery, persisted in sounding one, two, three, four, five, six, seven, eight strokes, quite proud of not resembling its sister in the church in Albany Street, which gives out a major third. Silence had kept me awake, these noises made me drowsy; the need of sleep became irresistible; I took a seat in front of Érard's grand piano, that musical marvel of the Exhibition; I leaned on my elbow on its sumptuous lid, and I was about to fall asleep, when Thalberg,[4] grasping my shoulder, said: "Now, colleague, the jury is assembling. Up with you! Summon your strength, for today we pass upon thirty-two musical snuffboxes, twenty-four accordions, and thirteen bombardons."

The musicians seem to be interested in my story: they remain silent and apparently expect me to continue.

The only thing to which I can compare the effect of the gigantic unison of the children at St. Paul's is the beautiful religious harmonizations written by Bortniansky[5] for the Imperial Russian Chapel, and given in St. Petersburg by the singers of the court with a perfection of ensemble, a delicacy of shading, and a beauty of tone of which you cannot form any idea. But instead of being the power resulting from a mass of uncultivated voices, it is a product of uncommon art; it is the result of painstaking and unremitting practice by a body of picked choristers.

---

[4] Sigismond Thalberg (1812–71), piano virtuoso and composer.
[5] Dmitri Bortniansky (1751–1825), Russian composer with whose works Berlioz became acquainted on his first trip to St. Petersburg in 1847. See below, pp. 239–400.

The choir of the Emperor of Russia's chapel is composed of eighty singers, men and boys. They perform works in four, six, and eight real parts, some of a rather lively turn and complicated with all the artifices of the fugal style, others calm and seraphic in expression and taken in an extremely slow tempo which calls for unusual voice-control and practice in sustaining it. The chapel appears to me superior to anything of the kind that we have in Europe. It includes basses of a depth unknown in our climes, going down to the low A below the staff of the F clef. To compare the choral singing of the Sistine Chapel in Rome with that of these marvelous singers is to compare the wretched little troupe of fiddle-scrapers in a third-rate Italian theater with the orchestra of the Paris Conservatoire.

The effect of this Russian choir and its music on nervous temperaments is irresistible. Under the impact of these unheard-of expressive accents one is seized by almost painful spasmodic movements that are beyond one's control. I have on several occasions tried by a determined effort of will-power to remain calm, but without success.

The ritual of the Orthodox Church forbids the use of musical instruments, including the organ, in the churches; the Russian choristers consequently sing without accompaniment. Those of the Emperor have actually achieved the further feat of dispensing with a conductor to beat time for them. Her Imperial Highness the Grand Duchess of Leuchtenberg having one day in St. Petersburg done me the honor of inviting me to hear a Mass sung specially for me in the chapel of the Palace, I was able to judge with what amazing self-assurance these choristers thus left to their own devices pass abruptly from one key to another, from a slow to a brisk tempo, and even sing recitatives and unmeasured psalmody with the same unshakable ensemble.

The eighty singers in their rich costume stood facing each other in two equal groups on either side of the altar. The basses were farthest from the center; in front of them were the tenors, and in front of these again the child sopranos and contraltos. Motionless, with downcast eyes, they all waited in profound silence for the time to begin, and at a sign doubtless made by one of the leading singers—imperceptible, however, to the spectator—and without anyone's having given the pitch or indicated the tempo, they intoned one of Bortniansky's biggest eight-part concertos. In this harmonic web there were complications of part-writing that seemed impossible, there were sighs, vague murmurs such as one sometimes hears in dreams, and from time to time accents that in their intensity resembled cries, gripping the heart unawares, oppressing the breast, and catching the breath. Then it all died away in an incommensurable, misty, celestial decrescendo; one would have said it was a choir of angels rising from the earth and gradually vanishing into the empyrean. Fortunately the Grand Duchess did not say a word to me on that day, for in the state of mind I was in at the end of the ceremony, it is likely that I would have seemed uncommonly stupid to Her Highness.

Dmitri Stepanovich Bortniansky, born in 1751 at Glukhov, was forty-five years of age when after a rather prolonged stay in Italy he returned to St. Petersburg and was appointed director of the Imperial Chapel. The choir, which had been in existence from the time of the reign of Czar Alexis Michailovich, still left a good deal to be desired when Bortniansky took charge of it. An able man, he devoted himself wholly to his new task, made every effort to perfect the workings of this worthy institution, and to attain this object confined himself mostly to the composition of religious works. He set to music forty-five psalms in four and eight parts, besides a Mass in three parts and a large number of separate pieces. In all these works true religious feeling obtains, which frequently becomes a kind of mysticism that plunges the hearer into a profound ecstasy. He shows rare skill in the grouping of vocal masses, a miraculous sense of nuance and resonant harmony, and—still more surprising—an incredible freedom in the handling of the parts, a sovereign contempt for the rules respected by both his predecessors and his contemporaries, especially by the Italians whose disciple he is supposed to be.

He died on September 28, 1825, at the age of seventy-four. After him the direction of the chapel was entrusted to Privy Councilor Lvov, a man of exquisite taste and possessed of a wide practical knowledge of the masterworks of all schools. An intimate friend and one of the most fervent admirers of Bortniansky, he deemed it his duty to follow scrupulously in his footsteps. The Imperial Chapel had become a splendid and remarkable institution by 1836 when, after the death of Councilor Lvov, his son, General Alexis Lvov, was appointed its director.

Most connoisseurs of string-quartet music and all the great violinists of Europe know this eminent musician, who is both virtuoso and composer. His talent as a violinist is remarkable, and his latest work, which I heard in St. Petersburg four years ago, the opera *Ondine*, which has just been translated into French by M. de Saint-Georges,[6] contains beauties of the highest order: it is a fresh, lively, youthful, and charmingly original work.

Ever since he became director of the Imperial Chapel, General Lvov has carried forward his predecessors' work as regards the perfecting of execution, while also applying himself to extending the already rich repertory of the chapel. This he has done both by composing religious music of his own and by engaging in fruitful scholarly research in the musical archives of the Russian Church, thanks to which he has made several discoveries of great importance to the history of music.

Choral music has carried us a long way, gentlemen, but I could not let go unnoticed so important a fact as the perfection of performance attained by the singers of the Russian Emperor. The thought of them naturally occurred to my mind as the antithesis of the English children at St. Paul's.

Now to come back to London, and before I describe the music of the Chinese, Hindus, and Highlanders that I heard there, I must tell you that England—as is insufficiently recognized on the Continent—has witnessed during the last few years the creation of some very important institutions in which music is not an object of financial speculation as in the opera houses, but rather an object of cultivation on the grand scale, with ability, attention, and genuine love. Such are the Sacred Harmonic Society[7] and the London Sacred Harmonic Society,[8] both in London, and the Philharmonics of Manchester and Liverpool. The two London societies, which give oratorios in the huge Exeter Hall, number nearly six hundred choristers. The voices are not of the finest, it is true, though they

---

[6] Jules Henri Vernoy, Marquis de Saint-Georges (1801–75), the prolific librettist referred to above (p. 205) and parodied in the "analysis" of *The Lighthouse*.
[7] Founded 1832.
[8] An offshoot of the former (1848–56).

seemed to me far superior to the Parisian voices properly so called; but their massiveness produces an imposing and essentially musical effect. These singers, after all, are capable of correctly performing the complex works of Handel and Mendelssohn, which are so often dangerous as regards intonation—in other words, the most difficult choral music there is. The orchestra that accompanies them is inadequate in numbers only, given the generally simple instrumentation of oratorios; it leaves little to be desired in other respects. It was this well-trained group of amateurs, supported by a few professionals, that gave the magnificent sacred poem *Elijah*, Mendelssohn's last work, when I heard it performed at Exeter Hall before two thousand deeply attentive listeners.

Between such institutions and those that have enabled our Parisian workmen to sing publicly once a year some wretched program of old warhorses, there is an abyss. So far I have had no chance to judge the worth of the Liverpool Society.[9] The one in Manchester, led at the present moment by Charles Hallé,[1] that model pianist, that musician "without fear and without reproach," is perhaps superior to the London societies, if impartial judges are to be believed. At all events the beauty of the voices there is very remarkable, the musical sense very keen, the orchestra large and well trained.

As for the enthusiasm of the dilettanti, it is such that four hundred would-be subscribers on the waiting list pay half a guinea simply for the right to buy a ticket when one becomes available through the absence or illness—which is very rare—of some regular subscriber. With such zeal to support it a musical institution is bound to prosper no matter how heavy the expenses. Music makes herself beautiful and charming for those who love and respect her; she has nothing but scorn and contempt for those who sell her. That is why she is so bad-tempered, so insolent, and so stupid nowadays in most of the great theaters of Europe, which are sunk in speculative finance, and where she is accordingly treated like dirt.

Among other musical institutions of London I must also mention the Old Philharmonic Society of Hanover Square, which has been famous for too long a time to need comment from me.

---

[9] Founded in 1840, active from 1849.
[1] Now the Hallé Orchestra.

As to the New Philharmonic Society, recently founded at Exeter Hall, where it has had a brilliant career, you readily understand why I must confine myself to a few purely statistical details: in my capacity as conductor of that Society it would ill become me to sing its praises. I will only say that the directors of the Society have given me the means of performing the great works in noble style, and the possibility, hitherto almost unexampled in England, of holding enough rehearsals. Orchestra and chorus together number two hundred and thirty, among whom are to be found the best English and foreign artists in London. All of them combine acknowledged talent with energy, zeal, and the love of art, qualities without which the most genuine talents usually turn out only average results.

There are also in London several quartet and chamber-music societies, the most flourishing of which at present bears the name of Musical Union.[2] It was founded by Mr. Ella, a distinguished English musician, who directs it with a care, intelligence, and devotion beyond all praise. The object of the Musical Union is to popularize not solely the taste for quartets, but the taste for all good instrumental chamber music, with the occasional addition of a song or two, almost always of the German school. Although himself a talented violinist, Mr. Ella is modest enough to content himself with being the organizer and director of these concerts, without taking any part as performer. He prefers to bring the most able virtuosos in London together with the foreigners of high renown who may be passing through, and thus it is that this year he has been able to unite with Messrs Oury and Piatti: Léonard, Vieuxtemps, Mlle Clauss, Mme Pleyel, Sivory, and Bottesini. The public is well satisfied with a system that brings it both superior performance and a variety of style not to be obtained from one and the same group of virtuosos.

It is not only to the performance of the masterpieces offered at his concerts that Mr. Ella gives his attention; he also wants the public to develop a taste for and an understanding of them. So the program of every matinee, which is sent in advance to the subscribers, contains a synoptic analysis of the trios, quartets, and quintets to be performed. These analyses are generally very good.

---

[2] Founded in 1844. John Ella (1802–88), well known as a violinist, was the initiator of analytical program notes, as shown below.

They speak at once to the eyes and to the mind through the use of musical quotations on one or more staffs, showing either the theme of each movement, a phrase or figure that plays an important part in it, or the remarkable harmonies or modulations that deserve notice. Thoughtfulness and zeal could go no further. As a motto on his programs, Mr. Ella prints the following words in French, the truth and sound sense of which are unfortunately not much appreciated in our own country; they were originally uttered by the learned Baillot: *"Il ne suffit pas que l'artiste soit bien préparé pour le public; il faut aussi que le public le soit à ce qu'on va lui faire entendre."* [3]

O ye sad composers of dramatic music, if you possess both genius and soul, go and put your trust in listeners who prepare themselves to hear your works by stuffing on truffles and champagne and who go to the Opéra to digest—poor Baillot was dreaming!

It remains for me to say a word to you about the Beethoven Quartet Society,[4] whose sole object is to produce Beethoven's quartets at frequent intervals. Each evening program presents three quartets; nothing less and nothing else. Usually, each quartet represents one of the composer's three styles, and it is always the quartet of the third period (that of Beethoven's alleged incomprehensibility) that excites the most enthusiasm. You see these English people following on little miniature scores, printed in London for the purpose, the unpredictable flight of the master's thought—which would suggest that quite a few of them can manage to read the score. But I have had my suspicions of these score-mongers' ability ever since the time when looking over the shoulder of one of them, I discovered that his eyes were glued to page four though the players were already at page six. This amateur no doubt belonged to the school of that King of Spain whose passion was to play first violin in the quintets of Boccherini, though he always lagged behind, and who would say, when the muddle got too appalling: "Go on, go on, I'll catch up with you!"

This interesting society, founded, unless I am mistaken, ten or

---

[3] "It is not enough that the performer should be thoroughly prepared for the public's sake. The public should be just as well prepared for what it is about to hear." Pierre Baillot (1771–1842), a famous player and teacher of the violin, whose *Art of the Violin* is still in use.

[4] Founded in 1843.

twelve years ago by Mr. Alsager, an English amateur [5] who came to a tragic end, is now directed by my fellow countryman M. Scipion Rousselot, who has been in England a long time. A man of the world and a man of parts, an accomplished cellist, a learned and ingenious composer, an artist in the full sense of the term, M. Rousselot was better fitted than most to make this enterprise a success. He has gathered around him three first-rate virtuosos as full of zeal and admiration as himself for these extraordinary works.

The first violin is the German Ernst,[6] nothing less, Ernst, more captivating and more dramatic than ever. The second violin is Mr. Cooper, an English violinist whose playing is always impeccable and of perfect clarity even in the most complicated passages. He does not, however, seek to shine out of turn, as is the habit of many of his colleagues, and he never gives his own part more than the relative weight assigned to it by the composer. The viola is Mr. Hill, also an Englishman, one of the first viola-players in Europe and the owner, moreover, of a wonderful instrument. The cello, of course, is in the safe hands of M. Rousselot. These four virtuosos have already given all the Beethoven quartets some twenty times; and still they hold long and detailed rehearsals before each public performance. You can infer that this quartet is one of the most perfect to be heard anywhere.

The meeting-place of the Beethoven Quartet Society bears the name of Beethoven Room. For a while I occupied an apartment in the same house.[7] The music room, which can accommodate at most two hundred and fifty people, is often hired for concerts that appeal to a small audience; there are many such. Now, as the door of my apartment gave on the staircase leading to the concert room, it was easy for me to keep it open and hear everything that was going on below. One evening I heard Beethoven's Trio in C minor: I open wide the door—come in, come in and be welcome, proud melody! Heavens! how noble and beautiful it is! Where, oh where

---

[5] Thomas Massa Alsager (1779–1846), one of the owners of the London *Times* and an intimate of Lamb, Wordsworth, Leigh Hunt, and their circles. As a passionate amateur player and listener, he sponsored many concerts at his own house and was the first to engage a professional music critic for a daily paper.
[6] See above, note 3, p. 198.
[7] At No. 27 Queen Anne Street.

did Beethoven find all those thousands of phrases, each more poetically characterized than the rest, each different, each original, and without even that family resemblance one finds among the melodies of masters that are known for their fertility? And what ingenious developments! What unexpected turns! How swiftly the indefatigable eagle flies! How he hovers poised in his harmonious sky! He dives into it, loses himself in it, soars, swoops again, disappears; then returns to his starting-place, his eye more brilliant, his pinions stronger, intolerant of rest, quivering, thirst for the infinite!—A splendid performance—who has been playing the piano like that? My servant tells me it is an Englishwoman. A real talent, without question. But what's this? A grand aria for prima donna? John, shut the door, quick, quick. I can still hear the creature. Shut another door—and a third, is there a fourth? Ah, I breathe easier!

The singing female below reminded me of one of my neighbors of the rue d'Aumale, in Paris. Having made up her mind to become a diva, she worked as long as she had strength to emit a sound, and she was very strong. One morning a milkwoman, passing under her window on her way to market, heard her piercing shrieks and said with a sigh: "Ah, married life isn't all roses!" By midafternoon, returning home the same way, the compassionate milkwoman heard again the efforts of the tireless singer. "Heavens!" she cried, crossing herself, "the poor woman! Three o'clock, and she's been in labor since dawn!"

The transition will not be too abrupt now if I speak to you of the Chinese singers, about whose out-of-the-way specialty you were curious to hear.

I wanted first to hear the famous Chinese woman, the Small-footed Lady, as the English posters and advertisements styled her. My interest in hearing her centered in the matter of the Chinese tonality and division of the scale. I meant to find out whether, as so many people have said and written, they differ from ours. After my experience I concluded that there is no truth in the report. This is what I saw and heard: a Chinese family, consisting of two women, two men, and two children, sat on a small stage in the drawing-room of the Chinese House, at the Albert Gate. The concert began with a song of ten or twelve stanzas sung by the music master, accompanied on a little instrument with four metal strings like those on our guitars. This he played with a piece of leather or wood instead of the quill plectrum used in Europe to pluck the strings of the mandolin. The neck of the instrument is divided into sections marked by frets that come closer and closer together as they near the sound box, exactly as on the fingerboard of our guitar. One of the last frets, owing to the maker's error, was badly set and gave a sound that was too high, just as our guitars do when badly made. Still, this division of the neck gave notes entirely in keeping with those of our own scale.

As for the joining of the voice with the accompaniment, it was such one could only conclude that this Chinaman at least had not the slightest notion of harmony. The air (grotesque and loathsome from every point of view) ended on the tonic, like the commonest of our romances, and never departed from either the tonality or the mode set at the beginning. The accompaniment consisted of a rhythmic figure that was fairly lively and always the same, the mandolin chords going hardly or not at all with the notes of the voice. The most excruciating part of it all was that the young woman, in order to enhance the charm of this strange concert and paying no attention to the notes her learned master was emitting, kept scratching with her fingernails the open strings of another instrument of the same kind during the whole duration of the piece. She was like a child in a drawing-room where music is being played, and who amuses himself by striking at random the keyboard of a piano.

To sum up, it was a song accompanied by a bit of instrumental confusion. As to the Chinaman's voice, nothing so strange had ever struck my ear. Imagine a series of nasal, guttural, moaning, hideous tones, which I may without too great exaggeration compare to the sounds a dog makes when after a long sleep it stretches its limbs and yawns. None the less, this ludicrous melody was quite intelligible, and if required could have been noted down. Such was the first part of the concert.

In the second, the roles were reversed; the young woman sang and her master accompanied her on the flute. This time the accompaniment produced no discord; it simply followed the song in unison. The flute is rather similar to our own; it differs from it only by its greater length and by the embouchure, which is almost in the middle of the tube instead of near the top as with us. For the rest, its tone is rather sweet, fairly in tune, which is to say fairly out of tune, and the player gave us nothing outside our own scale and tonal system.

Compared with her master, the young woman was gifted with a celestial voice. It was a mezzo-soprano resembling in quality the contralto of a boy nearing adolescence and whose voice is about to break. She sang fairly well—always comparatively speaking. I thought I was listening to one of our provincial cooks singing "Peter, friend Peter" as she washes the dishes. The melody, the tonality of which was, I repeat, well defined, contained neither quarter tones nor half-quarters, but only the simplest of our diatonic sequences. It struck me as a little less eccentric than the male singer's romance, yet so angular and of a rhythm so elusive in its oddity that I should have found it very hard to take down exactly on paper if I had had a mind to do so.

It goes without saying that I do not take this *exhibition* as an example of the actual state of singing in the Celestial Empire, in spite of the "quality" of the young woman, which, if the leader of the troupe, who spoke English fairly well, is to be believed, was of the highest. The "quality" who sing in Canton or Peking, are content to stay in their own country and do not come to show themselves off in ours for a shilling. They must, I suppose, be as far above this one as Countess Rossi [8] is above the Esmeraldas of the crossroads. This is the more likely as the young lady was perhaps not so small-footed as she would have us believe. Her foot, the distinctive mark of the women of the upper classes, may well have been natural and plebeian, to judge from the care she took to let only the tip of it be seen.

At any rate I cannot help considering my experience as decisive with regard to the division of the scale and the sense of tonality among the Chinese. But to give the name of music to what they produce by this sort of vocal and instrumental noise is, in my opinion, a strange abuse of the term. And now, gentlemen, let me tell you about the *soirées* of music and dance given by the Chinese sailors on the junk they have anchored in the Thames. Believe me if you can.

At these affairs, after the first unavoidable pang of terror, you are overcome with laughter, you laugh yourself silly and sick. I

[8] That is, the great Henrietta Sontag. Esmeralda is the gypsy girl in Victor Hugo's *Notre-Dame.*

have seen English ladies end by swooning on the deck of the celestial ship, so great is the power of this Oriental art. The orchestra consists of a big gong, a small one, a pair of cymbals, a kind of wooden pan or bowl set on a tripod and struck with a couple of drumsticks, a wind instrument rather like a coconut, into which the player merely blows to emit a howling "hoo-hoo," and lastly a Chinese violin. But what a violin! It is a thick bamboo tube six inches long, into which is let a very thin wooden rod about a foot and a half long, forming something like a hollow hammer, the handle of which is fitted near one end of the mallet instead of in the center. Two fine silken cords are stretched anyhow from the end of the handle to the head of the mallet. Between these two strings, which are lightly twisted one over the other, comes the horsehair of a fabulous bow which, when pushed or drawn, makes both strings vibrate simultaneously. The two strings are discordant and the resulting sound is hideous.

The Chinese Paganini, with a serious mien worthy of the success he meets with, rests the instrument on his knees and uses the fingers of his left hand on the upper part of the double string to vary the pitch, just like a cellist, but without regard to any division having to do with tones, semitones, or any interval whatever. He thus produces an endless series of grating sounds or feeble mewings which suggest the wails of the newborn offspring of a ghoul and a vampire.

In the *tutti* the hubbub of the gongs, cymbals, violin, and coconut is more or less frenzied according as the man with the bowl (who, by the way, would make an excellent kettledrummer) speeds up or slows down the roll of his sticks on the wooden instrument. Sometimes, at a signal from this virtuoso, who is all at once conductor, kettledrummer, and singer, the orchestra stops for a moment and, after a brief silence, strikes a single smart stroke. The violin alone keeps on wailing. The melody passes from the conductor to each of his men in succession, forming a dialogue; these two, uttering head notes intermixed with a few chest or rather stomach notes, seem to be reciting some famous legend of their country. Perhaps they are singing a hymn to their god Buddha, whose fourteen-armed statue adorns the interior of the ship's saloon.

I shall not attempt to describe these wildcat howls, these death-rattles, these turkey cluckings, in the midst of which, despite my closest attention, I was able to make out only four distinct notes (D, E, B, and G). I will only say that the small-footed lady and her music master must be adjudged superior to this. The singers of the Chinese House are clearly artists, while those on the junk are merely bad amateurs.

The dancing of these strange men is on a par with their music. Never have I witnessed such hideous contortions; you think you are looking at a horde of demons twisting, leaping, and grimacing to the hissing of all the reptiles, the bellowings of every monster, the metallic din of all the tridents and caldrons in hell. I shall with difficulty be persuaded that the Chinese are not demented.

There is no city in the world, I am sure, where so much music is consumed as in London. You are pursued by it into the very streets, and the music made there is by no means always the worst. For a number of talented artists have discovered that the profession of itinerant musician is infinitely less arduous and more lucrative than that of an orchestra player in any theater whatever. Playing in the street takes only two or three hours a day, as against eight or nine in the theaters. In the street you are out in the open, you breathe fresh air, you move about, and you only have to play a little piece from time to time. In the theater you stand a stifling atmosphere and the heat of the gas, you have to keep sitting and play without interruption, sometimes even during the intermissions. In a theater, moreover, a second-class musician earns hardly more than six pounds a month ($30). That same musician making a debut in the public squares is almost sure to take twice that amount in a month, and often more. The result is that one can hear with actual pleasure in the streets of London small groups of good English musicians, who are as white as you and I, but who have deemed it advisable to attract attention by blackening their faces.

These sham Abyssinians accompany themselves on a violin, a guitar, a tambourine, a couple of kettledrums, and castanets. They sing little five-part airs, most agreeably harmonized, quite melodious, and sometimes original in rhythm. And the men, too, are lively and full of spirit, which shows that they like their work and are happy. Shillings and even half-crowns rain down around them after each of their pieces.

Besides these strolling bands of real musicians one will also stop and hear a fine Scot garbed in the curious costume of the Highlands and accompanied by his two children, also wearing the plaid and the checkered kilt. He plays on the bagpipes the favorite tune of the clan MacGregor. He too is excited by the sounds of his rustic instrument; and the more his pipes chirp, drone, squeal, and frisk, the more his gestures and those of his children become swift, proud, and menacing. One would think these Gaels were going to conquer England, just the three of them.

Next you see coming toward you, drowsy and melancholy, two poor Hindus from Calcutta with their once white turbans and once white robes. Their whole orchestra is made up of two small drums shaped like kegs, such as one saw by the dozen at the Exhibition. They hang the instrument in front of them by a string around the neck, and gently beat both sides of it with the extended fingers of each hand. The feeble noise produced has a rather peculiar rhythm, which in its continuity resembles the rapid click-clack of a wind-mill. One of them sings to it, in some dialect of India, a pretty little melody in E minor that stays within the compass of a sixth (from E to C). It is so sad in spite of its brisk movement, so full of pain, so exiled, so enslaved, so disheartened, so sunless, that as you listen to it you fall a prey to homesickness. Here again there are neither thirds of tones, quarters, nor half-quarters—and it is singing.

Judging from the instruments sent by India to the Universal Exhibition, the music of the East Indians must differ but slightly from that of the Chinese. I have examined, among those childish machines, mandolins with three or four strings, and even with only one, whose fingerboards were divided by frets, as with the Chinese. Some are small, others of very great length. There were big drums and small drums, the sound of which differs little from that produced by tapping with your fingers on the crown of a top hat. There was a double-reed wind instrument akin to our oboe, whose tube, having no holes, produces only a single note. The leader of the musicians who came to Paris some years ago with the nautch-girls of Calcutta used this primitive oboe. He would make an A hum for whole hours, and those who love this particular note got their money's worth.

The Exhibition's collection of Oriental instruments also contained: traverse flutes, in all respects similar to that of the Small-footed Lady's music master; an enormous, crudely built trumpet of a pattern differing only slightly from that of European trumpets; several bowed instruments as clumsily worthless as the one used on the junk by the Chinese fiend I mentioned; a sort of dulcimer whose strings are stretched over a long sounding-board, and are apparently supposed to be struck with a stick; a ridiculous little harp with ten or twelve strings attached to the body of the instrument without pegs to stretch them, and which are as a result constantly discordant with each other; and lastly a great wheel fitted all around with small gongs, the din of which as the wheel moves is as delightful as the noise of the bells on the harness of a carter's horse. That's the battery: take off your hat to it!

To sum up, this is my conclusion: the Chinese and Indians would have a music similar to ours if indeed they had one. But they are still plunged in the dark depths of barbarism, and in a childish ignorance where one can hardly detect some vague and impotent instincts. The Orientals moreover give the name of music to what we should call a din: for them, as for the witches in *Macbeth*, "foul is fair."

G LUCK'S *Iphigenia in Tauris* is being performed.
The entire orchestra is filled with a religious respect
for this immortal work and seems afraid of not being
able to rise to the occasion. I notice the deep, sustained attention of the musicians as they keep their
eyes on the conductor, the precision of their attack,
their keen sense of expressive accent, the delicacy of their accompaniment, their ability to produce a wide range of nuances.

The chorus also is impeccable. The Scythians' scene in the first
act rouses the enthusiasm of the select public that fills the house.
Orestes is inadequate and almost ridiculous; Pylades bleats like a
lamb. Iphigenia alone is equal to her role. When she comes to her
aria "Unhappy Iphigenia!" whose color of antiquity, solemnity of
accent, and desolate dignity of expression in melody and accompaniment recall the sublimities of Homer and the simple grandeur
of the heroic ages, while filling the heart with the unfathomable
sadness inseperable from the memory of a glorious but vanished
past, Corsino turns pale and stops playing. He puts both elbows on
his knees and buries his face in his hands, as if overwrought by inexpressible emotion.

I can see his breathing become more and more rapid and the
blood rushing to his reddened temples. At the entrance of the
women's chorus on the words "To her lament we join our plaintive cries," at that instant when the prolonged outcry of the priest-
esses blends with the voice of the royal orphan and swells with a
heart-rending tumult in the orchestra, two streams of tears force
their way from his eyes and he sobs so vehemently that I am compelled to lead him out of the house.

We go outside . . . I see him home. Seated in his modest room,
lit up by the moon alone, we stay a long time motionless. Corsino
raises his eyes for an instant to the bust of Gluck that stands on his
piano. We gaze at it. . . . The moon disappears. He sighs painfully, flings himself on his bed, and I leave. We have not uttered
a single word.

Gluck and the Conservatory in Naples

A Saying of Durante's

THEY are giving etc., etc., etc.

The orchestra still seems under the spell of the previous night's emotions. No one plays, yet there is little talking. All ruminate upon the sublime. Corsino comes up and holds his hand out to me.

"My dear fellow," I say to him, "I was once like you. But the brutish insensibility of the public I have lived with for so long has crushed my feelings: mine don't respond like yours any more, their strength is gone, and when the expressiveness of great art moves you as it did last night, I feel nothing more than a painful anguish. Just think, dear friend, that barely two years ago,[1] I conducted at a concert this same scene from *Iphigenia*, and while conducting in an ecstasy similar to yours, I could see listeners near the orchestra showing signs of complete boredom. Then I heard the singer, in despair at her lack of success, curse the work and its composer. I had to endure the reproaches of a number of amateurs, and even of distinguished artists, for having, as they said, 'exhumed that rhapsody.' Shown the truth by this rugged and decisive experience, I soon became absolutely certain of one thing: three quarters of the European public is today as impervious to musical expressiveness as those Chinese sailors. We have no surer means of knowing what it likes and dislikes than to observe what charms and delights us and vice versa. It blasphemes what we worship, and relishes what we—eliminate.

"Now consider the great to-do about the rule of harmony that Gluck so daringly violated at the close of Iphigenia's aria. It is precisely where the conjunction of notes that is absolutely prohibited

---

[1] On March 19, 1850, at a concert of Berlioz's own Philharmonic Society in Paris.

by the theorists occurs that the greatest and most dramatic effect is produced. In this connection the story goes that one day in Naples, where the *Clemenza di Tito*,[2] from which this number is drawn, was being performed, the students of some conservatorio (who, being students, naturally detested Gluck) became wild with joy at finding in this aria the so-called incorrect chord progression and ran to their teacher Durante [3] with the new score by the 'German donkey,' submitting it to his indignation without telling him the composer's name. Durante studied the passage for a long time and then remarked: 'There is no rule, of course, to justify this combination of sounds; but if it is a fault, I must admit it can have been committed only by a man of rare genius.'"

DIMSKY: Well spoken! This one remark is enough to show that Durante was a scholar and a gentleman.

"His saying is all the more remarkable because none of his fellow countrymen have ever understood the masterpieces of the German school. They have no access to them—in another sense—for lack of any singers to interpret them in the true style."

"Have we any right to be proud of our own?" puts in Corsino. "With the exception of Mme M., I fail to see who among last night's cast would qualify as tolerable." (*Turning to me*) "Have there ever been singers in Paris that were really up to these roles?"

"Yes. Dérivis the elder.[4] He was no singer, but he could make you understand Gluck's Orestes. Mme Branchu was an incomparable Iphigenia, and Adolphe Nourrit [5] has often electrified me in the part of Pylades. The silly languid manner of your shepherd-like tenor can't give you any notion of Pylades' heroic strength in the aria 'Oh divinity of noble souls,' in which Nourrit has never been equaled."

"I'm sure we had to guess at a good many things. But is there anything harder than to get such works well performed? No one would say, for example, that the effect produced by our Iphigenia was due to the scenery and stage direction."

---

[2] An early opera of Gluck's (1752).

[3] Francesco Durante (1684–1755), wrote only church music, but taught virtually all the leading composers of Italian opera in the second half of the eighteenth century.

[4] See above, note 3, p. 88.

[5] A famous tenor (1802–37) who made his debut in this role just two months before Berlioz's arrival in Paris (November 1821).

"I'll say not!" exclaim several musicians, for on this occasion our theater's stingy ways, most noticeable when the older masterpieces are produced, reached the point of cynical indecency.

"What did the scenery cost for the vile thing that was put on tonight?"

"Four thousand thalers."

"That's as it should be: ugly women need expensive accouterments. Nudity befits only goddesses."

The Huguenots is being performed.

The musicians take good care not to read or speak. "Another evening of music," I tell my neighbors during intermission. "It will be my last. I go back to Paris shortly."

"What, so soon?"

"Three days more."

"Well then, we must all have dinner together. The theater shuts down day after tomorrow *for repairs*."

"Fine, but since tomorrow the theater plans to stay wide open so as to favor us with that long and stringy opera recently imported from Italy, our friend Corsino must kindly conclude our literary evenings by reading us the story he's just finished writing and of which I indiscreetly read a few pages at his house."

"Good! That's settled."

"Quiet! I want to hear this tremendous chorus and the no less tremendous duet that follows."

Euphonia, or the Musical City

a tale of the future

THEY are giving etc., etc., etc.

Hardly have the first chords of the opera resounded before Corsino unrolls his manuscript and reads what follows, to an accompaniment of trombones and bass drum. We can hear him all the same, by virtue of the strength and peculiar timbre of his voice.

"Gentlemen," he says, "this is a tale of the *future*. The time, with your permission, is the year 2344."

Euphonia
or the Musical City

CHARACTERS

XILEF, a composer, prefect of voices and stringed instruments
in the city of Euphonia
SHETLAND, a composer, prefect of wind instruments
MINA, a celebrated Danish singer
MME HAPPER, her mother
FANNY, her maid

First Letter

Xilef to Shetland

SICILY, JUNE 7, 2344

I have just taken a swim in Etna! What a delightful time I have
been having, my dear Shetland, gliding through the pure waters of
that cool, calm lake! It is a huge basin whose circular shape and
steep banks make its surface reflect sound in such a way that my
voice can reach without difficulty from its center to the most distant parts of the shore. I noticed this from hearing the handclap-
ping of some Sicilian women who were taking a balloon jaunt
about two miles away from where I was flopping about like a
dolphin. I'd been singing as I swam a melody I composed this
morning to a poem in old French by Lamartine. The look of the
place I am in had brought it to my mind. I think the poem ravishing.
You'll be able to judge for yourself, for Enner has promised to
translate "The Lake" into German.[1]

You should be here; we'd go riding together. I feel full of the
spring of youth, full of strength, intelligence, and joy. Nature
all around is so beautiful! The plain where Messina stood is an en-
chanted garden—flowers everywhere, orange groves, palm trees
dipping their graceful heads. It is the fragrant crown of this divine
vessel, the bottom of the crater where today the dreamy lake stands
that has subdued the fires of Etna. What a strange and terrible
struggle that must have been! What a spectacle! The earth quaking
in horrible convulsions, the huge mountain collapsing on itself, the
snows, the flames, the seething lava, the explosions, the cries, the
death-rattle of the volcano in its agony, the ironic hissing of the
waters that rush in from a thousand subterranean springs, pursue
their enemy, grip it, close in on it, smother and kill it, then suddenly
become calm again, ready to smile at the slightest breath of wind.

Well, would you believe that this spot, which was once so frightful and is now so enchanting, is almost deserted? The Italians hardly
know about it; it's nowhere spoken of. The lust for business is so
strong among the inhabitants of this beautiful region that they take

---

[1] Lamartine's *Le Lac* appeared in his *Méditations Poétiques* (1820).

an interest in nature's magnificent sights only in so far as they can see a connection with the matters of trade and industry which engross them night and day. That is why to the Italians Etna is merely a big hole filled with stagnant water that can't be put to use. From one end to the other of this country formerly so rich in poets, painters, and musicians, this soil which after Greece was the second great temple of art, where the people themselves had a feeling for it, where eminent artists were honored almost as much as they are today in northern Europe, you see nothing but factories, workshops, mills, markets, warehouses, workers of every sex and age, burning with the thirst for gold and the fever of cupidity. You see anxious crowds of traders and speculators. From top to bottom of the social scale you hear nothing but the clink of money; the talk is all about woolens and cottons, machinery and raw materials from the colonies. In the public squares are men armed with field-glasses and telescopes who do nothing but spy out and report the arrival of carrier pigeons and airships.

Compared to modern Italy, France is the home of the arts—as well as of indifference and mockery. Yet it is to Italy that our Minister of Choruses sent me to find singers! What an idea! Prejudices without end. We must be strangely self-centered not to know how *barbarescent* are the manners of this country where the orange tree still blooms,[2] but where art, long since defunct, has not left even a memory.

I have all the same accomplished my mission. I looked for voices and found them in abundance. But Lord! What types! what minds! After this experience, I am proof against surprise. I spoke to a young woman whose clear strong speech made me suspect that her vocal equipment was remarkable and asked her to sing. She said: "Sing! Why should I? How much will you give me? For how many minutes?—That's not enough. I can't afford the time."

When I persuaded others less grasping to let me hear a few notes, I found their voices were often powerful and of wonderful quality, but uncultivated to an astounding degree—no sense of rhythm or tonality. One day while I accompanied a woman who had begun an aria in E flat, I suddenly modulated into D at the re-entry of the

[2] An allusion to Mignon's song in Goethe's *Wilhelm Meister,* "*Kennst du das Land . . .*"

theme. The young barbarian did not turn a hair but continued singing in the original key. It is still worse with the men. They shout at the top of their voices all the time. If they can sing one note more loudly than the rest, they try, whenever it occurs in the melody, to sustain that one note as long as posssible; they dwell on it, loll in it, blow it up, swell it out abominably. You think you hear the sinister howling of a melancholy wolf.

These horrors are but a slight extension of what the professional vocalists allow themselves. These "artists" shout a little less badly, that's all. And yet it's from Italy that five hundred years ago we had such singers as Rubini, Persiani, Tacchinardi, Crivelli, Pasta, Tamburini—those gods of florid song! But for whom and for why would they sing if they returned to earth today? One has to see one of the things now called operas in Italy to believe that such insults to art and common sense are possible. The theaters are stockyards, curb markets where people talk so loud that it's almost impossible to hear any sound from the stage. (Critics of olden days say it was always so, even in the time of the great composers and virtuosos who were Italy's glory. I don't believe it. *Artists*, surely, would not have stood for such defamation.)

In order to divert these brutish traders a little after their deals on the Exchange, someone has had the happy thought of putting billiard tables in the center of the ground floor of the theater; and these gentlemen play, shouting at every lucky stroke, while the tenor and the prima donna blow out their lungs on the stage. In Palermo day before yesterday they were giving *Il re Murate*, a sort of hodgepodge by twenty different authors of twenty different periods. After supper—for everyone takes supper in his box, and always during the performance—the ladies, annoyed at seeing the men preparing to go and smoke and play downstairs, rose up in arms and asked that the billiard tables be removed and a dance improvised in the free space, which was done. A few young men got hold of violins and trumpets and began to play waltzes in an upper corner of the dress circle, while couples whirled around on the floor without the performance being interrupted in the slightest degree. I hardly knew whether to laugh or cry when I saw this incredible opera-ballet under my very eyes.

As a result of this bottomless contempt for music on the part of the Italians, they no longer have any composers and the names of the great masters from 1800 to 1820,[3] for instance, are known only to a small number of scholars. The amusing name *operatori* (operators, workmen, makers) has been given to the poor devils who, for a pittance, go into the libraries to compile into operatic scores some airs, duets, choruses, and ensembles culled from all and sundry masters and from all periods, whether the pieces suit or don't suit the situation, the characters, and the words—which they also pull together. These people are their composers; they have no others. I was curious enough to question an *operatore*, so as to know fully and exactly how they carry on their operations. This is what he said:

"When the director wants a new score, he assembles the singers and submits to them the scenario of the piece, and comes to an understanding with them about the costumes they will wear. The costumes really come first, being the only thing which momentarily attracts the public's attention at the première. Formerly, dreadful fights occurred between the managers and the vocal stars on this point. (Of course, the authors are never invited to these sessions nor consulted in these arguments. A libretto is bought like a meat pie, which one is free to eat or throw to a dog when one has paid for it.) But today managers have acquired some sense; they don't worry whether the costumes are appropriate; they realize it's not worth while alienating the stars over a trifle, and they make it their main business to satisfy them all on that one point—which is no easy matter.

"At the reading of the scenario, then, the object is to find out what kind of costume the actors want, and to see to it that no two among them intend to dress the same way, for an accident of that kind can lead to indescribible scenes of fury, making the impresario's position, to say the least, embarrassing. Thus in the new opera *Il re Murate*, Cretinone,[4] who was cast for the part of Napoleon, wanted to resemble an antique statue and appear in the breastplate of Pompey, an ancient general who lived more than three hundred years before Napoleon and was killed by a cannon-ball at

---

[3] This accounts for the discrepancy between the reports given by Stendhal, who was in Italy at the earlier period, and Berlioz, who first went there in 1831.
[4] An imaginary singer, of course, whose name suggests "cretin"—nitwit. Caponetti, below, bears a parallel interpretation, and so on throughout the tale.

the Battle of Pharsala." (You see that my poor *operatore* is about as weak in ancient history as he is in music.)

"But it so happened that Caponetti, who plays Murat,[5] had the same idea, and it would have been impossible to get either to yield had not Luciola, our prima donna, suggested a big bearskin head-gear with a white plume for Napoleon, and a blue turban with a diamond cross for Murat. These toppers satisfied our virtuosos and seemed in their eyes to mark a sufficient difference between them to permit them both to wear the Roman breastplate. Without this compromise the opera could not have been performed.

"Once the great question of costumes has been settled, one proceeds to the vocal numbers. And now begins a painful time for the *operatore*, you may be sure, a most humiliating time if he has any knowledge of music and some self-esteem. The singing ladies and gentlemen look over the range and substance of the melodies, and after cursory inspection one of them says: 'I will not sing in F my phrase in the trio: it is not brilliant enough. *Operatore!* You must transpose it into F sharp for me.'

" 'But, sir, it's a trio, and the other two voices have to stay in the original key; what can I do?'

" 'Do as you please, modulate before and after, add a few bars, I don't care what, but I insist on singing that theme in F sharp.'

" 'I don't like this tune,' says the prima donna; 'I want another.'

" 'Signora, it's the theme of the ensemble, which all the voices take up after you one by one, so you'll really have to sing it.'

" 'What do you mean, "have to"? The impertinence of the man! Give me something else, at once! That's the "have to" in this case. Do as you are told and no argument.'

" 'Hum! hum! *tromba! tromba! già ribomba la tromba!*'[6] shouts the basso on his high D. 'Oh dear, my D is not so strong as usual; it's my last illness; I must have time to let it recover. *Operatore!* you'll have to take out all these D's for me; I don't want any in my parts till September. Put in some C's and B's instead.'

" 'I say, Facchino,' growls the baritone, 'do you want to feel the tip of my boot in a likely place—you've forgotten my E flat? It comes in hardly twenty times in my aria. I'll thank you to add at

---

[5] Napoleon's marshal, brother-in-law, and appointee to the throne of Naples.
[6] "Already the horn—the horn resounds!" Syllables appropriate to practicing a deep voice.

least two E flats in every bar; I don't intend to lose my reputation.'—

" 'And yet,' resumes the wretched *operatore*, 'there are some very pretty passages in my music, if I do say so. But look how they've ruined my prayer—seems to me I've never hit upon anything better!'

"I take a look at 'his' music and—imagine my surprise—I recognize the beautiful, majestically effective prayer in Rossini's *Moses*,[7] which we occasionally play of an evening in the gardens of Euphonia. The old master of Pesaro, who is said to have made light of his own compositions, would have had to be very philosophical or, rather, culpably indifferent in matters of art, if he had been able to foresee without indignation the monstrosity which one of his finest inspirations would some day become.

"In the first place, the simple and vibrant modulation from G minor to B-flat major, which imparts so much splendor to the unfolding of the second phrase, has been changed to a horribly dry and hard modulation from G minor to B natural. Next, instead of Rossini's harp accompaniment, they have taken it into their heads to put in a flute variation full of ridiculous turns and ornaments. Finally, at the last return of the theme in G major, they have seen fit to substitute—what do you think? You'll never guess—if you did, you'd blush—why, the refrain of the French national anthem: 'To arms, ye citizens!' accompanied by a dozen snare drums and four bass drums!

"It is an established fact that this old Rossini, who was certainly not lacking in ideas, never missed an opportunity that came his way to appropriate the ideas of others if fate had willed that a felicitous tune should fall into the lap of a lout. He made no fuss about admitting it, and would even mock the man he was robbing. *E troppo buono per questo coglione*,[8] he would remark, and would make either a charming or a magnificent piece according to the nature of the lout's ideas. It was a case of seizing a cannon (no pun intended!) from the enemy, and like the great Emperor, erecting his memorial column! [9] Today, alas, the column is broken, and out

---

[7] See above, pp. 198–9.
[8] "It's too good for that bastard."
[9] The Colonne Vendôme, made by Napoleon from the bronze of captured guns.

of its fragments, of which we still collect a few with veneration, the Italians make kitchen utensils and disgusting caricatures."

Thus do certain glories depart from the very peoples they have bathed in their most burning rays. We Euphonians, it is true, preserve all those which art has firmly consecrated; but we are not "the people" in the highest sense of the term. We represent, admittedly, a very small fragment of the people, lost amid the mass of civilized populations. Glory is a sun that lights up in succession certain points of our petty sphere, but as it travels through space it describes such a huge orbit that the most advanced knowledge cannot foretell with certainty the time of its return to the places it has forsaken. Or to borrow another comparison from nature, the same is true of the great oceans and their mysterious evolution. If, as science has shown, the continents on which today our sad humanity travails were formerly submerged, must we not conclude that the mountains, valleys, and plains over which the dark billows of the ancient sea have rolled for so many centuries were at one time covered with a flourishing vegetation, affording bed and shelter to millions of living, perhaps of intelligent beings? When will it be our turn to be at the bottom of the abyss?

And on the day when that tremendous catastrophe occurs, will there be any glory or power, any strength of genius or of love, any might or beauty, that will not be extinguished? If so, what does anything matter?

Forgive me, my dear Shetland, this geological digression and this fit of philosophic despair. I am in pain. I have fears, anxiety; my face is flushed, my heart throbs, I scan all of space; the mail-balloon is not in sight, and yesterday's did not bring me anything. No news from Mina! What has happened to her? Is she ill, or dead, or unfaithful? I love her so frightfully. It is so painful to be a child of art, the art with flaming wings. Reared on its burning bosom, we suffer dreadfully, we whose poetized passions ruthlessly plow heart and brain to sow inspiration, that rough seed which lacerates heart and brain afresh when its germs develop. We die so many deaths before the last. Shetland, Shetland, I love her. I love her as you yourself would, if you could feel a love other than the one you have confessed to me. And yet, in spite of the greatness and the brightness of her talent, Mina often seems to me a very ordinary mind. Shall I tell you? She prefers the florid style to the great expressive accents of the soul. She is a stranger to reverie. She heard your first symphony in Paris without shedding a tear from beginning to end. She thinks Beethoven's adagios are *too long*. Oh, female of Homo sapiens!

On the day she confided this last opinion to me, I felt a sharp icicle pierce my heart. But there's worse. She is Danish, born in Elsinore, and owns a villa built on the old site and with the sacred fragments of Hamlet's castle. Yet she sees nothing extraordinary in that, and refers to Shakespeare without any special emotion. To her he is a poet like so many others. She laughs, laughs, the wretch, at Ophelia's songs; she considers them "quite improper," that's all. Oh, female of the monkey tribe!

Forgive me again, dear friend. I confess I am ashamed, but in spite of everything, I love her, I love her to the point of saying with Othello, whose example I could follow if she should deceive me: "Her jesses are my dear heartstrings." Art and glory may perish. She is everything to me, I love her.

I can see her with her swaying walk, her large sparkling eyes, her goddess-like air; I hear her Ariel tones, silvery, frolicsome, penetrating. I fancy myself beside her, speaking to her in her Scandinavian dialect: *"Mina, sare disiul dolle menos? Doer si men? Doer? Vare, Mina, vare, vare!"*)[1] Then, with her head on my shoulder, we gently murmur intimate secrets, speak of our first days together, and of you.

She wants very much to meet you, wants to go to Euphonia solely for that reason. She has heard so much about your amazing new works. She has formed a rather strange idea of you, one that luckily is not at all like you. I remember how interested she was, just before my departure from Paris, in every report of your recent triumphs. I even chaffed her about it and she made a remark about my jealous humor. I said: "Jealous of Shetland? Certainly not! I have nothing to fear; he's one person who will never love you; his heart is already possessed, and by far too strong a love; it would have to be extinguished first, and that's impossible." Mina shut her eyes and was silent. An instant later she opened them, more beautiful than ever, and said as she kissed me: "It's I who will never love *him*. But as for him, my lord, if I set my mind on it, I could show you, I think—" She was so beautiful at that moment

---

[1] This seems to be gibberish invented for the occasion.

that I admit I was very glad to know my friend Shetland—faithful as he is—to be nine hundred miles away, occupied with trombones, flutes, and saxophones.[2] You won't hold my frankness against me, will you?

Alas, I feel alone. After so many protestations, so many sworn promises not to let a week go by without writing, not a line has come from Mina.

Here's another mail-balloon coming in: I'm off. . . . Nothing!

You must be almost happy compared with me. You suffer pangs, it's true, but the one you love is no more. You cannot be jealous; you neither hope nor fear; you are free and great. Your love and art are twins, calling for inspiration; your life is the expansive life; you are radiant. I—let's not talk of ourselves nor of them. A curse on all beautiful women—when they're not ours!

Let me try to resume the sketch I began of Italy's musical manners: no question here of passion, imagination, heart, soul, or mind, but of dull realities. And so I continue.

In all the theaters there is in front of the stage a black pit filled with wretches who blow and scrape, equally indifferent to what is shouted on the stage and to what buzzes in the boxes and seats. They are possessed by one thought only: earning their supper. This assemblage of poor creatures is what is called an orchestra, and this is how an orchestra is generally constituted: two first and two second violins, usually; very rarely a viola and a cello; almost always two or three double basses, though the players, regardless of the salary you could offer, would be hard put to it to play anything in which they cannot use their three open strings—as in B major, for example, where their three notes, G, D, and A natural, do not figure. For they still use the three-stringed double bass tuned in fifths.

This formidable regiment of stringed instruments is pitted against an enemy consisting of a dozen keyed bugles, six piston trumpets, six valve trombones, two tenor tubas, two bass tubas, three ophicleides, a horn, three piccolos, three small clarinets in E flat, two clarinets in C, three bass clarinets (for lively tunes), and an organ (for ballet music). I should not forget four bass

---

[2] This tale first appeared as a serial in the *Gazette Musicale* beginning in February 1844, when the first saxophone had just been made and played by its inventor in a piece specially written for it by Berlioz.

drums, six snare drums, and two gongs. There are no longer any oboes, bassoons, harps, kettledrums, or cymbals, these instruments having been consigned to deepest oblivion.

The reason is obvious: the sole object of the orchestra being to produce noises capable of drowning out from time to time the tumult in the theater, the small clarinets and piccolos can emit sounds far shriller than oboes; the ophicleides and tubas are to be preferred to bassoons, snare drums to kettledrums, and gongs to cymbals. I confess I do not see why the one horn has been kept when they delight in blotting it out with the other brass instruments: it serves no purpose. And the four wretched violins and three double basses can hardly be heard any better.

This singular conglomeration of instruments taxes the skill of the *operatori* when they "adapt to the requirements of the modern orchestra"—that's the regular cliché—the instrumentation of the old masters. They proceed to *operate*, dismember, and recast it into an olla-podrida in keeping with the method I described at the beginning of my letter. And these operations, of course, are carried out in a manner worthy of everything that is manhandled here under the name of music. The oboe parts are given to the trumpets, those of the bassoon to the tubas, those of the harp to the piccolos, and so on.

The musicians (the musicians!) play approximately what is written, but almost without any variation in dynamics. The *mezzo forte* is not uniform but continual. The *forte* comes in with the bass drums, the snare drums, and the gongs, the *piano* when these keep quiet: such are the recognized nuances in use. The conductor looks like the deaf leading the deaf. He beats time with heavy blows of his baton on his wooden stand, never going any faster or slower, even when he ought to restrain a group that is growing too passionate (no one, to be sure, ever gets passionate) or to arouse a group that is falling asleep. He gives way to nobody, but moves mechanically like a metronome. His arm goes up and down; the players can look at him if they like, it's nothing to him. This human machine functions only during the overtures, dance tunes, and choruses. For it is absolutely impossible to foresee the rhythmical whims of the singers in the airs and duets. Unable to follow them, orchestral conductors have long ago given up indicating any tempo whatever. The players are on the loose, they accompany by instinct as best they can, until the mess becomes a trifle too colossal. The singers then signal them to halt, which they hasten to do, and the accompaniment stops altogether. I have only been in Italy a short time, but I have frequently had the pleasure of admiring this wonderful orchestral effect.

Farewell for tonight, dear friend. I thought I had greater strength: the pen drops from my fingers. I am hot, feverish! Mina, Mina, no letters! What do I care for the Italians and their barbarism? Mina! I can see the chaste moon gazing at its reflection in Etna. Not a breath! Mina . . . far away . . . alone . . . Mina! Mina! . . . Paris!

Second Letter

From the Same to the Same

SICILY, JUNE 8, 2344

What martyrdom our Minister consigns me to—I must stay here, kept in Italy by the promise I too lightly gave, not to leave until I have engaged the number of singers we need—when the smallest ship could carry me through the air to the spot where my life is. What does her silence mean? I am most unhappy! To have to be busy about music in this feverish dizziness of mind, this turmoil of the senses, in the midst of a stormy conflict among a thousand harrowing impulses. And yet it has to be. Oh, my dear friend, the cult of art is joyful only for the serene. I know this by the indifference and disgust I now feel about the things that formerly aroused my deepest interest. Never mind! Back to the job.

Having heard about my mission and the duties I perform in Euphonia, the members of the Sicilian Academy wrote to me this morning, asking how our musical city is organized. They have heard much about it, yet not one of their members, in spite of all the modern facilities for travel, has had the curiosity to visit it. Please send me by return mail a copy of our charter, with a brief account of the city, which is a true conservatory of the great art we adore. I'll read both documents to the learned assembly. I am eager to see at close range the astonishment of these good academicians, who are so far from knowing what music is.

I've said nothing to you about either concerts or festivals in Italy, for the good reason that these occasions are most infrequent here. They would not arouse any interest among the people, and even if they did, the performances would not greatly differ from what I have heard in the theaters. As for sacred music, there isn't any either—at least from our point of view, which implies the noble use of all the resources of art in the divine service. Recent popes have prohibited in the churches any music but that of the ancient choirmasters of the Sistine Chapel, such as Palestrina and Allegri, and by this grave decision they have put an end forever to the scandal which certain critics who seem the most judicious complained of so bitterly a few centuries ago. You no longer hear violin concertos played during Mass or cavatinas sung in a falsetto voice by an entire man, and the organist no longer plays grotesque fugues or the overtures of comic operas.

Yet it is none the less regrettable that the papal ban, for which there were excellent grounds in the form of offensive and ridiculous monstrosities, should have brought in its train the exclusion of high and noble works of art. The works of Palestrina could never be in our eyes, nor in those of any person possessing the now widespread rudiments of the real religious style, completely musical or absolutely religious. They are a tapestry of consonant chords whose woven texture is sometimes interesting to the eye—or even to the mind, when one considers the difficulties with which the composer amused himself while solving them—and whose gentle and soothing effect on the ear frequently induces a deep reverie. But this is not the whole of music, since it makes no use of melody, expressiveness, rhythm, or instrumentation. The Sicilian scholars will, I think, be greatly surprised to learn what care we take to forbid in our schools any regard for these puerilities of counterpoint except as exercises. We reprove any desire to see in them an artistic end rather than a means, the danger of taking them thus seriously being to transform musical scores into tables of logarithms or chess problems.

On the whole, though, however much one regrets not being able to hear in a church anything but calm vocal harmonies, one must at the same time rejoice at the decision that has abolished the impudent style. Of two evils let us be glad that we suffer only the lesser. Moreover, the popes have long since permitted women to sing in church, believing that their presence and participation in the divine service was natural and proper, and far more moral than the barbarous custom of castration that used to be tolerated, in fact encouraged, by their predecessors. It took centuries to make this discovery. In earlier days women were allowed to sing during the service only on condition that they sang badly; as soon as their knowledge of music enabled them to sing well, and consequently to appear in an artistically assembled choir, composers were forbidden to use their voices. When one reads history, one concludes that at certain times our art has been despotically ruled by idiocy and madness.

Italian church choirs are, generally speaking, small in numbers—twenty to thirty voices at most on great festal days. The singers seem to me to be well chosen. They sing without dynamic shading, it is true, but in tune and with good ensemble. They must obviously be classed as far superior to the wretched brawlers of the theaters, about whom I refrain from speaking.

Farewell, I leave you and write to Mina once more: shall I be lucky this time, and will she at long last answer me?

Your friend,
XILEF

Paris

(*A richly furnished drawing-room*)

MINA (*alone*): Why, I almost feel as if I were going to be bored. Am I the butt of a practical joke? Not one of my gentlemen has so far come forth with a diverting idea for today. So here I am, alone, forsaken for the past four hours. The Baron himself, the most attentive of the lot, the most assiduous, hasn't yet put in an appearance.

After all, perhaps they did right to leave me in peace, they're all so stupid, these beaux who adore me. They never talk to me about anything but parties, intrigues, scandals, the races, and fashion—not a word that suggests mind or the love of art; nothing that springs from the heart. And I am above all an

artist, an artist to the bottom of my—soul, of my—heart. Why
do I hesitate to say those words? Am I quite sure I have a soul and
a heart? Pshaw! I know one thing: I don't feel the slightest love
for Xilef any more. I haven't even answered his glowing letters.
He accuses me, he is in despair, and I think of him—sometimes,
not often. Really it's not my fault if, as my fool of a baron says,
"absence is always a mistake, *presents* invariably right." Far be
it from me to try and change the world. Why did he have to go
away? A man really in love should never leave his mistress; he
should see only her in the whole world, and count all else as
nothing.

FANNY (*entering*): Madam, here are the papers and a couple of
letters.

MINA (*unfolding a newspaper*): Ah, the Gluck Festival at Euphonia next week. I'm going. I want to sing there. (*Reading*)
"The *Song of Praise* composed by Shetland is the talk of the
town. No one before him, in our opinion, has expressed noble
enthusiasm with more magnificence. Shetland is a man apart. He
differs from other men not only by his genius and character,
but also by the mystery in his life." Fanny, ask my mother to
come.

FANNY (*going out*): You've forgotten your letters, madam; I
think there's one from your fiancé, M. Xilef.

MINA (*alone*): My fiancé! What a funny word! A fiancé—what a
ridiculous thing! And he can call *me* fiancée, which makes me
ridiculous too! The silly girl, with her absurd expressions! I
loathe it all, it infuriates me, gives me convulsions. She guessed
right; it *is* a letter from my faithful Xilef. There he goes—
reproaches—his misery—his love—the same old story. Young
man, you get on my nerves. Xilef, my dear fellow, you're
through. These everlastingly passionate characters are really
unbearable. Who wants their constancy? Who ever asked him
to adore me? Who? Come to think of it, I did. He was busy
about other things. Now that he's lost his peace of mind for my
sake (as they say in novels), it's rather low of me to send him
packing. Yes, but—we live only once.

Now let's see the other letter. (*Laughing*) Oh, oh, here's
brevity for you! A horse—neat drawing, I must say—and not a
word. It does for a signature and a hieroglyph. It means that my

brute of a baron expects me to come for a drive with him in the park. He can go by himself. (*Mme Happer comes in with heavy tread.*) Good Lord, Mother! the time it takes you to come in when I call you. I've been champing here for over half an hour, and there's no time to lose.

MME HAPPER: What's the matter? What crazy new idea have you taken into your head? You seem all excited.

MINA: We are going away.

MME HAPPER: You are going away?

MINA: We are going away, Mother.

MME HAPPER: But I am quite comfortable here; I have no desire to leave Paris—especially if it is (as I suspect) to join your pale-faced lover. Let me say it again, Mina, your conduct is outrageous; you show respect neither to me nor to your real self. This marriage is unsuitable in every way; you know that that young man's fortune is not satisfactory. And then he has ideas, strange ideas, about women! I tell you, you are mad, out of your mind—forgive my saying so—an utter fool, for all your wit and talent. No one in her senses could choose such a man. And why this passion for getting married? I'd thought that the real blue-blood who came here had brought you back to your senses. But it looks as though your whims are like a fever, they come and go, and the fit is on again.

MINA (*bowing with exaggerated respect*): My honorable mother, you are sublime! I won't say you improvise magnificently because I'm sure you were working out this lecture while you kept me waiting so long. But never mind; eloquence is rare. Only, you've been preaching to a convert. As I just told you, we're leaving; we're going to Euphonia; I am singing at the Gluck Festival. Xilef is out of my mind. To begin with, we'll change our names so as to put him off the track. I shall call myself Nadira and you will pass as my aunt. I am a new Austrian singer making her debut, and the great Shetland takes me under his wing; I am a tremendous hit; everybody goes wild over me; as for the rest—we'll see.

MME HAPPER: O merciful God, bless her soul! I've found my daughter again. At last, at last, good sense has—give me a kiss, you beautiful thing—I'm choking with joy. No more silly notions of the plighted word, so called. Bless you!—Yes, let's go.

As for that little fool of a Xilef, who had the impudence to have designs on my own Mina and wanted to take her from me, oh, but I'd like to tell him to his face what I think of him, that *marrying man*. I'm going to, too, it's my business and concerns me—the brat! A talented singer like you, and a beauty besides! Ah, yes, my lad, she is yours for the asking—not if *I* know it! I'll get rid of him in ten words; in two hours we're all packed, make the mail-boat, and tomorrow we're in Euphonia, where we score a triumph—while the little gentleman hunts high and low for us in the opposite direction. Yes, indeedy, I'll give him plenty to do! (*Exit Mme Happer breathing like a whale and crossing herself repeatedly.*)

FANNY (*who has come back within the last few minutes*): So you're giving him up, madam?

MINA: Yes, it's over.

FANNY: But he loved you so! He put all his faith in you! You don't love him any more, not the least little bit?

MINA: No.

FANNY: It frightens me. Something awful's going to happen; he'll kill himself, madam.

MINA: Nonsense!

FANNY: He'll kill himself for sure.

MINA: Come on now, that's enough!

FANNY: The poor young man!

MINA: Will you be quiet, you little fool? Go and help my mother get ready for our trip. And no remarks, mind, if you want to remain in my service. (*Exit Fanny.*)

MINA (*alone*): Kill himself?—Perhaps I really ought to— Anyhow, can I help it if—if I don't love him any more?

(*She sits down to the piano and sings for a few minutes. Then her fingers wander over the keyboard, recapturing the theme of Shetland's First Symphony, which she heard six months before. She talks to herself as she plays:*) It's really beautiful. That melody has something so exquisitely tender, so capriciously passionate. (*She stops.—A long pause, then she resumes the symphonic theme.*) Shetland is a man apart—He differs from other men—by his genius, his character (*continuing to play*), and the mystery in his life. (*She goes into the minor key.*) According to Xilef, he will never love me. (*The theme reappears in fugal imi-*

tation, dislocated, broken up. A crescendo. An explosion in the major key. She gets up, goes to a mirror and tidies her hair, humming the first bars of the theme. Another pause. She notices the Baron's letter with the horse drawn in outline, takes a pen and draws a loose bridle around the neck of the animal; then she rings. A footman in livery appears.) Take this to the Baron; it is my reply. (*Aside*) He is stupid enough not to understand it.

FANNY (*entering*): Madam, everything is ready.

MINA: Has my mother written to—?

FANNY: Yes, madam, I have just put the letter in the box.

MINA: You two go ahead and into the ship; I'll be right behind you.

(*The maid goes out. Mina sits down on a sofa, folds her arms across her breast, and remains for an instant absorbed in thought. She bows her head, an imperceptible sigh escapes her lips, a slight flush tinges her cheeks. Finally, she picks up her gloves and walks out, muttering with an ill-tempered gesture:*) Ah well, let *him* worry!

Third Letter

Shetland to Xilef

EUPHONIA, JULY 6, 2344

Here, my poor dear friend, is the musical charter together with the description of Euphonia. These documents are in some ways incomplete, but your enforced leisure will enable you to go over my hasty scribble, and by drawing on your own experience you can complete the account without too much trouble. I couldn't send you the bare text of our musical rules and policies; I had to give your Sicilian academicians an approximate idea of our City of Harmony by means of a brief but precise description. So I had to write out a sketch of Euphonia as well as I could. I'm sure you'll forgive the slips in my text, as well as what is diffuse and unfinished about it, when I tell you the strange emotion under which I have labored for some days past. I was appointed, as you know, to take charge of everything connected with the Gluck Festival. I had to compose the *Song of Praise* to be given outside the temple.

I had to superintend the rehearsals of *Alcestis* (performed in the Thessalian palace), lead the chorus rehearsals of my song, and also substitute for you in the management of the strings.

But all that was mere child's-play; the grave meditations, painful memories, and deep despondency which I owe to my old and incurable sorrow have at least freed me from the influence of passion and given my mind a sober calmness that does not hamper but assists its activity—a calmness which, I am sorry to say, you do not share. Acute suffering does paralyze the artistic faculties; it is suffering with its searing embrace that alone cripples the noble impulses of the heart; it is suffering that destroys us, turns us to stone, drives us mad, makes us stupid. I became free, as you know, from such consuming griefs, my heart and my senses knew peace, they partook of the sleep of death, from the moment when a certain star vanished from my heaven. My mind and secret fancy grew all the more alive on this account. I could then use almost all my spare time as art dictated. So far I have not failed, and this has been less from love of fame than from love of the beautiful, toward which we both instinctively tend with no ulterior motive of vainglorious satisfaction.

What has lately upset me, stirred me, ravaged me, was not the composing of my Song, nor its enthusiastic reception by our musical population, or the praises of the Minister, nor the pleasure it gave the Emperor, who, if His Majesty is to be believed, is transported by my music. It was not even the very great impact that the work produced on me—none of those things. It was a strange occurrence which worked upon my mind more than I thought possible, and whose deep impression unfortunately does not fade.

As I was taking the cool of the evening after a long rehearsal, lounging in my little ship, and from the height I had reached, gazing at the dying day, I heard coming out of the cloud I was skirting a woman's voice, high and strong yet pure, and resembling by its amazing agility, its capricious turns and charming flights in mid-air, the song of some marvelous invisible bird. I stopped my engine suddenly. After a few minutes I saw through the mists purpled by the setting sun a balloon heading rapidly in the direction of Euphonia. A young woman was standing in the forepart of the ship, bending in an enchanting pose over a harp. She swept the strings from time to time with her right hand, which was sparkling with diamonds. She was not alone; several other women were inside the ship and could be seen flitting past the windows of the cabin. At first I thought they were some of our young choristers from Soprano Street who were, like me, on an air stroll.

She was singing (and ornamenting with all kinds of extravagant vocalises) the theme of my First Symphony, which I thought almost unknown except among Euphonians. But on looking closer at the charming creature who was warbling so brilliantly, I knew that she was not one of us and had never come to Euphonia. Her look was both abstracted and inspired and it startled me by its strange expression. The thought flashed into my mind that it would be a calamity for a man to love a woman like that unrequited. Then I thought no more about it. The high mountaintops of the Harz were already cutting off the sun on the horizon; I made my ship rise perpendicularly some hundreds of feet in order to see the fleeing sun once more, and I gazed at it for some minutes in that ecstatic silence of which one has no idea upon earth. At last, tired of dreaming and being alone in the sky, and hearing wafted on the west wind the distant harmonies of our Tower ringing out the Hymn of Night, I came down, or rather swooped arrow-like on my house, which is, as you know, outside the town walls.

I spent the night there in fitful sleep. A dozen times I saw in my dreams the beautiful stranger bending over her harp as she emerged from her rose-gold cloud. In the end I even dreamed that I was maltreating her and that my brutal behavior made her very unhappy; I saw her at my feet, broken up, in tears, while I was coldly congratulating myself on having tamed a graceful but dangerous animal. Strange vision for a mind like mine, which is remote from feelings of the sort!

Immediately after getting up I went and sat in my rose garden, and without thinking about it threw wide open the double door of my Æolian harp. In an instant, floods of harmony poured into the garden; *crescendos*, *fortes*, *decrescendos*, and *pianissimos* followed each other haphazard under the fitful breath of the wild morning breeze. I was painfully shaken, yet not in the least tempted to escape my suffering by closing the doors of the mournful instrument. On the contrary, I found pleasure in my pain and listened motionless. Just as a gust of wind stronger than the rest drew from the harp, like a cry of passion, the chord of the dominant seventh, and carried it wailing through the arbor, it so happened that the decrescendo formed an arpeggio containing the opening bars of the theme I had heard my unknown sing the day before—the theme of my First Symphony. Amazed at this freak of nature, I opened my eyes, which I had shut at the beginning of the Æolian concert and—there she stood before me, beautiful, strong, imperious—a goddess!

I sprang to my feet. "Madam!"

"I am happy, sir, to find you at a time when the spirits of the air have just addressed you a graceful compliment. It will perhaps dispose you to grant me the favor I have come to ask. Favors, I have been told, are something the great Shetland is not lavish of."

"But who is it I see, madam, bringing life so early into my solitude?"

"My name is Nadira; I am a singer; I have just come from Vienna; I want to be at the Gluck Festival; I want to sing in it; I have come to beg you to give me a place in your program."

"But, Madam—"

"Oh, you must hear me first, that is only fair."

"It is unnecessary; I have already had the pleasure of hearing you."

"When? Where?"

"Last evening, in the sky."

"So it was you I noticed sailing all alone as I emerged from my cloud. I saw you just as I was singing your wonderful melody; those heavenly notes were apparently fated to serve as our musical introduction in both our meetings so far."

"Yes, it was I."

"And you could hear me?"

"I saw you and—what I saw I admired. . . ."

"Good heavens! The man is a wit and will make fun of me, and I'll have to take his jokes as compliments!"

"God forbid, I am not joking, madam; you are beautiful."

"What, again? Very well: I am beautiful and, in your opinion, I can sing?"

"You sing—too well."

"What do you mean, 'too well'?"

"I mean, madam, that in the Gluck Festival florid singing is not allowed. You shine especially by the lightness and grace of your ornaments; hence there is no room for it in a ceremony that is eminently in the grand, epic style."

"So you turn me down?"

"Alas, I can do nothing else."

"Oh, but that is unbelievable!" said she, reddening with anger and tearing from its stem a lovely rose, which she then crushed in her hand. "I'll speak to the Minister—" (I smiled) "to the Emperor."

"Madam," I replied calmly but earnestly, "the Minister of the Gluck Festival is my humble self; the Emperor of the Gluck Festival is likewise myself; the management of the ceremony is in my hands. I am absolute master, my word is law without appeal—and" (looking at her with only half the anger I felt) "you will not sing in it." Whereupon the beautiful Nadira with a shaking hand wipes from her eye a few tears of vexation and hurries away.

My half-angry mood once gone, I could not help laughing at the naïveté of that young madcap, accustomed by her Viennese worshippers, of course, to seeing everything and everybody bow to her whims. It never occurred to her that anything could prevent her coming and spoiling the unity of our festival after imposing her will on me.

I saw no more of her for a few days. The festival took place. *Alcestis* was nobly given, after which the six thousand voices in the amphitheater sang my *Song of Praise*, which I had scored quite simply for a hundred families of clarinets and saxophones, another hundred of flutes, four hundred cellos, and three hundred harps. The effect, as I've told you, was very impressive. The storm of applause being over, the Emperor rose and, after complimenting me with his customary courtesy, was graciously pleased to bestow on me his right to designate the woman who should have the honor of crowning Gluck's statue. Renewed shouts and applause from the assembly. In that glorious moment of enthusiasm my eye fell on the beautiful Nadira, who, from a distant box, was fixing a humble and saddened gaze on me. Suddenly a feeling of tender pity, even a kind of remorse gripped my heart at the sight of beauty vanquished and eclipsed by art. It struck me that as a magnanimous victor art should now yield to beauty part of its glory; and I pointed to Nadira, the frivolous Viennese singer, as the one to crown the god of expressiveness.

The universal surprise cannot be described. No one knew her. Flushing and turning pale by turns, Nadira rose, took from the hands of Gluck's acolyte the crown of flowers, leaves, and sheaves that she is to place on the divine brow, comes slowly into the amphitheater, ascends the steps of the temple, and on reaching the foot of the statue, turns toward the multitude and makes a sign to show that she wished to speak. All are silent, all admiring; even the women are struck with her extreme beauty.

"Euphonians," she begins, "I am not known to you. Only yesterday I was but an ordinary woman gifted with a brilliant and agile voice, and nothing more. High art had not been revealed to me. I have just heard *Alcestis* for the first time in my life, and with you I have admired the splendid majesty of Shetland's Song. Now I understand, I have heard, I have come to life: I am an artist. The instinct of genius alone, Shetland's genius, could have divined this. Allow me therefore, before crowning the god of expressiveness, to prove to you, his faithful worshippers, that I am worthy of this signal honor, and that our great Shetland was not mistaken."

At these words, tearing the pearls and gems from her hair, she flings them to the ground, tramples them underfoot (as a symbol of recantation), places her hand over her heart, bows her head to Gluck, and in a voice sublime in its accent and quality, begins Alcestis' aria, "Inexorable deities!"

It is impossible, my dear Xilef, to describe to you with any hope of success the extraordinary emotion produced by her amazing singing. All the heads gradually bowed down, every heart was overflowing; here and there people would join their hands or raise them absent-mindedly to their heads; young women burst into tears. But at the end, at the return of the immortal phrase:

> *It cannot be that I offend you*
> *When I implore your hastening my death,*

Nadira, accustomed to the clamorous enthusiasm of her Viennese, must for a moment have felt appalled; no one applauded. The entire amphitheater was silent and aghast. A minute later, each one recovering breath and voice—and in this you see again our Euphonians' musical sense—without either the prefect of the choruses or myself making the slightest sign to suggest the harmony, ten thousand voices burst out spontaneously on the chord of the diminished seventh followed by a magnificent cadence in C major.

Nadira, who had begun to falter, stood erect once again at this harmonious clamor, and raising her statuesque arms, glowing with admiration, joy, beauty, and love, she placed the crown on the Olympian head of Gluck. Inspired in my turn by this majestic scene, and wanting to temper an enthusiasm that was getting out of hand—perhaps, too, feeling already jealous—I gave the sign for the march from *Alcestis*. Falling fervently to our knees, we Euphonians paid homage to the sovereign master with his own religious incantation.

On rising, we all looked for Nadira; she had disappeared.

Hardly had I got into my house when I saw her approaching. She came up to me, bowed, and said: "Shetland, you have initiated me into art, you have given me a new life; I love you: can you love me? I give you my whole being—my life, my soul, and my beauty are yours."

After a moment's silent doubt in which I thought of my former love now fading away, I replied: "Nadira, you have made me see beyond art a sublime ideal. I love you with all my heart. I take what you give. But if you deceive me, now or later, you are a lost woman."

"Neither now nor later can I ever deceive you; but even if I have to pay with a cruel death the happiness of belonging to you, I want that happiness, I want it, I ask it—Shetland!"

"Nadira!" Our arms . . . our hearts . . . our souls . . . the infinite . . . There is no Nadira any more: it is I; no Shetland: it is she.

I am ashamed, dear Xilef, to be telling you such things, you whose heart bleeds, torn by absence and longing. But passion and happiness are selfish absolutely. And yet my happiness suffers interruptions and its bright skies are sometimes crossed by fearful shafts of darkness. I remember that on the instant when I said to Nadira: "I love you with all my heart!" three strings of my harp broke with a mournful sound. I feel superstitious about the incident. Was it a farewell from the art I am lost to? For it does seem to me I am no longer in love with it. But listen further.

Yesterday, a scorching day of scorching summer, we were hovering, she and I, high up in the skies. My ship, which I was not

steering, was wandering at the will of a feeble east wind. Intoxicated with love, clasping each other ecstatically as we lay stretched
out on the soft couch of my flower-strewn car, we were on the
threshold of another world. A single step, a single exertion of the
will, and we could step across it! "Nadira!" said I, straining her to
my heart.

"My beloved?"

"See: life has nothing more to offer us in this world; we have
reached the summit; shall we return to the earth? Let us rather die."
She gave me a surprised look. "Yes, let us die," I continued, "let us
fling ourselves over the ship's side in each other's arms. Our souls,
fused in a last kiss, will rise heavenward as one breath even before
our bodies whirling through space have reached the prosaic earth
again. Will you? Come!"

"Later," was her answer. "Let us live a little longer."

Later! thought I. But later, will we know another such minute
together? Oh, Nadira, you are a mere woman after all!

So here I am, since she wants it so. Farewell, dear friend. I
haven't seen her these two hours that I have been writing to you.
And during the whole of that time spent away from her, I have
felt an icy hand slowly tearing the heart out of my bosom.

SHETLAND

Mme Happer's letter, in which that worthy dame cynically informed Xilef that her daughter was giving him up and releasing
him from his engagement, also notified him of Mina's departure for
America, where she had been called by the attractive offer of a
theatrical manager and the "friendship" of a wealthy shipowner.

It would be difficult to form an accurate idea of the shock, the
distress, the indignation, the grief, and the boundless fury of a
man like Xilef, at once affectionate and violent, when he read that
masterpiece of brutality, insolence, and bad faith. He shook from
head to foot; tears and fire alike sprang from his eyes; and the notion of a punishment fitting the crime immediately took hold of
his mind. On the spot he decided, first to let Shetland know what
had happened to him, and then to leave at once for America and
seek out his perfidious mistress.

He was thus breaking away from everything that bound him

to Euphonia, losing his position, and at one stroke destroying his present and his future. But what did it matter? Could he now have any object in life but revenge? Shetland's letter containing the description of Euphonia reached him just as he was leaving Palermo, and he had only time to send the document to the Sicilian Academy, with a few words in which he apologized for being unable to present the paper in person as he had promised. Shetland's manuscript follows, exactly as the president of the Academy read it at a public sitting; Xilef had made no alterations in it.

A DESCRIPTION OF EUPHONIA

Euphonia is a small town of twelve thousand souls, situated on the slopes of the Harz, in Germany. The whole town may be looked upon as a great Conservatory of music, since the exercise of this art is the sole purpose of its inhabitants' labors.

All Euphonians, men, women, and children, are exclusively occupied with singing, with playing instruments, and with whatever else has a direct bearing on music. Most of them are both instrumentalists and singers. A few who do not perform devote themselves to the manufacture of instruments or to the engraving and printing of music. Others give their time to acoustical research and to the study of that branch of physics which relates to the production of sound.

The singers and players of instruments are grouped by categories in the several quarters of the town. Each type of voice and instrument has a street bearing its name, which is inhabited only by the section of the population which practices that particular voice or instrument. There are streets of sopranos, of basses, of tenors, of contraltos; of violins, of horns, of flutes, of harps, and so on.

Needless to say, Euphonia is governed in military fashion and subjected to a despotic regime. Hence the perfect order which obtains in study and the marvelous results that ensue for art.

For the rest, the Emperor of Germany does all he can to make the Euphonians' life a happy one. All he asks in return is that they send him, two or three times a year, a few thousand musicians for the festivals which he organizes in different parts of the Empire. Seldom must the whole city move at one time. On the contrary, when the solemn festivals whose sole object is art take place, it is the listeners who travel in order to come and hear the Euphonians.

An amphitheater, somewhat similar to the amphitheaters of Greek and Roman antiquity, but built to provide superior acoustic conditions, is devoted to the monumental performances. It can accommodate an audience of twenty thousand, and performers to the number of ten thousand.

The Minister of Fine Arts selects from the population of the several cities of Germany the twenty thousand privileged listeners who are permitted to attend these festivals. The choice is always determined by the greater or less intelligence or musical culture of the individuals. In spite of the extraordinary interest aroused by these gatherings throughout the Empire, no extraneous consideration would entitle anyone to attend if he were known to be unworthy.

The education of the Euphonians is carried out in the following manner: the children are trained from an early age in all kinds of rhythms; within a few years they reach the point where the subdividing of the beats in the bar, the syncopated forms, the combining of incompatible rhythms, and so on, are like play to them. Next comes the study of solfeggio parallel with that of an instrument, and later on, of singing and harmony. At puberty, the inception of life's flowering, when the passions begin to make themselves felt, it is sought to develop in them a sense of true expression and, as a result, a sense of style.

The rare ability of appreciating truth of expression, whether in a composer's work or in its performance, ranks above all others in the minds of the Euphonians. Whoever is shown to be absolutely lacking in that faculty, or whoever takes pleasure in works that are false as to expression, is inexorably banished from the city, however eminent his talent or exceptional his voice, unless he consents to descend to some inferior employment, such as the preparation of catgut for strings or the tanning of skins for kettledrums.

The teachers of singing and of the various instruments have under them a number of assistant masters whose duty it is to teach certain specialties in which they are known to excel. Thus, as regards the classes for violin, viola, cello, and double bass, in addition to the principal master who directs the main study of the instrument, there is one who teaches exclusively the pizzicato, another the use of harmonics, another the staccato, and so on. Prizes have been established for agility, precision, and beauty, as well as fineness of tone. Hence the wonderful degrees of *piano* which in Europe the Euphonians alone know how to produce.

The signal for working-hours, meals, and meetings by streets and wards, as well as for rehearsals in small or large groups, is given by a huge organ situated at the top of a tower rising above all the buildings of the town. This organ is worked by steam, and so powerful that its tones can easily be heard ten miles away. Five centuries ago, when the ingenious manufacturer Adolphe Sax,[3] to whom we owe the valuable group of brass reed instruments bearing his name, put forward his idea of a similar organ designed to perform in more musical fashion the function of bells, he was looked upon as a lunatic—just like the unfortunate man who still earlier had talked of applying steam power to navigation and railways, or like those who two centuries ago steadfastly worked at the means of steering aerial flight, which has changed the face of the world.

The language of the tower organ, this aural telegraphy, is hardly understood by any but Euphonians; they alone are familiar with telephony, an invention whose importance was foreseen by one Sudre in the nineteenth century,[4] and which one of the prefects of harmony in Euphonia developed and brought to the degree of perfection it has reached today. The Euphonians also communicate by visual telegraph, and the rehearsal leaders have only to make a simple sign with either or both hands and the conductor's baton, to indicate to the performers that they are to give out, loud or soft, such and such a chord followed by such and such a cadence or modulation; or to perform a given classical work either all together or in a small body, or again in crescendo, by having the divers groups enter in succession.

When some important new work is to be performed, each part is studied separately for three or four days. Next, the organ announces the rehearsal in the amphitheater of all the voices by them-

---

[3] See above, note 2, p. 237.
[4] Jean-François Sudre (1787–1862), at first a violinist and composer, later devoted his life to developing a musical language for civilian and military communication. He received offical praise and awards for his system, which ultimately became a purely rhythmic code for teaching the deaf, dumb, and blind.

selves. There they sing, under the direction of the singing-masters, by "centuries"—each hundred constituting a complete chorus. At this rehearsal, all the breathing-places are decided on, and so arranged that never more than one fourth of the singers take a breath at the same time. In this way the vocal output of the entire mass never suffers any appreciable interruption.

The first rehearsals aim at literal exactitude; then come the broad nuances; lastly style and EXPRESSION. Any marking of the rhythm by bodily movements during the singing is strictly forbidden to the choristers. They are also trained to silence, a silence so absolute and profound that if three thousand Euphonian choristers were assembled in the amphitheater or in any other resonant place, one could still hear the buzzing of an insect, and a blind man in their midst might think he was quite alone. They are so highly practiced that even after such a long silence in which they may have counted hundreds of rests, they have been known to attack a chord en masse without a single singer missing his entrance.

A similar system is employed for orchestra rehearsals; no section is allowed to take part in the ensemble before it has been heard and severely examined separately by the prefects. The entire orchestra then rehearses by itself; the vocal and instrumental masses are brought together only when the prefects have declared themselves satisfied that each group has been sufficiently rehearsed.

The grand ensemble next undergoes the composer's criticism. He listens from the upper part of the amphitheater, which the public will occupy; and when he finds himself the absolute master of this huge intelligent instrument, when he is sure that nothing remains but to communicate to it the vital nuances that he feels and can impart better than anyone else, the moment has come for him to become a performer himself. He climbs the podium to conduct. A tuning-fork attached to every desk enables the instrumentalists to tune noiselessly before and during the performance; trial runs or any other noises, however slight, are absolutely forbidden. An ingenious mechanism, which might have been invented five or six centuries earlier if someone had taken the trouble to design it, and which is actuated by the conductor without being visible to the public, indicates to the eye of each performer, and quite close to him, the beats of each measure. It also denotes precisely the several degrees of *piano* or *forte*. In this way the performers are immediately and instantaneously in touch with the conductor's intention, and can respond to it as promptly as do the hammers of a piano under the hand pressing the keys. The master can then say with perfect truth that he is *playing the orchestra*.

Chairs of musical philosophy are held by the most learned men of the time and serve to spread among the Euphonians sound ideas as to the purpose and importance of art. They learn the laws on which it is based, and acquire accurate historical notions of the revolutions it has undergone. It is to one of these professors that we owe the peculiar institution of concerts of bad music, which the Euphonians attend at certain periods of the year in order to hear the monstrosities admired for centuries throughout Europe, the rules for producing which were then taught in the conservatories of Germany, France, and Italy. The Euphonians hear and study these works in order to get a clear idea of what to avoid—for example, the majority of the cavatinas and finales of the Italian school of the beginning of the nineteenth century, and the vocal fugues of the more or less religious compositions of periods antedating the twentieth.

The first experiments thus made on a population whose musical sense is today extraordinarily fine, well-nigh impeccable, led to rather odd results. Some of the masterpieces of bad music that were false in expression and ridiculous in style but were nevertheless effective in a certain way, and though not agreeable, at least bearable to the ear, aroused in the Euphonians a feeling of pity. They thought they were listening to the productions of children lisping a language that they do not understand. Other works made them laugh so much that it became impossible to continue the performance. But when it came to singing the fugue on *Kyrie eleison* from the most celebrated work of one of the greatest masters of our ancient German school, and they were assured that this had been written, not by a madman, but by a very great musician who was merely following the example of other masters, and who in turn became an example to others for a very long time, their consternation cannot be portrayed. They were shocked and grieved at the thought of this humiliating malady to which, as they could see, even genius was not immune. Their religious sense and their musical sense joined in revolt against these unbelievable blasphemies, and with one accord they sang the celebrated prayer *Parce Deus*,[5] the expression of which is so true, as if to apologize publicly to God in the name of music and musicians.

Since everybody has some kind of voice, every Euphonian is duty bound to exercise his and acquire some idea of the art of singing. The result is that the orchestral players of string instruments who can both sing and play at the same time form a second reserve choir, which the composer can draw upon in certain circumstances, and whose unexpected entrance occasionally produces remarkable effects.

On their side, singers are required to master the mechanism of certain string and percussion instruments and are able, if need be, to play them while singing. Thus all of them are also harpists, pianists, and guitarists. Many of them can play the violin, the viola, the viola d'amore, and the cello. The children play the modern sistrum and the harmonic cymbals, a new instrument, each stroke on which gives off a chord.

The parts in works for the stage and the solos for voice or instruments are entrusted only to Euphonians whose native gifts and special talents fit them best for right performance. They appear at a competition held publicly (and patiently) in the presence of the entire population, which makes the final choice. All the time necessary is devoted to it. When it was required not long ago to celebrate Gluck's decennial, an eight months' search was made among the women singers for the one most capable of playing and singing Alcestis, and nearly one thousand women were successively heard for the purpose.

In Euphonia no privileges are granted any artists to the detriment of art. There are no leading singers, no property rights in title roles, even though such roles should be obviously unsuited to their special talent or physique. The composer, the minister, and the prefects determine the essential qualities required to fill such and such a part, to represent this or that character; a search is then made for the individual best equipped with these qualities, and even if he is the most lowly in Euphonia, he is elected as soon as discovered. Occasionally our musical government's search and labor are in

---

[5] *Parce Domine*—"Spare Thy people, O Lord!" a chant used at the benediction of the Holy Sacrament in a time of penance. Which setting Berlioz had in mind does not appear.

vain. Thus in 2320, after having sought a Eurydice for fifteen months, we were compelled to give up the idea of staging Gluck's *Orpheus*, for lack of a young woman beautiful enough to represent that poetic figure and intelligent enough to understand the part.

On the literary education of the Euphonians much care is lavished; they are all able up to a certain point to appreciate the beauties of the great ancient and modern poets. Any among them who should be incurably ignorant or uncultivated in this regard could never aspire to a part in any of the higher musical functions. And thus it is that, thanks to the intelligent will of our Emperor and to his untiring solicitude for the most powerful of the arts, Euphonia has become a great conservatory of monumental music.

The academicians of Palermo thought they were dreaming as they listened to the reading of these notes drawn up by Xilef's friend, and asked themselves whether the young Euphonian prefect had not practiced on their credulity. It was accordingly decided then and there that a delegation from the Academy should visit the musical city and judge for itself of the truth of the extraordinary facts just laid before them.

We left Xilef breathing nothing but revenge, and ready to pursue his bold mistress by air to America, where in his simplicity he thought that she had gone. He left, accordingly, mute and gloomy as the thunderclouds that sweep across the sky before the coming of a great storm. He ate up space; never had his engine worked so furiously. If his ship ran into a contrary wind, she would meet it head on, or by soaring to a higher zone, would either seek a more favorable current or even rise to that region of eternal calm which probably no human being before Xilef had ever reached. In those almost inaccessible solitudes, on the borderline of life, the cold and dryness are such that the objects made of wood in the ship warped and cracked. Pilot on a sinister mission, Xilef remained impassible. He was half dead from the rarefaction of the atmosphere and unmoved at the sight of blood streaming from his nose and mouth. He waited until he could no longer stand the pain and was forced to come down in search of air fit to breathe, hoping that the direction of the wind would permit him to remain there.

Such was his headlong speed of flight that forty hours after his leaving Palermo he landed in New York. It is impossible to recount his relentless search, not only in the towns and villages of the United States, Canada, Labrador, and South America as far as the Straits of Magellan, but also in the islands of the Atlantic and Pacific Oceans. It was only after a year of these insane efforts that he saw their futility, and the idea finally came to him of looking for the two rascally women in Europe, where they had probably remained in order to put him off their track. He wanted moreover to see his friend Shetland, if only in order to ask him to replenish the means he had nearly exhausted. For it can readily be imagined that in the course of his furious exploration money had not been spared.

He consequently decided to return to Euphonia, and arrived there after three days of navigation, on the very evening when Nadira and Shetland were having a garden party at their villa. The grounds and reception-rooms were brilliantly lighted. Wishing to show himself only to his friend, Xilef waited concealed in a shrubbery for the opportunity of finding him alone. Overhearing from his hiding-place the noises of the party, he was startled to hear the tones of a voice that reminded him of Mina's.

"It's my imagination, it's delirium!" said he to himself. Shetland appeared at last and, suddenly seeing the exile before him, cried out: "Dear God, it's you! How wonderful! Now that you're here, our party is really complete."

"Not a word, I beg of you, Shetland; I cannot show myself. I am no longer a Euphonian; I have lost my post; I have come only to have a talk with you about something very serious."

"Do let's leave serious matters till tomorrow," replied Shetland. "You will have your post again, I promise you; you are still one of us. Come along, I must introduce you to Nadira, who will be delighted to meet you at last."

And with the cruel lightheartedness of those who are happy and cannot imagine the sorrows of others, he dragged Xilef willy-nilly toward the spot where the company was gathered. As chance would have it, when the two friends entered the room where Nadira was she was apparently engrossed in some flirtation and did not see them. She thus had no time to prepare herself for Xilef's shattering apparition. As for him, he had recognized his unfaithful mistress as soon as he came in. But hatred and suffering had in the past year given his character such strength, he had learned so completely to master his feelings, that he was able to control his emotion and conceal it entirely.

Xilef and Nadira were consequently brought face to face abruptly and in a way most likely to disconcert two less extraordinary beings. The beautiful singer, on meeting the lover she had so shamefully forsaken and deceived, and seeing at a glance that he did not want to recognize her, thought she could not do better than to follow his lead. She greeted him politely yet coldly, and without any sign of surprise or fear; such was the woman's amazing habit of dissimulation.

Shetland had therefore no inkling of the truth, and if he noticed a certain coldness in Xilef and Nadira's greeting, he attributed it, on the one hand, to a kind of instinctive jealousy which would make Nadira look unfavorably on any man who might steal from her the smallest part of her lover's affection; and, on the other, to the painful reflections on his own misery that Xilef could not help making when suddenly brought face to face with the intoxication and happiness of another.

The party went on without a single cloud to spoil its brilliancy. But long before the end, Xilef's penetration had shown him—in certain signs imperceptible to any other observer, in certain gestures and the tone of certain remarks—the undeniable fact that Nadira was already deceiving Shetland.

From that instant the idea of stoical resignation that Xilef had at first conceived, so as not to destroy his friend's happiness and keep him in ignorance of Nadira's antecedents, was swept away by sinister thoughts. These suddenly lit up the darkest recesses of his soul and revealed to him perspectives of horror he had never before known. His mind was soon made up. He told Shetland the next day that he had given up the idea of continuing his journey and that consequently he did not need to talk over with him the business he had had in mind. He disclosed his intention to remain in Euphonia, but retired, in obscurity, and inactive. He begged him to take no steps toward having his prefecture restored to him; peace and quiet were all he now required in life.

In spite of her astuteness, Nadira let herself be taken in by this pretense of resigned sorrow, and enjoined on her mother to imitate her reserve toward Xilef: he seemed so eager to forget a secret known in Euphonia only to themselves and him. In order to make the situation less dangerous, Xilef rarely emerged—or so it appeared—from the retreat he had chosen. He saw his friend only once in a while, pleading an unsociable disposition born of his incurable sorrows.

But variously disguised, and with the crafty caution of a cat on its nocturnal prowl, Xilef watched Nadira and followed her in all her secret rendezvous. Within a few months he held in his hands all the clues to her intrigues and could measure the full extent of her infamy. Then and there the denouement of the drama was settled in his mind. Shetland must at any cost be wrenched away from circumstances so defiling and dishonored. Even if death should be the consequence of his disillusionment, it was imperative that love, noble and wholehearted love, the sublimest sentiment of the human heart, which had inflamed two eminent artists for such an unworthy creature, should be avenged, and avenged in a terrible and fearful manner, the like of which had never been known. And this is how Xilef managed to carry out his duty.

In those days there was in Euphonia a celebrated mechanical genius whose inventions aroused universal wonder. He had just finished a huge piano whose variegated sound was so powerful that under the fingers of a single virtuoso it could hold its own with an orchestra of a hundred players. Hence the name of orchestra-piano given to it. Nadira's birthday being near, Xilef had no difficulty in persuading his friend what a magnificent present for his beloved the new instrument that everyone admired and talked about would be. "But if you wish to make her joy complete," he added, "you must give her as well the delightful steel pavilion that the same designer has just made. Its elegance is beyond that of any structure with which we are acquainted. It will make a delightful summer boudoir, airy, cool, just the thing for our hot season. You can inaugurate it by giving a ball which the radiant Nadira will open."

Shetland gladly and entirely approved his friend's idea and even deputed him to purchase both the masterworks. Xilef lost no time before calling on the inventor. After telling him the object of his visit, he asked whether it would be possible to add to the summerhouse a special and powerful mechanism, the nature and effect of which he described, and the existence of which was to be kept secret by both of them. The designer was startled by the suggestion, but tempted by its novelty and the considerable sum Xilef offered him to carry it out. After a moment's thought he replied with the assurance of genius: "It will take a week."

"That will do," said Xilef, and so the thing was settled. A week later the happy Shetland was able to present to his love the double present intended for her.

Nadira received it with transports of joy. The summerhouse especially delighted her; she never tired of admiring its elegant yet solid construction, its curious decorations, the arabesques with which it was covered, its exquisite furniture, and the coolness that made it so comfortable at night during the dog-days.

"It's a charming idea of Xilef's," she exclaimed, "to inaugurate it with a ball for our close friends, a gathering of which my darling Shetland will be the soul, improvising brilliant dance tunes on the new giant piano. But this magical instrument would be too powerful close to the audience. Xilef will therefore be kind enough to have it moved from the summerhouse to the big reception-room of the villa at the far end of the garden, where it will still sound marvelous. I am off to send out invitations."

This arrangement seemed most reasonable, it fitted in admirably with Xilef's plan and was promptly carried out. On the appointed day, Nadira, adorned like a fairy queen, and her huge mother, bedecked with heavy finery, received in the summerhouse all the young women who were in every respect worthy of the intimacy with which Nadira honored them, and all the young men she had marked out for *special distinction*. The trap was set. Xilef observed with frightening self-possession all his victims heading for the pit one after another.

Shetland, still unsuspecting, welcomed everybody most cordially, though he was weighed down by a feeling of sadness inappropriate to the occasion. Going up to Nadira, he said to her entranced: "How beautiful you are, dear heart! Why, then, do I feel so sad tonight? I ought to be so happy! I feel as if on the brink of some great calamity, some dreadful event. It must be you, naughty witch, whose beauty upsets and disturbs me till I am dizzy."

"Don't be silly! You and your visions! Why don't you go down to the piano. We could at least open the ball!"

"Yes," Xilef put in, "our beautiful Nadira is obviously right as usual. To the piano! Everybody here is dying to come to grips."

Very soon the strains of an irresistible waltz are heard, while groups of dancers form and whirl. Xilef, standing with his hand on a steel button in the outer wall of the summerhouse, follows them with his eyes. Something strange seems to be going on within him; his lips are bloodless, his eyes misty; from time to time he puts his hand over his heart as if to stop its frantic beating. He is still hesitating when he hears Nadira, leaning on the arm of her waltzing partner, say quickly to him: "No, not tonight, I can't; expect me tomorrow."

At this fresh proof of Nadira's shamelessness, Xilef can no longer master his fury. He presses the steel button with all his might, saying: "Tomorrow, you wretches! There is no tomorrow for you!" He runs to Shetland, who, all absorbed in his inspiration, was flooding villa and garden with harmonies now sweet and tender, now wild and despairing.

"What do you think you are doing, Shetland?" shouts Xilef; "you're asleep on the bench; everybody's complaining of your slow tempo. Faster, faster, I tell you. Those dancers are full of the devil! That's better! Oh, what a beautiful phrase, what a marvelous harmony, what a threatening pedal! How this theme in the minor groans and wails, like a song by the furies! You are a poet, you are a seer. Listen to their shouts of joy! Oh, your Nadira is very happy!"

Fearful shrieks were in fact to be heard from the summerhouse; but Shetland, more and more excited, was letting loose from the orchestra-piano a torrent of sound that drowned out the cries and disguised their import.

The instant Xilef had pressed the spring that released the secret mechanism of the summerhouse, the steel walls of the little circular building had begun to roll in on themselves slowly and noiselessly, so that the dancers, finding less space in which to move, thought at first that their numbers had increased. Surprised, Nadira exclaimed: "Who are these newcomers? I'm sure there are more of us than before; it's unbearable, we shall suffocate. Even the windows seem smaller and let in less fresh air!"

Mme Happer, red and pale by turns, was crying for help; "Merciful God, what has happened? Please, gentlemen, help me out of here! Open, open up!"

But instead of opening, the summerhouse turns on itself with a sharply accelerated motion which masks the doors and windows with an iron wall. The space inside shrinks rapidly; the screams grow in intensity, those of Nadira can be heard rising above the din. And the beautiful singer, the poetic fairy queen, feeling herself hemmed in on all sides, pushes back those around her with gestures and words of horrible bestiality, her low nature shown up by the fear of death and standing out in all its hideousness.

Xilef has left Shetland in order to see the infernal spectacle at close range. Panting like a tiger licking the prey it has struck down, he roams round the summerhouse, shouting with all his might: "Oh, Mina, what ails you, my sweet, that you should get into such a state? Is your steel corset too tight? Ask one of the gentlemen to unlace it for you; they're used to it. And your hippopotamus of a mother, how is she? I don't seem to hear her dulcet tones."

And indeed, to the horrible and anguished screams under the ever-tighter straining of the steel partitions, has succeeded the hideous noise of flesh mangled, the cracking of fractured bones, bursting skulls; eyes are torn from their sockets and streams of foaming blood spurt out from beneath the roof of the summerhouse, until the hideous machine stops exhausted over the unresisting mass of bloody clay.

And Shetland is still playing, unaware of the party or the dances, when Xilef with haggard eyes tears him from the keyboard and drags him toward the summerhouse just reopened, its tessellated floor a smoking charnel-house in which human forms are no longer to be discerned.

"Come, now, come, you poor wretch," he cries, "and see what's left of your worthless Nadira, who was my worthless Mina; of her execrable mother, and of her eighteen lovers! Look! And tell me if justice is done."

At the sight of this unspeakable horror, this scene which divine vengeance spared the damned of the seventh circle, Shetland sinks to the ground. When he rises again, he is laughing; he rushes distractedly across the garden, singing, calling Nadira, gathering flowers for her, gamboling; he is mad.

Xilef, on the contrary, had quieted down and suddenly recovered his coolness. "Poor Shetland, he is happy. But I think there is nothing more for me to do, and so I may as well take a rest. 'Othello's occupation's gone!' " Taking a deep breath from a flask of cyanide that he always carried with him, he fell dead.

Six months after this catastrophe Euphonia in mourning was still under the vow of silence. Alone the organ of the tower scattered across the skies a slow dissonant harmony, like a wail of horrified grief. Shetland had died a few days after Xilef, without recovering his mind for even a moment. At the funeral of the two friends, whose appalling end remained, like the rest of the drama, incomprehensible to the entire town, public consternation was such that not only song but funeral music was prohibited.

Corsino rolls up his manuscript and goes out.

After a few instants' silence, the musicians get up. The conductor, whom they have invited to the farewell dinner in my honor, bows to them on his way out, and says: "Till tomorrow."

BACON: You know, Corsino frightens me.

DIMSKY: To write such dreadful things a man must be rabid.

WINTER: He is an Italian!

DERVINCK: He is a Corsican!

TURUTH: He is a gangster!

MYSELF: He is a musician!

SCHMIDT: It's plain he's not a literary man. When a man has nothing in his head but absurd improbabilities like that, he'd do better to write—

KLEINER (*interrupting*): *A Visit to Tom Thumb*, eh? You're jealous, that's all.

SCHMIDT: Kettledrummer!

KLEINER: Buffoon!

SCHMIDT: Bavarian!

MYSELF: Gentlemen, gentlemen, such home truths are out of place right now. Save them till tomorrow when we have time to tell them to one another—*inter pocula*.[6]

BACON (*going out*): Really, our guest makes me tired with his Greek. To hell with him!

---

[6] "In our cups."

The Farewell Dinner

*Corsino's toast—the conductor's toast—Schmidt's
toast—the author's toast*

The End of the Kleiner Brothers' Vexations

A T SEVEN o'clock I come into the room assigned for the stirrup-dinner.[1] I find assembled there all my good friends of the orchestra of X, including their worthy leader, and even the player of the bass drum, who has never looked upon me with favor. But it is an institutional function, and the good fellow thought he should set aside his personal dislike in order to attend. Moreover, since the occasion is clearly a *tutti*, he must have thought: "How can there be one without the bass drum?" The gathering is like all get-togethers among artists, noisy and gay. Comes the time for the toasts.

Glass in hand, Corsino is the first to rise. "Here's to Music, gentlemen," he declares; "her reign has come! She protects the drama, dresses up comedy, glorifies tragedy, gives a home to painting, intoxicates the dance, shows the door to that little vagabond, the ballad opera, mows down those who oppose her progress; flings out of the window the representatives of routine; and triumphs in France, Germany, England, Italy, Russia, and even in America.

"She levies huge tribute everywhere; she has flatterers too stupid to understand her and detractors who cannot perceive either the greatness of her designs or the learned audacity of her intentions, but all fear and admire her instinctively. She has worshippers who

---

[1] So called for the nonce by analogy with the stirrup-cup, which the hostess at the inn gives the rider when on his horse and about to depart.

sing odes to her, would-be assassins who always miss, a guard which will die for her and never surrender.[2] Several of her soldiers have risen to be princes, princes have made themselves her soldiers. People take their hats off to foul misrepresentations of her only because they are passed off as her portraits. But on the great days when they see her in person, her brow resplendent with glory and genius, they bow down, they shout, and praise her with their hands. She has passed through the Terror, the Directorate, and the Consulate; having now reached the Empire, she has made up a court out of all the queens she has dethroned. *Long live the Emperor!*"

Rising in his turn, the conductor says: "Well put, my good Corsino. I'll give a cheer with you, *Long live the Emperor!* For although I rarely speak of it, I love our art passionately. Yet I am very far from thinking, as you do, that it is at the height of its power. Europe's state of ferment makes me fear the worst. True, everything is quiet right now. But didn't the last storm cruelly bruise and exhaust her? [3] Are music's wounds healed, and will she not wear hideous scars for a a long time to come?

"In the minds of those nations of warring ants among whom we live, of what use are we poets, artists, musicians, composers— crickets of every species? None whatever. You know how we were treated during the latest European tornado. When we complained, the warring ants asked: 'And what were you busy with yesterday?'—'Singing.'—'Singing? Congratulations! Now you can go and dance!' [4]

"When you come to think of it, what interest can you expect the nations to take at this time in our insights, our strivings, or even our most dramatic effects? What signifies our music on the Blessing of the Daggers, our choruses on revolt, our Witches' Sabbaths, our Brigand Songs, our Infernal Dances, our abracadabra of all sorts,[5] beside the colossal hymn to suffering, rage, and destruction which is being sung across Europe by millions of voices? What are our orchestras compared to these formidable hordes roused by thunder and fire to perform hurricanes, led by the indefatigable

---

[2] An allusion to the Imperial Guard at Waterloo and the saying attributed to General Cambronne, who led it.
[3] The revolutions of 1848, which lasted in effect four years.
[4] Quoted from La Fontaine's "The Ant and the Cricket."
[5] Berlioz is alluding to portions of contemporary works, notably Meyerbeer's and his own, that express something akin to war and destruction.

Kapellmeister whose bow is a scythe and whose name is Death?

"And what kind of ideas and men do these upheavals suddenly bring into prominence? What are the voices that make themselves heard above these many sinister clamors? The startled nightingale returns to its thicket, shuts its eyes to the lightning flash, and answers the thunder only with silence. We who are not nightingales do the same; the chaffinch crouches in the hollow of the oak, the lark in its furrow; the rooster goes back to the henhouse, the pigeon to its dovecote, the sparrow to its barn. The turkey and the peacock perch on their dung-heap, the osprey and the owl in the old ruins. Only the rook and the crow wander in the fog and join their discordant voices to greet the storm.

"No, today the difficulties in the path of our art are mighty, the obstacles many, the achievements laborious and slow. And yet I still have hope. I believe that constancy, courage, and dignity can still save art. Let us therefore band together and be patient, energetic, and proud. Let us prove to the peoples distracted by so many grave concerns that if we are the last-born of civilization's children and have only for a moment enjoyed its deepest affection, we were worthy of it. Possibly they will then understand how much art would suffer if we were to perish.

"I drink to those artists whom nothing can debase or dishearten, the true, the valiant, and the strong!" (*Applause.*)

BACON (*whispering to Kleiner*): He doesn't often speak, our chief, but when he does, he is anything but tongue-tied.

"Yes," says the younger Kleiner, "but all this is dry stuff." (*Rising*) "As for me, I drink to our good comrade Schmidt, so that he'll enliven us a little, for we're getting into politics and I know of nothing more—vexatious."

Schmidt makes a face and, glass in hand, stands on his chair. "Gentlemen," he says in his rattling voice, "not to change the subject too abruptly, I must confess that Corsino's faith and enthusiasm, and the chief's clinging to a hope I thought had died within him, give me the greatest pleasure. Maybe in time faith and hope will come to me too—just a minute! I have a queer feeling, as if faith and hope together were coming back to me right now. I don't feel quite strong enough to move mountains—yet; but, God forgive me, I'll get there, for on my honor I believe that I believe.

"On what trifles do the revolutions of the human mind hinge!

Just now I was more skeptical than an algebra-teacher. I did think that two and two made four, but, like Paul-Louis Courier, the French vine-cutter,[6] I wasn't so sure about it. Now, as a result of the fine sermons we have just heard, if I were told that M. —— had done . . . ; that Mlle —— had not . . . ; and that Mme —— had never said . . . , I should be capable of believing it.

"Notice, by the way, how kind my blunderbuss was not to fire its shots! What a chance I had, if I were really mean, to let a sentence so charged with ammunition go off! I could attribute good deeds to scoundrels, works of genius to blockheads, common sense to fools, and talent to Kleiner—"

"A hit! A palpable hit! You got what was coming to you, Kleiner, you wanted to be 'enlivened' (*hisses*), now you *are!*"

SCHMIDT (*resuming*): Yes, in my present mood I could ascribe a
public to our theater, voice and style to our singers, beauty to
our actresses, a feeling for art to our manager—really my
blunderbuss might create fearful havoc. But no: its open mouth
shall remain silent; I lock the trigger, and for greater security
(*swallowing a large glass of wine*) I dampen the powder. For
just as one has heard of unloaded shot-guns that went off, so one
ought to suppose the same thing can happen to a loaded blunderbuss that is merely uncocked.

"I want to be kindness itself today, as kind as the heavy guns on the ramparts that bask harmlessly in the sun and in whose mouths fowls build their nests. I want to propose a simple, well-meant toast, which my two honorable predecessors should have proposed first. They have left the honor to me and I take advantage of it— too bad for them! I drink, then, to the guest whom we all love and who is about to leave us. May he soon return to help us out once more with our work on the night shift!" (*Prolonged cheers, clapping, and handshaking.*) "Didn't I tell you?" cries Schmidt triumphantly. "It's the jokers who have the most heart."

I rise in turn. "Thank you, my dear Schmidt. Gentlemen, my opinion as to the present and future of art is rather like Corsino's, and even more like that of your distinguished leader. I sometimes find myself sharing the fervid enthusiasm of the former, but the fears of the latter quickly come to cool it. The memory of many a

---

[6] A famous pamphleteer who assumed the role and style of a country man to talk common sense on political questions.

disheartening experience adds to my despondency, if not to my discouragement. Political disturbances are no doubt a great obstacle to the thriving of music as we understand it. Unfortunately, if it is ailing and languishing, the primary causes are quite close by, and it is there, I believe, that we must look for them.

"Our art, inherently complex as it is, needs for the deployment of its full strength the co-operation of many agents. Now, to give indispensable unity to their action there must be authority—strong and absolute authority. This point Corsino thoroughly grasped in the organization of his Euphonia. But to that artistic authority, which we shall suppose to be intelligent and devoted, we must add the sinews of war and industry: money. Where are these four powers—authority, intelligence, devotion, and money—to be found constantly together? I could not say if I tried. Their union subsists but transiently and in rare, exceptional circumstances. The troubled and precarious life that music leads in Europe today is chiefly the result of the disastrous connections it has suffered to be imposed upon it, and of prejudices that sway it now this way, now that. It is the plight of Virgil's Cassandra, the inspired virgin over whom Greeks and Trojans contend, and whose prophetic words are not heeded. She raises her eyes to heaven—only her eyes, for her hands are in chains. Many and all too true are the sad things that have been said on this subject at our recent evenings in the orchestra, during what Schmidt calls 'the work of the night shift.' Allow me to sum them up here.

"From its connection with the theater, a connection that once produced, and could again produce, magnificent results, have come music's slavery and shame—every kind of degradation. As you well know, gentlemen, it is not only with its sisters, dramatic poetry and the dance, that music must join nowadays in the theater, but far more with certain inferior arts clustering around to stir up a childish curiosity and distract the attention of the crowd away from the main point. The managers of the great 'lyric' theaters so called, having noticed that only enormous works brought in enormous receipts, no longer find any merit except in compositions of enormous length. But being also convinced, and rightly, that the public's attention at its best cannot be kept alert during five hours by music and drama alone, they have introduced into their five- or six-act operas all that the most restless imagination can conceive by way of din and bustle and dazzle for the crude excitement of the senses.

"Ability in a manager of large opera houses now means his greater or lesser skill in making the public *endure* music when the music is beautiful, and preventing that same public from noticing when the music is worthless.

"Next to this method of speculation, we must mention the ambition of singers who also aim at making money by every means possible. The strange disease that seems to have overtaken the entire flock of theatrical singers during the last few years, a disease whose symptoms you are familiar with, does not generally come from a love of fame, or from competition and vanity: it is the mean love of lucre, it is avarice, it is the passion for luxury, the insatiable desire for material enjoyment. They want applause and hyperbolic praise only because these move the hesitant crowd and push it toward this one or that. And it is to the crowd the appeal is made because it alone brings in the cash. In that world of theirs they do not want, as we would, money *for* music, but *from* music—and in despite of music.

"Hence the taste for tinsel, bombast, volume above all; the contempt for the primary qualities of style, the outrageous defiance of expression, common sense, and language; the destruction of rhythm, the introduction into singing of the most revolting stupidities; hence finally the naïvely erroneous conviction of the public at large that these are essential conditions of dramatic music, which it confuses with theatrical music. Teaching itself has come to serve the same ends. You have no idea what certain masters teach their pupils. With rare exceptions, one may say that today a singing-teacher is a man who is a little more stupid than the next man, and who imparts the ways of murdering good music while giving an appearance of life to bad.

"As for the poets and musicians who write for the stage, it is not in our time that one would find a majority (some are still to be met with, I admit) filled with a genuine respect for art. How many among them are capable of limiting themselves to the production of a few works of high excellence, though but moderately lucrative, and of preferring this modest and finished output to the continual exploiting of their talent, exhausted though it be? They are like a meadow mown and mown again down to the roots, with no time allowed for the grasses to grow again. With or without ideas, one must write and write often; one must pile act upon act so as to pile royalties upon royalties and amass capital and interest, and finally corner all that can be cornered and absorbed, like those infusoria called *vortex*, which create an eddy in front of their ever-gaping mouths, so as to engulf without cease all the animalcules that go by. And to justify themselves our authors modestly cite Voltaire and Walter Scott, who, quite unlike them, grudged neither time nor pains to bring their works to perfection.

"Others with no ambition to become wealthy, as so many think they have a right to be nowadays, content themselves with seeking in art their livelihood. They do not hesitate to turn their very real talent into a stock-in-trade, and so must scratch down to bedrock a soil capable of producing fine fruit if it were wisely cultivated. This is less blameworthy, to be sure; necessity is not the mother of art. But it is very deplorable all the same, not only as regards the self-respect of these intelligent men, but as regards the public which pays for the enjoyment of certain products and finds the sellers only too often bringing shoddy to the market.

"From both kinds of suppliers in this relentless and more or less hurried production, come forth, wriggling together and disgustingly intermixed, formulas and devices, slickness and commonplace. These it is that cause all the works of the same period that are written under like conditions to look alike. It takes too long to wait for the birth of an idea and to find for it a fresh form. One knows that by putting together notes or words in this or that fashion, combinations result that will be accepted by the public of all Europe. Why then look for other ways of putting them together? These combinations are merely the wrappers of ideas; to change the colors of the labels is enough, it will take a long time for the public to find out that the wrapper contains nothing. The important thing is not to produce a few good works, but a quantity of mediocre ones that will succeed and bring in quick returns.

"The extent of public tolerance has been measured to a hair and although its good nature, close to indifference, has gone far beyond the limits of taste and common sense, the journeymen say: 'Let's go that far, pending the time when we can go farther. Let us seek neither originality, nor naturalness, nor probability, nor elegance, nor beauty; let's not worry about vulgarities, platitudes, barbarisms, or tautology. The choice is dictated by the relative speed

with which we can write works endowed with either set of qualities. The public would feel no gratitude for our delicacy. Let us
save time, for time is money, and money is everything.'

"And so it is that in works which are certainly not without merit
in other respects, the carpers can find incredible faults, which it
would not have taken the author twenty minutes' attention to spot
and correct. But twenty minutes are worth possibly twenty francs,
and for twenty francs one is willing to allow the septet in the third
act of *The Huguenots* to sing: 'Whatever may happen or befall' [7]
—a notorious but not a unique line, which by the way was the
cause of my losing a sizable bet recently. Someone swore that no
such line was to be found in the text, and that no one could sing so
outstanding a piece of asininity at the Opéra. I maintained the
opposite; a bet was made and the matter looked into: I lost. What
they sing is: 'Whatever may befall or happen.' "

Roars of laughter from the guests. Bacon alone keeps a straight
face and wonders what there is to laugh at in the line. The reader
has already been told that he is no descendant of the Bacon who invented gunpowder. [8]

I go on: "These practices of the theater spread even to artists
outside, whose intentions are of the highest, whose convictions are
sincere. We see some who, in order to attract applause, not so
much to themselves, but to the things they care for, commit acts of
positive cowardice. Would you credit the fact that for a great
many years at the concerts of the Paris Conservatoire it was
customary to tack on the final chorus of *Christ on the Mount of
Olives* to Beethoven's *Coriolanus* Overture? For what reason? Because the overture ends *smorzando* with a *pizzicato* and it was
feared that it would meet with insulting silence from the public,
whereas the brilliant peroration of the chorus could be counted
on to secure applause for Beethoven. Oh pettiness! Oh worship of
the *claque!* What if the house did not applaud this heroic inspiration, was that an excuse for destroying the deep impression it undeniably makes and for compounding an offensive hodgepodge, a
burlesque anachronism, coupling together Coriolanus and Christ,

---

[7] "*Quoi qu'il advienne ou qu'il arrive.*" The librettists were Scribe and Émile
Deschamps.
[8] Meaning, according to the French adage, that he is slow-witted: *il n'a pas
inventé la poudre*—will never set the Thames on fire.

blending the clamor of the Roman Forum with the choir of angels on Mount Zion? Please observe, too, that the perpetrators of this wretched scheme guessed wrong. I have elsewhere heard the *Coriolanus* Overture performed by itself and it was applauded twenty times harder than ever was the chorus that used to be fastened to it as a parachute at the Conservatoire.

These examples, gentlemen, and many others that I refrain from citing, bring me to a conclusion that is severe but, in my opinion, just: nowadays the theater is to music . . . *sicut amori lupanar.*" [9]

"What does that mean?" ask Bacon and a few others. Corsino translates the second part of my comparison, which I have not dared to put into French. Whereupon comes a burst of applause, shouts, and exclamations: "True, true!" The approval is such that the drinking-glasses are violently banged on the table and smashed to pieces. You cannot hear yourself think.

"All this being so, gentlemen, is the reason why we must ever show the warmest regard for theatrical compositions in which music is respected and passion nobly expressed, and in which are displayed common sense, naturalness, plain truth, grandeur without bombast, and strength without brutality. They are the respectable girls that have withstood the contagion of bad example. A work in good taste, truly musical and coming from the heart—why, in our times of exaggeration, vociferation, dislocation, mechanism, and manikinism, we must adore it, throw a veil over its defects, and put it on so high a pedestal that the mud splashing around it cannot reach it.

"We shall be told: 'You are the Cato of a lost cause.' So be it, but that cause is immortal. The triumph of the other is only temporary, and the support of its deities will fail it sooner or later, together with the deities themselves.

"All this being so, again, we must never conceal our contempt—and you, I must say, barely hide it—for the products of the low musical industry exposed on the stalls of the theatrical butchers.

"All this being so, finally, our duty is never to set forth except in its most majestic attire the music that is independent of stage requirements, music that is free—in short, Music. If she has to be more or less humiliated in the theater, let her be all the prouder elsewhere. Yes, gentlemen—and here I agree heart and soul with

---

[9] —"as is to love a bawdyhouse."

the views of your leader—the cause of great art, of pure and true art, is compromised by the theater; but it will triumph in the theater itself if we artists defend it and fight for it with unremitting strength and constancy.

"The opinions of our judges vary, it is true; the interests of individual artists appear opposed to one another; many prejudices still flourish in the schools; and the public taken as a whole is not very bright, but frivolous rather, unjust, indifferent, changeable. But though its intelligence has weakened or disappeared about certain elements of our art, it seems to be developing as regards others. Its changeableness, which so often leads it to modify its first verdict, makes up for its injustice; and if its ear for expression in particular is atrophied, the cause lies in the contemptible products of bad art. The frequent hearing of works rich in poetic and expressive qualities will perhaps succeed in restoring to life this apparently dead nerve.

"Now, if we consider the position of the artist within the social milieu in which he lives, we see that misfortune has often pursued and crushed inspired men, yet it is not only the illustrious ones of our art and our time that it has persecuted. The great musicians share the fate of almost all humanity's pioneers. Beethoven was lonely, misunderstood, looked down on, and poor. Mozart, forever in pursuit of the necessaries of life, was humiliated by unworthy patrons, and at his death left nothing but six thousand francs' worth of debts; and so with many others. If we look outside the domain of music, at poetry for instance, we find Shakespeare, tired of the lukewarmness of his contemporaries, retiring to Stratford in the prime of his age, wanting to hear no more about poems, dramas, or the stage, and writing his epitaph to curse those who might 'disturb his bones.' We find Cervantes crippled and poor; Tasso also poor and dying insane from wounded pride as much as from love, in a prison.

"Camoëns was still more unfortunate. He was a warrior, a venturesome sailor, a lover, and a poet; he was dauntless and patient; he had inspiration and genius, or rather he belonged to genius, which made him its prey, dragged him palpitating through the world, gave him the strength to struggle against winds, storms, obscurity, ingratitude, banishment, and pale hunger with its hollow cheeks—bitter billows that he breasted with a noble courage, raising above them with a sublime gesture his immortal poem. Then he died after much suffering, and without having ever had the chance to say: 'My country knows and values me; it knows the man I am, it sees the glory of my name reflected on its own, it understands my work and admires it; I am happy to have come, seen, and conquered; thanks be given to the supreme power that gave me life!' No, far from that, he died lost amid the mass of those who suffer, the *gente dolorosa*, still armed and fighting, pouring out in floods his thought, his blood, and his tears; indignant at his fate, indignant at finding men so small, indignant at himself for being so great, shaking with fury the heavy chain of material needs, *servo ognor fremente*. And when death claimed him, he must have gone out to meet it with the sad smile of the resigned slaves marching, under Cæsar's eyes, to their final combat.

"Then fame descended—fame!—O Falstaff! . . .

"The great musicians, then, are not the only ones that suffer. And against these all too well established cases of misfortune are to be set off numerous examples of the brilliant and happy destinies of men eminent in the arts. There have been some, there are, and there will be. We at any rate, who do not pretend to the role or to the fate of Titans, should at least acknowledge that our lot has compensations. Though our pleasures are few and far between, they are vivid and elevated. Their very rarity enhances their worth. A whole world of ideas and sensations is open to us which adds a life of luxury and poetry to the necessaries of prosaic life, and we enjoy it with a happiness unknown to other men.

"This is no exaggeration. The joys of the musician, deeper than all others, are really denied to the greater part of the human race. The other arts, some of which appeal only to the mind, while others are deprived of movement, can never produce anything comparable. Music (please understand what I mean by the word, and do not confuse different things that have only the name in common), music, I say, speaks first to a sense that it charms, and the excitation of which, spreading through the entire organism, produces a voluptuous feeling, now gentle and calm, now fiery and violent, that no one can imagine possible until he has experienced it. Then, by associating itself with ideas which it has a thousand means of engendering, music augments the intensity of its action with all the power of what is commonly meant by poetry. Already a flame by itself, when it expresses the passions, it appropriates their fire. Dazzling with its beams of sound, it decomposes their light through the prism of the imagination; it embraces at once the real and the ideal; as Rousseau said, it can make silence speak. By suspending the rhythm that gives it movement and life, it can assume the aspect of death. With the play of harmonic means at its disposal, it might confine itself (it has done so only too frequently!) to being a pleasant diversion for the mind; or, in its melodic sport, limit itself to tickling the ear. But when it concentrates at one and the same time all its powers on the sense of hearing which it skillfully charms or offends, on the nervous system which it excites, the circulation of the blood which it accelerates, the brain which it sets on fire, the heart which it fills and quickens, the mind which it enlarges beyond measure and launches into the infinite, then it is acting in its proper realm—that is to say, upon beings who truly possess the musical sense; then its power is enormous, and I hardly know what other power it could seriously be compared with. Then it is that we are gods, and if men on whom fortune has heaped its favors could understand our ecstasies and buy them, they would squander their gold to share them for a moment.

"So I repeat the toast your leader made: To those artists whom nothing can debase or dishearten, to true artists like yourselves, to artists who are persevering, valiant, and strong!"

Cheering broke out once more, but this time in chorus and with a harmony full of splendor.

At the final cadence of this musical clamor, just when all the empty glasses are lowered and strike the table together, I signal to the waiter who for some minutes past has been standing by the door. The Ganymede comes forward, his white apron tucked back under his left arm, his vest adorned with an enormous bouquet, carrying on a tray a tall dish cover which seems to conceal some delicacy. He goes over to the brothers Kleiner, who are sitting together, puts down the tray in front of them, takes off the cover, and the company can see that this unscheduled present consists of TWO ORDERS OF BAVARIAN CREAM.

"At last, at last, at last!" comes in a crescendo of shouts from every part of the room. "That proves—that's the proof, now we can prove—" cackles little Schmidt as he jumps up on the table; "it's the ocular proof that given time and patience courageous artists end by getting the better of fate."

I slip out amid the tumult.

Corsino's Letter to the Author

The Author's Reply to Corsino

*Beethoven and his three styles—the inauguration of
Beethoven's statue at Bonn—Méhul's biography—
London once more—the Purcell commemoration—
St. James's Chapel—Mme Sontag—the suicide of an
enemy of the arts—Henri Heine's* Mot—*a fugue of
Rossini's—Falstaff's philosophy—M. Conestabile
and his life of Paganini—the adventures of Vincent
Wallace in New Zealand—the end*

 THIS BOOK having gone to all my friends in the
orchestra at X, the edition was naturally out of print,
and I hoped, as may be seen from the Prologue, that
that would be the end of it. I crowed too soon. It's
not the end of it. Authors always crow too soon.

Here is a letter from that fantastic fellow Corsino, a
letter bristling with question marks and full of rather unpleasant
comments, to which I must reply without hedging. This correspondence obviously means that my publisher has to bring out a
second, aggravated edition of *Evenings with the Orchestra.* For
there are fifty musicians in the opera at X, and I am not equal to
copying out my letter fifty times.

Just as I was about to prepare this second edition, M. Lévy [1]

---

[1] Michel Lévy, the publisher; see Translator's note, p. xvii.

asked me whether I have not also some friends in Paris, and whether he shouldn't, with them in mind, increase the number of copies to be printed.

"Yes indeed," I replied, "I have many good friends, even in Paris. Still, I shouldn't like to involve you in a heavy outlay. Why not go ahead as if I had none?"

"What about enemies?" he rejoined with a smile full of hope. "Now those are really useful people. They often go as far as to buy books which they mean to—you know. Wouldn't it be funny if with their help we managed to sell a few hundred copies of your *Evenings*, at a bad time in the publishing business, when sales are reckoned by tens only?"

"Enemies, me? You flatterer! No, I have no enemies, not a single one, do you hear? But since you're obsessed with the strange idea of printing me from here to eternity, why, act as if I had lots of enemies, print as much as you like; print and reprint—we'll deposit some everywhere."

My last words suggest in a rather unfortunate manner the famous line in the scene of the little dogs in *Les Plaideurs*.[2] Never mind. Let me go on; or, rather, don't let me. Let me on the contrary reproduce at once the letter of my friend Corsino and try to clear myself of the charges he brings against me; while helping him by my reply—him and his colleagues—to ward off the threatening musical danger to which a wretched composer is about to expose them.

To the Author of *Evenings with the Orchestra*, Paris

DEAR SIR:

The musicians of the *civilized town* have received your book. A few of them have read it. Here is what they think of it:

---

[2] Racine's comic masterpiece, in which a dog is tried for killing a chicken. Other dogs are witnesses (Act III, Scene iii), from which the allusion in the text above can readily be imagined.

They are of opinion that they are represented in your book in a rather discreditable light. They maintain that you have committed an unspeakable breach of trust in letting the public know of their doings, their conversations, their malicious jokes, and especially the liberties they take with mediocre works and mediocre performers. To be frank, you have taken liberties with them. They never imagined they were such intimate friends of yours.

As far as I personally am concerned, I can only thank you for having made me play a part that I like and that I find as un-hackneyed as it is true. I shall none the less seem ridiculous in the eyes of the literary men and musicians of Paris who read your book. But I don't care a hoot. I am what I am; *honi soit qui sot me trouve!* [3]

Our tenor-god is furious, so furious that he pretends the mischievous things you write about him are "charming." Only yesterday, in an attempt to prove his goodwill toward you, he was pestering our manager, Baron F., to have him put on one of your operas, in which he claims to be able to fill the main role to your entire satisfaction—and to his own, I suppose, for even doing his best he would butcher the opera without mercy. Fortunately I am familiar with this sort of vendetta, and I would not allow your falling a victim to it here. I dissuaded His Excellency from following up the treacherous singer's suggestion, and I replied to the latter's reproaches with a French proverb slightly recast for the occasion. I am sure he understood it, for he has kept quiet ever since:

Dis-moi ce que tu chantes et je te dirai qui tu hais. [4]

The baritone is pleased and altogether happy that in the part of Don Giovanni you considered him worthy of the Montyon Prize. This critical judgment flatters him more than I can say.

The woman singer of whom you wrote: "we thought she was in labor," retorted sourly: "At any rate, he'll never be the father of my children." Here I cannot congratulate you, for she is an enchanting little fool.

Both the Figaro and the Almaviva, fortunately, are still unaware

---

[3] "Shame to him who calls me fool."

[4] Corsino adapts the proverb *"Dis-moi qui tu hantes, je te dirai qui tu es."* This means "Tell me the company you keep and I'll tell you what you're like"; whereas the paraphrase, which sounds almost exactly the same, means: "Tell me whose music you sing and I'll tell you whom you hate."

of the remarks about them which you attribute to me in your book. They are not highly educated, though I believe they can read.

Moran, the horn-player, thinks that the pun made on his name is unworthy of you.[5] I agree with him.

The bass drum is the only one of our colleagues who did not receive a copy of your book; he borrowed one from Schmidt, who wasn't using his, and read it with care. He was hurt at the ironical tone in which you refer to him, but he permitted himself only one remark. "The author," he said, "gives an inaccurate report of my dealings with our manager over the six bottles of wine that were sent me last winter by way of encouragement. I did tell the manager that I needed no encouragement—that much is true; but it is not true that I sent the bottles back."

Our conductor seems thinner since you pointed out the "bouncing of his potbelly." Obviously he now wears a corset. He seems rather pleased with you.

The brothers Kleiner have just got married; they have taken as wives two Bavarians. They always keep the sweetest memory of the pair you so handsomely treated them to on the night of our farewell dinner. They thought then that they had reached the end of their vexations, but there remained one more for them to undergo: their father died. For the rest, your book did not entertain them much; they read only ten pages of it.

Bacon is vainly trying to find out why you twice tell your readers that he is not descended from the Bacon who invented gunpowder.

And last, I must confess that Dimsky, Dervinck, Turuth, Siedler, and I will be hanged if we know what you meant in your speech when you said apropos of Camoëns: "Then fame descended—fame!—O Falstaff!"

Who is Falstaff? What's the connection with Camoëns? What kind of name is that anyway? Was he a poet? a soldier? I am lost, they are lost, we are lost in conjecture.

Two final and most important questions: We've just performed a charming opera translated from the English, called *Maritana;* the composer's name is Wallace. Do you know him?

An Italian pamphlet on Paganini came our way lately, which

---

[5] Moran the horn-player = *le cor Moran* = the cormorant.

supplements your sketch of this great virtuoso. But you are pretty badly manhandled in it. Have you read it?

Good-by, my dear sir. Pending your next visit, please be good enough to reply to me in full—a letter two and a half hours long. It will be invaluable for our first performance of *Angelica and Roland*,[6] a very dull opera we are rehearsing just now. The third act especially is to be feared.

Your devoted and
co-fanatical musician,
CORSINO

The Author's Reply to M. Corsino
Concertmaster of the Orchestra of X

MY DEAR CORSINO:

You frighten me! An opera called *Angelica and Roland*, in 1852, and what's more, in three acts! The part of Angelica is no doubt sung by the pretty little fool in whose bad books I am; that of Roland by the highly moral Don Giovanni, and that of Medor by my insidious tenor? My poor fellow, I can share your feelings and I pity you. You have all my sympathy, and in spite of my dislike of long letters, I do see that I must proportion the size of the present one to the length of the imminent opera you mention.

First I shall put into it something that was not intended for you —everything is grist to the mill—but God grant that you'll be pleased with it. It has to do with Beethoven, being a study of his three styles, written by a Russian who is passionately fond of music. Lacking this book, which I regret I can't send you (though you, Corsino, must get it from St. Petersburg sooner or later), our friends may be kind enough to be content with the review I have just written about it. It will be a protection for you all against Act I of *Angelica and Roland*. I also have ammunition that can be used against Act II, and if you ask me the right questions (which I am quite pre-

---

[6] An imaginary score, though in 1843 Ambroise Thomas had produced a one-act comic opera entitled *Angélique et Médor*.

pared to answer) I have hopes I can help you conquer Act III, the toughest and most ruthless of the three, I am told. So at seven o'clock this evening, after the overture to *Angelica and Roland* (you can't, after all, omit the overture), you will be reading the following pages:

Beethoven and His Three Styles

BY M. W. DE LENZ [7]

Here is a book of great interest to musicians. It is written under the influence of a passionate admiration, justified and accounted for by its subject, but the author—unlike most critics—always keeps an open mind, which enables him to reason out his admiration, to censure occasionally, and to acknowledge that there are spots on his sun. M. de Lenz, like M. Ulibichev, the author of a biography of Mozart,[8] is a Russian. It is worth noting by the way that among the thoughtful works of musical criticism published during the past ten years, two have come to us from Russia.

I shall have much to praise in M. de Lenz's work, and that is why I want to dispose at once of the objections to which I think he has laid himself open in this book. The first has to do with the many German quotations with which the text bristles. Why did he not translate these fragments into French, since the bulk of the book is in French? Being a Russian, M. de Lenz speaks a quantity of languages, known and unknown, and he doubtless said to himself: "Who is there who doesn't know German?" like the banker who used to say: "Who hasn't got a million?" Alas, we French do not speak German—we have trouble enough learning our own language and seldom succeed even in that. As a consequence it is most unpleasant for us to read with feverish interest the pages of a book and stumble at every moment into traps like the following: "Beethoven said to M. Rellstab: *Opern, wie* Don Juan *und* Figaro, *konnte ich*

---

[7] Wilhelm von Lenz (1809–83), Councilor of State in St. Petersburg, wrote this first work in two volumes and in French (1852). A second work on Beethoven in six volumes appeared in German in 1855–60.

[8] Alexander von Ulibichev (1795–1858), another amateur musicologist, reawakened an interest in Mozart by his three-volume biography in French, published in Moscow in 1844.

nicht componiren. Dagegen habe ich ein Widerwillen." [9] Well,
what *did* Beethoven say? I want to know. It is annoying. And I did
not even choose a good example, since the author has taken the unusual trouble of translating this particular quotation, as he has not
done with a host of other words, sentences, anecdotes, and documents, the significance of which is surely important for the reader
to know. Shakespeare's way is less trying: in *Henry IV*, instead of
giving the Welshwoman's reply to her English husband, he just puts
in the stage direction: "(*The lady speaks in Welsh*)."

My second objection is to a remark of the author's concerning
Mendelssohn, a remark already made by other critics, and which I
shall ask M. de Lenz's leave to argue with him.

"One cannot discuss modern music," he says, "without mention-
ing Mendelssohn-Bartholdy. . . . We are second to none in the
respect due to a mind of that caliber, but we think that the Hebraic
element discernible in Mendelssohn's thought will keep his music
from becoming the property of the whole world, without distinction of time or place."

Is there not a little prejudice involved in this way of judging that
great musician, and would M. de Lenz have written these lines if he
had not known that the composer of *St. Paul* and *Elijah* was descended from the famous Jew Moses Mendelssohn? I find it hard to
believe. "The chants of the synagogue," he goes on to say, "are the
prototypes of what one finds in Mendelssohn's music." Now, it
would be difficult to imagine how these chants of the synagogue can
have influenced Felix Mendelssohn's musical style, when he never
professed the Jewish creed. Everybody knows that he was a Lu-
theran, and a fervent and sincere one at that.[1]

Moreover, what kind of music is it that can ever become "the
property of the whole world, without distinction of time or place?"
None, most certainly. The works of the great German masters such
as Gluck, Haydn, Mozart, and Beethoven, who all belonged to the
Catholic—which is to say, "universal"—religion, will no more
achieve universality than the rest, however wonderfully alive, beautiful, healthy, and powerful they may be.

---

[9] "I couldn't possibly compose operas like *Don Giovanni* and *Figaro*. It goes
against the grain."
[1] Berlioz and Mendelssohn became close friends at Rome in their youth and remained on excellent terms of mutual help throughout their musical careers.

Apart from this question of Judaism, which, it seems to me, was quite irrelevant, M. de Lenz judges with great insight and delicacy Felix Mendelssohn's musical worth, the nature of his mind, his filial love of Handel and Bach, the education he received at the hands of Zelter, his somewhat exclusive sympathy with German life and the German hearth, his exquisite sentiment, and his tendency to limit himself to the circle of ideas prevailing in a given town or public. From the comparison he draws in the same chapter among Weber, Mendelssohn, and Beethoven he reaches conclusions that seem to me true in every respect.

He also has enough daring to say some very sensible things about fugue and the fugal style, their genuine musical importance, the use made of them by the true masters, and the ridiculous abuse of them by musicians who have no other preoccupation but with this form. He quotes in support of his views the opinion of a consummate contrapuntist who has spent his life in the study of fugue, and who might therefore have been expected to see in it the sole means of salvation in music, but who preferred to speak the truth. "He is," says M. de Lenz, "too honorable an exception to the narrow-minded ideas of the professionals for us not to do the reader [who knows German] the service of reproducing it. It occurs in an article by M. Fuchs, of St. Petersburg: *'Die Fuge, als ein für sich abge-schlossenes Musikstück . . .'* " [2] and so on. (He speaks Welsh.)

I would give a great deal right now to know what Fuchs said on the subject, but I must give it up.

Having established some most ingenious comparisons between Beethoven and the great German masters who were his predecessors and contemporaries, M. de Lenz takes up the delineation of his hero's character, the analysis of his works, and lastly the distinctive qualities of the three styles in which he wrote. This was a difficult task, but there can be nothing but praise for the manner in which the author has carried it out. No one could enter more fully into the spirit of all those marvelous musical poems, nor better grasp the whole and the parts, nor follow with greater energy the eagle's impetuous flight and discern more clearly when he rises or when he sinks, nor say it with more frankness. On this last point M. de Lenz has, in my opinion, the advantage over M. Ulibichev, for he does full justice to Mozart, while M. Ulibichev is far from being fair to

---

[2] "A fugue as an isolated piece of music for its own sake. . . ."

Beethoven. M. de Lenz admits without hesitation that several of Beethoven's works, such as the overture to *The Ruins of Athens* and certain parts of the piano sonatas, are weak and hardly worthy of him; that other compositions which, to be sure, are hardly known, are totally devoid of ideas; and finally that some two or three scores seem to him complete riddles.

As against this, M. Ulibichev admires everything in Mozart. Yet heaven knows the glory of *Don Giovanni* would not be dimmed if quantities of Mozart's childhood compositions had been destroyed instead of impiously published.[3] M. Ulibichev would like to create a void round Mozart; he seems unable to stand with equanimity the mention of other masters.[4] M. de Lenz is full of genuine enthusiasm for whatever is beautiful in art, and his passion for Beethoven, though not blind, is perhaps deeper and more vivid than that of his colleague for Mozart.

The tireless researches which M. de Lenz has pursued throughout Europe for twenty years have brought him much curious information, little known to the general public, about Beethoven and his works. Some of the anecdotes he tells are valuable in that they explain the musical anomalies one finds scattered through the works of the great composer, and which hitherto one had vainly tried to interpret.

It is well known that Beethoven professed a strong admiration for those masters of austere mien to whom M. de Lenz refers, who made an exclusive use in music of that "purely rational element in human thought which can never fill the place of grace." But do we really know what Beethoven admired, and how much? I doubt it. His taste reminds me rather of the fancy of certain wealthy gastronomers who, when they are tired of their Lucullan feasts, take pleasure in lunching off a herring and a dry biscuit.

M. de Lenz relates that one day while taking a stroll with his friend Schindler, Beethoven said: "I have found two themes for an overture. One lends itself to treatment in my own style, the other in Handel's; which do you advise me to do?" Schindler (believe it or not) advised him to use the second theme. This pleased Beethoven

---

[3] An Allegretto for piano, violin, and cello, written when Beethoven was fourteen, will have its premiere on the B.B.C. in November 1955.—News item dated London, July 29, 1955.
[4] Lenz later attacked Ulibichev on this point and was counterattacked in *Beethoven, ses critiques, et ses glossateurs* (Leipzig and Paris, 1857).

by reason of his predilection for Handel. He unfortunately followed Schindler's advice and was not long in repenting of it. It has even been said that he was annoyed with Schindler on this account. Handel's overtures are not in fact the most striking part of his work, and to compare them to those of Beethoven is to compare a bed of mushrooms to a forest of redwoods.

"This overture, op. 124," [5] says M. de Lenz, "is not a double fugue, as some have said. We must suppose that the theme Beethoven would have treated in his own style would have been the germ of a far more important work [no question but we must suppose this!], coming as it did at a period when the artist's genius was at its height and the physical man was enjoying his last days free from bodily pain. Schindler should have known that Beethoven's genius was unrivaled in the free symphonic style; that in this genre he need not be anyone's follower; that on the contrary the severe style was for him at best a hurdle to jump; he was not at home in it. The overture produced no effect whatever; it was even described as unperformable, and *possibly* it is."

The overture is indeed difficult, I may say to M. de Lenz, but it is quite performable by a good orchestra. Thanks to the many flashes of the Beethovenian style that come through the heavy web of the Handelian imitation, the entire coda and numberless other passages move the hearer and carry him away when they are properly played. I have conducted two performances of this overture; the first at the Conservatoire with an orchestra of the first rank. The audience found the style of Handel's overtures so badly reproduced that the work was rapturously applauded. Ten years later, when poorly performed by an inadequate orchestra, it was severely criticized; everybody agreed that Handel's style had been imitated to perfection.

At this point M. de Lenz quotes Beethoven's conversation with Schindler on the subject: *"Wie kommen Sie wieder auf die alte Geschichte?"* [6] etc. (He speaks Welsh.)

In such a minute and able review of the great composer's works the story of the indignities committed upon them was bound to have a place. That story is indeed told, but most incompletely. M. de Lenz, who handles Beethoven's improvers very roughly, makes

[5] The "Consecration of the House" (*Weihe des Hauses*) Overture.
[6] "Why do you always bring up that old business?"

fools of them, and subjects them to the lash, does not know the fourth part of their misdeeds. One must have lived for a long time in Paris and London to know the full extent of their ravages.

As to the alleged mistake in engraving which M. de Lenz believes is to be found in the Scherzo of the C-minor Symphony [7] and which consists, according to those who share his view, in the inappropriate repetition of two bars of the theme on its reappearance in the middle of the movement, I can say this much: in the first place, there is no exact repetition of the four notes, C, E, D, F, which make up the melodic figure. The first time they are written as half notes followed by a quarter note; the second time as quarter notes followed by a quarter-note rest, which entirely alters the character. Second, the adding of the two disputed measures is not in the least an anomaly in Beethoven's style. There are not a hundred, there are a thousand examples of a similar willfulness in his compositions. The fact that the two added bars destroy the symmetry of the phrase was not enough to deter him from writing them if the idea crossed his mind. No one has more often than he flouted what is known as *squareness*. There is a striking example of his daring in this regard in the second part of the first movement of that same symphony, on page 36 of the small score published by Breitkopf and Härtel, where a bar of silence, which seems *de trop*, destroys the whole rhythmic regularity and makes the re-entry of the orchestra a ticklish problem of ensemble.

Now, returning to the melody, I would have no trouble proving that its lengthening was done absolutely on purpose. The proof lies within the melody itself, which, when it recurs a second time immediately after the organ point, contains *two supplementary bars* (D, C sharp, D, C natural), about which no one ever says a word. These bars differ from the two that people want to cut out, and are added this time after the fourth bar of the theme, whereas the other two come into the phrase after the third bar. The whole period is thus composed of two phrases of ten bars each; hence there is a perfectly clear intention on Beethoven's part in making this double addition, there is even *symmetry*, a symmetry which is destroyed if we omit the two disputed bars while retaining the two others which have not been a subject of attack.

The effect of this passage in the Scherzo is not in the least dis-

---

[7] The Fifth.

agreeable; on the contrary, I must say I like it very much. The symphony is performed in this way in all corners of the globe where the great works of Beethoven are heard. All the editions of the score and parts contain these two bars. Finally, when in 1850 apropos of the execution of this masterpiece at one of the concerts of the Philharmonic Society of Paris,[8] a newspaper criticized me for not omitting them, obviously considering this error in engraving as a fact known to all, I received a few days later a letter from M. Schindler. M. Schindler's purpose was to thank me for *not* having made the correction. M. Schindler, who spent his life with Beethoven, does not believe in an engraver's mistake, and he assured me that he had heard the two famous bars in every performance of the symphony that had taken place *under Beethoven himself*. Will anyone believe that if the composer had detected an error there he would not have immediately corrected it? Whether in the last years of his life Beethoven changed his mind on this point, I am of course unable to say.

M. de Lenz, who is otherwise very moderate in discussion, loses his composure when he comes head on against the absurdities that are still being written and will continue to be written about Beethoven's masterpieces. On such occasions all his philosophy deserts him; he is irritated, miserable, he reverts to adolescence. Alas, I am free to admit that on this same subject I myself was hardly past infancy just a few years ago. But today I no longer let myself be annoyed. I have read and heard so many incredible things—not only in France, but also in Germany—on Beethoven and the noblest products of his genius, that nothing of that sort can now disturb me. I even think I can understand fairly exactly the various causes that give rise to these conflicting opinions.

The impressions of music are fugitive and quickly obliterated. Now, when a musical work is really new, it requires more time than other works to exert a strong influence on the organs of some of its hearers and leave in their mind a clear perception of what has taken place. It achieves this end only by dint of acting upon them again in the same fashion, of striking again and again on the same spot. Operas written in a new style, however original or even eccentric that style may be, are more quickly appreciated than concert works, and this in spite of the distractions that the accessories may cause in

---

[8] Founded and directed by Berlioz.

the hearer. The reason for this is very simple: an opera that does not fall flat at the start is always given again several times in succession in the theater that has just produced it. If successful, it is repeated later in twenty, thirty, forty other theaters. The hearer who on listening to it for the first time understood absolutely nothing becomes acquainted with it at a second performance, likes it more at a third, and sometimes ends by growing passionately fond of the work which at first he had found offensive.

This cannot happen with symphonies that are given only at wide intervals. Instead of obliterating the bad impressions they produced on their first appearance, the interval gives these impressions time to take root and to produce theories, indeed written doctrines, to which the talent of the writer who utters them lends more or less authority according to the degree of impartiality he seems to show in his critique and the apparent wisdom of the advice he gives the composer. Frequency of performance is therefore a prerequisite to the redress of errors of opinion about works such as Beethoven's, which were conceived outside the musical habits of those that hear them.[9]

But no matter how frequent, excellent, and bewitching we may imagine these performances, they will not of themselves change the opinions either of the dishonest or of decent men to whom nature has denied the faculty for perceiving certain sensations and for understanding a certain class of ideas. In vain will you say: "Admire this rising sun!"—"What sun?" they will reply, "we don't see anything." And truly they do not, some because they are blind, others because they are looking west.

Considering now the question what qualities of performance are necessary for the original, poetical, and daring works of the founders of musical dynasties, one should never forget that these qualities must be present in proportion to the novelty of the work and its style. It is often said: "The public does not notice slight inaccuracies, or nuances omitted or exaggerated, errors of tempo, defects in ensemble, in correctness, expression, or warmth." True, the public is not shocked by these imperfections, but it remains cold, it is not moved, and however delicate and graceful or great and beautiful

---

[9] No better account could be given of the reasons for the long misrepresentation of Berlioz's own works. What put an end to it was the frequent repetition made possible by recordings.

the composer's idea may be, when it is thus cloaked it passes by the public without the latter's perceiving its forms, for the public makes no practice of divination.

What is needed then, let me repeat, is that Beethoven's works should receive frequent performances of irresistible power and beauty. But I do not honestly believe there are six places in the whole world where one can hear, say, six times a year all his symphonies properly performed. In one place the orchestra is unselected, in another it is too small in numbers, in yet another it is badly led, or the concert hall is no good, and the players have no time to rehearse—in short, almost everywhere one runs into obstacles which, in the last analysis, bring disaster upon these masterpieces.

As regards his sonatas, in spite of the untold number of persons who go by the name of pianist, I must say it again, I do not know of six virtuosos able to play them faithfully, correctly, powerfully, poetically, without paralyzing their verve or extinguishing the ardor, the fire, the life that seethe in these extraordinary compositions; able to follow the capricious flight of the composer's thought, able to dream, to meditate, to share his passion with him—in a word, to identify themselves with his inspiration and reproduce it intact.

No, not six pianists in the world for the piano sonatas of Beethoven! His trios are more available. But his quartets? In all of Europe how many quadruple virtuosos are there, four-persons-in-one, who are capable of unveiling the mystery of the quartets? I dare not guess. There were consequently good reasons why M. de Lenz need not have taken the trouble to reply to the lunacies that these works of Beethoven have called forth. The sort of unpopularity these marvelous inspirations suffer is an inevitable misfortune. Come to think of it, is it even a misfortune? I doubt it. It may be better that such works should remain inaccessible to the multitude. There are enough composers who are full of charm, brilliance, and power and who are adapted, if not to the lower classes, at least to the intellectual third estate. The glorious geniuses, such as Beethoven, were created by God for sovereign hearts and minds.

He himself was fully conscious of the strength and greatness of his mission; his occasional outbursts leave no doubt as to that. One day when his pupil Ries dared to point out in one of his new works a harmonic progression termed incorrect by the theorists, Beethoven replied: "Who forbids it?"

"Who? Why, Fuchs, Albrechtsberger, all the professors."

"Well, *I* permit it."

On another occasion he remarked candidly: "I partake of the nature of electricity; that is why my music is so wonderful."

The celebrated Bettina [1] relates in her correspondence that one day Beethoven said to her: "I have no friends; I am alone with myself; but I know that God is nearer to me in my art than He is to others in theirs. I have no fears about my music; it cannot have an adverse fate; he who feels it fully will forever be delivered from the woes that beset other men."

In recording the peculiarities of Beethoven in society, M. de Lenz says that he was not always as uncouth as in his last years; that he even attended balls, but that he could not dance in step. This seems to me a rather strong assertion and I take the liberty of doubting it. Beethoven possessed in the highest degree the sense of rhythm, as his works attest; and if someone really said that he did not dance in step, it may be because making this childish remark seemed amusing in retrospect, as the record of a curious anomaly. There are people who have maintained that Newton did not know arithmetic and denied that Napoleon was brave.

It would seem, nevertheless—if we are to believe a considerable number of German musicians who played Beethoven's symphonies under him—that he was an indifferent conductor of his own works. There is nothing incredible in this; the conductor's talent is as specialized as the violinist's. It is acquired only by long practice, and only if one has in addition a very marked natural aptitude for it. Beethoven was a skillful pianist, but a very bad violinist, though he had taken violin lessons in his childhood. He could have played both instruments very badly, or even been unable to play either, without being on that account any less prodigious as a composer.

It is commonly believed that he composed with great speed. It did happen that he improvised one of his masterpieces, the *Coriolanus* Overture, in a single night. But generally speaking he worked, remodeled, kneaded his ideas to such an extent that the first sketch bore only a very slight resemblance to the final form he settled on

---

[1] Bettina von Arnim (1785–1859), a youthful and adoring friend of Goethe's and Beethoven's who wrote much about them. She lived long enough to be interested in Berlioz's fame, and the year after this essay came to one of his German concerts.

before he was satisfied. One must see his manuscripts to know what this meant. He rewrote the first movement of his Seventh Symphony three times. For several days he roamed about in the fields near Vienna to find the theme of the "Ode to Joy" that begins the finale of his "choral" Symphony. The sketch for this passage is extant. After the first phrase that came to Beethoven's mind is written in French the word "bad." The melody reappears a few lines farther down modified and accompanied by the remark, again in French: "This is better." Finally we have it in the form we admire, decisively elected by the two syllables which the stubborn seeker must have written with delight: "That's it!"

He worked for a very long time at his Mass in D. He rewrote his opera *Fidelio* two or three times, and composed for it, as everybody knows, four overtures. The story of what he had to endure to have the opera performed, through the ill will and hostility of all his performers, from the first tenor down to the double basses in the orchestra, would be sadly interesting to relate, but would carry us too far. Despite its many vicissitudes, the work has remained and will remain in the repertory of over thirty theaters in Europe. Its success would be still greater, in spite of the many difficulties of performance it presents, if it were not for the undeniable disadvantage of a melancholy play in which the whole action takes place in a prison.

When Beethoven was carried away by the subject of *Leonora, or Conjugal Love*,[2] he saw in it only the emotions it afforded him the opportunity of expressing; he never took into account the somber monotony of the spectacle it entails. The libretto, of French origin, was first set to music in Paris by Gaveaux. Later an Italian opera was made out of it for Paer, and it was after hearing in Vienna the music of the latter's *Leonora* that Beethoven had the candid cruelty to say to him: "I like the subject of your opera; I must set it to music." It would be revealing nowadays to hear the three scores in succession.

I must stop. I have said, I hope, enough about M. de Lenz's book to make Beethoven's admirers want to read it. I will only add that besides the high virtues he displays as critic and biographer, they will find in the catalogue and classification of the master's works a proof of the devoted care with which M. de Lenz has studied every-

---

[2] By the French playwright Bouilly in his revolutionary phase (1798).

thing relating to them, and of the learning that has guided him in his investigations.

These pages are unfortunately not enough: I have just timed them and find that they take only three-quarters of an hour to read. What can I tell you next so as to fill out the whole first act of your opera? Wait—I have it! I remember a journey I made to Bonn, at the time of the inauguration of Beethoven's statue. This will go pretty well with what precedes, so let us suppose that the date is the morrow of August 14, 1845 and that I am writing to you from the banks of the Rhine. You may read:

Supplement for Act I

THE MUSICAL CELEBRATION AT BONN [3]

KÖNIGSWINTER, AUGUST 15

The festival is over. Beethoven stands in the main square of Bonn, and already the children, heedless of the great, play around the base of the statue. His noble head is at the mercy of wind and rain, while the mighty hand that wrote so many masterpieces serves as a perch for common birds.

Artillerymen are now busy sponging out the mouths of their guns after so many salutes belched to the skies; the Quasimodos [4] of the cathedral let their bells, tired of pealing "Hosannah!" stay silent; students and guardsmen have put off their picturesque uniforms; the phalanx of singers and instrumentalists has dispersed; the throng of admirers, dazzled by the éclat of such fame, departs dreamily, to tell all the Echoes of Europe with what great beating of wings, with what fire in its eyes, it swooped down on the city of Bonn to crown the image of the greatest of her sons.

Quick, then, before the inevitable moment when everything cools down and goes out, when enthusiasm becomes a tradition, when suns break up into planets, let us be quick to record the pure and sincere piety of this vast assemblage, brought together on the banks of the Rhine with the sole object of doing homage to genius.

---

[3] Originally published in the *Journal des Débats*, August 22 and September 3, 1845.
[4] The hunchback of Notre-Dame.

Not much effort, to tell the truth, had been spent on gathering them there. The invitations addressed to foreign musicians by the Bonn Committee were merely superficial courtesies, which did not even ensure the guests a seat of any kind at the ceremonies. On the other hand, the principal institutions in which music is taught in Europe, including the very ones that have long lived and still live off the works of Beethoven, showed, as will be seen, but small eagerness to be represented. Almost all the artists, men of letters, and scholars who were present had been moved to come solely by the impetus of their personal sympathies and their admiration. Perhaps we should congratulate ourselves and conclude that it was to this scarcity of official representatives that we must ascribe the enthusiasm, the cordiality, the religious joy which united the members of this nearly Europe-wide meeting of the sons and friends of music. I say nearly, because of the predictable and understandable absence of musicians from Italy. All other nations *truly initiated* into the cult of the art of sound were represented by delegates, artists, critics, or amateurs, making together the most unexpected mixture.

From Berlin had come: Their Majesties the King and Queen of Prussia; M. Meyerbeer; the Earl of Westmorland (the English envoy); Messrs Möser senior, Möser junior, Rellstab, Ganz, Bötticher, Mantius; Mlles Jenny Lind and Tuczek.

From Vienna: Messrs Fischoff and Joseph Bacher, delegates from the Conservatory; Prince Frederick of Austria, Messrs Vesque von Püttlingen and Holtz.

From Weimar: Messrs Chelard and Montag, representing the ducal chapel.

From Salzburg: M. Aloys Taux, director of the Mozarteum.

From Karlsruhe: M. Gassner, director of the ducal chapel.

From Darmstadt: M. Mangold, director of the ducal chapel.

From Frankfurt: M. Guhr, director and Kapellmeister of the theater; Mlles Kratky and Sachs.

From Kassel: M. Spohr, Kapellmeister, special guest of the Bonn Committee.

From Stuttgart: Messrs Lindpaintner, Kapellmeister; and Pischek.

From Hohenzollern-Hechingen: M. Techlisbeck, Kapellmeister.

From Aix-la-Chapelle: M. Schindler.

From Cologne: the entire orchestra, invited by the Bonn Committee.

From Leipzig: Mlle Schloss.

From Paris: Messrs Félicien David, Massart, Léon Kreutzer, Vivier, Cuvillon, Hallé, Seghers, Burgmüller, Elwart, Sax; Mmes Viardot-García and Seghers.

From Lyon: M. George Hainl, conductor of the Grand Theater.

From Brussels: Messrs Fétis senior, Blaes, Véry, and de Glimes, representing the Conservatoire of which M. Fétis is director; Mme Pleyel.

From The Hague: M. Verhulst, Kapellmeister.

From Liége: M. Daussoigne, director of the Conservatoire.

From Amsterdam: M. Franco-Mendès.

From London: Their Majesties Queen Victoria and Prince Albert; M. Moscheles, Sir George Smart, members of the Philharmonic Society, M. Oury and Mme Oury-Belleville.

From everywhere: Franz Liszt, the soul of the celebration.

Among the press correspondents were: Jules Janin, Fiorentino, and Viardot, from Paris; Dr. Mattew from Mainz; M. Fétis junior from Brussels; Messrs Davison, Gruneisen, Chorley, and Hogarth, from London; M. Gretsch, editor-in-chief of the Russian newspaper *L'Abeille du Nord*, from St. Petersburg. Several other distinguished writers in the English press also attended, but I was unable to collect their names.

The conservatories and theaters of Naples, Milan, and Turin, together with the Pope's Chapel, did not figure in any formal capacity in this gathering of illustrious pilgrims. The reason is patent: in Italian eyes Beethoven is an enemy. Wherever his genius has sway or his inspiration has a hold on hearts and minds, the Italian muse is bound to consider herself humbled and seeks safety in flight. Italy, moreover, is aware of its national fanaticism and consequently dreads the opposing fanaticism of the German school. It is sad to have to acknowledge that she was not altogether wrong in recognizing the fact and staying away.

But our own Conservatoire, the Paris Conservatoire, which is or ought to be imbued with totally different ideas—what did it mean by neglecting to send an official delegation? And the Société des Concerts,[5] which for eighteen years has known no glory, no success —in short, no life—but the glory, success, and life bestowed upon it by the works of Beethoven—that it also should have wrapped

---

[5] For its origin and purpose, see above note 1, p. 159.

itself up in frigid reserve, as it did earlier when Liszt requested it to give one solitary benefit concert in aid of the project which, thanks to him, we have just seen realized—that is an enormity.[6] Its leading members, headed by their chiefs, should have been the first to make their appearance at Bonn; just as it was the Society's duty a few years ago not to reply by silence to Liszt's entreaties but to forestall them and give not one or two, but ten concerts, if necessary, for the erection of a monument to Beethoven. Either this needs no demonstration, or else gratitude and admiration are empty words.

Among the composers and leading conductors whose absence from Bonn astonished everyone, and whom surely only serious reasons can have kept away, are: Messrs Spontini, Onslow, Auber, Halévy, Ambroise Thomas, Habeneck, Benedict, Mendelssohn, Marschner, Reissiger, R. Wagner, Pixis, Ferdinand Hiller, Schumann, Krebs, Louis Schlösser, Theodore Schlösser, the brothers Müller, Stephen Heller, Glinka, Hessens senior, Hessens junior, Snel, Bender, Nicolai, Erkel, the brothers Lachner, and the brothers Bohrer. One of the last-named (Anton) was unfortunately detained in Paris by anxiety over his daughter's health; had this consideration not held him back, he would have made the journey afoot and slept in the open, rather than miss the occasion.

Despite all these gaps, the impression received by the latest comers on entering the concert hall the first day beggars description. This collection of celebrated names, great artists who had come of their own accord from all parts of Germany, France, England, Scotland, Belgium, and the Netherlands; the expectation of the divers sensations all were about to experience; the respectful passion felt by the whole assembly for the hero of the occasion; his melancholy portrait seen above the platform through the lights of a thousand candles; the huge hall, decorated with foliage and shields bearing the names of Beethoven's various works; the imposing dignity conferred by the age and talent of Spohr, who was to conduct the performances; the youthful and inspired fervor of Liszt,[7] who went through the ranks prodding the lukewarm, rebuking the indifferent, and imparting to all a little of his fire; the triple row of

---

[6] Liszt and Berlioz together and without any official support gave a concert in Paris for the benefit of the Beethoven Statue. This was on April 25, 1841, after Liszt's efforts to raise money by gifts had been generally fruitless.

[7] Liszt was thirty-four, Spohr sixty-one.

young women in white; and, above all, the shouts across the hall between friends who were seeing one another after three or four
years' separation and were now meeting almost unexpectedly in
such a place and for the realization of such a dream—all this was
enough to create the fine intoxication that art and poetry and the
noble passions that are their daughters sometimes excite in us. And
when the concert began, when the sheaf of lovely, well-trained, and
confident voices raised its harmonious clamor, I assure you it took
a certain amount of will-power to keep one's emotion within
bounds.

That day's program, as you can imagine, contained nothing but
Beethoven's music.

On the strength of the early rehearsals, the public in general had
been led to entertain exaggerated fears as to the competence of the
performers. From what had been told me I almost expected a musical debacle, or at the very least a very incomplete rendering of the
master's works. These fears proved groundless. During the three
concerts and on the day of the singing in church of the Mass in C,
with the exception of one item, only slight faults could be noticed.
The chorus was nearly always admirable for its precision and ensemble; and the orchestra, though weak, it is true, in several respects, maintained an average level of performance that showed it
to be as far from the inferior orchestras as from the heroic phalanxes
of instrumentalists whom it is possible to recruit in Paris, London,
Vienna, Brunswick, or Berlin. It occupied a position halfway between a Roman or Florentine orchestra and that of the Société des
Concerts in Paris. And this precisely is what the organizers of the
festival were most blamed for: everybody agreed that then or never
was the time to have a superb, regal, powerful, magnificent, un-
matched orchestra, worthy of the father and sovereign master of
modern instrumental music.

The thing would have been not only possible, but very easy. All
that needed to be done was to apply, six months in advance, to the
leading instrumentalists of the large towns I have named, obtain at
an early date (I have not a doubt that it would have been forthcoming) their definite promise, and keep clear of any narrow ideas
of nationalism. In circumstances of this kind they can only have
disastrous results and are bound to appear infinitely ridiculous to all
right-minded people.

Nothing could have been more appropriate than that Spohr and Liszt, both of them Germans,[8] should have been entrusted with the direction of the three concerts of this German celebration. But in order to form an orchestra as impressive by its strength as by the eminence of its virtuosos there should have been not the slightest hesitation in drawing on all the musical nations. What harm if, for example, instead of the inadequate oboist who performed the solos in the symphonies so poorly, Vény or Verroust had been brought from Paris, or Barrett from London, or Evrat from Lyon, or any other man of certified talent and high musicianship from anywhere? Far from doing that, they did not even think of calling upon the excellent instrumentalists who were in the audience. Massart, Cuvillon, Seghers, and Véry would not, I presume, have disgraced the rather meager violin section; Blaes, one of the best clarinetists extant, was close at hand, Vivier would have felt highly honored to take a horn part, while George Hainl, who, though he has become an admirable orchestra-leader, has none the less remained a first-rate cellist, and who, forsaking his theater and his pupils in Lyon, had traveled six hundred miles to come and bow down before Beethoven, would certainly not have refused to join forces with the eight or nine cellists that tried to struggle against the dozen double-basses.

As to the latter, they were in truly good hands, and I have rarely heard the figure in the Scherzo of the C-minor Symphony so energetically and cleanly played as by them. Even so, Beethoven was worth being treated to the luxury of bringing Dragonetti from London, Durier from Paris, Müller from Darmstadt, and Schmidt from Brunswick. Of course, to have staffed the lower parts in that style would have meant more stringent demands throughout the rest. Dorus would have had to figure among the flutes, Beerman among the clarinets, Willent and Baumann among the bassoons, Dieppo leading the trombones, Gallay the horns, and so on—plus some twenty of our most astounding violins, violas, and cellos from the Conservatoire. As for Liszt's cantata they might even have managed to get *one harp* (Parish-Alvars, for instance), so that the harp part would not have had to be played on the piano, as is done in small provincial towns. In sum, without being bad, the orchestra did

---

[8] Liszt was a Hungarian, but before the unification of Germany, all of central Europe was thought of—at least in casual contexts—as "the Germanies." The revolutions of 1848, which were to intensify the "narrow ideas of nationalism," were still three years in the future.

not come up in either size or quality to what the character of the festival, the name of Beethoven, and the instrumental riches of Europe gave us the right to expect.

The choir, contrariwise, would have seemed fully equal to its task if the quantity and quality of the men's voices had been sufficient to balance those of the women. The tenors made several shaky entrances, but the basses were unexceptionable. As for the one hundred and thirty sopranos, one had to admit that outside Germany no one has any notion of such a women's chorus, its ensemble, its rich sonority, its fervor. It was made up wholly of young girls and young women from the Bonn and Cologne musical societies, most of them good musicians, with voices of broad range, pure and resonant. They were consistently attentive, refrained from chatting, simpering, and laughing as the women in our French choruses too often do, and never lifted their eyes from their music except to look at the conductor's beat. As a result the effect of the upper parts of the chorus was unimaginably beautiful, and the palm for musical execution at these three concerts of Beethoven's works must by rights be awarded to the sopranos.

The *Missa solemnis* in D is written, like the Ninth Symphony, for chorus and four solo voices. Three of the soloists acquitted themselves very creditably in these vast compositions.

Mlle Tuczek [9] boldly approached the many perilous and frequent high notes with which Beethoven has unfortunately studded the soprano parts in all his works. Her voice is brilliant and fresh, though not possessed of great agility. She was, I feel, the best that could have been found for this difficult and dangerous part. Mlle Schloss [1] had no such great risks to encounter, the contralto part being written well within the limits of her natural range. She has moreover made substantial progress since I had the pleasure of hearing her in Leipzig, and she may be considered today one of the best singers in Europe, as much because of the beauty, strength, and accuracy of her voice as because of her musical sensitivity and the excellence of her style. The tenor, whose name escapes me,

---

[9] Leopoldine Tuczek (1821–83), who was descended from a large family of Czech musicians, began her stage appearances in Vienna at the age of thirteen. She was the leading ingénue at the Berlin Court Theater when she was invited to Bonn.
[1] Sophie Schloss, born in 1822, was then the leading singer at the Gewandhaus. She gave up singing for married life in 1848.

seemed feeble. The bass, Staudigl,[2] well deserves his high reputation; he sings like a consummate musician and has a superb voice
of great enough range for him to take the lower F and the high F
sharp without hesitation.

The effect produced by the "Choral" Symphony was marked by
depth and grandeur. The first movement, with its gigantic proportions and the tragic accent of its style, the Adagio, so poetically
expressive of nostalgia, the Scherzo, sparkling with such lively
colors and scented with such sweet rustic odors, successively astonished, moved, and enraptured the audience. In spite of the difficulties in the soprano chorus part in the second half of the symphony,
the ladies sang it with admirable vivacity and beauty of tone. The
martial stanza with the tenor solo: "Like a hero to victory marching," lacked decisiveness and clarity. But the religious chorus:
"Bow, ye millions," burst forth, strong and awe-inspiring as the
voice of a whole people in a cathedral. It was of a stupendous
majesty.

Spohr's tempos in this colossal work are the same as Habeneck's
at the Paris Conservatoire, with the one exception of the recitative
for the double basses, which Spohr takes much faster.

At the second concert, the immortal *Coriolanus* Overture was
warmly applauded, despite its silent ending.

The canon from *Fidelio* is charming, but away from the stage it
seems a trifle bob-short.

The air of the archangel from *Christ on the Mount of Olives*,
which was well done by the orchestra and the chorus, calls for a
more agile voice than Mlle Tuczek's if its vocalises and ornaments
are to be sung effortlessly.

The E-flat Concerto for piano is generally considered one of
Beethoven's best works. The first movement and Adagio especially
are of incomparable beauty. To say that Liszt played it, and that he
played it in a superb, exquisite, poetical, and yet ever-faithful manner, is mere tautology. It brought forth a hurricane of applause and
orchestral fanfares that must have been heard outside the hall. Then
Liszt moved to the podium and conducted the C-minor Symphony,

---

[2] Joseph Staudigl (1807–61), a great singer who was also a universal genius. He was
adept at composing and painting and notable as a linguist and chess-player, besides
having an amiable disposition and a cultivated mind. His career had been difficult and it ended in insanity in 1856.

the Scherzo of which he gave us just as Beethoven wrote it—not cutting out the double basses at the beginning, as was done for so long at the Paris Conservatoire, and playing the finale with the repeat indicated by Beethoven, a repeat that is still audaciously left out even today at the concerts of the said Conservatoire. I have always had so much confidence in the taste of those who improve the great masters that I was quite surprised to find the Symphony in C minor still more beautiful when executed entire than when corrected. I had to go to Bonn to make this discovery.

The finale of *Fidelio* closed the concert; this magnificent ensemble did not have that rousing effect which it always has on the stage, and which has made it famous. I think the weariness of the players and the audience had a good deal to do with this deficiency.

The celebration over, I went to collect my thoughts in a village whose peace and quiet contrasted strangely with the tumult that but yesterday reigned in the neighboring town. It is called Königswinter and is situated on the other bank of the river, opposite Bonn. The peasants there are quite proud of the glory reflected upon them. Several old men lay claim to having known Beethoven in his youth. He would frequently cross the river in a boat, they say, and come to muse and work in their meadows. Beethoven had indeed a great love of the countryside, a feeling which has strongly influenced his style. It occasionally makes itself felt even in those of his compositions whose intent is in no wise pastoral.

To the end of his days he kept the habit of wandering alone through the fields, taking no thought for the night's lodging, forgetting to eat and sleep, and of course paying scant attention to game-preserves and trespass notices. It is said that one day, in the environs of Vienna, he was arrested by a gamekeeper who insisted that he was a poacher setting traps for quail in the field of full-grown wheat where he was sitting. Already deaf at that time, and unable to make out the complaint of the inflexible guardian of the law, the poor great man, with the naïveté common to poets and great artists, who never doubt that their fame has seeped down to the lower ranks of society, shouted himself hoarse with repeating: "But I am Beethoven! You're making a mistake! Leave me alone! I am Beethoven, I tell you!" To which the official replied very much like the one in Brittany when Victor Hugo, returning from a trip out to sea, a few miles from Vannes, could not produce his passport: "What do I care whether you are Victor Hugo, man of letters, and that you have written *Mon Cousin Raymond* or *Télémaque!* [3] You have no passport, so come along with me, and quietly, too!"

I nearly missed hearing the Mass in the cathedral on the second day, owing to the scant ceremony with which the committee treated all its invited guests: it did not trouble itself about them in the least. To get near the doors of the church was impossible; the crowd obstructed every approach to it, and the crush was disgraceful. In such a mob the pickpockets who had come from London and Paris must have made their finest hauls. It occurred to me at last that there must be a stage entrance for the orchestra and chorus. I went in search of it, and thanks to a kind burgher of Bonn, a member of the committee who, hearing me called by name, did not take me for the author of *Télémaque*, I managed to get in with my clothes intact. From the other end of the church one could hear cries and tumult that made one think now and then of the clamor of a town taken by assault.

The Mass did finally begin and I found the performance remarkable. This score is in a less daring style than that of the *Missa solemnis* and is conceived on a smaller scale. But it contains a number of very fine movements, and recalls by its character the best *Messes solennelles* of Cherubini. The music is forthright, vigorous, brilliant; there is even occasionally, from the point of view of the right expression of the sacred text, an excess of vigor, motion, and brilliancy. But according to a widespread opinion, most of the movements in this work were written by Beethoven for motets and hymns, and then adapted—with great skill, it is true—to the words of the divine service. Here again the sopranos of the choir did wonders, and they seemed to me to be better supported by the men's voices and by the orchestra than at the previous concerts.

The clergy of Bonn were fortunately less strict than the French clergy, and had seen their way to allowing women to sing at this service. I am aware that otherwise the performance of Beethoven's Mass would have been impossible; but this reason might have seemed of little weight, despite the unusualness of the occasion. In

---

[3] It is perhaps needless to say that Victor Hugo wrote neither of these works.

Paris, I know, it would have been unavailing. There women may make themselves heard in church only on condition that they are neither singers nor musicians. For quite a while one could go and admire, at the services in the Church of Sainte-Geneviève, a canticle sung by the Ladies of the Sacred Heart to the air of: " 'Tis love, 'tis love, 'tis love," borrowed from the repertory of the Théâtre des Variétés. But women musicians would not have been allowed to perform within those church walls a hymn by Lesueur or Cherubini. It would seem that in France, when our musical institutions or their influence on our morals are involved, we take a genuine delight in not showing common sense.

Immediately after Beethoven's Mass came the inauguration of the statue in the adjoining square. It was then especially that I had to make persevering use of my fists. Thanks to them, and to my bravely climbing a fence, I managed to get a place in the reserved enclosure. Taking all in all, the invitation I received from the committee in charge of the Bonn festival did not positively prevent me from witnessing it. We stood there packed close together for an hour, awaiting the arrival of the King and Queen of Prussia, the Queen of England, and Prince Albert, who were to behold the ceremony from the top of a balcony fitted out to receive them. Their Majesties having arrived, guns and bells began their racket once more, while in another corner of the square a military band struggled to gain a hearing for a few scraps of the *Egmont* and *Fidelio* overtures.

Silence having been nearly restored, the president of the committee, M. Breidenstein, delivered a speech the effect of which on the audience might be compared to that of Sophocles reciting his tragedies at the Olympic games. I beg M. Breidenstein's pardon for likening him to the Greek poet, but the fact remains that only his immediate neighbors heard a word he said; his speech was lost on nine hundred and ninety-nine thousandths of his audience. It was about the same with his cantata. Even had the atmosphere been calm, I should certainly not have taken in much of that composition; the futility of vocal music in the open air is notorious; but the wind blew violently toward the choristers, and my portion of M. Breidenstein's harmony was unjustly conveyed in its entirety to the listeners at the other end of the square; and gluttons that they were, they still thought it small rations. A similar fate was reserved for the German song which had been chosen by competition, and crowned by a jury that had doubtless heard it.

How can the composers of these works have entertained for a single instant any illusion regarding their reception? A score that is not performed may still pass for wonderful—there are people whose business it is to build up a reputation for unknown works; but a work presented in the open air and consequently making no effect is always reputed mediocre. It remains under the influence of this prejudice until such time as a proper performance indoors allows the public, if there is cause, to reverse its first judgment.

The sudden stopping of the lively conversation among the listeners who could not hear proclaimed the end of the speeches and cantatas; whereupon everyone's attention turned to the unveiling of the statue. When the monument was uncovered, applause, cheers, trumpet fanfares, drum-rolls, volleys of gunfire, and the pealing of bells—in fact all the noises expressing admiration that constitute the voice of fame among civilized nations, burst forth anew and paid respect to the statue of the great composer.

Today, then, the thousands of men and women, young and old, who have spent so many sweet hours with his works, whom he has so often carried away on the wings of his thought to the highest regions of poetry; the enthusiasts whom he has excited to the point of delirium; the humorists whom he has diverted by so many witty and unexpected turns; the thinkers to whose reveries he has opened immeasurable realms; the lovers whom he has moved by reawakening the memory of their first tender affection; the hearts, wrung by an unjust fate, to which his energetic accents have given strength for a momentary revolt, and who, rising in their indignation, have found a voice to mingle their screams of fury and grief with the furious accents of his orchestra; the religious souls to whom he has spoken of God; the nature-lovers for whom he has so faithfully depicted the carefree contemplative life of the countryside in the beautiful summer days, the terror of the hurricane, and the consoling ray threading its way through the tattered clouds to smile on the anxious shepherd and restore hope to the terrified tiller of the soil—today all these intelligent and sensitive souls, on whom his genius has shed its radiance, turned to him as toward a benefactor and a friend.

But it was too late; this Beethoven in bronze is unconscious of all this homage. And it is sad to think that the living Beethoven whose memory is thus honored might perhaps not have obtained from his native town in his days of suffering and destitution—of which there were so many during his difficult career—the ten-thousandth part of the sums lavishly spent on him after his death.

Still, it is fine to glorify in this way the demigods who are no more. It is fine, too, not to make them wait too long; and we must thank the city of Bonn, and Liszt above all, for having understood that the judgment of posterity on Beethoven had long since been rendered.

A last great concert had been announced for nine o'clock on the following morning, so it was imperative to get there by half past eight. According to report, the departure of the kings and queens, who were to attend in the morning and return to the castle of Brühl in the course of the day, was the cause of this unseasonable hour. The hall was filled long before the appointed time, but Their Majesties did not appear. We respectfully waited for them a whole hour, after which perforce things had to begin without them, and Liszt conducted his cantata.

The orchestra and chorus, still excepting the sopranos, gave this beautiful work with a slackness and inaccuracy which looked like ill will. The cellos in particular played an important passage in such a fashion that one could have thought it rendered by students devoid of technique and experience. The tenors and basses made several false, divided, or uncertain entrances. And yet it was possible to see at once the great superiority of this composition over the usual "occasional music," so called, and even over the expectations based on the great gifts of the composer.

Hardly had the last chord sounded when an extraordinary commotion at the doors heralded the arrival of the royal families and brought the audience to its feet. Their Majesties Queen Victoria, the King and Queen of Prussia, Prince Albert, the Prince of Prussia, and their suites having taken their places in the large box reserved for them to the right of the orchestra, Liszt bravely began his cantata over again. That is presence of mind for you, and self-confidence besides. He had made a lightning calculation which the event proved correct: "The public will think that I am starting over again by the King's command, and I shall now be better performed, better listened to, and better understood." Nothing in truth could be more dissimilar than these two performances of the same work ten minutes apart. In proportion as the first had been colorless and flabby, the second was accurate and full of life. The first had done duty as a rehearsal, and no doubt the presence of the royal families spurred the orchestra and choristers' zeal and overawed the ill-intentioned who, in the mixed ranks of that musical army, had a short while before tried to make their weight felt.

It may be asked why and how there could be any ill will against Liszt, the eminent musician whose eminence is unquestionable and moreover Germanic, whose fame is widespread and generosity proverbial, who is rightly credited with being the instigator of everything that has been successful at the Bonn Festival, who has scoured Europe in all directions giving benefit concerts to cover the expenses of this festival, and who has even offered to make good the deficit if there is one. What feelings could subsist in the crowd other than those which meritorious deeds such as this should naturally inspire? Alas, the crowd is ever the same, especially in small towns. It was precisely these noble and meritorious deeds that gave offense. Some had a grudge against Liszt because of his extraordinary talent and exceptional success, others because he is witty, still others because he is generous, because he has written too fine a cantata, because the other works composed for the festival and given the previous day were not a success, because he has hair and not a wig,[4] because he speaks French too well, because he knows German too thoroughly, because he has too many friends, and doubtless also because he hasn't enough enemies.

The motives of the opposition, it is clear, are many and important. Be this as it may, Liszt's cantata, once well performed and warmly applauded by three quarters and a half of the house, is a great and beautiful thing, which at once puts him very high among living composers. The expression is true, the tone fitting, the style elevated and original, the plan well conceived and skillfully carried out, and the instrumentation remarkable for its variety and power. We never hear in his orchestra a succession of similar sonorities such as make certain works, in other respects estimable enough, so tiring for the hearer. He knows how to make the right use of small and large means, he does not ask too much from either instruments or voices—in a word, he has shown at one stroke that he possesses

---

[4] I.e., because he is young and a modernist, not an old fogy.

something one might have expected not to find in him so soon—*style* in instrumentation as in the other departments of music.

His cantata begins with a phrase of interrogative accent, as required by the sense of the first verse, and this theme, which is treated with rare ability in the course of the introduction, returns in the peroration in a fashion as felicitous as it is unexpected. Several choruses of the finest effect succeed one another until a decrescendo in the orchestra seems to bespeak our attention for what is to follow. What follows is certainly most important, since it is the adagio variations from Beethoven's B-flat Trio, which Liszt has had the happy idea of introducing at the end of his own cantata, to make of it a sort of hymn of praise glorifying the master. This hymn, presented first in its original character of sad grandeur, finally bursts forth with the majesty of an apotheosis; then the theme of the cantata reappears in dialogue between chorus and orchestra, and everything ends with an impressive ensemble. Let me say it again, Liszt's new work, large in its dimensions, is truly beautiful in every respect. I say this in no spirit of partiality toward the author,[5] and my opinion is also that of the most severe critics who were present at its performance; its success was great and can only keep on growing.

The program of this concert was of a richness one may properly call excessive. The timing of the numbers had not been accurately computed, and it was seen too late that to carry it through would be impossible. And so it turned out. From the outset the King saw at a glance that he could not stay until the end of so long a session, and pointed out the pieces he wanted to hear, after which he would leave. The royal will was complied with, and at its dictate a sorting out took place, which yielded the following program:

(1) *Egmont* Overture, Beethoven; (2) Piano Concerto, Weber; (3) Aria from *Fidelio*, Beethoven; (4) Aria, Mendelssohn; (5) "*Adelaide*," cantata by Beethoven.

The King of Prussia is excellent at drawing up programs. The *Egmont* Overture was splendidly played; the coda in common time, spiritedly given by the orchestra, was electrifying. Mme Pleyel played with rare acuteness of perception and elegance Weber's en-

---

[5] It was well known in artistic circles that Liszt and Berlioz were close friends and co-workers.

chanting concerto.[6] Mlle Novello sang in a splendidly proud manner the beautiful aria from *Fidelio* with three horns obbligato. Mlle
Schloss sang Mendelssohn's air with great breadth of style, a magnificent tone, faultless intonation, and a true and deeply felt expressiveness. What a loss to opera-composers that this admirable singer
refuses to take up a dramatic career! She at any rate understands
French thoroughly, and I know of a large opera house where she
could render invaluable service.

I cannot say as much of Mlle Kratky; she gave that sweet elegy,
Adelaide, one of the most touching of Beethoven's compositions, in
a thick, heavy, commonplace manner, and sang flat throughout. To
this Liszt had to play the piano accompaniment! One had to hear
this work sung by Rubini,[7] whose tradition came from Beethoven
himself, to know all the sorrowful tenderness and passionate pining
it enshrines.

After these pieces, Their Majesties having left, it was decided to
carry on with the program. M. Ganz, first cello of the Berlin Opera,
played with great talent a fantasia on themes from *Don Giovanni*.
Then young Möser, whose success at the Paris Conservatoire a year
ago will be remembered, played a concertino of his own on themes
by Weber. Whatever one may think of his score, one must admit
that nobody could have more control over intonation, more purity
of style, or more concentrated fervor. Besides, M. Möser masters
difficulties with as much felicity as aplomb; at the present time he
is unquestionably one of the first violinists in Europe. His success
had not been expected, and he played the entire piece amid the
most profound silence, without any applause, without the slightest
approving murmur; it burst out suddenly; the bravos never stopped,
and the young virtuoso was so surprised that in his joyous stupor
he knew neither how to leave the platform nor what countenance
to assume while staying on it. August Möser is a pupil of Charles de
Bériot, who must be very proud of him.[8]

M. Franco-Mendès was unfortunate enough to insist on playing
his cello solo, despite the fact that Ganz had preceded him, and the

---

[6] Mme Pleyel, it will be remembered, was the former Camille Moke, Berlioz's
faithless light o'love satirized in earlier pages as Hortense and then as Mina-Nadira.
[7] See above, p. 44 n. and ff.
[8] Möser, born in Berlin in 1825, died in the United States in 1859.

still more unlucky idea of choosing as themes for his fantasia some arias from Rossini's *The Lady of the Lake*. He consequently met with a very poor reception. And yet the air "O early dawn!" is a very fresh and poetic inspiration, and M. Franco-Mendès plays the cello delightfully; but he is Dutch and Rossini is Italian—hence the twofold anger of the perfervid German nationalists, all of which is, I must say, deplorable.

There remained to be performed an aria from Spohr's *Faust*, by Mlle Sachs, a song of Haydn's by Staudigl, and a batch of choruses. But the sitting had lasted nearly four hours, the audience was flowing out gently without asking for more, and the stream swept me out. True, I made no desperate effort to hold back. Another concert was in store for me that evening. The King of Prussia had been graciously pleased to ask me to the musicale he was giving his guests at his castle in Brühl, and for more reasons than one I was eager to save enough strength to go and enjoy it.

On reaching Brühl amid fairyland illumination and a pouring rain, I found another brilliant crowd to fight my way through with blunted weapons. Spurs clanked on the great staircases; on every side it was a sparkling of beautiful eyes, epaulets, white shoulders, medals, coiffures studded with pearls, golden helmets. The wearers of black coats cut a sorry figure, I can assure you. But owing to the kindness of the King, who came and talked with them a few minutes and welcomed them as "old acquaintances," places were found for them, and we were able to hear the concert.

Meyerbeer was at the piano. A cantata he had just composed in honor of Queen Victoria was first on the program. It was sung by Mantius, Pischek, Staudigl, Bötticher, and a chorus. It is forthright, lively, sinewy in its brevity—a harmonious hurrah vivaciously uttered. Next Mlle Tuczek sang a delicious romance from the opera *The Tournament* by the Earl of Westmorland.[9] Liszt played a couple of pieces—*his* way—and we heard for the first time the highly belauded Jenny Lind, who has taken Berlin by storm.

Truly, hers is a talent greatly superior to what we hear today in French and German opera houses. Her voice has an incisive, metallic timbre, great power, and incredible agility, lending itself

---

[9] The Eleventh Earl, John Fane (1784–1859) and better known in music as Lord Burghersh. He was a prolific composer in every genre, but is remembered for his perseverance in founding an Academy of Music in London.

equally to the softer shades, to impassioned expression, and to the most delicate ornamentation. Her talent is magnificently complete, yet if we are to believe good judges who admired her in Berlin, we could appreciate but one facet of it, for it requires the stimulus of the stage to disclose its full range of power. She sang the duet in the third act of *The Huguenots* with Staudigl, the finale of *Euryanthe*, and an aria (with chorus) of enchanting originality and freshness, strewn with unexpected turns, full of piquancy in its dialogue between chorus and soprano solo, of vibrant and elegant harmony, of coquettish and incisive melody; it was called on the program: "Aria from Pacini's *Niobe*." Never was there a more ingenious hoax: it was a cavatina from Meyerbeer's *An Encampment in Silesia*.[1]

Pischek and Staudigl sang a duet from *Fidelio*. Pischek's voice is altogether beautiful and it admirably matched Staudigl's, whose power I have already praised. The timbre of Pischek's voice is the most perfect I know of. If I add that he is young and handsome and that he sings with inexhaustible vitality, you will conceive how eagerly the King of Württemberg took him away from the Frankfurt Theater and attached him for life to his own chapel.

Mme Viardot-García also sang three pieces with her usual exquisite skill and poetic expression; the pieces were a dainty cavatina by Charles de Bériot, the infernal scene from *Orpheus*, and a song of Handel's—this last by request of Queen Victoria, who knew how admirably Mme Viardot interprets the old Saxon master. Midnight was striking and the sinking stars invited sleep. I luckily found a seat in a railway coach to return to Bonn; I went to bed at one o'clock and slept till noon, dead drunk with harmony, worn out with admiring, a prey to the irresistible need of silence and quiet, and coveting the cottage in Königswinter, where I now am and where I propose to muse for a few more days before returning to France.

Don't you wonder at my good memory, dear Corsino, and the ease with which I was able, seven years later, to muster and arrange my recollections for this antedated narrative? The impression the Bonn festival made on me was so deep and vivid! I feel sunk in sad-

---

[1] A three-act opera (1844), also known as *Wielka,* which met with success only when Jenny Lind sang the main role in Vienna.

ness merely from telling you about it. Beethoven is no more! Our poetic world is a desert! We shall never again experience the upheavals, the conflagration of the soul caused by the first hearing of his symphonies! The glorious realities of our youth now seem to be vanished dreams, vanished forever. Did spring and summer really exist? The cold, stormy wind blows day and night with such cruel persistence! No more green meadows, bubbling brooks, mysterious woods; no more azure in the sky; the grass is scorched, the water frozen, the forest bare; leaves, flowers, and fruit have fallen, the cold earth has gathered them, and we—soon—shall follow them.

Forgive me, I wander. I must get busy about your second hour of anguish. You managed to get through the first somehow, didn't you? I shouldn't say "somehow"—none of you can complain: during the entire first act of *Angelica and Roland* you had nothing but Beethoven! Will you now have some Méhul? Here is a short account of this classical composer, that I wrote for my musical colleagues in Paris.[2] It may suit yours, for in the course of my travels I have often noticed how little biographical knowledge foreign artists have about our French masters of the great period.

(Change your reader: the first one must be exhausted.)

For the Second Act

MÉHUL

It will appear strange to many that anyone in 1852 should take it into his head to write in France a biography of Méhul. "What!" they will say, "are the French so forgetful of their national glories that it is already necessary to remind them of the author of *Euphrosine*, to say when he lived, to name his works and describe the style of his compositions?"

Fortunately it is not so; we do not forget so easily, and very few people, surely, among those who took an interest in music thirty years ago, could be told anything new about Méhul. But the present generation, the one which for the last fifteen or eighteen years has diligently attended the Opéra-Comique, which has become accus-

---

[2] The article was prepared in connection with the revivals of Méhul's *Joseph* in June 1850 and September 1851.

tomed to the ways of the modern Parisian muse, a muse of whom it could be said that aside from a few pleasant works she has inspired her Pindus is the Butte-Chaumont and its Permessus the river Bièvre —that generation is as ignorant of the musical world as La Fontaine's little mouse was of the universe, and like the beastie takes a mole-hill for the Alps; [3] it is afraid of cockerels and full of love for cats—and consequently knows very little about Méhul.

Were it not for the concerts where the overture to *La Chasse du jeune Henri* and the first air from *Joseph* are occasionally heard (or for the posted programs about these which they have seen), this generation would hardly know this great master even by reputation. They never have known and never will know anything about Gluck and Mozart; they are quite ready to attribute *Don Giovanni* to Musard, who admittedly wrote quadrilles on the themes of that opera. But even so, only the erudite among them will know that there is an opera *Don Giovanni* "by Musard." All the same, these connoisseurs must be forgiven; they go to the Opéra-Comique from time to time *to relax*. This they do by listening to more or less interesting plays, the dialogue of which is written in a language that is theirs and interspersed with bits of music more or less catchy, more or less—simple-minded. They easily retain the melody, for it, too, is theirs. If by chance the melody, such as it is, is only conspicuous by its absence (in which case they can hardly remember it), they then enjoy the pleasure of believing that here is *learned* music; and the particular opera gets known as such. They get used to it, so great is their good nature; they adopt it, and when they speak of the composer, they no longer say just So-and-so, as they do of the composers they like, but *Monsieur* So-and-so. The former are their friends, the latter is their superior. No, this particular public must neither be attacked nor made fun of; it is a gem of a public, always happy, always merry, incapable of finding fault with anything at the Opéra-Comique, always eager to recall at every première all the actors, all the authors—unless they are dead (and even if they are); a public most inoffensive and inoffensible, a public that takes its fun wherever it can find it and fully as much where it cannot.

What seems to me far less pardonable is the ignorance of the young musicians, or at any rate the young people who would like to be considered such. It is extremely unwise of them not to learn

---

[3] In the fable "The Cockerel, the Cat, and the Little Mouse."

something about the past of their own art; they ought to reflect that among those they will meet in good society there are some who are tolerably well-informed about what they themselves are ignorant of, and the more educated will not fail to put them in their place if opportunity offers. It would not be a heavier burden on them to learn the titles of the works of the great masters (I do not ask them to know the works themselves) than to stuff their memory with so many shameful names, school it to retain what goes on daily in the theatrical houses of ill fame, and soil it with the endless trash among which they live and die because they were born there.

We should then no longer see what we see now—professors, prize winners with laurels and pensions, attributing *The Marriage of Figaro* to Rossini, calling Gluck the author of *Dido*, and believing that Piccinni was a conductor at the Porte-Saint-Martin; knowing by heart and singing, or making their pupils sing, all the low-grade music of the day, and not knowing as much as eight bars of the masterpieces that were, are, and will ever be the true glory of European art.

I refrain here from going into what such a state of things might produce; it would take me too far. I shall only say, without going back to primary causes, that in general the historical ignorance of the young generation living in and around music in Paris is lamentable; it surpasses anything that can be imagined as parallels in literature or the graphic arts. Yet one has to reckon with it every time that an illustrious name which happens to have disappeared from the horizon for a few years reappears there. When this happens, the critics must bear in mind that they are addressing readers brought up in Tasmania, at Borabora, or in the island of Ombai, and be sure to tell them that Napoleon was born in Corsica, an island surrounded on all sides by water; that he was a great general and won a number of battles, among which Fontenoy must not be reckoned; that he was actually Emperor of the French and King of Italy, and not Marquis de Buonaparte, a general in the army of His Majesty Louis XVIII, as certain historians have asserted.

The upshot of all this is that in dealing with Méhul we shall repeat some ancient anecdotes that all civilized musicians and connoisseurs of music know very well, but which, for thousands of young barbarians, are downright new news.

It is to them I speak, then, when I say: Méhul is a famous French composer. I have heard some learned amateurs in the provinces class him among the German masters and assert that his name should be pronounced Mehool, and not Mehül, but this is wrong. Recent and conscientious inquiries have convinced me that Méhul was born at Givet, in the department of Ardennes, a French department if ever there was one. I cannot give you the precise date of his birth, for I have not personally examined the register of births at Givet. Messrs Fétis and Choron, his biographers, agree that he was born in 1763, but M. Fétis says positively that the date was June 24, whereas Choron is above such details and says nothing about it at all.

The former permanent secretary of the Academy of Fine Arts of the Institute, M. Quatremère de Quincy, has written a paper on Méhul in which he tells us that Méhul's father was an inspector of the fortifications of Charlemont. There are various ways of dealing with truth, and this assertion of M. Quatrèmere illustrates one. Méhul's father was an ordinary cook who much later, when his son had acquired fame, owed to the latter's influence the subordinate post he held. Its title undoubtedly sounded better than the other at a public session of the Institute; it has in any event a luster of its own and a slight scientific flavor which is rather flattering.

A poor blind organist gave young Méhul his first music lessons, and the child made rapid enough progress for him to be appointed, at the age of ten, organist in the church of the Récollets at Givet. A fortunate circumstance having brought a German musician of ability, Wilhelm Hauser, to reside at the Abbaye de Lavaldieu, in the Ardennes near Givet, the boy Méhul managed to get himself taken on by him as a pupil. He became in fact a boarder at the Abbaye. His parents thereupon hoped that he would become a monk; and this might have happened if the colonel of a regiment garrisoned at Charlemont had not had prescience of what the young organist might some day become and persuaded him to go to Paris with him.

I do not know how long he was in Paris, very likely struggling with something close to poverty, when an unusual incident brought him into contact with a master far more learned and a patron far more powerful than those he had had up to that time. This detail comes from an habitué of the Opéra, an intimate friend of old Gardel (the famous ballet-master of that theater), who had long been close to the main character in the scene I am about to recount.

There was in Paris at that time a German composer named Gluck (pronounced Gloock),[4] whose works engrossed public attention to a degree you cannot imagine. Believe me or not, as you like, but it is a fact that all by himself he was more famous, more admired, and more admirable than three popular composers of today taken jointly—perhaps more than three members of the Institute. And yet this Gluck had so far written only a very small number of works for the Opéra; in those days scores were not as plentiful as berries. He had just finished one called *Iphigenia in Tauris,* which you have very likely never heard of, but which none the less aroused in Paris an enthusiasm greater than all the preceding works of this same Gluck, and for which, even today, many people feel one of those fierce passions that would petrify you if you should witness it. No need to tell you the cause of this abnormality.

Well, then, Méhul, having crept, I don't know how, into the rehearsal of this *Iphigenia in Tauris,* was so struck by what he heard, so moved, so upset, that he wished at all costs to hear the first performance on the following day. But how to manage it? All the tickets were sold, and besides Méhul, in his capacity as a young composer, had a large vacuum in his purse. So he conceived the idea of hiding at the back of a box, hoping to remain there undetected till the following night, and to be well inside the gates at the solemn hour. Unfortunately a house attendant found him in his hiding-place, called him down sharply, and was about to usher him out. Gluck was still on the proscenium, engaged in settling a few details of the Scythian ballet—an extraordinary piece which you do not know—for this devil of a man meddled with everything; he insisted that not only the words, but the staging, the dancing, the costumes, and everything else should be completely in keeping with his music, and he worried the life out of everybody to that end. We have long since risen superior to such ideas, have we not?

Be this as it may, the altercation in the box had attracted Gluck's attention, and he inquired the cause of it. Whereupon Méhul came forward trembling and explained matters, addressing the great master as *Monseigneur*. At bottom this Gluck was a goodhearted man,

---

[4] This direction is given because the French have a habit of pronouncing the *u* as in their own language—and with such determination that they frequently spell Gluck's name with an umlaut.

in spite of the fact that he had wit, genius, an iron will, and had brought about a musical revolution. He was touched by the enthusiasm of the young intruder, promised him a ticket for the first performance of *Iphigenia*, pressed him to call for it at his house, he, Gluck, being desirous, as he said, of making Méhul's acquaintance. You can guess the rest and conceive the influence that such a man's counsels must have exercised over the protégé's talent. For this Gluck, I repeat, was truly a composer of great ability, and what is more, a *Knight*, and very wealthy to boot, which, to you people, must be superabundant proof of his merit.

Hardly anyone today would spend more than two hours in a box without food or drink for the sake of hearing a masterpiece. The reason must be either that formerly masterpieces were scarce, or that there are in our day very few Méhuls. As for the *Monseigneur*, it has completely fallen into disuse. When speaking to an illustrious composer, one is more apt to say "old boy." It is true that *seigneur* comes from *senior*, the comparative of the Latin word *senex* (old); hence the expression "elder," "ancient," "senior," "old boy." The respect is just as deep: it is merely expressed differently.

It was under Gluck's direction that Méhul then wrote—as exercises only and with no idea of having them performed, three operas: *Psyche*, *Anacreon*, and *Lausus and Lydia*. Nowadays, when one has written three romances with an eye on a publisher, one begins to deem oneself possessed of an inalienable right to the attention of opera managers. Méhul was twenty years old when he submitted to the examining committee of the Opéra a serious score: *Alonzo and Cora*. Marmontel's *Incas* had no doubt supplied the subject of the poem. *Cora* was accepted, but not performed. So when after six years the young composer saw himself no better off there than in the beginning, he turned to the Opéra-Comique and submitted to it a three-act opera of domestic manners, *Euphrosine and Coradin*, based, if I am not mistaken, on a tale by Hoffmann. For a beginning, it brought Méhul a striking success. It was lucky for him that his first opera had not been staged; for it is said that when, having seen the triumph of *Euphrosine*, the Royal Academy of Music made up its mind to produce *Cora*, which it had kept pigeonholed for so long, this pale and frigid work had no success.

Despite the considerable number of beautiful or charming works that followed it, I must confess that for me *Euphrosine and Coradin* has remained its author's masterpiece. It has grace, delicacy, dash, plenty of dramatic movement, and passionate outbursts of terrific violence and veracity. The character of Euphrosine is delightful, that of the physician Alibour is of a somewhat satirical geniality. As for the rugged knight Coradin, everything he sings is magnificently headlong. In this work, which appeared in 1790, and is still radiant with life and youth, I shall content myself with citing the physician's two arias: "When the Count sits down to dinner" and "Minerva, O divine wisdom!"; the quartet for three sopranos and a bass, in which appears very felicitously the oft-repeated theme: "Dear sisters, leave it to me"; and the tremendous duet: "Beware of jealousy," which has remained the most overwhelming example of what music coupled with dramatic action can do by way of expressing passion. This amazing piece is the worthy paraphrase of Iago's speech: "Beware of jealousy, it is the green-eyed monster," in the *Othello* of Shakespeare, a great English poet who lived in the time of Queen Elizabeth.

The story goes that at the dress rehearsal of *Euphrosine*, Grétry (you know—Grétry, an ancient composer born in Liége, in Belgium, whose wittily melodious work *The Speaking Likeness* has just been put on again by the Paris Opéra-Comique)—the story goes, I say, that having heard the "jealousy" duet Grétry exclaimed: "It's enough to break open the roof of the house with the skulls of the audience!" The *mot* is not excessive. The first time I heard *Euphrosine*, twenty-five or twenty-six years ago, I was the cause of a regrettable incident at the Théâtre Feydeau, because of the fearful cry I was unable to repress at the peroration of the duet: "Ungrateful wretch, I have breathed into your soul!" Since little credence is given in theaters to emotions so naïvely violent as mine was, Gavaudan, who still sang the role of Coradin, in which he excelled, was sure this was an attempt to ridicule him by some outrageous prank, and he made his exit in a temper. The fact remains that he had never produced a more genuine effect. Actors more often deceive themselves the other way around. To perform this duet requires very powerful voices. I should like to hear Mlle Cruvelli and Massol sing it.

A little later Méhul wrote *Stratonice*, in which he had to depict the sorrows of the grand passion, the concentrated love that kills. From this work I must cite first the overture; then a charming invocation to Venus; the song: "Pour out all your sorrows"; the quartet of the consultation ("I tremble, my heart throbs") during which the physician Erasistratus, at the sight of the deep emotion the dying Antiochus feels at Stratonice's presence, discovers the young prince's love for her and diagnoses the cause of his illness; finally, the beautiful aria of Erasistratus and the last phrase, so true and touching, of King Seleucus:

> *Take from my hand your dearest Stratonice,*
> *And from this painful sacrifice*
> *Infer the love your father has for you.*

Méhul then wrote *Horatius Cocles; The Wise Young Girl and the Silly Old Fool,* a sort of petty ballad opera; *Doria,* obscure to this day; *Adrien,* a fine unpublished score (we have a manuscript of it in the library of the Conservatoire); [5] and *Phrosine et Mélidore,* the music of which is often inspired and contains orchestral effects entirely new at the time, such as the use of four horns in their hollowest hand-stopped notes to accompany, like a sort of instrumental death-rattle, the voice of a dying man. After this, Méhul, in the hope of overwhelming Lesueur, whom he detested, and whose opera *The Cavern* had just scored an immense success— (I almost forgot to tell you that Lesueur was a celebrated French composer, born at Drucat-Plessiel, near Abbeville, in the same year as Méhul; he was superintendent of Napoleon's chapel, of Louis XVIII's and Charles X's; he wrote a quantity of Masses, oratorios, and operas, and left among his papers an *Alexander in Babylon* which has never been performed). Méhul, then, angry at the success of Lesueur's *Cavern,* set to music an opera on the same subject and with the same title. Méhul's *Cavern* fell flat. I know that the library of the Opéra-Comique owns this manuscript and I should, I confess, be very curious to see with my own eyes how far this catastrophe was deserved.

Another failure sealed the fame and glory of Méhul, that of *La Chasse du jeune Henri,* an opera whose overture was so enthusiastically encored and made such an impression that the audience would not listen to the rest of the score, which, it is said, was rather ordinary.

---

[5] Berlioz had been librarian of the Paris Conservatoire since 1850.

Among the very fine works of Méhul that enjoyed but little success, *Ariodant* must be given first place. The subject of this opera is virtually the same as that of the *Montano and Stephanie* by Berton (a French musician, born in Paris, where he acquired a great reputation with his operas). Both are borrowed from a tragicomedy by the English poet Shakespeare, whom I mentioned a while ago; its title is *Much Ado about Nothing*. In *Ariodant* there is a jealousy duet which is nearly good enough to be a companion piece to the one in *Euphrosine;* there is a love duet so plain and true as almost to verge on indecency; a superb aria: "Oh, most faithful of lovers!" and the very popular romance which you surely know:

> *Oh tender woman, do you hear the singing*
> *Of birds about us carrying on their loves?*

Bion, in which there is a pretty rondo; *Epicure, The Treasure Hunt, Helena, Johanna, Happy in Spite of Himself, Gabrielle d'Estrées, The Troubadour Prince,* and *The Amazons* were not successes; they probably belong to the category of works justly consigned to oblivion. *The Angry Man, A Mad Try, Uthal, The Blind Men of Toledo, A Day of Adventures, Valentine of Milan,* and *Joseph*, on the other hand, are those to which success has been meted out rather fairly, I think, in proportion to their merit. The least-known of these operas, *The Blind Men of Toledo*, begins with a charming overture in the style of a Spanish bolero. *The Angry Man* was written to hoax the First Consul and the people about him, who denied the gift of melody to all but the Italians, and denied it especially to Méhul. The work was given out as the translation of a Neopolitan opera. Napoleon took care not to miss the first performance; he applauded with all his might, and declared for all to hear that no French composer could ever write such charming music. Whereupon, the public having called for the author's name, the stage manager flung to the astonished house the name of Méhul. An excellent hoax which will always succeed, at any time or place, and which demonstrates the unfairness of prejudice without ever destroying it.

Uthal, with its Ossianic subject, again clashed with Lesueur's *The Bards*, which was continuing its brilliant career at the Opéra, and which Napoleon had moreover taken under his wing. Méhul, to give the orchestration of *Uthal* a melancholy coloring of the cloudy, Ossianic kind, conceived the idea of using no strings but violas and cellos, the whole violin section being entirely omitted. The result of protracting this veiled timbre was a monotony more fatiguing than poetic, and Grétry, when asked about it, said frankly: "I'd give a gold soverign to hear an E string."

Joseph is the best-known of Méhul's operas in Germany. Its music almost throughout is simple, touching, rich in felicitous, though not very daring, modulations, full of broad and vibrant harmonies and graceful figures in the accompaniment, while its expression is always true. The second part of the overture does not seem to me equal to the colorful introduction that precedes it. The prayer "God of Israel!" in which the voices are supported only by occasional chords in the brass, is beautiful from beginning to end and in every respect. In the duet between Jacob and Benjamin: "O thou worthy prop of an aged father!" occur some rather vivid reminiscences of *Œdipus at Colonus*, they doubtless came into Méhul's mind through the similarity between the situation and the sentiments of this duet and certain parts of Sacchini's opera.

Méhul also wrote a great deal of music other than the operas I have enumerated. He made, or arranged, three ballet scores: *The Judgment of Paris*, *The Dance Craze*, and *Perseus and Andromeda*. He composed choruses and a good overture for Joseph Chénier's tragedy *Timoleon;* several symphonies; a large number of pieces for the solfeggio classes at the Conservatoire; cantatas; more operas whose titles I need not mention since they were never performed; operas composed for an occasion, such as *The Bridge of Lodi* [6] and others in which he had collaborators; a piece for two orchestras, of which the second follows the first in canonic imitation, like an echo. This was played on the Champ-de-Mars at a public festival held in celebration of the victory of Marengo; [7] he wrote the music for a melodrama at the Théâtre Porte-Saint-Martin, and some patriotic songs, among which *Le Chant du Départ* ("Victory sings to us") has held its ground beside the *Marseillaise*.

Méhul died on the 18th of October 1817, at the age of fifty-four. He is said to have been an engaging conversationalist and a man of wit and learning, with a taste for gardening.

---

[6] The occasion was Bonaparte's victory of that name in his first Italian Campaign (1796).

[7] In the second Italian Campaign (1800).

His musical system, if one may call system a doctrine such as his, was that of plain common sense, which is so disdained in these times. He believed that operatic music, or any other intended to be joined to words, should show a direct correlation with the sentiments expressed in these words; that sometimes, even, when this can be done without awkwardness and without damage to the melody, it should seek to reproduce the accent of the voice, the declamatory accent, so to speak, which certain words and phrases call for and which one feels to be nature's own. He thought that a question, for instance, cannot be sung to the same arrangement of notes as an assertion. He believed that for certain impulses of the human heart there are special melodic accents, which alone can truly express them, and which it is necessary to find at whatever cost, under penalty of being false, inexpressive, and cold, and failing to attain the supreme goal of art.

He was moreover fully convinced that in truly dramatic music, when the importance of a situation deserves the sacrifice, the composer should not hesitate as between a pretty musical effect that is foreign to the scenic intent or dramatic character, and a series of accents that are true but do not yield any surface pleasure. He was convinced that musical expressiveness is a lovely flower, delicate and rare, of exquisite fragrance, which does not bloom without culture, and which a breath can wither; that it does not dwell in melody alone, but that everything concurs either to create or destroy it—melody, harmony, modulation, rhythm, instrumentation, the choice of deep or high registers for the voices and instruments, a quick or slow tempo, and the several degrees of volume in the sounds emitted. He knew that a man can show himself a learned or brilliant musician and yet be wholly lacking in the sense of expression; and contrariwise that one can possess this sense in the highest degree and yet be a musical mediocrity; and that the real masters of dramatic art have always been more or less gifted with a combination of highly musical qualities and the sense of expression.

Méhul had none of the preconceived ideas held by some of his contemporaries with regard to artistic method. He made adroit use of certain devices whenever he considered them suitable, even though the professors of routine prohibit them in all cases. He was therefore truly and completely of Gluck's school. But his style was more chastened, more polished, and more academic than the German master's, and also much less majestic, less gripping, less *rugged to the heart*. In Méhul one finds fewer of those tremendous flashes of lightning that light up the depths of the soul. And then, if I may be allowed to say so, Méhul seems to me somewhat sparing of ideas; he made music of high quality, true, agreeable, beautiful, and touching, but well-behaved to the point of severity. His muse has intelligence, wit, heart, and beauty; but she retains the ways of the housewife, her gray gown lacks fullness, and she worships economy.

Thus it is that in *Joseph* and in *Valentine of Milan* simplicity is carried to a point which it is dangerous to approach so closely. In *Joseph*, again, as in most of Méhul's other scores, the orchestra is treated with perfect tact and a highly respectable common sense; not a single instrument is *de trop*, not one sounds a note that is out of place; but in its learned soberness this orchestra lacks color, energy, movement, and the indescribable something that gives life. Without adding a single instrument to those Méhul used, it would, I think, have been possible to give to the whole the qualities one regrets not finding in it.

I hasten to add that this defect, though undeniable, seems to me a thousand times preferable to the loathsome and repellent error which characterizes the majority of modern dramatic composers and which one may as well give up trying to correct—the error which makes the art of instrumentation too often give ground, in operatic orchestras, to coarse and ridiculous noises, coarsely and ridiculously introduced. These are the enemies of expressiveness and harmony, the annihilators of melody and the human voice; their only role is to give greater stress to deplorably vulgar rhythms, which in spite of their violence actually destroy energy; for energy in sound is only relative, and it results only from contrasts adroitly and sparingly used. Noises that have nothing musical in them are a standing criticism of the taste and mind of the public that tolerates them, and they have ended by making our operatic orchestras the counterpart of those manned by mountebanks and quack doctors at village fairs.[8]

Now you must admit that although you held Méhul and his works in high esteem, you did not know all this. And it is to *Angelica and Roland* that you are indebted for this unlooked-for education. It's an ill wind that blows nobody good.

---

[8] See above, note 9, p. 88.

But I'm afraid your second act is not over. So let us chat awhile. I am once again back from London. This time, except for two women singers, I heard nothing there by way of music but what was rather painful. At Her Majesty's Theatre I saw a performance of Mozart's *Figaro* that was trombonized, ophicleided—in a word, copper-bottomed like a ship of the line. That is an English habit. Neither Mozart, nor Rossini, nor Weber, nor Beethoven has managed to escape *re-instrumentation*. Their orchestra is not sufficiently spicy, and it is deemed imperative to remedy the defect. Besides, if the theaters have regular performers on the trombone, ophicleide, bass drum, triangle, and cymbals, they are obviously not hired to twiddle their thumbs. This is an old story and it would seem about time to drop it.

Cruvelli [9] played the page, and for the first time in my life I heard the part sung intelligibly. Yet Mlle Cruvelli puts rather too passionate an accent into it; she makes Cherubino too big a boy; she almost converts him into a young man. Mme Sontag *was* Susanna. The existence of a talent of this magnitude is hard to believe even by those who are under its spell. Here is a singer who understands the art of nuances, possesses a full keyboard of them, and knows how to choose and apply them!

> *Strew for her lilies,*
> *Armfuls of lilies.*[1]

I attended the Purcell Commemoration at Westminster Abbey. A small choir of mediocre voices sang with organ accompaniment hymns, anthems, and motets by this old English master. A small, devout audience attended the ceremony. It was cold, stagnant, sleepy, and slow. I exerted myself to feel admiration, but fell back into the opposite feeling. Then the memory of the children's chorus in St. Paul's assailed me and set up in my mind an unfortunate comparison, so that I left, leaving Purcell to slumber with his faithful.

Sir George Smart was good enough, one Sunday, to do me the honors of St. James's Chapel, of which he is the organist. Alas! music has forsaken this little nook since kings and queens have given up residing at the Palace. A few choristers without any voice, eight

---

[9] Sophie Crüwell (1826–1907), of German birth, Italianized her name on going to England, where she made her debut as the Countess in *Figaro*.

[1] Adapted from Virgil's *Æneid* (VI, 883), where it is applied to young Marcellus.

choirboys with too much, a primitive organ—that is all that one can hear there. The chapel was built by Henry VIII, and Sir George showed me the little door by which this good King used to come in to give thanks to God and sing some hallelujas of his own composition every time he had invented a new religion or beheaded one of his wives.

I also heard at a concert Rossini's brilliant *Stabat Mater*. You don't know, do you, the story of the fugue with which the score concludes? This is it.

Rossini, that great musician, had, despite his great wit, the weakness to believe that a respectable *Stabat*, a true *Stabat*, a *Stabat* worthy to stand beside those of Palestrina and Pergolesi, absolutely must end with a fugue on the word *Amen*. Actually, as you know perfectly well, this practice produces the most abominable and indecent nonsense. But Rossini lacked the courage to defy the settled prejudice on this question. Now, as fugue is not his strong point, he sought out his friend Tadolini,[2] who has the reputation of being a cast-iron contrapuntist, and said to him in his most coaxing manner: "*Caro Tadolini, mi manca la forza; fammi questa fuga!*"[3] Dear Tadolini sacrificed to friendship and composed the fugue. When the *Stabat* appeared, the professors of counterpoint found it detestable, these gentlemen being in the habit of giving credit for ability in fugue exclusively to themselves and their pupils. So if we are to believe them, Rossini might just as well have written his fugue himself.

Such is the story going the rounds; but between ourselves the truth is that the fugue is Rossini's own.

We have just suffered a serious blow in Paris, and you'll be very lucky if you don't feel its aftereffects. Z.,[4] the great insulter of art and artists, in despair at having lost, through stock-market speculation, three fourths of the enormous fortune he had amassed you-know-how, was unable to resist an impulse to suicide. He made a will, leaving, it is said, the remains of his fortune to the headmistress of a girls' school. This pious duty fulfilled, he made his way to the Place Vendôme, where he had the door of the column [5] opened to

---

[2] Giovanni Tadolini (1793–1872), an opera-composer who divided his time between Paris and Italy.
[3] "Dear Tadolini, I haven't the strength; do the fugue for me!"
[4] This person, like Heine's poem about him, has not been identified.
[5] See above, note 9, p. 264.

him. On reaching the gallery at the top of the monument he took off his hat, tie, and gloves—I owe these horrible details to the custodian of the column—gazed calmly at the abyss beneath him, then going back a few steps from the parapet, as if for a fiercer spring, he abruptly gave up the idea.

Heinrich Heine, whom I have just seen, recited to me in French prose a little elegiac poem he has composed in German on this catastrophe. It would make you laugh till you cried.

Poor Heine! Bedridden for the last six years by an incurable paralysis, and almost blind, he none the less retains his terrible gaiety. He will not as yet consent to die; as he says, "God must wait." He first wants to see "how it will all end." He makes *mots* about his enemies, about his friends, about himself. The day before yesterday, on hearing me announced, he called out from his bed in his weak voice, which seems to come out the grave: "Well, well, my dear fellow, it's you? Come in! So you haven't given me up?— Always original!"

If your second act hasn't ended yet, I am sorry for you, Corsino, but I have nothing more to say right now. Resign yourself to fate, pick up your violin, and play the finale as if it were good. It won't kill you. The fact is, I want to read your letter over again. I want to answer it so that I shan't have to part company with you until the very end of the third act, which you diagnose as the most dangerous.

For the Last Act

When I began this letter, I had no intention of taking the slightest notice of certain passages in yours. I now revert to them.

And so! My four or five readers think I did wrong to refer to the recreations they indulge in with their colleagues when they have to play music they do not like—recreations which I freely confess to have shared. That's just like an artist! If he does something reasonably well, he expects the five hundred and thirty thousand voices of fame (not counting her trumpet) to announce it all over the five continents—and how, with what fanfare! I know all about it. But if by chance he lets himself be involved in some action or piece of work that gives the smallest handle to criticism, then in spite of all the pussyfooting and all the smiles of much-abused Criticism, in spite of the friendly form it takes in order to be kind, gentle, and a good fellow, the mere mention of that action or piece of work is a shameful crime. Listen to artists and you'll be persuaded it is outrageous, a mean trick, a breach of trust—each indignantly cries out with Othello:

> *Are there no stones in heaven*
> *But what serve for the thunder?*

I must say, dear good friends, that I feel sorry for you. I thought you less old-fogyish and I did think myself one of your intimates. I was wrong. When I write to you now, I am going to put on kid gloves. I will never show up in your orchestra except in a white tie and wearing *all my medals;* I will speak to you, my lords, only hat in hand.

Joking aside, your susceptibility is childish (be thankful that I don't say "infantile"). But as I know you well enough to guess that by now you're laughing at it yourselves, let's change the subject and not bring it up again.

As for you, Corsino, who imagine you will seem "ridiculous in the eyes of the Paris musicians and men of letters who read your book," let me tell you that your fear is entirely groundless, for the good reason that men of letters in Paris read only their own books, while the musicians never read anything.

Let me also give you heartfelt thanks for shielding me from the roundabout vendetta of the outraged tenor, and for taking a stand against my being played. I am doubly obliged to you, since the danger would be double if my opera were to be performed at X. I think your colleagues fully capable of transforming it into *a conversation piece:* they would start reading *Clarissa Harlowe* at the première.[6]

I freely admit the silliness of my pun on Moran's name, but yours apropos of the Kleiners' two Bavarians is just as bad.

I cannot bring myself to share your suspicion about your conductor's corset. More likely the rehearsals of *Angelica and Roland* have made him lose weight. It's pretty grueling, isn't it?

If I have said twice that our sweet Bacon (a pleasant-sounding

---

[6] Richardson's *Clarissa* is, among classic novels, possibly the longest: it is often printed in six volumes.

phrase) is not descended from his famous namesake, it is because his unusual mind and wit might lead one to think he was. And *that* supposition would be a slander against the scientist Roger Bacon, who invented gunpowder, for Bacon was a monk, and monks do not marry. This explanation will, I hope, completely satisfy our friend.

But that Dimsky, Dervinck, Turuth, Siedler, and you, Corsino, should not know who Falstaff is! And have the nerve to admit it! If true, you are all of you more Bub-Bub-Bub-Bacon than Bacon himself. Falstaff a poet! a soldier! and you pretend to know your Shakespeare! Know then, gentlemen and musical friends, that Sir John Falstaff is a main character in three of the English poet's plays —the two tragedies of *Henry IV*, and the comedy entitled *The Merry Wives of Windsor;* and that he also claims the public's attention in a fourth drama by the same author, in which he does not appear, though his last moments are recorded. Know ye also that he was a favorite of Queen Elizabeth's, that he is the archetype of the English buffoon, the English Gascon, the English hector, one might say the true English Punchinello, and the embodiment of five or six cardinal sins: gluttony, wenching, and cowardice are his outstanding qualities. But in spite of his obesity, his rotundity, his meanness, and his poltroonery, he captivates women, making them pawn their silver to satisfy his greedy tastes.

Shakespeare has made him Prince Hal's companion in his orgies and nocturnal escapades in London, and the Prince allows Falstaff to treat him with incredible familiarity, until the time when the "royal Hal," as Falstaff has the insolence to call him for short, becomes King under the name of Henry V. Then, eager to have his youthful follies forgotten, he banishes from the court the fat companion of his carousing and sends him into exile. You must know too that this incomparable cynic, in whom one takes so much interest in spite of oneself that his sad end almost brings tears to the eyes, this Falstaff, when he is compelled to take part in a great battle at the head of a rabble of vagabonds in rags and tatters of whom he is the captain, runs away at the very beginning of the action, and in the corner where he has gone to hide, delivers himself of the following monologue:

"Honor pricks me on. Yea, but how if honor prick me off when I come on? How then? Can honor set a leg? No. Or an arm? No.

Or take away the grief of a wound? No. Honor hath no skill in surgery, then? No. What is honor? A word. What is in that word *honor*? What is that honor? Air; a trim reckoning! Who hath it? He that died o' Wednesday. Doth he feel it? No. Doth he hear it? No. 'Tis insensible, then? Yea, to the dead. But will it not live with the living? No. Why? Detraction will not suffer it. Therefore I'll none of it. Honor is a mere scutcheon: and so ends my catechism.

I have transcribed this famous speech in the original for those of you, gentlemen, who do not know English but would like to pretend you do. But here is the translation, for the use of those whose pretensions do not go beyond that of knowing French.[7]

You see now, don't you, why in speaking of Camoëns's career and belated glory, I had reason to exclaim: "O Falstaff!" and to think of his philosophy. Nothing escapes you.

But to come, my dear Corsino, to your final question: The author of the *Life of Paganini* you mention recently wrote to a friend of mine asking him to induce me to review his work in the *Journal des Débats*. He hoped, he said, that I would not let myself be influenced in my judgment by my hatred of the Italians and their music. I therefore read his little book. I found it easy to reply to the virulent rebukes addressed to me. But when I had finished my rejoinder I was dissuaded from publishing it in a newspaper, so as not to start a polemic which, as it concerned me alone, would necessarily be out of place in its columns. Here the circumstances are different, and since you have read the accusation, I am glad to lay my defense before you.

A Reply to M. Carlo Conestabile, author of the book entitled Vita di Niccolo Paganini da Genova

M. Conestabile of Perugia appeals to my impartiality in asking me to review this little book in which he treats me most unkindly. I thank him for believing me capable of doing full justice to his work. I should do so very willingly, accustomed as I am to finding myself in this titillating situation, but unfortunately the work is such that I cannot express an opinion of any value about it. I can neither pass upon the historical merits of the book, not being in a

---

[7] Berlioz's translation is omitted here for obvious reasons.

position to know the truth of the facts it reports; nor upon the style of the author, since the niceties of the Italian language are necessarily beyond my grasp; nor upon the correctness of the author's estimate of the great virtuoso's talent, *for I never heard Paganini play*. I was in Italy at the time this extraordinary artist was turning everyone's head in France. When I knew him later, he had already given up playing in public; the state of his health no longer permitted it, and it will be readily understood that I did not dare ask him to play once more for me alone. If I conceived so high an opinion of him, it is, in the first place, because of his conversation; because of the radiance which seems to emanate from certain distinguished men, and which surrounded Paganini with an aura of poetry; and second, because of the ardent and reasoned admiration he inspired in certain artists in whose judgment I place implicit trust.

I should like to think that M. Conestabile has drawn on the best sources for his life of the illustrious virtuoso whose appearance in Europe aroused such extraordinary emotions. I can see that on the subject of my own relations with Paganini, he has gathered several particulars that are in the main correct; his errors are confined to a few details of only slight importance.

Perhaps this is as far as I should go in judgment. Yet the book contains a passage well calculated to arouse my violent indignation, were the slander that it conveys not mitigated by its own absurdity. The reader must forgive me if I cannot refrain from giving it a brief reply.

After relating an anecdote about me which is public property, and in which Paganini played toward me a role of such magnificent cordiality; and moreover after kindly bestowing on my works excessive compliments, M. Conestabile exclaims:

"Now, who would believe it possible? The very same man who owes to an Italian the triumph of his own genius, the acquisition (*conseguimento*) of a considerable sum,[8] this Berlioz, who belongs to a nation so greatly indebted to the belovèd country of Palestrina, Lulli, Viotti, and Spontini, *no longer remembers*, Paganini once dead, the favors he has received. Having sucked in the venom of ingratitude, he delights in vomiting harsh words against *our* music,

---

[8] In the original, a note signed by the French publisher recounts the incident mentioned above in note 8, p. 196.

against *us*, who, with our traditional kindliness, are accustomed to endure the insults and outrages of foreign nations and meet their coarse sarcasms with disdainful silence. [I am translating literally.] No, the name of Hector Berlioz will not perish [you are too kind!], nor that of Paganini [a fortiori, this is mere tautology]; and if our contemporaries are silent [not all of them are silent], at least our descendants, on hearing about the adventure I have just related, will reward Italian philanthropy with their plaudits and devote a page to French ingratitude."

To this I would reply: "Really and truly, sir, if you knew how ridiculous your tirade is, you would be sorry that you permitted yourself to publish it. You live, apparently, in an exclusive circle, which wants to stay outside the musical movement of Europe. You are passionately fond of *your* music, as you call it, without being able or willing to establish useful comparisons between it and the music of other nations. Hence your religious faith in Italian art, and your irritability when anyone ventures to question its dogmas. You forget that the majority of artists and critics of any standing are more or less acquainted with the masterpieces of all countries, and that these same critics and artists attach real value only to genuine, great, original, and beautiful music. They love music for its qualities or detest it for its vices without worrying about the land of its birth. Perhaps you were not aware of this. If so, allow me to instruct you: whether the author of a musical work is Italian, French, English, or Russian is a matter of small concern to those whose judgment counts. The question of national origin is, in their eyes, altogether childish.

"The proof of this is to be found in your own book itself, when in speaking of Spontini's death, you say that I 'could not refrain' (for twenty-five years now I have been 'unable to refrain'!) 'from paying his works a liberal tribute of admiration.'

"Now let me show you the injustice of the offensive accusation you bring against me, the consequences that would follow if it were deserved, and the material error you have committed with regard to the fundamentals of the question.

"I note first in your invective an indication that you, at least, will not 'meet sarcasm with disdainful silence' and that you are almost exempt from the 'traditional kindliness' of your compatriots. You believe, moreover, that because a great Italian artist did what Paganini did for me, I am therefore bound, wholly on that account, to find excellent, perfect, irreproachable, everything that is done in Italy; I must praise the theatrical customs of that beautiful country, the musical predilections of its inhabitants, as well as the effect of predilection and custom on the practice of the freest among the arts, which is to say, I am to admire the fatal constriction of the art of music.

"Though I am French, sir, I owe a great deal to France. According to you, then, I should consider good all the music produced in France. That would be a very serious matter, for almost as much bad music is made in France as in your country. I am also greatly indebted to Prussia, Austria, Bohemia, Russia, and England;[9] I am loaded down with debts of this sort incurred almost everywhere. So I am bound to declare that all is for the best in the best possible world, and exclaim: 'All of you are sublime, let's kiss on it!' yet not adding: 'And never have another cross word again.'[1]

"What your argument amounts to is that with respect to any nation where one single individual may have been good enough to find merit in me, I must ignore my artistic conscience and, regardless of the truth, carry on a stupid make-believe of admiring everything.

"Paganini, sir, who did not share your opinion, would have despised me had I been capable of such conduct. Moreover, I know full well what he thought of his country's musical habits, though he never had occasion, happily for him and perhaps for you, to express his opinion in writing. I tremble at the thought of letting you even suspect what Cherubini and Spontini likewise thought on this same point—they whose fame and works you now lay claim to although Italy cared little enough for either. Paganini, Spontini, and Cherubini were accordingly greater monsters of ingratitude than I, for even if the rest of Europe afforded them a loftier career than that open to musicians in Italy, and forced their genius to take a higher and prouder flight while showering on them gold, honors, and glory, Italy gave them—birth. I do not say that this one not very costly present is not worth something.

"Kindly take note also that Paganini is not Italy any more than I am France. These two countries, of which you justly glorify the

---

[9] The reference is to Berlioz's repeated concert tours in those countries.
[1] The allusion is to a common phrase for ending a lovers' quarrel.

one while unjustly castigating the other, can in no sense be answerable en masse for the private beliefs of a couple of artists. Even if we could admit what you have so naïvely expressed, that all Italians are 'philanthropists,' I cannot grant you that all Frenchmen are 'ingrates.'

"Let me, moreover, take you into my confidence on an important point: however passionately fond you may be of 'your' music, I am almost certain of being much more so of music *itself;* to such a point, indeed, that I feel quite capable of affectionate sympathy for a bandit with genius who might have tried to murder me, and of hardly any for an honest man to whom nature has denied intelligence and the artistic sense.

"No doubt your convictions are sincere and you are a thorough scholar and gentleman. But please believe that Paganini's ideas on the matter in hand differed hardly at all from my own monstrous manner of thinking. Finally, to conclude my profession of faith, let me say that I am deeply grateful to the men whose works kindle admiration in me; but I can never admire mediocrities, even if their treatment of me has inspired me with the liveliest gratitude. You may infer from this the extent of the right I take upon myself *not* to praise the mediocre or worse-than-mediocre works and talents of people to whom I owe no debt whatever.

"Now for a mistake in date which is not without importance. The critique of mine that you quote, incidentally altering the meaning by substituting 'melodic sense' for 'sense of expression'—a very different thing, I assure you—this sketch of musical tendencies in Italy which is the basis of the charge in reply to which I now have the pleasure of conversing with you, was written in Rome in 1830. It was printed for the first time in Paris, during the course of the same year, by the *Revue européenne,*[2] and afterwards reproduced in various publications (among them *L'Italie pittoresque*) and in the *Revue musicale* of M. Fétis,[3] who at first taxed my opinion with exaggeration, but later on admitted its accuracy and justness. You can satisfy yourself of this point by reading in the *Gazette musicale* the account M. Fétis published about his journey to Italy. Now, I

---

[2] Berlioz's memory plays him false here, though this does not affect the argument: the article was written in 1831 and first published in 1832.

[3] F. J. Fétis (1784–1871), famous theorist and musicologist, whose authority in the last century was acknowledged throughout Europe.

saw Paganini for the first time in 1833. You can therefore see that no ingratitude can be charged upon my article, since it was written, printed, and reproduced long before I had even met the immortal virtuoso of whom you are the biographer, and before he had honored me with his friendship.

"This, I suppose, is enough to weaken somewhat the force of your accusation. Yet it does not prevent my having at the present moment the same ideas about such of the musical practices of 1830 as may still obtain in Italy, nor my still claiming the right to express them without deserving in the least the reproach of ingratitude with which you have had the patriotism to charge me.

"This, sir, is all I can say regarding your book, which for the rest seems to have been written with an honorable purpose and the best intentions.

I can now answer, *caro* Corsino, the other important question contained in your letter. Yes, I do know Wallace, and it is a pleasure to me to learn that you like his opera *Maritana*.[4] It has been very well received in Vienna and London, but so far I have not heard it. As to the author, here are a few improbable details about him which may interest you. Take them for true, for I have them from Wallace himself, and he is much too lazy, in spite of his vagabond humor, to take the trouble of lying.

The Adventures of Vincent Wallace in New Zealand

Vincent Wallace was born in Ireland.[5] He began as a distinguished violinist, and won great success in London as well as in India and Australia. Later he gave up the violin to devote himself to teaching the piano, an instrument of which he is master, and to composition. He is a first-class *eccentric*—as phlegmatic in appearance as certain Englishmen, at bottom rash and violent like an

---

[4] Première at Drury Lane, November 15, 1845.
[5] William Vincent Wallace (1814–65). The story to follow, though dressed up for retelling, is factual at most points and truly represents the hero's character, wanderings, and abilities.

American. When together in London, we spent many a late night over a bowl of punch, he narrating his strange adventures, I listening to them eagerly. He has carried off women, he has fought several duels that turned out badly for his opponents, and he has been a savage—yes, a savage, or pretty nearly one—for six months. This is how I have heard him tell, with his customary impassiveness, this strange episode in his life:

"I was in Sydney [Wallace says: 'I was in Sydney,' or 'I am off to Calcutta,' the way we say in Paris: 'I am off to Versailles,' or 'I am back from Rouen'] when I ran into the commander of an English frigate whom I knew and he suggested to me, between cigars, that I accompany him to New Zealand.

" 'What are you doing there?' I asked him.

" 'I'm going to chastise the inhabitants of Tewaewae-Punamu Bay, the most ferocious of New Zealanders, who took it into their heads last year to loot one of our whaling-ships and eat its crew. Come along with me, the crossing is not long, and the expedition will be fun.'

" 'All right, I'll come with pleasure. When do we start?'

" 'Tomorrow.'

" 'Count on me, I'm going along.'

"The next day we set sail and the voyage was soon over. On sighting New Zealand our commander, who had made straight for the bay, gave orders to put the ship in disorder, tear a few sails, split a couple of spars, close the ports, carefully screen our guns, conceal our soldiers and three fourths of the crew between decks —in a word, give our frigate the appearance of a poor devil of a ship half disabled by a gale and no longer answering the helm.

"When the New Zealanders caught sight of us their customary caution made them stay quiet. But after counting only ten men on the frigate, and believing from our wretched appearance and the indolence of our movements that we were shipwrecked mariners asking for help, rather than an attacking party, they seized their weapons, jumped into their canoes, and came at us from every corner of the shore. Never in my life have I seen so many canoes. They kept coming from the land, the sea, the bushes, the rocks, everywhere. And remember that several of these boats contained as many as fifty warriors. It was like a school of huge fish swimming toward us and closing ranks.

"We let ourselves be surrounded like men unable to offer any resistance. But when the canoes, which were divided into two groups, came within half pistol range, and so closely packed that they could not turn, a slight push of the tiller made our frigate wear and turn its beam to the two flotillas, whereupon our commander shouted: 'Battle formation, all hands! Open the ports! Broadsides for the vermin!' Port and starboard guns, simultaneously poking their muzzles out of the ship's sides just like inquisitive folk putting their heads out the window, began to spit on the tattooed warriors a regular hailstorm of up-to-date grapeshot, ball, and shell. Our four hundred soldiers accompanied this concert with a heavy and well-directed fusillade. Everybody worked hard; it was superb.

"From the top of one of the mainmast yards, to which I had climbed with my pocket full of cartridges, my double-barreled gun, and a dozen grenades handed me by the master gunner, I, for my part, destroyed the appetite of many New Zealanders who very likely had already dug the oven in which they hoped to roast me. I can't tell you how many I killed. (Of course you know that in those countries you think nothing of killing men.) You can't imagine the effect of my grenades especially. They burst between their legs and sent them sky-high to drop into the sea like flying fish, while the twenty-four- and thirty-six-pounders, with their big cannon-balls, raked whole batches of canoes, splitting them apart with a cracking noise like lightning striking a tree. The wounded yelled, the runaways drowned, while our commander stamped about, shouting through his speaking-trumpet: 'One more broadside! Give them bar-shot! Shoot that chief with the red feathers! Out launch, out cutter, out yawl! Finish the swimmers off with your handspikes! Knock them on the head, my lads! God save the Queen!'

"The sea was strewn with corpses, limbs, weapons, paddles, and wreckage from the canoes, while here and there the green waters were flecked with big crimson patches. We were beginning to weary, when our men in the launch, who were less infuriated than the commander, having contented themselves with sending another dozen swimmers to kingdom come with pistol-shots and blows of their oars, hauled out of the water a couple of magnificent New Zealanders, two chiefs who were exhausted. They were hoisted half dead on to the deck, and in another hour the two Goliaths were on their feet again, as lively as panthers. The interpreter we had brought from Sydney went up and assured them that they had nothing more to fear, white men not being in the habit of killing their prisoners.

" 'Then why,' said one of the two, enormously tall and of terrifying aspect, 'why did the whites fire on us with their big guns and little guns? We weren't yet at war.'

" 'Do you remember,' said the interpreter, 'the whalers whom you killed and ate last year? They belonged to our nation and we came to avenge them.'

" 'Oh,' exclaimed the big chief, stamping violently on the deck, and gazing at his companion with savage enthusiasm, 'that's all right, then. The whites are great warriors!' Our conduct evidently filled them with admiration. They judged us from the standpoint of art, like connoisseurs, noble rivals, great artists.

"The New Zealanders' fleet destroyed and the butchery finished, our commander tells us, rather late in the day, that he must now sail for Tasmania, instead of returning to New South Wales. I was greatly annoyed at having to go on this new journey, which would take some time. Just then up comes the frigate's surgeon and expresses the desire to remain at Tewaewae-Punamu to study the New Zealand flora and enrich his collection of plants, provided the commander would pick him up on his way back to Sydney. This was readily agreed to. And then and there the idea of seeing these terrible savages at close range took hold of me and I volunteered to accompany the surgeon. The two chiefs were to be set free, on condition that they would vouch for our safety. The arrangement suited them very well, and they promised to protect us while we were among their people who, they said, would welcome us. '*Tayo, tayo* (Friend)!' they repeated, rubbing noses with us according to custom. '*Tayo rangatira* (Friends of the chiefs).'

"The pact was concluded. We were taken ashore, the surgeon, the two chiefs, and myself.

"I must admit I felt a cold chill on setting foot on the now deserted beach, which only a few hours before had been covered with enemies in arms, and which we now trod, we conquerors, with no other protection against the fury of the vanquished than the word and doubtful authority of a couple of cannibal chiefs."

"I must say," I broke in amid Wallace's recital, "you both deserved to be roasted over a slow fire and eaten. Your folly and presumption are inconceivable!"

"Anyhow, nothing happened to us. On rejoining their tribe, our chiefs explained that peace had been concluded and that they owed their freedom to us. Thereupon they made us kneel at their feet and lightly tapped both of us on the nape of the neck with a battle-ax, making certain signs and uttering words that made us sacred.

"Men, women, and children shouting '*Tayo!*' in their turn approached us with curiosity, but without the slightest sign of hostility. They seemed to be flattered by our trust in them and all responded to it. Besides, the surgeon won them over by dressing the wounds of the few who had survived the grapeshot, among whom several had frightful injuries and fractures. After a few days he left me to explore a forest in the interior with Koro, the big chief, as his guide.

"The year before, I had learned in the Hawaiian Islands a few words of the Kanaka language, which in spite of the enormous distances that separate these various archipelagoes is in use in Hawaii, Tahiti, and New Zealand. To begin with I used these words to make friends with two charming little native girls, as lively and coquettish as Parisian working girls, with large, sparkling black eyes, and eyelashes the length of my finger. Their shyness once conquered, they followed me like a couple of llamas, Meré carrying my gunpowder and bullets, Moïanga the game I brought down during our excursions; at night when we slept in the open, each of them in turn served me as a pillow. What nights! what stars! what a sky! That country is paradise on earth.

"In spite of it all, would you believe that I was smitten there by the most infernal and unexpected of woes? Emaï, my protector and chief, had a daughter of sixteen who had not shown herself at first, and whose bewitching beauty, when I set eyes on her, implanted in my heart a fearful love, with all the tremors, breathlessness, and other abominable nervous sensations that ensue.

"Do let me dispense with drawing her portrait. I thought all I had to do was to introduce myself to be welcomed with open arms; Meré and Moïanga had spoiled me. I therefore tried after a few honeyed words to take her into a field of phormium (the flax of the country), there to spin golden and silken hours. But no; she resisted, with a stubborn resistance. I then resigned myself to courting her in due form and assiduously. The father of Tatea (that was her name) warmly espoused my cause; often, in my presence, he scolded the pretty little rebel. I offered Tatea one after the other, then all together: the gilt buttons off my waistcoat, my knife, my pipe, my only blanket, and over a hundred blue and pink glass beads. I killed a dozen albatrosses to make her a cloak of white down. Finally I proposed that she should herself cut off my little finger. This seemed to shake her for a moment, but still she refused. Her indignant father was on the point of breaking her arm, and I had great trouble dissuading him. My two other women then took a hand in the matter and tried to overcome her obstinacy. For jealousy is ridiculous in New Zealand, and my women were not ridiculous. Nothing came of it.

"At that point I broke down in the dumps. I gave up eating, smoking, sleeping. I hunted no more, and spoke not a word either to Moïanga or to Meré. The poor creatures wept; I took no notice of them, and was about to blow out my brains, when the idea occurred to me of offering Tatea a small keg of tobacco which I always wore strapped to my back.

"That was the thing! And I'd never guessed it!

"The most rewarding smile greeted my offering. She put out her hand to me, and as I touched it I felt my heart melt like a lump of lead in a forge. The wedding gift had been accepted. Meré and Moïanga hurried off to carry the good news to Emaï, while Tatea, delighted with the ownership of the precious keg—she had persisted in not asking for it from pure coquettishness—loosened her hair at last and dragged me all palpitating toward the field of phormium. . . .

"My dear fellow, don't talk to me about our European women!

"At sunset my first two little women and my queen Tatea and I all sat down together in a corner of the wood to a riotous family supper consisting of fern roots, *kopanas* (potatoes), a magnificent fish, an iguana (a large arboreal lizard), and three wild ducks, all baked in an oven of red-hot stones according to native custom, and washed down with a few glasses of the brandy I still had.

"Had anyone offered me, that evening, to transport me to China into the Emperor's porcelain palace and to give me the celestial princess, his daughter, as wife, with a hundred mandarins bearing the crystal button to wait upon me, I should have refused.

"On the day following the private nuptials, the surgeon returned from his botanical expedition. He was covered with vegetable matter in various degrees of dampness and looked like a walking haystack. His chief and mine, Koro and Emaï, our two mahouts, resolved to celebrate the reunion and the marriage with a splendid official feast. They had just caught a young female slave in the very act of stealing in their pah (village), and they had determined to punish her with death on the occasion of our festivities. This was done, though I protested that we already had a very fine dinner and that I would not eat a bit of her.

"The fact is, you can believe me, that at the risk of alienating our chiefs, who had gone out of their way to entertain us, at the risk even of irritating Tatea, who thought my repugnance absurd, I could not face it. I was offered the best cut from the shoulder of the slave, served on a green fern leaf and surrounded by succulent *kopanas;* I simply could not touch it. Our European education is really strange! I am ashamed of it. But this feeling of horror at human flesh inculated from childhood becomes second nature, and it's vain to try to go against it.

"Out of bravado, the surgeon attempted to taste the shoulder I had declined, but he was almost immediately punished for his experiment by violent spasms of nausea, to the great anger of Kae, Koro's cook, whose self-esteem was hurt. But my first two girls, my darling Tatea, Koro, and my father-in-law soon mollified him by paying signal homage to his culinary skill.

"After dinner the surgeon, who had a rather respectable bottle of brandy, handed it first to Emaï, who, after having drunk, said to him gravely: '*Ko tinga na, hia ou owe* (May you enjoy good health and be happy)!' So natural is the custom of toasting, for which England is sometimes blamed! Koro followed his example and, addressing me, repeated Emaï's kind wish. Meré and Moïanga gazed at me tenderly. Then, while the chiefs were smoking a few pinches of tobacco from the small keg, generously passed around by the new bride, Tatea snuggled close to me, nonchalantly rested her head against mine, and sang into my ear, as if telling me a secret, three stanzas, of which this is the refrain; I shall never forget it:

> *E takowe e o mo toku mei rangui*
> *Ka tai ki reira, aku rangui auraki*

(When you have reached the haven where you want to go, my affectionate feelings will follow you.)

"Shame on our cold music, our impudent melody, our heavy harmony, our Cyclopean song! Where in Europe will you find this mysterious voice of a bird in love, whose secret murmuring made my whole being quiver with a new and fearful voluptuousness! What warblings of the harp can imitate it? What delicate web of upper harmonics can give an idea of it? And the sad refrain in which Tatea, associating by a strange whim the expression of her love with the thought of our separation, spoke to me of the far-off haven to which her affectionate feelings would follow me—

"Beloved Tatea! Sweet bird! While singing like an Indian finch under the foliage at noon, she was with her left hand twining a long tress of her beautiful black hair about my neck, and with her right toying with the knuckle-bones of the slave's foot that she had just eaten. An enchanting blend of love, childishness, and reverie! Did the old world ever suspect such poetry? Shakespeare, Beethoven, Byron, Weber, Moore, Shelley, Tennyson, you are merely rough men of prose!

"During this scene, Kae had indulged in an endless whispered chat with the bottle, which told him so many things that Koro and the surgeon had to help him along to his hut, where he dropped down dead-drunk.

"More drunk than the cook, but drunk with love, I carried rather than led Tatea away; and my two other little women once again slept peacefully through the night.

"Tatea had noticed that often in my moments of reverie, when we sat together on the shore, I traced with my ramrod in the sand the letter *T*.

"She finally asked me why I continually drew this sign, and I succeeded, not without difficulty, in making her understand that it recalled her name to me. This greatly astonished her. She probably doubted that such a thing was possible, but one day when I was absent, having herself scratched a rough *T* on a rock, she showed it to me and clapped her hands when she heard me at once exclaim: 'Tatea!'

"You may be thinking that when I tell you these trifles I am laughing at myself, and am about to make ironic remarks about my drift toward the pastoral, the Daphnis-and-Chloe game. Not at all;

I was just happy, not being French.

"Many like days and nights passed by. Though I did not realize it, they came to weeks and months; I had forgotten the world and England when the frigate showed up again in the bay and reminded me that 'there was a port to which I must go.' A surprising thing was that after the first chill the sight of it spread through my veins, I almost felt courage. The Union Jack flying at the mast produced on me the effect of Rinaldo's adamantine shield; it now seemed possible, not to say easy, to tear myself from the arms of my Armida.[6] And yet, when I announced my departure to her, what tears, what despair, what convulsions of the heart! At first Tatea showed herself the more resigned of the two. But when the cutter from the frigate had come to shore, when she saw the surgeon get into it and wait for me, when I had made my last presents to Emaï and Koro, she threw herself distractedly at my feet and entreated me to give her one more proof of my love, the last—a strange proof, which would never have occurred to me.

" 'Yes, yes, anything you ask,' I said to her, raising her from the ground, and clasping her frantically, 'what is it you want—my gun, my powder, my shot? Take them, take them, whatever belongs to me is yours.' She shook her head. Then, grasping her father's knife (he stood by, the impassive witness of our farewells), she brought its point close to my bare chest and gave me to understand, for she could no longer speak, that she wished to make a mark there. I consented. Tatea thereupon slashed me twice, making a cross-shaped incision, from which the blood spurted forth in jets. On the instant the poor child flung herself on my chest, which was streaming with blood, laid against it her lips, cheeks, neck, bosom, and hair, and drank my blood, which mingled with her tears; she screamed, she sobbed. Oh, my old England, on that day I surely proved to you that I loved you!

"Meré and Moïanga had sprung into the water before the cutter's departure; I found them at the frigate's companion. It was another scene full of heart-rending shrieks. In vain did I keep my eyes fixed on the flag, my strength failed me for a minute. I had left Tatea fainting on the beach; beneath my feet the two other

---

[6] The allusion is to a scene in the fifth act of Gluck's *Armide,* an opera based on the famous episode of Rinaldo's enchantment by the witch-queen Armida in Tasso's *Jerusalem Delivered.*

dear creatures swam with one hand and waved farewell with the other, repeating in their moaning voices: 'O Walla, Walla!'—which is how they spoke my name.

"The effort it cost me to climb that ship's ladder! As I climbed each step, I felt as if I were being broken on the wheel, limb by limb. On deck I could not endure it any longer; I turned round and was on the point of leaping into the water, swimming ashore, and embracing all three of them, to flee with them into the forest, letting the frigate sail away loaded with my curses, when the commander, guessing my rash impulse, made a sign to the regimental musicians on board. 'Rule, Britannia' rang out, a supreme, heartbreaking upheaval shook me and, three-fourths insane, I rushed into the saloon, where I remained till evening, stretched out on the floor like a living corpse.

"On recovering consciousness my first impulse was to run up on deck, as if I should find there—we were already far away—no land in sight—nothing but sky and water. Then only did I give a long maddened scream of pain.

"It relieved me. My chest was still bleeding. Wanting to make the scar ineffaceable, I procured some gunpowder and coral, which I pounded together and put in the wound. I had learned this method of tattooing from Emaï. It succeeded perfectly. Just see" (here Wallace opened his waistcoat and shirt and showed me a large bluish cross), "it means to me Tatea in the language of New Zealand. If you ever come across a European woman capable of thinking up as innocent an idea, I will permit you to believe in her affection and to remain faithful to her."

Wallace would have found it difficult to continue imparting his secrets that evening. He was not crying, but red streaks flecked the whites of his eyes, his lips foamed, he went and stood before a mirror and remained there a long while, gazing darkly at Tatea's signature. It was now three o'clock in the morning and I left, a prey to a feeling of deep oppression. On reaching home, I could not go to sleep; I kept thinking for a long time about the hospitality of the New Zealand warriors, the prejudices of Europeans against slaves, the influence of small kegs of tobacco, polygamy, savage love, and the fanatical patriotism of the English.

Two years later Wallace called on me in Paris. Frederick Beale,[7]

---

[7] See above, note 4, p. 232.

that king of English publishers, that intelligent and generous friend of artists, had commissioned him to write a two-act opera for a London theater. Wallace counted on using his Paris leisure to write this short work; but an acute inflammation of the eye, which occurred almost immediately on his arrival and which nearly deprived him of his eyesight, kept him from doing so and forced him to go through a period of long and dreary inactivity.

Having recovered at last under the care of the learned Dr. Sichel, whom I had brought in to see him, he returned to London with the intention, first of finishing his opera, then of making another trip round the world to divert himself—also, I like to think, in order to revisit New Zealand. He did in fact start on the journey; but reasons I know nothing about have made him tarry in New York, where on the pretext that he is making thousands of dollars out of drawing-room compositions that the Americans are crazy about, he forgets his friends, men and women, and he is satisfied to live a dull life among people who are sunk in the deepest civilization.

I would give a good deal to know whether the tattooing on his chest is still visible. Poor Tatea, I am afraid your knife did not go deep enough!

Which does not prevent my saying to him across the Atlantic: "Good morning, my dear Wallace; do you think, too, that I have committed a breach of trust in publishing your Odyssey? I bet you don't!"

I flatter myself, gentlemen, that your opera is now nearing the end. In any case, if my letter does not last two and a half hours, I am very sorry, but I cannot drag it out further. To me it seems good for ten mortal hours.

So farewell, Corsino; farewell, Dervinck; farewell, Dimsky; farewell, all of you. We may meet again—Lord, how sad I am!

That's epilogue enough.

Adam, Adolphe, 207 *n.*, 211 *n.*
Adelaïde (Beethoven), 340–1
Aeneid (Virgil), 81 and *n.*, 105 and *n.*, 159 *n.*, 208 and *n.*, 213, 237 and *n.*, 302, 356 and *n.*
Albrechtsberger, Johann Georg, 324
Alcestis (Gluck), 147, 166, 276, 279–81
Allegretto for piano, violin, and cello (Beethoven), 318 *n.*
Allegri, Gregorio, 270
Alsager, T. M., 245 and *n.*
Armide (Gluck), 374 and *n.*
Arnim, Bettina von, 324 and *n.*
Auber, Daniel François Esprit, 67, 171 *n.*, 216, 329

Bach, Johann Sebastian, 317
Bacon, Roger, 360
Baillot, Pierre, 223, 244 and *n.*
Balzac, Honoré de, 5, 80 *n.*
Barber of Seville, The (Beaumarchais), 95 *n.*
Barber of Seville, The (Rossini), 182, 200, 312
Bards, The (Lesueur), 167, 226–7, 352
Barilli, M., 171, 224
Barilli, Mme, 171, 224
Barnum, P. T., 99 ff.
Beale, Frederick, 232 *n.*, 375–6
Beaumarchais, Pierre Caron de, 95 and *n.*
Beethoven, Ludwig van, 74, 116, 155, 158, 182, 187, 225, 232 *n.*, 244, 266, 305, 307, 314–44, 356, 373
Beethoven and His Three Styles, (Lenz), x, 314–26
Bellini, Vincenzo, 60 and *n.*
Bériot, C. de, 343

Berlioz, Louis Hector (1803–1869)
LIFE—ix ff., 11 *n.*, 19 *n.*, 21 *n.*, 27 *n.*, 33 and *n.*, 47 *n.*, 53 and *n.*, 54 *n.*, 73 *n.*, 80 and *n.*, 81 and *n.*, 90 *n.*, 91 *n.*, 109 *n.*, 114 and *n.*, 116 *n.*, 135 and *n.*, 140 *n.*, 153 *n.*, 164 *n.*, 195 ff., 196 *n.*, 213 *n.*, 226 *n.*, 228 ff., 238 ff., 245 and *n.*, 254 and *n.*, 255 *n.*, 262 *n.*, 267 *n.*, 316 *n.*, 321 *n.*, 340 *n.*, 341 *n.*, 351 *n.*, 364 *n.*, 365 *n.*
WORKS—*Benvenuto Cellini,* 19 *n.*, 90 *n.*; *Grotesques de la Musique,* 228 *n.*; *Harold in Italy,* xiii, 196 *n.*; *Infant Christ,* xviii; Mass of 1825, 80 and *n.*; *Memoirs,* ix, xiii, 11 *n.*, 196 *n.*, 197 *n.*; *Queen Mab* Scherzo, 33, 40, 41, 50; *Requiem,* 80 *n.*; *Romeo and Juliet* Symphony, xiii, 33 *n.*, 34; *Soirées de l'Orchestre,* ix ff., xvii–xviii, 310 and *n.*, 311; *Symphonie Fantastique,* xiii, 196 *n.*, 299; *Voyage Musical en Allemagne et en Italie,* 10 *n.*
Berton, Henri Montan, 172, 352
Boccherini, Luigi, 244
Boïeldìeu, François Adrien, 158
Bortniansky, Dmitri, 238 and *n.*, 240–1
Bottesini, Giovanni, 243
Bouilly, Jean Nicolas, 325 *n.*
Bourgeois Gentilhomme, Le (Molière), 48, 182, 203
Boyce, William, 231
Branchu, Mme, 80, 144–5, 147, 150, 157, 165–6, 255
Burgmüller, Friedrìch, 115 and *n.*
Byron, George Gordon, Lord, 373

Cambronne, Pierre Jacques Étienne, Baron, 299 and *n.*

Index

Camoëns, Luiz Vaz de, 307–8, 313, 361
Carnival of Venice, The, 197
Castil-Blaze (François Henri-Joseph
 Blaze), 53 and n., 59, 168
Cellini, Benvenuto, 10 ff., 17 n., 21 n.
Cervantes Saavedra, Miguel de, xiii, 66,
 68, 109, 307
Césole, Conte di, 197–8
Charlet, Nicolas Toussaint, 125, 127
Chasse du jeune Henri, La (Méhul),
 345, 351
Chénier, Joseph, 353
Cherubini, Maria Luigi Carlo Zenobio
 Salvatore, 155, 156, 166, 335, 336, 364
Chopin, Frédéric-François, 139
Chorley, Henry F., 185 n., 328
Choron, Alexandre, 194 and n., 234,
 347
Christ on the Mount of Olives (Beetho-
 ven), 305, 333
Cimarosa, Domenico, 140, 154, 223 n.,
 224
Clarissa Harlowe (Richardson), 359
 and n.
Clauss, Wilhelmine, 243
Clemenza di Tito, La (Gluck), 71, 255
 and n.
Colbran, Isabella Angela, 163
Concerto in E flat (Beethoven), 333
Concerto in G Minor (Mendelssohn),
 216 ff.
Conestabile, Carlo, 362–6
Cooper, James Fenimore, xiii
Coriolanus Overture (Beethoven),
 305–6, 324, 333
Cortez (Spontini), 116, 152, 155, 165,
 167, 168–71, 173, 176–8
Cosmos, The (Humboldt), 5, 64
Courier, Paul-Louis, 301 and n.
Cramer, J. B., 232 and n.
Crescentini, Girolamo, 222 and n., 224
Crivelli, Gaetano, 171, 261
Cruvelli, Sophie, 350, 356 and n.

Dante (Durante Alighieri), 14
Daussoigne-Méhul, Louis Joseph, 328
David, Félicien, 328
Dérivis, Henri Étienne, 80, 88 and n.,
 144–5, 150, 166, 255 and n.
Deschamps, Émile, 305 n.
Dickens, Charles, xviii, 5

Don Giovanni (Mozart), 55, 117, 171,
 221, 314, 315, 318, 345
Don Quixote (Cervantes), 66, 68, 109
Donizetti, Gaetano, 114–15, 189 and n.
Duponchel, M., 54–5, 90, 94
Duprez, Gilbert Louis, 93, 95, 232
Durante, Francesco, 255 and n.

Egmont Overture (Beethoven), 336,
 340
Elijah (Mendelssohn), 242
Eliot, George, 232 n.
Ella, John, 243 and n., 244
Elleviou, Jean, 156 n.
Erard, Pierre, 174, 216 ff.
Ernst, Heinrich, 198 and n., 245
Euphrosine et Coradin (Méhul), 155,
 344, 349–50
Euryanthe (Weber), 343

Favorita, La (Donizetti), 189 and n.
Festa, Francesca, 171
Fétis, François Joseph, 328, 347, 365
 and n.
Fidelio (Beethoven), 187, 325, 333, 334,
 336, 340, 341, 343
Fifth Symphony (Beethoven), 158,
 320–1, 331, 333–4
Frederick William IV, 174, 327, 336,
 340–1, 342
Freischütz, Der (Weber), 38 ff., 52 ff.,
 116, 182
Fuchs, Georg Friedrich, 324

Ganthony, Joseph, 231
Gardel, Pierre Gabriel, 347
Gaveaux, Pierre, 225, 325
Generali, Pietro, 225
Geoffroy, Louis, 144 and n., 145
Gide, André, xiv
Gil Blas (Le Sage), 206 and n.
Glinka, Michael Ivanovitch, 329
Gluck, Christoph Willibald, 71, 72 n.,
 80, 109 n., 135, 146–7, 149, 154, 166,
 182, 253, 254–5, 272 ff., 288, 316, 346,
 348 and n., 349, 354, 374 n.
Goethe, Johann Wolfgang von, xiii, 260
 and n.
Goldschmidt, Otto, 104
Goss, Sir John, 229 and n.
Goudimel, Claude, 231 and n.

Grégoire, Abbé, 172 and *n.*
Grégoire (Napoleon's secretary), 222 ff.
Grétry, André Ernest Modeste, 350, 353
Guglielmi, Pietro, 223 and *n.*, 224

Habeneck, François, 128 ff., 329, 333
Halévy, Jacques François Fromental
  Elias, 54 *n.*, 67, 205, 329
Hallé, Charles, 241 and *n.*, 328
Hamlet (Shakespeare), 124 *n.*, 182, 266
Handel, George Frideric, 242, 317,
  318–19, 343
Haydn, Franz Josef, 155, 316, 342
Heine, Heinrich, xiii, 91, 357 *n.*, 358
Henry IV (Shakespeare), 308, 313, 316,
  319, 360–1
Hoffmann, E. T. A., 198, 349
Hugo, Victor, 226 and *n.*, 248 and *n.*,
  326 and *n.*, 334–5 and *n.*
Huguenots, The (Meyerbeer), 112, 257,
  299, 305, 343
Humboldt, Alexander von, 5, 64
Hummel, Johann Nepomuk, 140

Iphigenia in Aulis (Gluck), 131, 166
Iphigenia in Tauris (Gluck), 147, 166,
  253, 254, 255, 348–9

Janin, Jules, 196 and *n.*, 328
Jerusalem Delivered (Tasso), 374 *n.*
Joseph (Méhul), 352, 353, 355
Josephine, Empress, 156–7
Jouy, Étienne de, 83, 156 and *n.*, 168,
  206
Juive, La (Halévy), 54 and *n.*
Jullien, Antoine, 114 *n.*

"*Kennst du das Land*" (Goethe), 260
  and *n.*
Kratky, Mlle, 327, 341
Kreutzer, Rodolphe, 172, 223

Lablache, Luigi, 185 and *n.*, 186, 188
La Fontaine, Jean de, 91 *n.*, 106 and *n.*,
  127 and *n.*, 164 and *n.*, 299 and *n.*, 345
  and *n.*
Lalla Rookh (Moore), 173
Lamartine, Alphonse Marie Louis de
  Prat de, 259 and *n.*
Lemoyne, *see* Moyne

Lenz, Wilhelm von, 315 ff.
Léonore (Bouilly), 325
Le Sage, Alain René, 206 and *n.*
Lesueur, Jean François, 166, 167, 223,
  225–7, 336, 351, 352
Lind, Jenny, x, 100 ff., 327, 342–3 and *n.*
Liszt, Franz, 44 ff., 93, 328 ff., 338–40
Lost Illusions (Balzac), 80 *n.*
Lulli, Giovanni Battista, 362
Luther, Martin, 231
Lvov, Alexis Feodorovich, 241
Lvov, Feodor Petrovich, 240–1

Macbeth (Shakespeare), 252
Macpherson, James, 226, 352
Magic Flute, The (Mozart), 117
Malherbe, François de, 49 and *n.*, 236
  and *n.*
Mario, Giovanni, 113
Maritana (Wallace), 313, 366 and *n.*
Marmontel, Jean François, 349
Marriage of Figaro, The (Mozart),
  315–16, 346, 356
Mars, Mlle, 185
Marschner, Heinrich August, 329
Martin, John, 235 and *n.*
Martini, Giovanni Battista, 154
Mary Stuart (Schiller), 183
Mass in C (Beethoven), 330, 335
Mazarin, Jules, 107 and *n.*
Méditations Poétiques (Lamartine),
  259 *n.*
Méhul, Étienne Nicolas, 154, 156, 166,
  344–55
Mendelssohn-Bartholdy, Felix, 216, 218,
  219, 242, 316 and *n.*, 329, 340
Merry Wives of Windsor, The (Shake-
  speare), 360
Meyerbeer, Giacomo, 54 *n.*, 60 ff., 67,
  108, 109 *n.*, 299 and *n.*, 327, 342, 343
  and *n.*
Michelangelo, 13
Milton, John, 235 *n.*
Milton (Spontini), 156, 175, 176
Missa l'Homme Armé (Palestrina), 190
Missa Papæ Marcelli (Palestrina), 190
Missa solemnis (Beethoven), 332–3
Moke, Camille, *see* Pleyel, Mme
Molière (Jean Baptiste Poquelin), xiii,
  48, 85 *n.*, 122 and *n.*, 123, 146 and *n.*,
  182, 203

Index

Monsigny, Pierre Alexandre, 134 *n.*
Montyon, Baron Jean, 221 and *n.*
Moore, Thomas, 142, 173, 373
Moscheles, Ignaz, 328
Möser, August, 327, 341 and *n.*
Moses in Egypt (Rossini), 116, 198–9, 264
Moyne, J. B., 134, 136 and *n.*, 146
Mozart, Wolfgang Amadeus, 117, 155, 171, 182, 221, 225, 307, 315 ff., 345, 356
Much Ado About Nothing (Shakespeare), 352
Murat, Joachim, 263 and *n.*

Napoleon, 37, 150, 157, 194, 222 ff., 262, 263 and *n.*, 264, 299, 324, 346, 351, 352, 353 *n.*
Newman, Ernest, xiii
Newton, Sir Isaac, 324
Nicolai, Carl Otto, 329
Niedermeyer, Abraham Louis, 88 *n.*
Ninth Symphony (Beethoven), ix, 325, 333
Notre-Dame de Paris (Hugo), 248 and *n.*, 326 and *n.*
Nourrit, Adolphe, 255 and *n.*

O'Connell, Daniel, 94 and *n.*
Odry, Jacques Charles, 111 and *n.*
Offenbach, Jacques, 111 *n.*
"Old Hundred," 231 and *n.*, 235
Old Mortality (Scott), 191 *n.*
Olympia (Spontini), 154, 166, 172–3, 176–8
Ondine (Lvov), 241
Orfeo (Poliziano), 12
Orientales, Les (Hugo), 226 and *n.*
Orpheus (Gluck), 168, 289, 343
Ossian, *see* Macpherson, James
Othello (Shakespeare), 143, 182, 350, 359
Oury, Antonio James, 243, 328

Pacini, Giovanni, 343
Paer, Ferdinando, 171 and *n.*, 325
Paganini, Nicolò, 43, 163, 193, 194–9, 249, 313, 361–6
Paisiello, Giovanni, 140, 223 *n.*, 224, 225
Palestrina, Giovanni Pierluigi da, 270, 357, 362
Panseron, Auguste, 47 and *n.*

Parce Domine, 288 and *n.*
Pasta, Giuditta, 261
Pergolesi, Giovanni Battista, 357
Perseus (Cellini), 13, 19 *n.*, 23
Persuis, Luc Loiseau de, 147 and *n.*, 148, 167, 172
Piccinni, Luigi, 72 *n.*, 346
Pischek, Johann Baptist, 327, 343
Pleasants, Henry, xi *n.*
Pleyel, Mme, 140 *n.*, 243, 340–1
Poliziano, Angelo, 12
Pomare, Queen, 204
Prophet, The (Meyerbeer), 54, 61 and *n.*, 62, 113
Proudhon, Pierre Joseph, 210
Psalm cxxxvi, 107 *n.*
Purcell, Henry, 356

Quatremère de Quincy, M., 347

Rachel, Mlle, 94 and *n.*
Racine, Jean Baptiste, 212 *n.*, 237 and *n.*, 311 and *n.*
Rellstab, Heinrich Friedrich Ludwig, 315, 327
Richard III (Shakespeare), 145
Richardson, Samuel, 359 *n.*
Ries, Ferdinand, 323
Rigel, M., 223
Robert Bruce (Niedermeyer), 88 *n.*
Robert le diable (Meyerbeer), 60 ff., 109 *n.*, 114, 130
Rosenhain, Edward, 92 *n.*
Rosenhain, Jakob, 92 *n.*
Rossini, Gioacchino Antonio, 88 *n.*, 116, 156 *n.*, 182, 195, 199, 342, 346, 356, 357
Rousseau, Jean-Jacques, 168
Rousselot, S., 245
Rubini, Giovanni Battista, 44 and *n.*, 45 ff., 93, 261, 341
Ruggieri, Claude, 209 and *n.*
Ruins of Athens, The (Beethoven), 318

Sacchini, Antonio Maria Gasparo, 353
Saint-Georges, Jules Henri Vernoy, Marquis de, 205, 241
Saint-Huberty, Antoinette Cécile, 71, 144
Salieri, Antonio, 166 *n.*, 172
Sax, Adolphe, 237 and *n.*, 267 and *n.*, 285, 328

Schiller, Johann Christoph Friedrich von, 183
Schindler, Anton, 318–19, 321, 327
Schloss, Sophie, 328, 332 and *n.*, 341
Schumann, Robert, 329
Scott, Sir Walter, xiii, 191, 304
Scribe, Augustin Eugène, 62–3, 205, 305 and *n.*
Shakespeare, William, xiii, 57, 60, 123–4, 143, 145, 182, 235, 252, 266, 307, 308, 316, 350, 352, 359, 360–1, 373
Shaw, Bernard, xii
Shelley, Percy Bysshe, 373
Sivory, Ernesto Camillo, 243
Smart, Sir George, 328, 356–7
Sontag, Henrietta, 248 and *n.*, 356
Spohr, Ludwig, 327, 329 and *n.*, 331, 333, 342
Spontini, Gasparo Luigi Pacifico, 67, 72 *n.*, 80, 135 ff., 142 ff., 152–79, 196, 329, 362, 363, 364
Stabat Mater (Rossini), 357
Staudigl, Joseph, 333 and *n.*, 342, 343
Steibelt, Daniel, 140 and *n.*
Stendhal (Marie Henri Beyle), xv, 262 *n.*
Stoltz, Rosina, 94 and *n.*
Stratonice (Méhul), 350–1
Sudre, Jean-François, 285 and *n.*

Tacchinardi, Niccolò, 171, 261
Tadolini, Giovanni, 357 and *n.*
Talma, François Joseph, 185
Tamberlik, Enrico, 187 and *n.*
Tartufe (Molière), 122 *n.*
Tasso, Torquato, 307, 374
Télémaque (Fénelon), 335 and *n.*

Tennyson, Alfred, Lord, 373
Thalberg, Sigismond, 185, 238 and *n.*
Thomas, Ambroise, 314 *n.*, 329
Thumb, Tom, 184 ff., 188, 296
Trio in B flat (Beethoven), 340
Trio in C Minor (Beethoven), 245–6
Tuczek, Leopoldine, 327, 332 and *n.*, 333, 342

Ulibichev, Alexander von, 315–18

Vernet, Horace, 185
Vestale, La (Spontini), 116, 134, 135 ff., 142 ff., 155, 156–69, 176–9
Viardot, Pauline, 328, 343
Victoria, Queen, 327, 336, 338, 343
Vieuxtemps, Henri, 243
Vigny, Alfred de, 182
Viotti, Jean Baptiste, 362
Virgil, xiii, 14, 60, 81 and *n.*, 105 and *n.*, 159 *n.*, 208 and *n.*, 237 and *n.*, 302, 356
Voltaire (François Marie Arouet), 102 and *n.*, 120, 182–3, 206, 304

Wagner, Richard, xii, 329
Wallace, Vincent, 313, 366–76
Weber, Carl Maria von, 38 ff., 52 ff., 116, 178, 182, 194, 317, 340–1, 356, 373
Weihe des Hauses Overture (Beethoven), 319 and *n.*
Westmorland, Earl of, 327, 342 and *n.*
When Israel came out of Egypt, 213 and *n.*
William Tell (Rossini), 70–1, 73 and *n.*, 95, 116, 139, 156 *n.*

Zelter, Carl Friedrich, 317
Zingarelli, Niccolò Antonio, 224